Stories of Childhood

Stories of Childhood
Evolving Portrayals in Books and Films

Dean W. Duncan

McFarland & Company, Inc., Publishers
Jefferson, North Carolina

LIBRARY OF CONGRESS CATALOGUING-IN-PUBLICATION DATA

Duncan, Dean W.
  Stories of childhood : evolving portrayals in books and films / Dean W. Duncan.
      p.   cm.
  Includes bibliographical references and index.
  Includes filmography.

  ISBN 978-0-7864-7132-4 (softcover : acid free paper) ∞
  ISBN 978-1-4766-2140-1 (ebook)

  1. Childhood in motion pictures.   2. Childhood in literature.   I. Title.

  PN1995.9.C45D76 2015
  791.43083—dc23   2015035350

BRITISH LIBRARY CATALOGUING DATA ARE AVAILABLE

© 2015 Dean W. Duncan. All rights reserved

No part of this book may be reproduced or transmitted in any form or by any means, electronic or mechanical, including photocopying or recording, or by any information storage and retrieval system, without permission in writing from the publisher.

Front cover image © Jacek Chabraszewski, iStock/Thinkstock

Printed in the United States of America

McFarland & Company, Inc., Publishers
  Box 611, Jefferson, North Carolina 28640
  www.mcfarlandpub.com

To my wife, Sharon,
and to our children,
Caitlin, Drew, Sarah, Spencer,
Mathieson, and Claire,
for whom and from whom
I learned all of this great stuff.

Contents

Acknowledgments	ix
Introduction—The Roots and Branches of Children's Media	1

Part I: Books and Films

1. The Media: What Was I Scared Of?	11
2. From Confrontation to Conciliation: Not Worrying So Much and Learning to Love the Media	41

Part II: Defining Childhood— Evolving Representations and Realities

3. The Angel Child	77
4. Idealism, Sentimentality and the Advent of Film	100
5. The Problem with Perfection and Ways Forward	115
6. Bad Boys and Demon Seeds	143
7. Reconciling and Synthesizing Polar Positions	170
8. Adults and Children, Mutually Implicated	200
Chapter Notes	223
Bibliography	241
Filmography	261
Index	267

Acknowledgments

This book began when my wife, Sharon, and I started having kids, and realized that we weren't as knowledgeable about the language and lore of childhood as we thought. I am grateful to the individuals and institutions that helped us get up to speed, both for ourselves and, eventually, for the purposes of this publication.

First, I want to thank my parents, Don and Mona Duncan, for having established a household rich with story and song, principle and precept, and all of the material and emotional bounty that children need, and with which they grow and thrive.

I am grateful to and for my siblings. Our eldest brother, Scott, was an unfailing protector and great benefactor through the entire course of my childhood and youth. He taught and embodied the qualities of kindness, integrity, and generous world-curiosity, which qualities have been a motivation and a blessing to me ever since.

Among her many other excellencies, my late older sister, Susan, showed me that attitudes and methods that differed from mine were not automatically or necessarily to be dismissed or opposed. She was the first to teach me the counterintuitive, undeniable, and essential lesson that there is more than one right way to mow that lawn.

Lisa, the next in line after me, is a dear heart and a bright light, ever a kindred spirit and soul mate. Our youngest sister (also called Sharon) was most remarkably produced after we existing children importuned our parents to have just one more. Only later did we come to understand what a marvelous thing it was for them to actually comply with that request. Given those circumstances, Sharon arrived with a golden, graced, almost magical aura. She gave us to understand at an unusually early age that little children are indeed a heritage and a reward.

I am grateful for the narrative arts and for the antical, evocative, and nurturing children's programs that were there to greet me as I first emerged out of the hazes of infancy. I bless the edifying anarchy of *The Bugs Bunny Show* and *The Bugs Bunny/Road Runner Hour*, as well as the gentler tone and spirit of Ernie Coombs' *Mr. Dressup*, and *The Friendly Giant*. I remember *The Beachcombers*, I feel of *The Forest Rangers*, and freely admit to being a big fan of *Coming Up Rosie*.

I am grateful to our mother, who read us books. I am thankful that William Pène du Bois' eye-popping picture book *The Alligator Case* reached out to me from the stacks of the Meadowlark Elementary School library, when I was a lad back at the beginning of Grade One. Tove Jansson and J. R. R. Tolkien did the same thing, two years later, and my great-aunt Maude's full 1903 Collins edition of Charles Dickens four years after that. I am thankful for all of the blessed book repositories and for all the blessed books that beckoned to me then, and for all those that have been doing so ever since.

I remember with pleasure the rollicking screenings of a series of not particularly good Disney features in the church and school gymnasia of late-sixties, early-seventies Edmonton, Alberta, Canada. I am very glad for all of the late movies that the CBC and CTV ran for all those years—and for the way my parents indulgently pretended they didn't know I was sneaking down to watch them. I appreciate the years of Saturday afternoon films series that ran downtown at the Stanley A. Milner branch of the Edmonton Public Library and for the long and adventurous bus rides that took me there and back. I owe a great debt to the programmers and projectionists of Old Strathcona's Princess Theatre, which, from its refurbishment in 1978, provided me with a tremendously broad and abundant film education, long before I ever thought of becoming a film educator.

For all its myriad complexities and contradictions, I particularly love the National Film Board (NFB) of Canada. Early exposed to its individual productions—and less directly its core principles—I came to understand that profit wasn't always or only to be calculated on the black side of a ledger. With groundwork laid by founder John Grierson, with the productions of Norman McLaren and Bill Mason, of Tom Daly, Wolf Koenig, Roman Kroitor and Colin Low, with the civilized, almost Athenian tones of Stanley Jackson, Eldon Rathburn and Donald Brittain, the NFB ever gave me to understand that commerce and escape were never as important, nor as pleasurable, as the delights of intelligent discourse, of artistry applied for the benefit and education of others, of dedication to duty and community.

Acknowledgments

I am beholden to the instructive frustrations—for a small Anglophone in Western Canada, just needing to become aware of worlds beyond his own—of CBC Montreal's bi-lingual children's program *Chez Hélène*, not to mention all the Stanley Cups that the Habs won so relentlessly through the course of my childhood and youth. I also appreciate becoming aware of the Great Behemoth to the south. This consciousness probably started with the National Hockey League's American franchises, and the Canadian Football League's numerous, strictly apportioned American imports. But there was also that ever-increasing stream of bright, brash media imagery, equal parts appealing and unseemly. Who are those guys?

American children's programming helped me to process and reconcile these contradictory things. *Sesame Street* came onto the scene when my younger sister was still in pre-school. I watched her watch it, and we would come to appreciate its joyfully affirmative velocity and kinesis, its even-handed and forward-looking race and class and gender syntheses. In stylistic contrast, I am grateful for later instructions at the hands of the sublime Fred Rogers.

The various ways that these various practitioners went about doing good demonstrated to me that diversities of operation and motivation could always come together to serve common and constructive ends.

Leaping forward: I am grateful to the Department of Theatre and Media Arts (TMA) at Brigham Young University in Provo, Utah, USA, where I have taught since 1992. Together with the College of Fine Arts and Communications in which it is housed, TMA has been unstinting in its support of this project, and of the many things that led up and contributed to it. My appreciation goes to department chairs Harold Oaks, Eric Fielding, Bob Nelson, Rodger Sorensen, and Amy Jensen—and also to deans James Mason, Bruce Christenson, Newell Dayley and Stephen Jones—for their sequential and multifaceted support. This has been largely manifest in the establishment and nurture of our multifaceted children's media program, which it has been my privilege to serve in for many years and in a number of capacities.

As mentioned, my wife, Sharon, and I started to have children, only then realizing we didn't know enough about childhood's mythologies and attendant realities. I would like to thank Jim Jacobs and, especially, Mike Tunnell, of BYU's McKay School of Education, who helped set us on the path of being more than just kids' lit hobbyists. Soon after their tutelage, I started a children's media class, which was offered between the fall semester of 2000 and the winter semester of 2011. I am thankful to all of the students and teaching assistants who attended and leavened its many iterations. These include but are not limited to Mary Aagard, Randy Astle, Marta Becceril, Allison Belnap, Jen Bushman, Caroline Drake Calkins, Sarah Nielsen Cramer, Aislin Powell Dyer, Natasha Haught Fudge (really!), Carolyn Hanson, Benjamin Harry, Heidi Hathaway, Emily Hess-Flinders, Erika Hill, Megan Pugmire Hinmon, Bruce Holt, Kathy Cowley Johnson, Susan Kenney, Davey Morrison, Megan Whittaker Nesbit, Stephanie Ollerton, David Pearson, Noelani Sanchez Porter, Michael Potter, Jane Prince, Alyssa Whipple Rock, Charlotte Aldridge Sheppard, Seth Sherwood, Meg Gibson Singley, Janine Sobeck, Eva-Marie Stegeby-Luna, Becca Potter Summers, and Megan Wolfley Weiss.

I wish to express appreciation to those students who turned their hands to the productive stumble of our *Children's Media Review* (CMR), which ran from 2004 to 2007. These include Tom Archibald, Clark Edmunds, Wilhelm Haydt, Shawnda Moss, Sarah Olson, Matt Pierce, Nicola Taylor, Benjamin Thevenin, and Sarah Weech. Special thanks and commendation go to Stacey Snider Birk for her tremendously good writing, wise editing, and administrative efficiency.

The CMR was a part of a concentrated Children's Media Initiative at BYU TMA, which unfortunately did not survive the recent global economic crisis and the belt-tightening that followed. A number of scripts and films did make it through the meltdown, however. I am grateful for the tact, tractability, and talent of the many who contributed to these productions: Joshua Abboud, Rosemary Archer, Megan and Shane Atkinson, David Axelgard, Allison Belnap, David Bisson, Whitney Borup, Melissa Brady, Emily Burnworth, Trevor Campbell, Ryan Cannon, Jana Schurig Cardon, Gabe Casdorph, Justin Cook, Luke Drake, Mark Ellsworth, Jeremy Fisher, John Forbyn, Kohl Glass, Gloria Gong, Tony Gunn and Leslie Hart-Gunn, Jeff Gustafson, Wilhelm Haydt again, Jim Huffaker, Karla Huntsman, Kimi Isom, Jennie Bangerter Larsen, Brent Leavitt, Bryan Lefler, Berta Marquez, Johanna McEuen, Daniel Needham, William Newman, Chantelle Squires Olsen, Justin Partridge, Tony Petersen, Tyree Pini, Heidi Reed, Joel Remke, Ben and Kristen Sansom, Rodger Sorensen, Benjamin Thevenin (part 2), Paul Tuft, Ben Unguren, Manju Varghese, Cole Webley, Tyler Weston, Caitlin Wise, Danielle Palliser Wright, and Jason Yancey.

The rigorous, exhilarating experience of adapting the likes of Hans Christian Andersen, Anton Chekhov, Mary de Morgan, Emily Dickinson, Kenneth Grahame, the Brothers Grimm, Joseph Jacobs, Selma Lagerlof, G. E. Lessing, Frank Stockton, Leo Tolstoy, Walt Whitman, Oscar Wilde, and even Plato himself taught me immeasurably about the grandeur, range, and durability of canonical children's literature, and of contemporary kids' lit voices as well. Similarly, our production activities convinced me anew of the inexhaustible flexibility and expressiveness of the film medium. The same went for the capacities and potential of the young readers and writers with whom we had the privilege of working. I feel to honor particularly the superb, signal contributions of Meredith Bak, Stacy Snider Birk (again), Megan Pugmire Hinmon, Kimi Howington, Eleanor Rossell Potter, and Charla Ausman Williams.

Numbers of grown-ups were also most generous with their time and talents during the run of the Children's Media Initiative. Special thanks go to TMA colleagues Stan Ferguson, Darl Larsen, Kelly Loosli, Jeff Parkin, Tom Russell, Eric Samuelsen, Janet Swenson, and especially the unfailingly generous, unfailingly faithful Tom Lefler.

My dear friend and esteemed collaborator Ben Unguren was largely responsible for the success—and even the existence—of our decade-long documentary project, *Fit for the Kingdom* (2000–2010). This series of short films took some of the impulses that informed our work in the Children's Media Initiative and applied them to recording and preserving the real time, real place interactions of children and parents. These enriching and instructive experiences would not have been possible without, among others, Carrie Hakes Barrow, Whitney and Lynette Borup, Scott Christopherson, Ramona Cutri and family, Drew Duncan, Greg and Genna Gardner, Rusty Haupt, Ruston Jones, the late David Lange, Janice and Heather Lange and family, William Newman, Tennille and Becky Olsen, Jeff Parkin, Leroy Pratt, Juston and Mary Rindlesbach, the Russell and Kelly Robinson family in Casas Grandes, Chihuahua, Mexico, the late Angie Russell and her family, Hayley Smith, the LDS Kolob Eighth ward in Springville, Utah, the Wandsworth Common ward in South London, Christy Warnick, and Krystal Williams-Rowley.

Toward the tail end of the *Fit for the Kingdom* series, my friend Tom Russell (Angie's husband) joined me in undertaking a second documentary project, *Home Movies*. This one was devoted to domestic, amateur film production—and to our own home movies in particular. Our lengthy (2009–2012) and intensive collaboration led not only to an exhaustive website and a feature length documentary, but to the bringing together of all these various activities and energies into the culminating synthesis of this book.

In addition to Tom's superhuman efforts, which saw him very lovingly go any number of extra miles, *Home Movies* would not have been possible without the tremendous technological and editorial contributions of Jon Bell, Emma Hoskisson, Brooke Parker, and Seth Sherwood. I wish most especially to acknowledge the exceptionally gifted Becca Potter Summers for her skillful and sensitive oversight of this project, as well as Drew Duncan, whose artistry and inspiration in this and in so many other related things has practically approached the angelic.

I am grateful to numbers of administrators and artists associated with the Chicago International Children's Film Festival, the TIFF Kids International Film Festival in Toronto, and the East Lansing (Michigan) Children's Film Festival for their many years of hard work, artful programming, and most gracious hospitality. It was my privilege to be able to take nearly all of my children to one or another of these festivals over the course of time. These experiences, beyond being personally precious, raised and answered a number of extremely helpful questions about the place and the possibility of film in the lives of young people.

I am beholden to the chairs and members of generations of funding committees at BYU, in my department, and in my college, as well as the BYU Film Committee. In the latter connection, it was Tom Lefler, again, who was so often a combination of rigorous taskmaster and generous benefactor. These committees have provided me with years of financial and moral support.

All of these activities led eventually to the writing of this book, to which a number of people and institutions have especially contributed. The children's sections of the Strathcona and Southgate (Whitemud Crossing) branches of the Edmonton Public Library, of BYU's Harold B. Lee Library, of the Springville and Orem, Utah, public libraries, of the La Cañada/Flintridge and La Crescenta branches of the County of Los Angeles Public Library, of the Lincoln Park and Merlo branches of the Chicago Public Library, of the Hillhead Library on Byres Road in Glasgow, Scotland, of the Westminster City Council's Charing Cross Library, and of the Kensington & Chelsea and Barbican branches of the London public library system have all provided me with many, many happy hours of related reading and study.

I am grateful to our daughter and son-in-law, Caitlin and Colton Miller, who on a couple of occasions vacated and gave me the run of their house in Idaho Falls, Idaho, for the purposes of some uninterrupted writing. The same goes for our good friends, Steve and Erin Aste, and their cabin up in Utah's Heber Valley, and for Erin's father, John Day, who offered up his house in Holladay. Similarly, my thanks to my in-laws, Wallace and Anne Anderson, for so hospitably granting me extended residence in the upstairs family room in their La Crescenta, California, home through the spring of 2014.

Benjamin Thevenin, former student and current colleague, generously and patiently helped me fill in some large gaps relating to current conversations about media literacy. Amy Jensen and her executive committee provided me with further resources in order to prepare and then send out my manuscript for some editorial work. In the TMA office, Shannon Bingham, Lindsay Larsen, and Gabby Martinez assembled my bibliography and filmography, and that with much longsuffering. Kelyn Ikegami and Drew Duncan most capably and kindly cleaned up and even created my notes. Elizabeth Funk, also unfailing in her support, cheerfully oversaw this work.

I am most especially grateful to Jennifer McDaniel of BYU's Faculty Editing Service for her microscopically detailed pass through my entire manuscript. Her attention to detail was awesomely exact, her suggestions pointed and acute, but always sensitive to the run of the writing and the drift of its ideas. Jennifer's courteous and tremendously effective editorial ministrations have been one of the highlights of this entire process. Thomas Call, Emily Smith, and Felicity Warren had a part in all this, for which I am also most appreciative.

To close, I mention two more things. My colleagues and I at BYU work in a film program, and in an arts college, and we are occupied by all sorts of curricular, scholarly, student and administrative matters. However, writing this book, on this subject, has made me more aware of a very strong subtext, doubtless common to most any workplace. Over the course of these decades of meetings, plans, team-teaching and just loitering in the hallways, we have held another very lengthy, possibly unmarked conversation. It has been fraternal, and familial. We have all counseled and lived together, partaking of the mutual perplexities, pains and delights not only of work, but of our family lives. We have come to know each other's family members very well. We have mourned, and rejoiced, and expanded our affections to an incalculably diffusive extent. For this I love Ed Adams, Brad Barber, Brian Christensen, Jim D'Arc, Mary Farahnakian, Stan Ferguson, Elizabeth Funk, Larrie Gale, Daryl Hague, Barta Heiner, Wade Hollinshaus, Richard Hull, Amy Jensen, Susan Kenney, Darl Larsen, Daryl Lee, Tom and Laura Lefler, Kelly Loosli, George and Leslie Nelson, Jeff and Jana Parkin, Tom and Courtney Russell, Eric Samuelsen, Megan Sanborn-Jones, Rory Scanlon, Don Shelline, Marcus Smith, Rodger Sorensen, Kyle Stapley, Joe Straubhaar, Janet Swenson, Sharon Swenson, Benjamin Thevenin, Tim Threlfall, Ben Unguren, Bob Walz and Julie Williamsen.

Finally, I thank and pay tribute to my immediate family. Writing a book is not always easy or fun for the writer, or the people who live with him. For all that, everyone has been extraordinarily good-humored, patient, and constant during the course of this, our long captivity. But writing a book can be surpassingly instructive, and improving. The wonderful, interesting issues that I have been thinking about over these last few years have brought me back, always and ultimately, to my own home and family.

My wife has been, as ever, good-natured, even-tempered, level-headed, strong-backed, awesomely able, always faithful. And we have learned and gained so much from our children! Our daughter Caitlin is a vivid, bracing force of nature. Our daughter Drew is a fierce, bright intelligence. Our daughter Sarah, a plenitude and a wholeness. Our son Spencer is a compass and a straight path. Our son Mathieson, a hearty embrace and a loving heart. And, finally, our daughter Claire, the child of our old age, a sweet support and consolation. Although this is properly, mostly a work of scholarship, these children, and the process by which we all helped raise each other, lie between every line. How we love them!

And finally to you, dear Reader. Thank you for taking the time, and making the effort!

Introduction—
The Roots and Branches of Children's Media

In the early 1950s, the great French film theorist André Bazin wrote an important essay entitled "The Evolution of the Language of Cinema."[1] In this essay, Bazin considered and took issue with what had been a critical commonplace: that the mature silent film was the apex of cinematic art and that its eclipse at the coming of sound films in 1927–29 was an aesthetic disaster of near-tragic proportions.[2] Against this powerful, emotional view, Bazin held that the undoubted losses accompanying the advent of "talkies" had been counterbalanced by real gains and, more importantly, key continuities.

These continuities were both stylistic and philosophical. They could be seen most clearly in the silent films of directors like Erich von Stroheim, F. W. Murnau, and Robert Flaherty. Their work prefigured and anticipated sound films directed by Orson Welles, some of the Italian neorealists,[3] and especially the pioneering French filmmaker Jean Renoir.[4] Bazin observed that all of these artists scrupulously maintained "the continuity of dramatic space and, of course, of its duration."[5]

Bazin went on to emphasize that the continuity and duration of dramatic space were of much more than just stylistic significance. Deep focus and long takes were the basic markers of his preferred version of cinematic realism, which communicated regardless of whether or not synchronized sound was being recorded. These core realist techniques went beyond mere artistry, or mere technology. They had real-world correlations and real-world implications: "The image is evaluated not according to what it adds to reality but what it reveals of it."[6]

This was the evolution to which Bazin referred in his title "The Evolution of the Language of Cinema." Here was a trajectory that was natural, positive, and productive. Through it, the medium of film, contrary to some appearances and much dire commentary, was actually growing, and thriving. The strident battles of the formalists and the technologists had obscured the development of a cinematic language of real ontological and epistemological heft. Being, in other words, and knowing: Bazinian realism rendered the world in all of its ambiguity, multiplicity, and abundance, and it held the key by which reflective viewers could access and understand same.[7]

In the many decades since the appearance of this essay, André Bazin has quite properly been revised and challenged. In our present conversation, however, and with regard to continuity and harmonious evolution, his assertion simply, straightforwardly stands. Differences and similarities between silent and sound cinema are of limited interest to most people today. Much more present are brave and occasionally intransigent allegiances to tradition, coupled with resistance to and even fear of the next new thing (especially if it is technological). Just as present and even more pressing is another possibility: despite all contention, productive correlations and continuities do exist between apparently incompatible approaches and irreconcilable camps.

The broad subject of this study is the discourse of children and families. Discussions about this very important topic take place in all sorts of contexts. One of the more divisive of these closely echoes the dynamic explored in Bazin's essay. There is a prevalent, long-standing perception that, like the silent versus sound film controversy, also has to do with an ideal thing in danger of being eclipsed by a much lesser thing. Unlike the fall of the high silent film, though, it would seem that *this* eclipse could never be total or permanent. Still, for all of the supposed preeminence of this ideal, fewer and fewer young people seem to be availing themselves of it, such that, for them, it might as well be utterly and irretrievably lost.

This perception is that books are greater, media—other means of mass communication—lesser. Books are respectable, media isn't. Books are superior in quality, artfulness and substance. Most importantly, especially when it comes to children and families, books behave themselves and they help children do the same. On the other hand media, and in the present discussion movies in particular, are either frivolous or corrupting. They are either full of mayhem and profanity and promiscuity, or they are a complete waste of time.

"Media"—a term frequently used as both plural and singular—is a many-sided object. It comprises all means of mass communication, as well as the institutions and individuals who utilize those means ("the media"). The very expanse and ubiquity of these media feeds and sometimes justifies the fears to which I have just referred. During the course of this study, and unless otherwise indicated, I will be using "media" more specifically. They are the stories described in books, compared to and correlated with stories acted out on film and television.

Are film and television siblings, or are they cousins? The two media share many points of contact, but in a number of technological, aesthetical, and economical particulars, they are also quite distinct. Despite this fact, when it comes to the issues of appropriateness and corrupting capacity, television has tended to be lumped in with the movies. More recently the landscape has been cluttered by a dizzying proliferation of technologies, devices, and social media. But in many ways these new platforms have not really altered the basic situation, the basic problem, or at least certain perceptions related thereto.[8] Now that media can be accessed by so many means, at any time, and in any place, it really can seem like the sky has fallen.

There is some justice to these perceptions. And even when these perceptions are not entirely just they are still, in complicated and poignant ways, somewhat justified, given the responsibilities and fears that the perceivers have toward the children in their care. Still, this book most unequivocally echoes and endorses André Bazin's position, and the attitude that attends it. It needn't always be a matter of better and worse, still less of right and wrong; the differences between page and screen are not as important as the very substantial conceptual continuities that bridge both technological and temporal gaps. Literature, films, television programs, sound recordings, and most of the various new technologies all repeatedly reveal and reflect these points of contact.

André Bazin valorized a cinematic method that bound and unified seemingly separate, even incompatible eras. For him this method, regardless of the time or technological fashion in which it was plied, was most effective in conducting viewers to the realities that existed outside of art and of commerce. My book will likewise suggest that, for all the significance of medium and medium specificity, the most important thing is how artistic enterprises—books and movies both—lead us complementarily into a world of real relations, real problems, and real solutions.

The arts have long been successful and even essential in articulating and addressing the realities and possibilities of children's lives. Present difficulties related to the use and abuse of media should not blind us to the fact that these media constitute an incorporation and, in some ways, a culmination of their ancestral arts. As such, a genetical, hereditary principle pertains and applies. Media bear the traces and retain the characteristics of their artistic forebears. Like these forebears—and, in the present conversation, like literature in particular—media can contribute greatly to the healthy, instructive, and joyful conversations that have always taken place between young people and the grown-ups who love and care for them.

There are many, many productive points of contact between literature and film, manifested in and across the respective texts of each medium. Each of these is rooted in and radiates back out into actuality, into the aspirations and experiences of real individuals in their real circumstances. This book will concentrate on one of the most fundamental of these points of contact, which relates to the nature of childhood. But in the background of this specific study many more pertinent issues will become apparent, and indicate how very rich and far-reaching the conversation really is.

For instance, as one example among many, books and films have been very concerned with identifying the most appropriate ways to portray and explain the world, and the best course for children attempting to make their way safely through it. In this connection both books and films have tended at times toward didacticism—toward communication that prescribes and proscribes and generally knows what is best. At other times, literature and cinema, in part as a response to the sometimes smothering of didacticism, have opted for a more antic, even anarchic kind of story. They would have it that the child must not only be safe, but happy as well.

It has been easy, even customary to establish and inhabit camps in this conversation, and in all sorts of similar ones. Polarizing, unproductive partisanships have resulted. A more conciliatory approach echoes Bazin—or perhaps the Mean that Aristotle[9] and others have elaborated. As demonstrated by John Bunyan and Bugs Bunny, there is a need and place for both catechism and cutting up. The reality, or at least a perception of reality being urged by this publication, may also resemble a balanced diet, or a food pyramid, or a properly filled and distributed plate, perhaps with some dairy on the side. Proverbs and parables, as well as Professor Branestawm; *The Man Who Planted Trees* and *A Town Called Panic*.

This one binary suggests a very deep scratch across a very important surface. Further attending to this surface might reveal a positive cross-hatching of subjects and possibilities, and of productive syntheses as well: the adventure tale and the yarn, folk and fairy stories, pictorialism and a certain sense of wonder, modernist strategies and postmodernist proliferations, the political appropriation of childhood, realism and a kind of return or apotheosis of the traditional fairy tale, nonfictional (historical, scientific, and mechanical) media. Each, all of these multifarious subjects, can be rolled into a larger familial and societal narrative. It is a mass, and a puzzlement. It is also a totality, and a wholeness. The careful and considered, patient and positive contemplation of matters like these may alert us to and convince us of a real evolutionary advance, similar to the one discussed at the beginning of this introduction. Books and movies are apt, equal, and, in the current cultural and technological climate, even necessary for the ways that they address and illuminate the problems and the possibilities at hand.

* * * * *

There are multiple points of contact, then, between literature and film. For the present, this book will restrict itself to just two of these, each contained within a dedicated part. The first part, comprised of chapters 1 and 2, examines the nature of these two media. The first chapter—"The Media: What Was I Scared Of?"—lays out a genealogy of concerns about, even fear of and hostility toward, story, and enacted story in particular.

Concerns about enacted narratives have caused all manner of minders to act in a protective and often censorious fashion. These guardians, from Plato, through the Puritans, and up to a number of contemporary Anglo-American commentators, have had their good reasons. They have also had their severe limitations, which are laid out and countered in the second chapter, "From Confrontation to Conciliation." This chapter sets forth some of the qualitative differences between film and literature, as well as some of the methods and mindsets that will allow readers in both to make substantial use of both.

The book's second part seeks to substantiate the assertions of the first. In order to do so it moves from medium to matter, detailing the rich debates that both literature and the cinema have had about the nature of childhood, and of children. This second part begins with chapter 3, entitled "The Angel Child." It explores some of the rich range of child-related discussion in the Bible, then goes on to detail how one of the major strands of that discussion—the idealization of children and the concept of childhood—later took precedence and, for a time, rose to what sometimes seems an exclusive pre-eminence. This powerfully convincing idealization is examined through its appearance in a number of key literary texts, mostly from the nineteenth century.

The fourth chapter, "Idealism, Sentimentality and the Advent of Film," discusses how the idealization of childhood informs early film narratives. Many of these early films are as ardent and convincing as their literary antecedents. Others, in part because of the uncertain or elementary nature of some early films, reveal important gaps and ruptures in the ideal.

Chapter 5, "The Problem with Perfection and Ways Forward," provides a detailed analysis of these gaps in the ideal child. It further provides a number of solutions that both books and films have offered to the failings of unmitigated idealization. One of these solutions, or responses, is to actively counter idealization by exploring its opposite.

The sixth chapter, entitled "Bad Boys and Demon Seeds," expands on this idea and considers two important and influential alternatives. The first of these is that children are not inherently innocent, nor always angels and ministers of grace. Rather, they carry, and often carry out, the seeds of malice and corruption so often evident in the adult world. In addition to the idea of what we might call an original, fundamental sinfulness, chapter 6 also examines the institutions of literary naturalism, or the idea that heredity and environment determine the child's course, and not any fundamental pre-existing qualities, whether fair or foul.

Chapter 7, "Reconciling and Synthesizing Polar Positions," acknowledges the power and legitimacy of both childhood idealization and its various counters. It then goes on to posit that a synthesis of both strands might best reflect the realities that most families know, and that both books and films affirm in most consistent, impressive, and constant array. In making this synthesis, this book continues to address the underlying idea introduced in its first part. This is that, for all of our circumstantial preferences, both literature and film are complementary and absolutely, profoundly adequate to the challenge of telling this story, and illuminating these lives.

In exploring questions about the nature of childhood, we will also learn much about the nature of adulthood. The book's eighth and final chapter, "Adults and Children, Mutually Implicated," first considers a few powerful and problematical semi-slanders against adulthood that have often populated children's discourse. It concludes with the implied end, the obvious consummation of so many child-centered narratives—that the child grows to gainful and joyful adulthood, and then, perhaps, undertakes the entire journey again, on behalf of her own charges.

The comprehensiveness of this familial cycle affects this book's scope and, particularly, the scope of its references. André Bazin held that despite certain material and stylistic differences, silent and sound films could be of equal substance, both equally true. As explained, my own related conceit is that books and films can be similarly equivalent, especially to the sympathetic reader/viewer, and most especially on the subjects of childhood and family life. This fact actually invites us to extend our consultations beyond the confines of the kids' shelves.

Leonard Maltin and Richard Bann contrast Hal Roach's *Our Gang* comedies, which he began to produce in the early 1920s, with Sidney Franklin's *Fox Sunshine Kiddies* series. The latter series just predated the former, and it was very distinct in its approach. Franklin mounted expensive adaptations of well-known children's properties, and he aimed them exclusively at young audiences. Maltin and Bann hold that Franklin's effort was worthy but the result was stuffy; neither the kids nor their adult minders were much interested. Maltin and Bann contrast Franklin's worthy failure with the wildly more successful Roach, who had simply "hoped to entertain everyone who bought a theater ticket and targeted his backyard *Our Gang* capers at the entire movie-going public: adults and kids alike."[10]

Maurice Sendak made a related observation about picture books produced in the 1870s. "I'm never interested in these books specifically as children's books. That's dull. What makes them interesting is the fact that they're both for children and for everybody else. In my opinion there's no such thing as a book *just* for children."[11]

London's Victoria and Albert Museum of Childhood affirms the fluidity, the permeability of things that we have sometimes associated exclusively with childhood.

> The original meaning of the word "toy" was a thing of little value, a trifle, and in the past was not automatically associated with playthings or even children: some of the earlier toys in the [museum's] collection were intended as adult curiosities for the wealthy. Early optical toys, finely constructed automata—clockwork moving toys—and even dolls' houses were intended for grown-ups, before making the transition to the childhood realm.[12]

As with manufactured leisure objects, so too the stories that have come to be associated with children. It is well known that the tales collected by Jacob and Wilhelm Grimm were drawn from and, at first, distributed to adult communities.[13] Subsequent concerns about the tales being inappropriate for children are apt, since at some basic level they probably are. At the very least, they were not initially intended for children, so that a problematical, often quite productive ambiguity has continued to attend their subsequent dissemination.

Many of this book's points will be illustrated from texts that were created for children. Other sources will have been subscribed to by children, without necessarily having been expressly intended for them. In many cases, books and films *about* children will be consulted that were not necessarily intended and may not actually be appropriate for children. Publications more associated with adults will often feature perspectives that are relevant to the subject at hand, and will accordingly be cited.

The American cartoonist Charles Schulz's *Peanuts* comic strip features a number of small children who are often quite precocious in the subjects that they discuss, and in the perceptions they bring to those subjects. In one panel Linus, he of the constant security blanket, tells Charlie Brown that he has been reading Dostoyevsky's *The Brothers Karamazov*. He says that he enjoyed it very much, though he did find himself "bleeping over the [difficult] Russian names."[14]

Are such references any more than glancing? Are they simply gratuitous? They might be, at least if no further connection is made to the things being referenced. But here is an example of how a wide range of sources, together with an awareness of the continuities between media, can be tremendously beneficial. It may be that Schulz's Schroeder and his oft-declared interest in Beethoven provides little actual musical exposure, little actual musical benefit to young readers. But I am also thinking of those young readers' exposure to Vince Guaraldi's scoring of the *Peanuts* TV specials. His easy, swinging ensemble work served as a child's guide to the jazz ensemble for millions of young viewers. The happy musical tones of that Christmas special might very well have moved young listeners to try Dave Brubeck and Paul Desmond and Gerry Mulligan, or perhaps returned them to the recently abandoned bench at their very own piano.

In a similar sense, this study cites somewhat broadly, with the hope and confidence that readers are willing to adapt, and connect. As to the nature of this book's illustrations, it will need to surmount a challenge that is inherent in writing about the arts, or about film at least. As will be explored in some detail later on, film is a profoundly visual and aural medium. To discuss it in a book completely lacking in photographs or film frame enlargements and without audio recordings of any kind is to start out with a considerable and even preposterous disadvantage. To a degree, writing about and not having recourse to film relegates us to the realms of analogy and metaphor. As poetical and productive as these realms can be, they are always to a certain extent only "like" or "as" the actual object being discussed.

As a result, and as a kind of compensation, this book will quote from many of the literary texts to which it refers. Bibliographical convention, or at least certain very valid takes thereon, would have it that quotations are best kept to a minimum. Effective and sufficient citation means that readers can find the source and consider it as they see fit. The writer should be devoted to making and demonstrating his points, in his own words. This is, or can be true. However, since this volume is intended not only as an argument with illustrations but also as something of a celebration, then I will quote at some unusual length from a number of sources. In doing so this long essay, as well as the arguments that form it, will contain much of the sensibility of compilation, even of collage.

Silence, sound; books, films; children, adults—this fluid, expansive discussion will lead us through the center of this book and on to its conclusion, which has a parallel in the family life that it partially portrays. A Hegelian dialectic, as opposed to the conflicts explained and then espoused by Karl Marx, allows us to consider and reconcile binaries, proving all things and holding fast that which is good.[15] This constant, affirmative synthesizing will lead to a kind of horizontal integration. One text leads to another, or to another activity, or conversation, or journey, or course of study. Openness and expansiveness lead to education, adeptness, occupation, and joyful association.

Media reflects, media even causes, any number of social and familial tensions. It need not only be thus. The clear identification, categorization, and appreciation of the various points under review here can help previous partisans to leave their camps and meet in what may turn out to be a surprisingly familiar and fertile middle ground. The issues at play are complex and often contradictory, and they are very important. The lives of young people are becoming ever more affected by and even predicated upon media. Though we may be concerned and even distressed by the fact, the fact remains. Another fact is that we need not only bemoan; there are many positive things to be said and done. Media phenomena call for a great deal more thinking and defining, intervention and, yes, celebration. A simultaneous study of children's literature and children's media, rooted in the realities and possibilities that give them rise, can bring this to pass.

Part I: Books and Films

1

The Media: What Was I Scared Of?

In this book, I seek to affirm and demonstrate the great substance of media—and of movies most of all. Before proceeding, however, it would be well to address a few deep-seated concerns and objections. There are shortcomings—perceived and actual—and even dangers in film and television, especially as they relate to young people. In either case they are real, after a fashion, and not simply to be dismissed.

Suspicion of and resistance to media seems to be inscribed in the philosophical, even the mythological DNA of Western civilization. One of the most striking and resonant of media critiques predates modern media technology: Plato's Parable of the Cave (ca. 380 BC)[1] has at its heart an uncannily prescient picture of the excessive and even addictive consumption of cinematic images in a movie theater.[2]

In this primordial parable Plato, through Socrates, describes an underground prison space in which individuals are chained and immobilized, then exposed to an endless procession of shadows projected onto a wall in front of them. Though mere illusion, these shadows are presented compellingly, such that they come to be accepted by the prisoners as the sum and substance of reality. The result is that they adhere to a "truth [that is] literally nothing but the shadows of the images."[3]

This is a terrible deprivation, though the prisoners do not see it as such. Plato wittily elaborates upon this scenario with the emergence of what resembles a critical or academical class of prisoners: "They were in the habit of conferring honors among themselves on those who were quickest to observe the passing shadows and to remark which of them went before, and which followed after, and which were together;

and who were therefore best able to draw conclusions as to the future."[4] Still, for all of the seeming substance of having film reviews published by a university press, and notwithstanding the apparent accomplishment represented by that Oscar or *Palme d'Or,* in the end these critical or adulatory iterations are equally shadowy, equally insubstantial. Their seeming diversity and depth do not change the fact that the entire apparatus is utterly arresting, such that the imprisoned come to willingly accept and even embrace their captivity. They never leave, and they never want to.

This scenario does not admit the recreational benefits of a moderate media diet, and it certainly doesn't allow for the possibility of aesthetic or ethical substance in the consideration of story, image, or concept. The implications are simple, and they are clear: Plato's intent with the Parable of the Cave is to "show in a figure how far our nature is enlightened or unenlightened."[5] It would not be out of place to conclude that, adjusting for historical conditions and allowing for technological evolution, the compulsive and unreflective media addict continues to be the definitive emblem of unenlightenment, of ideological and intellectual servitude.

The parable describes clear means for a prisoner's deliverance, though they are not easily attained. He[6] must disengage and remove himself from this world of shadows. He will have difficulty as he does so, feeling a sharp and painful glare as he emerges into the light of reality, of real objects and real relations:

> He will require to grow accustomed to the sight of the upper world. And first he will see the shadows best, next the reflections of men and other objects in the water, and then the objects themselves; then he will gaze upon the light of the moon and the stars and the spangled heaven; and he will see the sky and the stars by night better than the sun or the light of the sun by day.[7]

Shadowy spectacle continues to exert a powerful hold, especially when contrasted with the bewildering brightness of the world outside. In the course of time, however, the former captive will become accustomed to the light of the sun. In its bright clarity he will come to understand things as they really are. As he does so he will also come to pity his captive brothers, wishing to provide for them the same deliverance that he now enjoys.

Plato's parable attests that the man who becomes enlightened must then enlighten his fellows. It also demonstrates how difficult, how very dangerous this necessary undertaking really is. The Parable of the Cave ends on a cautionary note, even a chilling, pessimistic one. "Men would say ... it was better not even to think of ascending; and if any one tried to loose another and lead him up to the light, let them only catch the offender, and they would put him to death."[8]

The Cave as Part of a Lineage of Engaged Critique and of Outright Repudiation

Plato's Cave brings contemporary situations to mind. Among other things it suggests how media, and movies particularly, can distract and enervate. However, although it is apt to reference the Cave in discussing historical suspicions about film, it is important to put that reference into proper context. The Cave relates to more than just movies. Modern media is merely the most recent iteration of a very longstanding problem, and such concerns are part of a long lineage of thinking about art in general, and narratives particularly.

This thinking comes in two registers. Both concern themselves with communication, with cultural apparatuses that distract and even disable the individual. "Between what matters and what seems to matter, how should the world we know judge wisely?"[9] The opening words to E. C. Bentley's pioneering 1913 detective novel, *Trent's Last Case*, reflect an ancient and endless perception, a measurable and undeniable disjunction. Surface and substance, appearance and reality, are not always the same. They are in fact in constant tension, if not outright opposition. These disjunctions are nowhere more evident than in the stories that men contrive, and the art that they create.

Conviction and concern about this gap lies at the core of any number of indelible, imperishable critiques, across centuries and continents: Plato's Cave would seem to qualify, as do the provocations of Aristophanes, the fables of Aesop, the satires of Juvenal; Boccaccio and Chaucer embody the sensibility, as in Rabelais or Cervantes it moves toward a kind of modernity; it is in Erasmus and his ironic praise of Folly, and in Thomas More's similarly antical Utopian counter. The gap between "seeming" and "being" attends the brute pragmatism of Machiavelli's *The Prince*, as well as Thomas Hobbes's more traumatical, metaphorical *Leviathan*; it is at the root of Jonathan Swift's sharply despairing *Gulliver's Travels*, and it infuses the sweeter, still eviscerating concoctions of Henry Fielding and William Makepeace Thackeray (1749, 1848); it motivates Bertolt Brecht (or Viktor Shklovsky, or Erwin Piscator) in pitting the modern theater against the epic theater, in enshrining alienation—*Verfremdungseffekt*—and its self-awareness against the passive identification, the self-abnegation of conventional commercial theater.

Instances multiply—the practically tectonical declarations of Martin Luther, the jolly provocations of Moliere, Voltaire's *Candide*, as informed by *The Philosophical Dictionary* and the *Treatise on Tolerance*, the encyclopedic fictions of Balzac and Zola, the dialectical dramas and comedies of George Bernard Shaw, the inquiring social excavations of Henrik Ibsen, or the violent psychological eviscerations of August Strindberg, not to mention Antonin Artaud's Theater of Cruelty. On the political stage there are Marx and Engels elaborating the workings of ideology, Antonio Gramsci elaborating the workings of hegemony, or Louis Althusser laying out the operations of any number of repressive state apparatuses. The motif continues to sound, even as it is brought, more or less, into the theoretical present. In a certain basic manner Peter Burger's take on the two avant-gardes, Jean Baudrillard's simulacra, Frederic Jameson on postmodernity—all of these voices and so many more continue to be concerned and engaged with the problem of the shadows on the wall.

As suggested, these are all critical engagements. They measure, describe in detail, take issue with perceived error. At the same time they also take a certain delight in that perceiving, from which one might infer that problems have some solution, and that the critic intends to contribute to it in some way. These various interventions characterize the first interrogative register just mentioned.

As it turns out the second register, to which the Cave more properly belongs, and of which it is in fact an emblematic, formative manifestation, is quite sharply separate from the first. Statements related to this second register are not just concerned with our credulousness, or of the workings of the institutions that exploit it. Their objections are more basic, more deeply, unwaveringly moral. These formulations are not so much critique as outright condemnation, more inclined to repudiate than to attempt, or even consider, any kind of reform.

This is the fleeing from the groves and from the fleshpots. These are the Lamentations of Jeremiah, the vanities laid out by the preacher in Ecclesiastes. This is Babylon, ever arrayed against the righteous, and Israel, delivered out of Egypt, gathered out from all the nations.[10] This is the call of thunder—"Depart ye, depart ye, go ye out from thence, touch no unclean *thing*; go ye out of the midst of her; be ye clean, that bear the vessels of the Lord"[11]—and a thunderous, everlasting victory. "And a mighty angel took up a stone like a great millstone, and cast it into the sea, saying,

Thus with violence shall that great city Babylon be thrown down, and shall be found no more at all."[12]

As it comes closer to the present, we can see more clearly the nature and implication of this particular project. Here the humorous, ostensibly optimistic earlier sections of *Gulliver's Travels* give way to the heartrending howls of the finale, where men are discovered to be irredeemable, and the despairing protagonist cannot even countenance the company of his own family, his own wife. A powerful, frequently prescribed antidote to the despair that Swift both describes and succumbs to is to withdraw from wickedness and to save oneself in so doing. The saving application of this antidote can be seen in the Franciscan embrace of poverty and selfless service, in the ascetical devotion of Thomas à Kempis's *Imitation of Christ* (ca. 1420), in the sweet and saintly disavowal of George Herbert's *The Temple* (1633). The same can be said, in broad terms, of any number of monastic regimes in both Christian and Buddhist traditions, as well as some of Islam's Sufi sects.

All of these iterations constitute a kind of line in the sand, with the World and all of its corruptions, occupations, even recreations, quite everlastingly on the other side. Separated from its original setting, the Parable of the Cave strikes the modern reader with its urbanity and sophistication. In its original context, however, and in the company of all of these other conscientious objectors, these are not at all the qualities that it avows. Rather it is written in stone, steadfast and immoveable, and much more of a refusal than many moderns will be willing to make.

Unwilling, that is, except when a child is involved. The critiques and repudiations just outlined have particular relevance in a discussion about children's literature and media. They have a particular appeal as well. This is because of the undeniable and defining vulnerability of children, and the irrefutable idea that adult worth and societal integrity can and must be measured by how well those children are protected. In this connection, severity and even plain opting out may suddenly seem like a more viable option. Indeed for many, they may appear as the only decent choice.

Plato on Story, Genre and Enacted Narrative

Many people are suspicious of movies. For many, the worst of their suspicions have been amply confirmed. There is a firm moral-philosophical core to this view and to the response that, quite logically, quite immediately, follows.

In *The Republic*, Plato establishes the characteristics of a just city-state, and of the kind of man who will best contribute to it. There is a place for art and artists in this ideal society. More specifically, there is a place for *techne*. This much-debated term, perhaps closer to "craftsmanship" than to "art" as a modern person might understand it, conveyed the idea of the fashioning of objects for practical ends, often in a domestic setting. These objects were practical, but not unbeautiful, and their beauty was of a very particular kind. *Techne*, or "making," was informed by the art of measure, which sought the mean between excess and defect. In other words, the craftsmanship espoused by Plato was of the most symmetrical and balanced variety. Not coincidentally, these are also the values and proportions most associated with the perfections of classical antiquity.[13]

A beautifully fashioned object, whether made for use or contemplation, pleases both hand and eye. Further, it refines the senses, and the mind as well. The mind's susceptibility to beauty and decorum constitutes a seemly appetite, and one that can be satisfied in more than just the manufacture of objects. Beauty and decorum may also be manifest in a poem or a speech or a play, to which the art of measure can also be applied. Of all of these decorous classical symmetries, the most important was the art of measure's relation to the art of living, and the art of governance especially.[14] These principles were universal. Regardless of setting or utility the best art, the art that could most easily be countenanced, reflected the mean.

Now we come back to the shadow of the Cave, and to the status of story in Plato's city-state. Story has a place in this ideal society, but it is a very particular, circumscribed place. This is basically because of the effects that stories can have on impressionable children. "A young person cannot judge what is allegorical and what is literal; anything that he receives into his mind ... is likely to become indelible and unalterable; and therefore it is most important that the tales which the young first hear should be models of virtuous thoughts."[15]

Indeed, Plato repeatedly returns to this motif of the child's susceptibility. Because of this susceptibility, he will only countenance a certain kind of story. "If [children] imitate at all, they should imitate from youth upward only those characters which are suitable to their [eventual] profession—the courageous, temperate, holy, free, and the like."[16]

A virtuous story inspires its hearer and inclines him to virtuous action. This coin has another side, of course. Many stories contain negative examples, and these also affect the hearer:

> Stories should not depict or be skilful at imitating any kind of illiberality or baseness, lest from imitation they should come to be what they imitate. Did you never observe how imitations, beginning in early youth and continuing far into life, at length grow into habits and become a second nature, affecting body, voice, and mind?[17]

Seemly stories have an edifying effect. On the other hand, the portrayal of impropriety—filial impiety, quarrelling among the gods, the violation of oaths and duties—has a corrupting influence, especially on children. Such tales ascribe inappropriate behavior to the gods, or, alternatively, posit that the sins of mortals are derived from the actions of the gods. These were perilous assertions, with tremendous jeopardy attached. If they were true then how could the gods be good? Or men? And to whom could the child look, or in what confide?[18]

Much more than the elegant, multivalent and movie theater–resembling Parable of the Cave, this is the root of a practically ancestral suspicion of film, and most especially of the actors that play such compelling parts on the stages of our lives. Too many tales feature, model and implicitly advocate bad behavior. For the credulous—and not only the young—representation too often, too easily leads to imitation. This is also the prevailing contemporary complaint, or criticism, often unto outright condemnation. But if the staunchness of *The Republic* resembles much modern resistance to media, the manner of its unyielding is subtle in ways too often absent from the contemporary debate.

It is not simply the story being told that is at issue, but the manner in which it is being told. Morality relates not just to content, but also to the form in which that content is rendered. Just as importantly, beyond what is said and how it is said there is also the tremendous significance of the medium in which this rendering takes place. Though *The Republic* will retain its severe tone, it also allows for the considerable difference between "saying" and "playing." We might carefully adapt for changing times, conditions and technologies and say that this is also the difference between the page and the stage. Adapting similarly, we might add that the stage and the screen have tremendous correlations between them. Plato will continue severe, but his points will suggest how, when viewed from a more sympathetic perspective, film need not, cannot, be simply dismissed.

Plato describes the manner in which stories operate by making a generic distinction. "You are aware, I suppose, that all mythology and poetry is a narration of events, either past, present, or to come" and that "narration may be either simple narration, or imitation, or a union of the two?"[19]

Simple narration, or imitation, or a union of the two: in some ways the whole of theatrical practice, throughout all theatrical history, is contained in this simple genre categorization. It hints at how oral description, or the storyteller's narration of incident, developed into theatrical enactment. Further, it prefigures the manner in which literature expands—not in the sense of superiority, but in the way that it literally engages more of the physical senses—into the cinematic.

The Republic would almost certainly be wary of either of these phenomena. Some forms are morally viable, while others entail great moral risk. Plato observes that simple narration allows the poet to maintain his own person, and that he communicates transparently when he does so. He goes on to describe the union of narration and imitation, or the epic. In the epic mode, the narrator can assume the role of the character that he has been describing in his tale. As he does so, if narration continues to outweigh imitation, then the epic maintains a similar transparency to that of unadulterated narration. When this transparency is combined with an edifying story that portrays exemplary behavior, then narrative art continues to perform its proper, positive function. With regard to the Cave, we might say that these are not shadowy illusions, but constructive communications, circulating in the full light of day.[20]

Once again, this conversation relates to much more than mere entertainment. It concerns the art, and specifically the narrative art that will best contribute to the formation and maintenance of a just city-state. Likewise, it also concerns the art that will help to form the virtuous man or woman in that community.

At this point, Plato considers a central component of theatrical art that contains much of its appeal, and most of its danger. Coming after straight narration and the hybridized epic, the most dangerous of the generic alternatives is the imitative. Here the imitator, or actor, does not speak for his own self.[21] Rather, he assumes a role, portraying the actions of the character that he has taken on. This is the pantomimist, who is gifted, and whom children prefer. Plato has it that by taking on and maintaining a role, this appealing imitator traffics exclusively in appearances, and in shadows.[22] "If he is a good artist, he may deceive children or simple persons."[23]

Here again is the importance of both manner and method, of content and form. Plato holds that in both what he says and in the way that he says it, the imitative artist waylays, drawing his patron further and further away from the truth. And yet, as one of Plato's auditors innocently observes, "the pantomimic, which is the opposite of the one chosen by you, is the most popular style with children and their attendants, and with the world in general."[24]

There's the rub. Plato holds that "all poetical imitations are ruinous to the understanding of the hearers, and ... the knowledge of their true nature is the only antidote to them."[25] And what is that true nature? In the *Poetics* (335 BC), Aristotle lists the six elements of drama, and of tragedy in particular, in order of descending importance. They are plot, character, reasoning, music, diction, and spectacle.[26] Though Aristotle's formulation obviously postdates Plato, we might still venture to assume that Plato might have objected to fully imitative theater for the following, still potent reason. "Reasoning" has to do with a protagonist considering his circumstances, coming to understand something of their cause and consequence, and then both doing something about and learning something from them.[27] He "take[s] Arms against a Sea of troubles, And by opposing end[s] them."[28] Or at the very least, by opposing he comprehends them. It is through this process that the protagonist's tribulations, as well as the dramatic flow and fall of the play itself, actually make him a better man. In his apparent failing lies his moral triumph.

Reasoning resembles the modern notion of theme, and it has much to do with the likewise ancient institution of the moral tale, or fable. Like themes and morals, reasoning was to have led to some kind of a lesson for the dramatis personae, one that was also to have been apprehended by audience members. Plato held that the imitative nature of theater caused a shifting of these priorities, and a frustration of their worthy aims. He would hold that most enacted narratives combined plot and character with theatrical spectacle, which would be the least in and the last of Aristotle's hierarchy.[29] Such performances too easily, too universally, obscured the processes of reasoning or the moral lessons to which these processes properly led.

It is here that the dramatic, theatrical storyteller distracts the mind and waylays the heart. The more effective the spectacle, the more thorough the beguiling. The imitative poet "awakens and nourishes and strengthens the feelings and impairs the reason.... [He] implants an evil constitution, for he indulges the irrational nature which has no discernment of greater and less ...—he is a manufacturer of images and is very far removed from the truth."[30] The implications of this waylaying are tremendous. Once again, as always, innocent, unformed childhood is the key. A stirring imitation or a compelling theatrical spectacle can jeopardize the young person's moral education, his perception of reality, and his allegiance to righteousness.

It is performance itself, then, that contains the danger in enacted narrative. And it is performance in enacted narrative that demands our caution, and even disavowal. This is the theater, and it could well be the cinema, with its own species of spectacular imitations. At their very, frequent best, fictional narratives are arresting, compelling, convincing, and they may very well add up to some kind of irresistible force. For the Platonic sensibility, the conclusion is clear: This force must be resisted anyway.

> When any one of these pantomimic gentlemen, who are so clever that they can imitate anything, comes to us, and makes a proposal to exhibit himself and his poetry, we will fall down and worship him as a sweet and holy and wonderful being; but we must also inform him that in our State such as he are not permitted to exist; the law will not allow them. And so when we have anointed him with myrrh, and set a garland of wool upon his head, we shall send him away to another city.[31]

For all of its extremity, Plato's disavowal has much humanity to it, as in this superbly self-denying sentiment. With regard to all of these troubling things, he knew that "there is merit and gain here, but so as to choose the better part we will forego it."[32] This was the proper course, and for the most fundamental of reasons: "great is the issue at stake, greater than appears, whether a man is to be good or bad. And what will any one be profited if under the influence of honor or money or power, aye, or under the excitement of poetry, he neglect justice and virtue?"[33]

And so, the unyielding conclusion: "he who cannot conform to this rule of ours [is] to be prevented from practicing his art in our State, lest the taste of our citizens be corrupted by him."[34]

This is an intractable, practically geological response to the shadows that play upon the wall. Plato set the tone and established the terms for millennia of subsequent debate on the status of narrative art in civil society. This position, simultaneously so upright and intransigent, is difficult to deny in full, and even more difficult to counter. This is not because there are no gaps in its argument or alternatives to its perspective. It is because the stakes of the contest are so high and the consequences of failure so imponderable. There is the matter of the detrimental and possibly destructive effect of inappropriate imitations, and there is so much more besides: "For what shall it profit a man, if he shall gain the whole world, and lose his own soul?"[35]

Plato, Present in a Puritanical Milestone

So it is that in their various times and contexts, Plato's often wild-eyed successors tend not to be interested in discussion, negotiation, or compromise. Once again, they are concerned for the salvation of souls and with the confrontation and defeat of all that would endanger them. John Bunyan, the sublimely steadfast seventeenth-century English Puritan, takes up this Platonic torch (though he would not likely acknowledge, be aware of, or even appreciate the connection) with electrifying vigor and conviction. He finds that shadowy illusion holds sway, not only in Plato's Cave, but out in the broad daylight as well. It is not just the shadows, or the theater with which he takes issue, but all Vanity, all worldly affection or striving. For Bunyan, misrecognition and misapplication, error and sin, are the stuff of the entire fallen world. The only remedy is to remove oneself, as quickly and directly as possible. And yet, as one attempts to do so, there are so many valleys, so many shadows, through which he must pass.

The Pilgrim's Progress[36] illustrates this point quite multiply, and nowhere as powerfully as in the vision of that great worldly city, Vanity Fair:

> Then I saw in my dream, that when they [the Christian pilgrims that populate the parable] were got out of the wilderness, they presently saw a town before them, and the name of that town is Vanity; and at the town there is a fair kept, called Vanity Fair: it is kept all the year long.[37]

The Cave is geologic in its nature and power. Vanity Fair is more organic, more sentient and maliciously purposeful. And yet, its great long standing also gives it something of the tectonic, something of ancient heft and horror:

> This fair is no new-erected business, but a thing of ancient standing; I will show you the original of it.
> Almost five thousand years agone, there were pilgrims walking to the Celestial City ... and Beelzebub, Apollyon, and Legion ... perceiving by the path that the pilgrims made, that their way to the city lay through this town of Vanity, they contrived here to set up a fair; a fair wherein, should be sold all sorts of vanity, and that it should last all the year long: therefore at this fair are all such merchandise sold, as houses, lands, trades, places, honors, preferments, titles, countries, kingdoms, lusts, pleasures, and delights of all sorts, as whores, bawds, wives, husbands, children, masters, servants, lives, blood, bodies, souls, silver, gold, pearls, precious stones, and what not.[38]

This ringing catalogue speaks of and condemns the pursuit of material wealth, affected pomp, and striving for position. It condemns sensual indulgence, and even plain material or domestic comfort. Far from providing respite or refreshment, the recreational is considered to be as distracting, as potentially destructive as actual vice. "And, moreover, at this fair there is at all times to be seen juggling cheats, games, plays, fools, apes, knaves, and rogues, and that of every kind."[39] Perhaps this is because, whether on the stage or on the street, the stories being played out are identically depraved, and dangerous. "Here are to be seen, too, and that for nothing, thefts, murders, adulteries, false swearers, and that of a blood-red color."[40]

Bunyan grimly affirms that the way to the Celestial City lies through this town, and through its "lusty fair."[41] "He that will go to the city, and yet not go through this town, must needs go out of the world."[42]

And how are these pilgrims to accomplish this difficult thing? They may be humble, but Christ is omnipotent, and his grace is sufficient if they will take the proper course and follow his perfect example. The "Prince of princes himself," went of necessity through the fair, and was waylaid by Beelzebub.

> Yea, because he was such a person of honor, Beelzebub had him from street to street, and showed him all the kingdoms of the world..., that he might, if possible, allure the Blessed One to cheapen and buy some of his vanities; but he had no mind to the merchandise, and therefore left the town, without laying out so much as one farthing upon these vanities.[43]

Christ resisted temptation.[44] He is the exemplar, and this is how he came to prevail, and every pilgrim must do the same.

Whether he knows it or not, Bunyan's stirring formulation continues to inform every fundamentalist's fear of the media, and of the fallen world it reflects. It also suggests how these fears not only have considerable substance, but that they have been articulated with their own fierce beauty. It is not enough, as so often happens, to simply dismiss these objections, or the way that they are expressed. Rather, they deserve a measure of understanding and acknowledgment. Allowing for the importance and validity of people's perspective, they may even deserve a measure of agreement.

Sympathy for the Censorious: The Payne Fund Studies and *Movie Made America*

These ancient accounts are familiar, and still resonant. They inform almost every modern-day Puritan's concerns about the media, whether the Puritan knows it or not. Some people are inclined to censor, for the sake of the soul. They are more apt to intervene when that soul belongs to a young person. And intervention is much more likely when some kind of narrative is at hand, especially if it is imitative, enacted on a stage—or a screen—rather than being described in the pages of a book.

This censorious impulse has been an important, constant presence throughout the history of film. Those invested in the cinema have tended to view this censorship negatively, and with much good reason. Some regulatory impositions, taking place in a number of countries and over a number of years, have been presumptuous or high-handed. They have even been unnatural, undertaking to expunge from films reasonable traces of the ways that reasonable adults actually live and think and interact.

Filmmakers and free speech advocates quite naturally oppose all of this. However, as with Plato on the subject of imitation and spectacle, many parents, teachers, and other community leaders have not been especially moved by this opposition. Images of reasonable adult interaction, or the cause of liberty as applied to commercial creativity, are not nearly as important to them as the moral well-being of their children. This is especially true if these things are capable of jeopardizing that well-being. And who can blame the caretakers for their sentiments? Though there has been philistinism in the discourse and despotism in the methods of some of its participants—once again, the standard survey histories lay out the details—one must retain some sympathy for the media watchdog that vigilantly acts upon this basic and irreproachable motivation.

Many individuals and many organizations have been so motivated and have so acted. These efforts are international, and have attended the entire history of the film medium. The actions of the book-burning fascist fall outside of the purview of this study. The actions of the fearful parent, who under duress and in the midst of a multitude of pressures and perils may occasionally look or even act like a book-burning fascist, are of definite interest. Also of interest is the insufficiently acknowledged fact that the film-fearing naysayer has sometimes spoken quite sensibly. There are many instances; one of these, coming at a pivotal period and exerting tremendous influence, can give an indication of the entire conversation.

The year 1933 saw the U.S. publication of the Payne Fund Studies, which for the previous four years had gathered data about American children's film attendance, as well as their emotional responses to the films they had attended. The Motion Picture Research Council (MPRC), a non-industry body, had commissioned the study. In connection, 1933 also saw the publication of Henry James Forman's *Our Movie Made Children*, which summarized the findings of the Payne Fund Studies and adapted them for more popular consumption.

Some of Forman's intent is reflected in a quotation that he takes from

Will Hays, the president of the Motion Picture Producers and Distributors of America (MPPDA). Hays had been instrumental in establishing and implementing the American film industry's first self-regulatory regimes back in the early 1920s, and he would continue to play an important part in these conversations for decades to follow. In the following quotation, Hays encapsulates his entire mandate, at least as far as the public was concerned: "This industry must have toward that sacred thing, the mind of a child, toward that clean virgin thing, the unmarked slate, the same responsibility, the same care about the impressions made upon it that the best clergyman or the most inspired teacher of youth would have."[45]

This statement contains a shade of Plato, meaning not only the conscientious objector but also the strategical rhetorician. The child is certainly at issue, but here also are public relations and a degree of propaganda. A quick perusal of some of Forman's chapter titles—"Molded by the Movies," "The Path to Delinquency," "Movie-Made Criminals"—reinforce this same impression. They are heightened, to say the least, and have helped to form an impression, now fairly general, that Forman's book was alarmist and manipulative.

Film culture and kids' culture can have, and often have had, something of an adversarial relationship. ("Kids' culture" here refers to the complex and multifarious moral, logistical and, yes, commercial considerations that make of children a first priority, in most every instance.) But they might also understand each other. A closer look at Forman's book reveals that it is not wholly reactive. Other chapter titles—"The Blank Slate," "Movies and Conduct"—strike the ear as being much more reasonable, even necessary. From a parent's perspective, and removed from the barricades of partisanship, much of Forman's book actually reflects the real concern, and often, the good sense of Plato's original inquiry.

Like every adult with a stewardship over a child, Forman worries about "the influence of motion pictures and their impersonations upon the character, conduct and behavior of vast numbers of our nation and especially upon the more malleable and younger people." He is concerned because of the "excruciatingly realistic attitude" that children so often have toward movies.[46] "To the adult it may be good art or bad, it may be clever mechanism, good photography, effective direction, successful or unsuccessful story telling, a good movie, or hokum and trash. To the young child it is reality itself—the diffuse, chaotic reality of every-day life, intensely concentrated within the limited area of the screen."[47]

We have heard all of this before in *The Republic*: "a young person cannot judge what is allegorical and what is literal; anything that he receives into his mind ... is likely to become indelible and unalterable; and therefore it is most important that the tales which the young first hear should be models of virtuous thoughts."[48]

And so, good stories to reinforce the good. Forman understands that considerations such as these might not be of primary interest to the businessman or to the film craftsman. Although American films were not then protected by the first amendment to the American constitution,[49] the freedom to speak, to inquire, to conclude and to communicate, were still acknowledged to be an important part of the mix.

The original Payne Fund Study quotes Will Hays, again. "The proper treatment of crime as a social fact or as a dramatic motive is the inalienable right of a free press, of free speech and of an unshackled stage or screen."[50] Forman concurs, but only up to a point.

> With this opinion there is no quarrel whatever. The key to the situation, however, lies in his second word—"proper." That crime is a social fact in this country, and in virtually all countries, there is no doubt. That it is emphasized on the screen out of all proportion to its place in the national life is equally clear of doubt, indeed glaringly obvious. Were crime to receive similar emphasis in the life of any one of us as individuals, we should properly expect to be either in jail or in an insane asylum.[51]

The world is dangerous, and our films will reflect the fact. But in doing, so films may also distort the facts. Since this is true, then vigilance is required, on a number of fronts. "Man is by nature an imitative animal, and the types of imitation mentioned are as common and inevitable as any in the human curriculum. The aim in adducing them is to emphasize that the movies are a school, a school of conduct, a sort of supplementary system of education. And if the movies are that, they cease to be nobody's business."[52]

If this is the case, since this is the case—parents, teachers, and concerned citizens are obligated to be vigilant and to take action if needs be. As Plato himself held, and explained in very great detail, children are inclined to imitate, and imitation, compounded, will form the soul. For this reason, film stories cannot be seen simply as yarns, commercial products, or exercises of the franchise. "If we believe that good pictures have a beneficent effect, it is clearly useless to say that my child is proof against adverse influence, or that this crime picture will make no impression upon any particular child or some especially favored boy or girl."[53]

The very serious, potentially soul-threatening implications of all of these familiar Platonic things cannot be denied, for all the skepticism, all the scorn that the sophisticates may muster. Forman quotes William

James: "The drunken Rip Van Winkle, in Jefferson's play, excuses himself for every fresh dereliction by saying 'I won't count this time!' Well! He may not count it, and a kind Heaven may not count it, but it is being counted never the less. Down among his nerve-cells and fibres the molecules are counting it, registering and storing it up to be used against him when the next temptation comes."[54]

As indicated, Forman's book is not presently in fashion. Neither was it, or the Payne Fund Studies that informed it, universally embraced at the time of publication.[55] Film historian Richard Maltby views Forman's book as follows: "A widely circulated sensationalized digest of the Studies, Henry James Forman's *Our Movie Made Children*, made the MPRC's demands for federal regulation a profound threat to the industry."[56]

This characterization is significant, and emblematic. Community concerns for children were a threat to the film industry. For the film industry and many of its chroniclers, the threat held more weight than the concerns that brought it about. Maltby's account of the history of film censorship and regulation is thorough, balanced, and tremendously useful. It appears in one of the very finest survey histories of film. In this particular instance, he states a common perception, or perhaps a common assumption. The censors are sensationalist, with all the word implies about grandstanding, imbalance, and distortion. They constitute a threat not only to commerce, but to free discourse.

Our Movie Made Children contains hints of a now-superannuated behaviorism in the way that it discusses the child's susceptibility to external conditioning. Similarly, there is an unconscious, coincidental trace of the pessimistic Frankfurt School when it anticipates homogeneous response to what is actually a heterogeneic set of realities and possibilities. Since the publication of Forman's work, whole libraries' worth of works have been published on the subjects of phenomenology and reader response and on the ability of the individual to assert her own interests, for all the pressure that is brought to bear upon her.

Scholarly and attitudinal currency are very important, and yet something remains in Forman's work, and especially the concerns that it reflects, that cannot simply be dismissed. The present discussion concerns children's books and films, how they have often been placed in opposition, and how they might actually find some conciliatory common ground. But in doing so, and in referencing the aims of the artist or industry as sometimes arrayed against the child or his caretaker, we are entering into a more fundamental, primordial opposition.

This opposition is not just perspectival, or topographical. Scholarly camps, with their various values and cultures, will view the particular set of issues from here, or from there. The child's advocate cannot afford to be so dispassionate. From the trenches of children's discourse the opposition has been, and has only increasingly become, antagonistic.

Contemporary Manifestations of the Platonic Impulse

Things have changed since the depression of the 1930s. And they haven't. With television as the major culprit, a number of more contemporary voices have joined the immemorial outcry. It is significant that many of these concerned and even alarmist takes on the situation are much more informed, much more citing and seemingly scientific in their critique, than had often been the case previously. With all of this increased research, however, a stern, staunch unyieldingness has often remained.

Once again, out of a multitude of voices, a few examples will suffice. The last quarter of the twentieth century saw a number of vividly critical statements about the role of the media in the lives of young people: Marie Winn's *The Plug-in Drug* (1977, revised 1985) and *Children Without Childhood* (1984), David Elkind's *The Hurried Child* (1981), Michael Medved's *Hollywood vs. America: Popular Culture and the War on Traditional Values* (1992), Barry Sanders' *A Is for Ox: The Collapse of Literacy and the Rise of Violence in an Electronic Age* (1994), David Gauntlett's *Moving Experiences: Understanding Television's Influence and Effects* (1995, revised 2005), the American Medical Association's *Family Guide to Media Violence* (1996), and Shirley Steinberg and Joe Kincheloe's *Kinderculture: The Corporate Construction of Childhood* (1997, revised 2004).[57]

It is significant that these publications reflect a variety of ideological mindsets: conservative, often with a Christian tinge, or strictly secular, conventionally progressive, or social-democratic, or outright anti-corporate. It is also significant that for all of this political-philosophical diversity from across the spectrum, all of these publications share a consistent, apocalyptic tone. They are united in saying that the shadows on the wall, or the films and television programs that have replaced them, have multiplied and intensified to the point that they represent an imminent threat to most everyone, and to children most particularly.

American cultural critic Neil Postman raised one of the strongest and most consistent voices in condemning television and media culture generally, as well as the role of technology in extending their impact. Significantly, with regard to the present project, some of his most pointed criticism depends on a binarized opposition between books and media, between the power and substance of the word and the superficiality of the image. Postman's *The Disappearance of Childhood* (1982) holds that television is irreversibly altering the lives of children. Childhood has always been made up of a set of realities, or possibilities, that coalesced around a conceptual construct made possible by the printing press. Books defined and elaborated the construct, which was always informed and added unto by real lives. But now, Postman warns, after centuries of constructive evolution, this concept of childhood is on the brink of obliteration. And electronic media is the sole culprit.

For Postman, print created individuality. It led to the establishment of schools, of curricula and pedagogies that enabled children to learn all of the things that they needed to know. Until that process was completed, young people were kept from certain secrets, certain important adult prospects. This veil, as it were, allowed for the preservation of innocence until the time when innocence could be succeeded by experience, maturity, and increase.

Television, said Postman, has upset this longstanding equilibrium, to the point that it may even have eliminated it. As a "total disclosure medium," television has wrested control from the hands of parents. As a result, young people now have premature access to the mysteries that had previously been deferred until disclosure had been appropriate. They also have access to all manner of other mysteries, or depravities, which had never been countenanced, or considered, or even conceived of.

It would not be too much of a stretch to imagine that this was Plato's pantomimist, writ large and multiplied almost infinitely. The corruptions feared by the ancients had now taken root, and taken over. Tales, broadly speaking, were to blame; fictional and actual, whether shadowed suggestions or monstrously manifested in the light of day, our indulgent interest in and subscription to the groves of enacted narrative had brought all of this disaster to pass.

In the face of all of this apocalyptic alarm, a plaintive question might come to mind. Can parents not oppose all this, or prevail as they establish some footing on this slippery slope? Perhaps, but only in part. For Postman, even if parents were to do so, a more basic, insoluble difficulty remains. He holds print to be perfect for cognitive development. For its part, television is irrational, and as such, is beyond reforming. And it is ubiquitous. And it is here to stay.

This is the starting point for Postman's next major publication, *Amus-*

ing Ourselves to Death: Public Discourse in the Age of Show Business (1985). Postman writes with the basic assumption, the thorough conviction that books are basically, almost inherently good and that media are not. Like its predecessor, *Amusing Ourselves to Death* is an impassioned jeremiad about the destructive effects of mass media. Postman characterizes the book not only as an inquiry but as "a lamentation about the most significant American cultural fact of the second half of the twentieth century: the decline of the Age of Typography and the ascendancy of the Age of Television."[58] His argument begins with Plato, then ups the ante by proceeding to Moses, or rather Jehovah. The Hebrew Bible's injunction against graven images is then supplemented by Christ's New Testament discussion of the two great commandments.[59] In either case, Postman points out that the most thunderous of divine injunctions constitute a warning about and a proscription against the very enraptured, sated, even idolatrous immersion in imagery that is so emblematic of modern media culture.

To support this portentous assertion, *Amusing Ourselves to Death* lays out a systematic list of televisual culture's inherent shortcomings and of all their attached deleterious effects. Postman is critical about the brevity of televisual conversations, and how they are glancing unto emptiness. As will be the case throughout the book, he illustrates TV's dire concision by contrasting it with the inherent abundance of the book, or the word.

"Philosophy cannot exist without criticism, and writing makes it possible and convenient to subject thought to a continuous and concentrated scrutiny. Writing freezes speech and in so doing gives birth to the grammarian, the logician, the rhetorician, the historian, the scientist—all those who must hold language before them so that they can see what it means, where it errs and where it is leading."[60] Postman goes on to compare this self-perpetuating substance to the poverty of telegraphic communication. The telegraph, he says, provided information, but not background, leaving its subscribers "knowing *of* lots of things, not knowing *about* them."[61]

From the inadequacies of telegraphy, Postman proceeds to the visual, and to a bold conflation of all of its many iterations. "Like telegraphy, photography recreates the world as a series of idiosyncratic events. There is no beginning, middle, or end in a world of photographs, as there is none implied by telegraphy. The world is atomized. There is only a preset and it need not be part of any story that can be told."[62]

To reinforce this characterization, Postman reduces the visual, or more specifically the photographic, to the status of a mere reproduction of nature. For him Daguerre "invented the world's first 'cloning' device …

the photograph was to visual experience what the printing press was to the written word."[63] In addition to, as a result of this lack of agency, Postman avers that the photograph cannot be more than momentary, nor better than simpleminded. "By itself, a photograph cannot deal with the unseen, the remote, the internal, the abstract."[64]

At this point Postman makes another conceptual leap, bringing the partiality of the photograph back to bear on the entirety of television, and its ability to render or communicate complexity. The still image is very much like television's particular form of the moving picture. "Sustained, complex talk does not play well on television." As an advocate of the word, of writing, and of its engaged and continuous conversation, Postman finds that television ultimately, definitively accommodates the requirements of visual interest. In a final, cataclysmic conflation, Postman concludes thusly: "that is to say, to accommodate the values of show business."[65]

This back-and-forth continues throughout the whole of *Amusing Ourselves to Death*. Postman pulls out various elements of media culture, compares them to the bounty of the book, and finds them to be inadequate. In this, his earlier evocation of Plato is apt. He has consciously and thoroughly updated his exemplar's ancient argument. Like Plato, he has been mindful of different media and of how they work distinctly. He is concerned, and in very great and convincing detail. Postman does not go as far as John Bunyan in his repudiation of culture. In the end, though, his characterization of electronic media is basically puritanical, if not biblical: it is all vanity, and vexation of spirit.[66]

Amusing Ourselves to Death is convicted and conscientious, passionate and sincere in its polemicism. It is a provocation, but it is also principled, and not without its profundities. Deeply felt and decently motivated, anyone interested in its various issues would do well to consider it. The same is true of so many of Plato's philosophical descendants. But if Postman and Plato must not be dismissed, they must also be countered and added unto.

Actually, the Sky Is Not Falling

We have made this point: the objectors have their reasons, and they are deserving of proper respect and sympathy. And the second point is like unto it: for all of their emotional, parental justification, many of these objectors—and a great many of their objections—are compromisingly partial, and sometimes sorely lacking.

1. The Media

As mentioned, British media scholar David Buckingham characterizes some of the just-cited media critiques, Postman's included, as "apocalyptic." He acknowledges that these particular voices have their ample reasons, and that they pursue these reasons through use of actual data and a measure of scholarly methodology. Buckingham concludes, however, that as powerful and as emblematic as these voices may be, they are very often compromised by the way that they utilize that data, by the way that they generalize, and universalize.

> Ultimately the claims of Postman and the others rest on a view of media audiences as an undifferentiated mass. Children, in particular, are implicitly seen to be passive and defenceless in the face of media manipulation. Audiences are not seen here as socially differentiated, or as capable of responding critically to what they watch. Television, because of its inherently "visual" nature (one wonders what happened to the soundtrack), is effectively seen to bypass cognition entirely. It requires no intellectual, emotional or imaginative investment: it simply imprints itself on children's consciousness.[67]

Beyond the polemical instant, too much of this sharp criticism of the media does not stand up to scrutiny, or to any number of measurable, demonstrable proofs. And in fact, that worm lies at the very root of this entire censorious conversation. We have already appreciated and honored the magisterial Plato. Now it is fair to observe that some of his restrictive ideas are excessive, and suffer under scrutiny.

In Book III of *The Republic* Plato gives us a dialogue between Socrates and Adeimantus in which they criticize a number of specific story types, and go so far as to prescribe that they be outlawed. These include tales in which right does not prevail, or ambiguous tales in which divisions between right and wrong are obscured or unclear. Socrates and Adeimantus also disapprove of stories that are frightening, for reasons that any protective parent—or traumatized child—might imagine, or understand. Though *The Republic* is thousands of years old, these same categories, the same kinds of stories continue to be a concern for many moderns. And many moderns, especially when children are in the vicinity, proceed in the problematic way that Plato also records and endorses.

Socrates and Adeimantus continue forward, and they go too far. They also disapprove of stories that feature lamentation, as lamentation might affect morale or make hearers too excitable and effeminate. They disapprove of stories that feature laughter, given that laughter so often leads to violent reaction, and then, quite possibly, disorder. As these categories multiply, the protective, proscriptive project begins to seem unwieldy, and even unseemly. Depending on the inclination of the watchdog, every tale can be seen as objectionable, and so censored. Where does it stop?

The excesses of the exercise come into sharper relief when Socrates proceeds into the precincts of music. In the area of melody and music, he advocates outlawing harmonies that express sorrow and, of course, the soft or drinking harmonies.[68] He would further forbid, or at least seriously circumscribe, actual musical instruments, allowing only the lyre and the harp in the city, while of course leaving the shepherds their pipes in the country.[69]

The projects of reform or refusal, even in their most extreme particulars, contain at least two laudable things. One of these comes out of a pressing reality that is both ancient and modern, and of especial interest to those caring for and about children. It is that there is malice in the world, and danger, and the real possibility of harm or corruption. Since this is true, then the protective instinct, the guarding of one's charges against harm, is both natural and necessary. Similarly irreproachable is the impulse to identify, enact, and defend virtue. It is logical to think that good stories would promote good behavior, and who would not wish to promote and proliferate that?

Along with these two laudable things are two considerable problems. First, are right and wrong so clearly identifiable, or distinguishable? Melodrama, and moral/political naïveté, would posit that there is right and wrong, good and bad, always and only. History, law, and literature affirm that it is frequently otherwise. The second problem has to do with arbitration and authority. Who is to make these judgments? What authorizes them, legislatively, morally, or curricularly, to do so?

To these two problems we might add another, perhaps unconsidered and unsuspected at the time. "Poetry feeds and waters the passions instead of drying them up; she lets them rule, although they ought to be controlled, if mankind are ever to increase in happiness and virtue."[70] *The Republic* is consistent in holding that it is better to restrain and even repress feeling, particularly if it is excessive. Plato discusses the dignity and courage of the man who submits to evil fortune with equanimity. He compares him with the man who would rail and revile, and make a spectacle. He observes that the playwright always inclines to represent the latter and that even if he would do otherwise, the "promiscuous" rabble insists that he take the lesser course. This is another way in which narrative, in this case enacted narrative, embodies indignity and promotes disorder.[71]

For Plato, theater is far too demonstrative. In a certain sense, this description actually suggests that theater acts like a child. Concerns about stories in *The Republic* have to do with the State's responsibility to protect the vulnerable, including and especially children. One commonplace in our contemporary conversations about children—though it is not without its opponents—is that adults are always trying to make them grow up, or in other words, to stop them from acting like kids.[72] *The Republic* endorses this view, at least tacitly. In describing his project, and outlining some of its particulars with regard to protecting the vulnerable, Plato scorns those very vulnerabilities, not to mention the children who are subject to them.

Similarly, many modern voices are simply too insistent, too inflexible. This is partly the case because they are too removed from the particularities of the media, and, in the present instance, of film especially. Again, as it is past time to enumerate the substance of media, Neil Postman can stand in for the errors of the rest.

In *Amusing Ourselves to Death*, Postman's reference to Plato is partly practical, and it is definitely dispositional. As it turns out, he demonstrates the same faithful inflexibility as did his proscriptive philosophical forebear. Postman's fervor is connected with a problematic incuriosity, a consistent inaccuracy in his accounts of visual culture. His repeated assertion that the visual has no content does not take into account, for instance, André Bazin's theories of cinematic realism (discussed in this book's introduction) or the great richness of the deep, durational image. Neither does it allow for multiple readings or the operations of intertextuality. But the fact is that any of these can cause the allegedly telegraphic and superficial visual to multiply, or to increase in weight.

Bazin's notions are by now classical, even distantly Classical, at least in the film-philosophical sense. As with so many of his peers, Postman does not account for, is perhaps not aware of the generations of rich, conflicting, enriching critical discussion that has subsequently deepened our sense of the complexity and profundity of images. Also, since and even during the time of Postman's writing the discipline of media literacy has developed tremendously. Not only have its practitioners more thoroughly and helpfully identified difficulties and shortcomings, but they have also articulated and refined the ways in which the televisual actually functions positively.[73]

Postman states that the photograph lacks syntax, and therefore the capacity to argue with the world. To support this position he keys on the objectivity of photography, which is only a very small (and very tendentious!) part of generations of substantial, sophisticated, multiple documentary discourse. And, what, as David Buckingham suggested, of phenomenology? What of the capacity of the individual who looks, or views, and who considers as she does so? For instance: if the photograph is similar to telegraphy in its glancingness and poverty, then how is that limitation altered or deepened when any family gathers around its photo albums? And beyond such domestic discussions, what of photo archives, especially as they exist alongside of all manner of data and documentation, in all sorts of mediums?

Postman doesn't take the time to consider whether there are exceptions to his rule about talk and television—or films—being incompatible. It is certainly not in his interest to suggest that there are so many exceptions—Sacha Guitry, Preston Sturges, Billy Wilder, the Mankiewicz brothers, Chris Marker, Donald Brittain and Stanley Jackson, Roberto Rossellini's history films, Grigori Kozintsev's adaptations of Shakespeare and Cervantes, Eric Rohmer, and so on, and so on—that the rule no longer even stands. The same goes, exponentially, with his dismissive assertion that television—or film—is always and only devoted to the values of show business. What of Adolph Zukor's *Films d'Art*, German Expressionism, the Soviets, the '20s French avant-garde, the British documentary movement, the American Independents? What of Murnau, Lang, Dreyer, Renoir, Ray? Again the exceptions, both individual and institutional, approach the innumerable. Too many anti-film points can only be made when the actual history of film is not consulted, or even imagined.

Writing may freeze speech, but speech itself can and does reflect, honor, and often exalt the grammatical, the logical, the rhetorical and historical and scientific. And speech, for all that Postman seems to ignore the fact, has always had a dominant place, at least in a portion of the television universe.[74] Furthermore, the study of semiotics, or the science of signification, has long since demonstrated how much more there is to language and communication than the merely verbal. "It must have been clear from the beginning that photography and writing (in fact, language in any form) do not inhabit the same universe of discourse."[75] To illustrate this assertion, Postman, properly, discusses how television commercials of the 1950s crowded linguistic discourse as a basis for consumer decisions. Granted, and then not.

Semiotical inquiry has been going on for more than a hundred years, at least since Ferdinand de Saussure and Charles Sanders Peirce's early innovations in the field. It can no longer be disputed that many kinds of languages signify in ways that had not previously been suspected. As for film, Christian Metz's pioneering work in the field of cinematic signification is a half-century old, and it was only the beginning.[76] It is no longer a question among people who have attended closely and unprejudicially to the matter that with visual signification, most anything is possible.

Dire Dismissal, Trickling Down

Parents and teachers, concerned for the safety of their children, seek to protect them from the harmful effects of harmful media. Pilgrims and Puritans see those harmful effects everywhere. More informed polemicists tend to do the same, though they should know that things are actually a little more complicated. The result of all of this epidemical discourse is that much of the rest of the population takes it for granted that the whole of the media landscape is a wasteland, when it most definitely is not.

Aldous Huxley's *Brave New World* (1932) and Ray Bradbury's *Fahrenheit 451* (1953), among their other aims, take very famous pokes at what would eventually become television, or at television itself. These points are very well taken, of great use, and exceedingly partial. It might be said that they view technology in the manner of myths, or the sagas. Television is a dragon, a monster, a dire threat that must be vanquished. Unfortunately, it is a very short distance between mythological antagonisms and the dramatically, morally threadbare oppositions of melodrama.

Children's literature has often struggled with the distinction between mythological vividness and overly dismissive melodrama.[77] Two anti-television books, both by very estimable authors, characterize the conversation.

The Wretched Stone (1991), a picture book by the American children's author Chris Van Allsburg, concerns the voyage of the *Rita Ann*, its captain and crew. As the ship embarks the Captain's log informs us that many of the men are avid readers, vivid storytellers, tuneful musicians. Presently this accomplished crew encounters an uncharted isle, on which they find "lush vegetation that bears no fruit, bitter water, and an overpowering sickly sweet smell." They also find "a rock, approximately two feet across. It is roughly textured, gray in color, but a portion of it is flat and smooth as glass. From this surface comes a glowing light that is quite beautiful and pleasing to look at."[78]

The crew brings this mysterious and desirable object aboard the *Rita Ann*. The captain's log records that it immediately begins to fascinate the men. Soon they are neglecting their duties, not to mention their reading and playing and dancing. Instead, they just stare at the glass. The captain fears that they have caught some fever and suspects that the stone is the source thereof. The next day he finds that the men have locked themselves into the hold, with the stone. When the captain manages to gain entry, he is horrified to find that all of the men have turned into apes.

A storm hits. Without a crew to conduct it, the ship nearly perishes.

Its masts are broken, and the rudder is lost. And now, suddenly, the curious stone has also gone dark. In the hour of real and utmost need, it is completely useless. The men are still in their ape form. "As the boat drifts and waits for rescue, the captain discovers that playing the violin and reading to the crew has a positive effect."[79] He covers up the stone. Soon the men returned to normal. As the publisher's teacher's guide emphasizes, "those among them who knew how to read return most quickly to their natural forms."[80]

To ensure that these events are not replicated in the lives of young readers, Van Allsburg's publishers include the following strong suggestion in their online teachers' guide: "Read *The Wretched Stone* in the context of 'Turn Off Your TV' week. Have your students think of other things that can be done instead of watching TV and write about them. Post 'Turn Off Your TV' signs in the hallways of the school."[81] The TV Turn-Off Week began in the United States in 1994. It was based on the unexceptionable notion that children watch too much television and that in doing so they miss out on too many other healthy, edifying, and enjoyable activities. TV Turn-Off Week has spread increasingly in the intervening years, reaching into a number of other developed nations.[82]

Unexceptionable though its aims may be, however, the discourse surrounding this initiative has depended on an insufficient and frankly prejudicial characterization of film and media. They can be straw men, when they are not being subjected to out-and-out bigoted caricature. The best of kid culture minds, and hearts, are not immune to the effects.

In *Aunt Chip and the Great Triple Creek Dam Affair* (1996), the great American author/illustrator Patricia Polacco creates a town full of television addicts who no longer even remember how to read. The problem had started fifty years ago, when they built the TV tower. Aunt Chip, the town librarian, had warned them all, but they had ignored her and she had taken to her bed. Now all of her most dire predictions had come to pass. All of the color has seeped out of the town, leaving a uniform grey palate. There are still books, but they are now used exclusively for leveling furniture or stopping up holes in the roof. As a result of this long, uninterrupted exposure to television, and because of their isolation from literature's edifying influence, the town's adults have all become uniformly, unfailingly dim.

However there is still life in, still hope for a few of the children. A young relative manages to stir Aunt Chip back into action. She establishes a literacy campaign that lights a fire under the rest of the town's children. For all the reluctance and resistance of the grown-ups, the children's efforts eventually lead to the toppling of the tower. Everyone suddenly wakes back up when it falls. Terrible television's demise leads to a return of color, communication, light, love.

As stated in Polacco's afterward, and hinted at by small details in the illustrations, *Aunt Chip* is dedicated to the great American scholar and advocate of children's books, Charlotte Huck. In fact, comparisons between photographs and Polacco's illustrations reveal that Aunt Chip *is* Charlotte Huck, or at least a stylized, magical version of her. The victory of Huck's literary avatar bears some resemblance to the cause to which she dedicated her life. Causes, perhaps: it may have seemed, it must have been that advocating books also meant a contest with their perceived and often televisual foe.[83]

These piquant parables motivate their readers away from television's torpor and toward the Utopias of the printed page. They object to the medium itself and to the way that it allegedly, even demonstratively saps the energy and even the intelligence of its audiences. Van Allsburg, and Polacco particularly, are tremendous authors. The awesome draftsmanship of the former, and the latter's joyfully kinetic imagery, her great and loving heart, are still present in these two books. Here, however, on the subject of television, these authors are not at their best.

This type of systematic superstition and prejudice is of very long standing now. Patterns of misinformation, whether innocently or maliciously communicated, are often accepted as proverbs. These notions about the media permeate the culture of the developed Western nations at least, and their effect may be just as harmful as the shadows in that metaphorical Cave, or those very first, feared unedifying stories of so long ago.

All of this can be clearly seen when we move from the banners of prevalent publications to the trenches of the schools, with their various curricula and pedagogical methodologies. The following material is taken from the summer syllabus of our own eldest son's Grade 10 (2011–12) honors English course at Springville High School, Springville, Utah, USA. Among other things, that course included a unit on a film adaptation of a literary text. The discussion begins conventionally, and promisingly:

> **Overview:** The primary goals of the independent summer reading-writing course are to increase your experience as a close reader of literary and visual texts and improve your skills as an analytical writer. On a more personal level, the novel you select to read and the corresponding movie adaptation you view (no animated or cartoon versions) along with the novel you have been assigned (*Things Fall Apart* by Chinua Achebe) offers you the opportunity to engage in a private conversation with yourself and your peers within your scholarly community about not just literature, but ideas, values—in short, the human experience.

So far, so conventional. Also, unexceptionable, and very likely to be productive. Having established these basic objectives, the class instructors proceed to elaborate on the relationship between the reading and film assignments.

> 1. Novel to Film Comparison-Practice: Choose a novel ... that has been made into a movie. Read the selected novel and view the movie. Then compose a comparison-contrast essay that demonstrates your critical understanding and displays your analytical and persuasive writing skills.

Once again, this is conventional, and potentially productive. But it is in the nature of the comparing and contrasting or in the assumptions that inform it that the theme of this present book is renewed, and our long-standing problem reinforced. The instructors offer these prewriting considerations:

> a. What are you glad the director kept the same in his/her film version and why?
> b. What do you wish the director would have changed in his/her film version and why?
> c. What do you wish the director hadn't changed in his/her film version and why
> d. What are you glad the director did change in his/her film version and why?

This isn't all bad. In one very important sense these questions are inviting the students to think about what they enjoyed and what they didn't. They are being invited not just to consume but to consider their media, and how it makes them feel. But effective analysis and fair critique require a reasonable knowledge of the critical object. These four points fall far short in this respect, in their blithe and insufficient assumptions about the nature of film production, and the ways in which film images (and sounds, and speech) are apprehended and applied by viewers.

The problems here are, or should be, obvious. Films are created/manufactured by a collective. Directors can be primarily responsible for their message and manner, though even the most conspicuous auteur's work is profoundly affected and inflected by his or her collaborators. But an evaluation of a film adaptation would do well to consider the writer first, or equally.

Directors, or craft collaborators, or industrial collectives, are sometimes autonomous and in full control of their final product. More frequently they cannot fully control what is kept or changed. Clients, or producers, or the customers/public also have a place in this equation, and they can all be partly responsible, partly to blame for the eventual film.

This notion is especially important in a class assignment like this one. In the film adaptation, the writer has written, the designer designed, the director directed, the actor acted, and so on. But what of the reader or viewer? What of her rights, her related responsibilities? Theories of reader response are practically innumerable, and of very long standing. In this high school assignment they are nowhere to be seen. It may be that their existence is not fully comprehended, or even suspected.

These criticisms are fair and true. They may not appear to be fair, or kind, to the hard-working public school teachers that created the assignment and worked through a summer break to help the students complete it. In this, as in so much else, they deserve appreciation and support. The point is not to have anyone's head, nor to pillory any particular individual. It is rather to identify a broad cultural problem, a set of ideological assumptions that, for all their disproving, continue to be current, and even dominant. These bright young teachers are laboring, unconsciously, under a number of insistent, intractable misapprehensions. As film fans, as teachers in the humanities, they continue to reflect and propagate ideas that are not only hostile to film but are largely ignorant of the manifold ways in which film is actually shown and seen.

Here is the last prewriting consideration for the high school writing assignment on the subject of films adapted from novels: "In general, films fail to live up to the novels they are made from. What is your overall opinion of the movie adaptation of the novel and why?" The assertion in the first sentence is practically stated as a certainty, which rather leads young witnesses as they prepare their response. In anthropological or documentary terms, this is preconception,[84] which is that the cultural observer who goes in looking for certain things is very likely to find them, especially when they are negative, and whether or not they are actually true.

The film part of this English assignment falls short. Part of the problem, and some of the reason for it, can be seen in a much more effectively and authoritatively stated part of the adaptation assignment. "Compose your best analytical and persuasive comparison-contrast essay, using appropriate literary terminology and detailed examples of aspects and elements from both the novel and film (e.g., themes, characterization, point-of-view, plot development, etc.) to support your position." Now they're talkin', and sounding like they know what they are talking about. Everything here is very valid, but as has so often been the case when the literary folks take on movies, everything here is also strictly literary, print-derived, word-textual.

Films do indeed have themes, characterization, point-of-view, even voice—especially if one undertakes a conceptual transposition, one medium to the other. Films certainly have plot development, or at least plot-driven films do. But these English class considerations only scratch the surface of a medium that is only partially literary. Film is also visual, spatial, rhythmical, durational, aural, and any number of medium-specific, or other-medium-related things that do not feature in books.

Suspicion of and resistance to media seems to be inscribed in the philosophical, even the mythological DNA of Western civilization. Suspicion and resistance continue to be an insistent, influential part of the contemporary conversation. These things are very understandable, especially when it comes to vulnerable children and beleaguered young families. These things have too often become distorting factors in a conversation that is, and has been for a very long time, inadequate. Informed critiques of the media situate shortcoming as one part of a larger, decidedly more positive totality. And no one can benefit more from this broader view than children and families, who have at least as much to gain as they have to lose.

2

From Confrontation to Conciliation: Not Worrying So Much and Learning to Love the Media

Socrates and Plato's concerns about the theater—or, if we take the liberty of extending the conversation, about narrative generally—are very frequently shared by parents and teachers, by church and community leaders, by anyone with an investment and interest in protecting and promoting the interests of young people. The Greeks' unyielding response to these concerns continues to be commonly held, and with good reason. The cautious caretaker who accepts these formulations and proceeds on their assumptions has a good chance of safely ushering his child to his majority.

It is also possible that scarifying characterizations of the media and its effects, or of our lack of power in the face of these effects, can have a negative effect. Negativity unto alarmism and distortion could also produce zealots and xenophobes, holy warriors unwilling to take the time to actually consider, listen to, and learn from enemies that are perceived but not actual. This might result in a circumspection that also smacks of sanctimoniousness, producing enmity and even violence. Plato, Bunyan, Postman, and all of the rest of the conscientious objectors can be advantageously considered, but they might also be helpfully countered. Taken from another perspective, or met with a different set of lenses, families can not only survive the depredations of modern media but actually thrive on all of the good things the media have to offer.

This is certainly the thesis at hand, or in play, here. A corrupt world and the vulnerability of precious children aside, there must, at some point, be an end to proscription. The child must be exposed to literature and life, to harm and help, to consequences and abundances. Exposure, compounded, will lead to experience and hopefully a degree of capacity and wisdom. Even certain fundamentalists, possessed of a pluralistic bent, might well agree.

Also, more pointedly, helpful, fair-minded critiques of the film medium must at least be accurate in accounting for how the film medium actually works. Many parents combining care and reasonable moderation will want to take both these courses. But how to go about it? For an answer to that question, we have recourse to another ancient voice, more attuned to the full workings of imitative or enacted narrative than was Socrates. He, and Plato, were moral philosophers, powerfully persuasive, effectual, and ultimately quite polarizing in their prescribing and proscribing. Plato's protégé, Aristotle, provides an enormously helpful extension of, an enormously productive alternative to the outright prohibition of his predecessors.

Aristotle Weighs In: Balancing Criticism and Commendation

Aristotle can help the anxious parent, who nevertheless desires to positively engage with the culture, in a few important ways. We learn in Plato's *Republic* that "a master of any art avoids excess and defect, but seeks the intermediate."[1] This is the mean, which is desirable in making and in craftsmanship, and even more important in our interactions with others, in the realms of ethics and morality. Aristotle thoroughly explores the concept of the mean in *The Nicomachean Ethics* (ca. 340 BC). He argues convincingly and very beautifully that in these moral realms the midpoint between excess and defect is exactly where and how we find and enact virtue.

Numerous illustrations convincingly make the point: "With regard to feelings of fear and confidence courage is the mean; of the people who exceed, he who ... exceeds in confidence is rash, and he who exceeds in fear and falls short in confidence is a coward. With regard to pleasures and pains ... the mean is temperance, the excess self-indulgence." Liberality is the mean in matters financial; the prodigal is excessive, and the miser, defective. The mean also applies to each side of these moral equations. The prodigal finds himself at the midpoint of error, exceeding in spending and falling short in taking. Similarly, the miser takes too much and gives too little. As to sociality, or "pleasantness," the man who is properly pleasant "is friendly and the mean is friendliness, while the man who exceeds is an obsequious person if he has no end in view, a flatterer if he is aiming at his own advantage, and the man who falls short and is unpleasant in all circumstances is a quarrelsome and surly sort of person."[2]

Virtue lies at the midpoint between excess and defect. How might this idea apply to the present conversation? Socrates, Adeimantus, and so many other lovingly, fearfully proscriptive moral watchdogs right down to the present day are often motivated by the best of impulses. In the particular, however, and as they act upon their concerns, they are prone to situate themselves at the extreme edge of the conversation. A more moderate, Aristotelian approach might suggest that the mean lies at the midpoint between a licentious embrace of all of narrative's most dubious offerings and a joyless suspicion and even rejection of anything that might be contrived by the imagination of men, women, or children. The Cave and its images can distract, even endanger. They do not inevitably do so. Imitative art can waylay and even deceive, especially when the credulous are nigh. The wary spectator, however, or the engaged reader, will be less vulnerable. And beyond the cautioning, narrative art also provides innumerable benefits and edifications.

The concept of the mean can guide us in evaluating prevalent critiques of the media. It suggests that we respond warily to the loud voice and the pounding fist. It reminds us that in some conceptual or philosophical realms, virtue and vice, or the right and wrong of things, might not be so easily identified, or isolated. At the very least it warns us against undue haste, or impatience, in our judgments.

Here, as we try more gently to clarify problems and possibilities, the idea of the dialectic can also come to our aid. This synthesizing process will not be as tidy as the mean is, at least as it relates to character traits. Neither will it be as certain as were Marx's eventual prophecies, to cite only the most well-known example of dialectical synthesis, or speculation. All of this seeming lack of clarity could well be dispiriting. But it could also be humbling, allowing for unexpected illuminations and leading to more courteous interactions. We consider an idea from one perspective, and then we consider its counter. We repeat the process from a number of different angles, thus coming to understand that no object has merely two sides, or that no assertion can be complete. At the same time, we will find unsuspected sincerity and substance in positions that we had previously dismissed.

For examples, the Austrian psychoanalyst Bruno Bettelheim was a pioneer in combining the heritage of the traditional folk and fairy tale with the discipline of psychoanalysis, especially as it related to the raising of healthy, rounded children. That work is summarized in his superb book, *The Uses of Enchantment: The Meaning and Importance of Fairy Tales* (1976). In the midst of a series of tremendously insightful, edifying interpretations of a number of tales, Bettelheim also makes sweeping generalizations about the status of film and television. He sniffily states that these media inevitably turn fairy tales "into empty-minded entertainment."[3]

This is a possibility, and it has been a reality as well. It is also, as suggested, an insufficiently interrogated stereotype, one that will be jeopardized by closer and more thorough scrutiny. Here is Bettelheim, at the extreme of the conversation. But there is another strand for us to synthesize:

> The unconscious speaks to us in images rather than words, and it is simple when compared with the productions of the intellect. And ... it is viewed as the lowliest aspect of our mind when compared with ego and superego, but when well used it is the part of our personality from which we can gain our greatest strength.[4]

Now Bettelheim is speaking, quite wonderfully, of the substance of image culture, offering an effective, even Aristotelian, rebuttal to the very same careless generalization that he had previously made. In the so-often contentious precincts of book-film discourse, the mean helps us to value constructive contributions and make kindly allowance when these constructive contributions fall short.

In chapter one we discussed how Chris Van Allsburg and Patricia Polacco celebrate the power of books by making a straw man out of television. In doing so they make a fair point unfairly. Other children's authors have considered the shortcomings of enacted narrative in more moderate, conciliatory fashion. Chichester is the faithful, capable, and unimaginative coachman in Leon Garfield's 1974 novel for young people, *The Sound of Coaches*. As he so often did, Garfield set this story in nineteenth-century England. Chichester is alarmed when his beloved adopted son expresses a desire to begin traveling with a band of itinerant actors. His disapproval, and the suspicions that inform it, could well be applied to any number of modern communications media.

> The coachman grunted. Plays and players revolted him. Theirs was a world of fraudulent dreams and pretense, the ever-willing bedfellows of lying, thieving and the crooked way. What was an actor but a wretch living by deceit? How could such a fellow, filling his days with pretense,

ever know the difference between the truth and a lie? Habit must have corrupted him rotten.⁵

This good man, concerned as he was for the well-being of his adopted child, cannot be blamed for his fear. Indeed, some of his suspicions are quite valid, at least in part. But while Garfield understands, he does not endorse. Chichester's concerns may be valid, but they do not account for the whole of the thing. As it happens his adopted son does set out with this theatrical troupe. And he does, indeed, encounter theatrical shortcomings, both in the plays that are staged and in the attitudes and lifestyles that inform them. But as with any child who sets out on the perilous path, shortcoming is always accompanied by substance and by the opportunity to choose the better part.⁶

Turning to the subject of media theory, we might all respectfully give ear to Chichester's fears at the same time that we adhere to Garfield's more moderate, synthesizing perspective. In media theory, the mean is achieved by considering and incorporating the deeply felt, decidedly one-sided work of the media Cassandras, and then reading them against the more optimistic contributions of a group of media-sympathetic, sometimes mediaphilic scholars.

A few examples, out of many: in his 1974 work, *The History of Childhood*, the American psychohistorian Lloyd deMause balances the alarmist conversation by pointing out that the good old days were not always so good, especially for children. By assigning what amounted to a series of personality disorders to the prevalent child-raising practices that have operated through world history, deMause demonstrates how "childhood" has only recently emerged from out of the brutality and rampant infant mortality of mankind's numerous dark pasts. Far from decrying the technological and information present—at least circa 1974—he suggests that these are actually emblems of a signal accomplishment, the graduation of human communities into unaccustomed, even unprecedented civilization and decency.

As with Postman's *The Disappearance of Childhood*, Joshua Meyrowitz's *No Sense of Place: The Impact of Electronic Media on Social Behavior* (1986) allows that television has indeed given young people much quicker and much greater access to what had previously and exclusively been adult knowledge. But where it has been customary to bemoan this fact, Meyrowitz suggests that this increased access has increased the potential not only for trauma and corruption but also knowledge and power.⁷ In *Growing Up Digital: The Rise of the Net Generation* (1998), Don Tapscott expands upon this theme. He holds that digital technology's precipitous rise is linked to marked increases in access and openness and has led very clearly to more collaborative, democratic conversations.

For its part, Jon Katz's provocative *Virtuous Reality: How America Surrendered Discussion of Moral Values to Opportunists, Nitwits, and Blockheads like William Bennett* (1997) decries the smugly knee-jerking "mediaphobes" who use communications technologies as a convenient scapegoat for all of the world's ills. Though there are difficulties—as has always been the case with older media as well—new technologies and the conversations that they engender have, in the balance, been extremely positive and productive.[8]

David Buckingham summarizes the collective findings of this other, media-sympathetic faction.

> These new media are seen as democratic rather than authoritarian; diverse rather than homogeneous; participatory rather than passive. In this respect, they are seen to engender new forms of consciousness among young people that take them beyond the restricted imaginations of their parents and teachers.[9]

Buckingham goes on to chart something of his own Aristotelian midpoint, or Hegelian synthesis. He observes that the mediaphobes too consistently provide a not very helpful "combination of panic and nostalgia," while the utopians might be protesting too much, going so far as to use the rhetoric of the sales pitch.[10] The implication, not only in Buckingham but for any evenhanded consideration of the various issues, is once again quite unexceptionable. Valid perspectives stumble over their own limitations, sensible positions extend themselves into stridency and distortion. Careful consideration leads to an ecumenical understanding, with the whole of the ideological and pedagogical spectrum contributing to a thorough, balanced attack. Beware. Be grateful. Books, films.

How? To balance the systematic naysaying, we might return to an earlier point, from this book's first chapter. A long line of spirited, brilliant voices have addressed Plato's original provocation about the deceptive shadows on the wall. We have just been keying on those that took the route of repudiation. But the other option remains, that of engaged critique, coupled with a joy in exploring and utilizing media that do not always and only do harm. More recently, and for several generations, some of the most stirring statements about surface and substance have come from the still-too-underappreciated medium of film.

The pioneering generation of Soviet filmmakers consistently combined formal innovation with pointed cultural critique: Lev Kuleshov's *The Extraordinary Adventures of Mr. West in the Land of the Bolsheviks*

(1924) and *By the Law* (1926); Sergei Eisenstein's *Strike* (1924), *Battleship Potemkin* (1926) and, for all of the official outrage that it aroused, *Old and New* (1928); V. I. Pudovkin's *Mother* (1926) and *The End of St. Petersburg* (1927); Dziga Vertov's *One Sixth of the World* (1926) and *The Man with the Movie Camera* (1929). Significantly, each of these innovators, and many more besides—Dovzhenko, Shub, Room, Barnet, Medvedev—added volumes of penetrating written critiques to their multiply revolutionary films.[11] The result of all this was that, as so often before, immobilized and passive viewers were constantly urged and alienated into the light of formal and ideological self-awareness.

The Soviets were not without their inconsistencies; as one example among many, Eisenstein's *October* (1927) now seems as ideologically overdetermined, as melodramatically preposterous as the riven, hierarchical social and narrative models that it sought to expose. However, inconsistency does not invalidate an entire impulse, nor even its problematical individual manifestations. This is especially true when instances multiply. In this, film is no different from philosophy or any of the arts and letters, not to mention so very much of scientific discourse. Almost every great surge, every significant movement in the history of film production, and of film theory, concerns itself in some way with the shadows and the sun, with reality and the challenge of adequately accessing it.

Here: the first films of Louis and Auguste Lumière (from 1895), with their superbly sophisticated visuals, their blithe geographical expanse, their complicated ideological subtexts; the joyful, irrepressible abundance of Georges Méliès (from 1896); the cinematic syntheses and syntactical elaborations of the Pathé company, in France; D. W. Griffith's films for the American Mutuoscope and Biograph Company (1908–13; see also chapter four, q.v.); the pre–WWI coalescing and ascension of the feature film in Denmark and Italy, and in the expanding and ultimately obliterating US film industry; the simultaneously straightforward and surreally subversive pre-and wartime serials of Louis Feuillade; Charles Chaplin's practically comprehensive cinematic renewal of the *Commedia dell'Arte*; the elemental exteriors of Scandinavian cinema in the late 1910s and early 1920s; Erich von Stroheim's eviscerations of bourgeois pretense and hypocrisy; Robert Flaherty's elaboration of colonial mythology and indigenous process in the faraway places; the pictorialist cinema of Rex Ingram; Buster Keaton's mastery of the motion picture camera as the paradoxically humanizing apparatus in a mechanistic universe; the agonizing glories of Germany's expressionist and chamber films in the 1920s; France's unworried 1920s embrace of the entire medium as being capable of any artistic, philosophical, or social elaboration.

Here: the intractable, constantly evolving artistic integrities in the films of Carl Theodor Dreyer; the sublime, spiritual sensuality of Frank Borzage; the childlike sophistications in the early thirties films of René Clair and in the work of Stan Laurel and Oliver Hardy; the formal/technical advance and conceptual, ideological contradiction in the works of the Walt Disney corporation; the complex negotiations between state/corporate sponsorship and social activism in the British documentary film movement; the political provocation in the non-fiction films of Joris Ivens, or in Jean Renoir's *Boudu Saved from Drowning* (1932), *Toni* (1934), *The Crime of M. Lange* (1936), and *Rules of the Game* (1939); the genial class critique of screwball comedy; the modernist melancholy, rising to violence, of French Poetic Realism and American Film Noir; the pictorialist cinema of Michael Powell; the searing, scoring social critique in the films of Kenji Mizoguchi; the formalist flights of Len Lye and Norman McLaren; the gloriously, edifyingly entropic mud pie of the Warner Bros. cartoon; the historico-analytical World War II documentaries of Stewart Legg, and the analytico-pacifist World War II documentaries of Humphrey Jennings.

Here: the simultaneously archetypal and psychoanalytical filmscapes of Maya Deren; the Italian neo-realists, from the Rossellini trilogy (1945–48) to de Sica's *Umberto D.* (1952), or even from Olmi's *Il Posto* (1961) to Pasolini's *Theorem* (1967); Renoir's *The Southerner* (1946), and *The River* (1951), and *The Golden Coach* (1953); the shimmering, sad serenity in the middle and later films of Yasujiro Ozu; Robert Bresson's tender severities; Satyajit Ray's subcontinental elaborations of neorealist impulse from the Apu trilogy (1955–59) through *The Music Room* (1958) and *Devi* (1960), *Charulata* (1964) and *The Big City* (1963); Britain at the kitchen sink; the Enlightened, citizenly perfections of the National Film Board of Canada's Unit B, from *City of Gold* (1957) to the *Labyrinth* project at Expo '67; Britain, swinging, Fogo Island and the Challenge for Change, China's Second Wave, the rounding out and even apotheosis of neorealism in the expansive explorations of Iranian cinema. The French New Wave. *Cinema Novo*. Cassavetes. Jerry Lewis. Godard. Glauber Rocha. The Post-Oberhausen ferment in West Germany. Australia, subsidized. And, if we're still thinking of the Cave, we would do well to include the Wachowskis' self-consciously Baudrillardian, strainingly Cave-derived *Matrix* franchise.

This untidy, enthusiastic assemblage is both the tip and a great deal of the rest of the cinematic iceberg. It includes multitudes at the same time that it neglects, unconscionably, so much that is central, and essential.

But as we continue with and then conclude the discussion about whether books are in fact better than movies, this kind of assembly indicates the disposition of the present publication. More, it also illustrates an indisputable fact, for all those that continue to dispute it: film no longer needs any apology or permission or justification. It is vast and deep, perceptive and penetrating, rooted and reaching. If the world of adult discourse has been so enriched by the cinematic, then it stands to reason that, even before the specific illustrations and citations, children might be similarly served.

This book's primary thesis concerns the substantial continuities between literature and media. There is another central notion that supplements and strengthens that first thesis. It is that media (clay and marble; oil, water, or acrylic; print and electronic; and, in the narrative realm, books and films) are not properly subject to the hierarchies that we like to impose upon them.

One may, quite naturally, have preferences, but the fact is that media are not superior or inferior, better or worse, good or bad. There are differences between, strengths and limitations inherent in each medium. Beyond that, they are neutral, morally and practically, able to do both good and ill, according to the actions and dispositions of creators and receivers. The proper critical project, contrary to the fierce advocacies and hand-wringings that so often prevail, is to establish the characteristics of each medium. Thus informed, one can then go on to more effectively and helpfully consider and criticize individual expressions within media.

Aristotle's definition of the mean helps us in our general approach to the arts. His detailed, sympathetic critique of the theatrical medium itself can help us as we roll up our sleeves and address the specifics. After, in addition to, and instead of provocative polemical statements, one might also consider the actual object of study in more careful detail. That detailed scrutiny, in turn, may turn polemics into discourse, or discussion. Plato's engagement was moral, but not very theatrical. We might well err in identifying the effects of the theater if we do not understand or refuse to acknowledge how theater actually operates.

To his own profound moral philosophy, Aristotle added the perspectives and methodologies of a scientist and categorizer. Scientists, like formalist critics, or scholars that explicate poems, have moral views. But moral views, or the urging thereof, will not be the first or the central objective of scientists' work. Rather they provide or present data, leaving much of the moral interpretation to the reader. Aristotle's formative dissertations on the subjects of physics, astronomy, and zoology demonstrate his investment in the descriptive, scientific function. And science continues to inform his more pointedly moral work in the fields of ethics, politics, and rhetoric.

And art: As already mentioned, Aristotle both measured and morally categorized the theater in his *Poetics*, a slim volume that is surely the most influential and important analysis of theater/narrative ever written.[12] As we have already seen, the Greeks talked a lot about imitation and the many ways that people are drawn to it. Plato is an idealist, and in some ways a pessimist; for him, this propensity to imitate is dangerous. For his part, Aristotle brings a more practical set of considerations to the question and, as a result, is more flexible, more expansive in the possibilities that he sees.

Aristotle begins the *Poetics* by stating that art communicates when practitioners and patrons understand certain key, clear distinctions. Works of art, including stories, "can be differentiated from each other in three respects: in respect of their different media of imitation, or different objects, or a different mode."[13] Modern equivalents to these terms might be, first, the medium; second, the content or referent; and third, the individual artist's style or voice. Plato was also sensitive to these nice artistic distinctions when he distinguished between narration, imitation, and an epical combination of the two. The difference in Aristotle's project is that he exults in the art at hand, rather than fearing or condemning it. The result is that the possibilities of medium, content, and style now multiply before us, and proscription is replaced by the idea that these permutations can lead us to many possible, viable ideals.

The Republic warns unequivocally against theatrical imitation. Aristotle argues very convincingly—and most morally too—from the opposite perspective. Why do we imitate? He states that in earliest childhood humans learn to imitate and that they learn from imitating. In acquiring this skill, and especially in acquiring the many skills that follow upon that first acquisition, they derive great pleasure.[14] This is completely different from the unseemly pleasures that concern Plato. Instead of the swine running down the hill (to cite a familiar Christian reference), this is a pleasure predicated on learning, on the instruction that leads to increase and edification. Concerned contemporary observers may hasten to point out that Aristotle's standards do not at all correspond with current practices and responses—especially, perhaps, as they pertain to the media. Contemporarily we like to imitate, or, more passively, witness imitations, from which we expect and demand pleasure. Learning is often left out of the equation.

However, in considering Aristotle's formulation, we find that what *can* be is not the same as what *must* be. The worst case exists, but it is not inevitable or universal. If some would just as soon avoid the increase that substantial narrative offers, that increase is still plentifully available for any who would inquire. For that inquiring person, theatrical and cinematic imitation, the mutual creation of the speaker and hearer both, can still proceed on old and substantial lines. We create, we learn, we enjoy, and in that order.

And what is it that we most enjoy? Aristotle maintains that the theater is capable of providing great edification and that our empathetic faculties can be stirred by the involving, heartrending dramas that the theater lays before us. Plato sees almost unmitigated bad behavior. Aristotle sees noble aspiration and poignant, universal error intermingled. Far from corrupting the spectator, these invite him into an important kind of communion. By working upon our innate capacities to feel pity toward another and to be humbled by the enactment of that other's courageous struggles, the theater functions as a cathartic, cleansing agent. Further, even more profoundly, it is an epiphanic agent, which is to say that it is capable of providing revelatory insight and knowledge to the perceptive spectator.[15]

Aristotle's position constitutes an arts advocate's prescription for and description of enlightenment, the very same thing that Plato indicated was available to the person who removed himself from mere, paltry imitative shadow. Here is a paradox, to say the least.

Plato is a moral exemplar, a heroic beacon of integrity and honor. And, to a small degree, he is as fierce and unyielding about narrative as the cave dweller who would rather execute the would-be agent of his deliverance than be delivered.

If the reader will have it, if she sees any merit in a degree of cultural engagement, Aristotle emerges here as just as exemplary and a great deal more tractable. And he anticipates, practically demonstrates, why film can be, why it is the aesthetical and moral equivalent of any literature.

For Aristotle, theatrical imitation is most profitably demonstrated by and through tragedy. Here is the classic statement:

> Tragedy is an imitation of an action that is admirable, complete and possesses magnitude; in language made pleasurable ... performed by actors, not through narration; effecting through pity and fear the purification of such emotions.[16]

This elegant definition is dense with portent, and implication. It continues to suggest how theatrical imitation can lead to edification. More importantly, as part of the present argument, it makes important practical distinctions between narrative media.

For Aristotle, tragedy is an imitation of an action and not stasis; it must be complete, in the sense of a chronological coherence, and even more relating to the clear resolution of conflicts and questions. Tragedy possesses magnitude, which is to say that it is significant, it means something, and carries consequences for characters and spectators alike. For Aristotle, tragedy should also be sensuously attractive, utilizing the various elements of the medium in a way that creates a beautiful totality, which will provide sure and seemly pleasure. Tragedy should also contain heightened speech, as opposed to mere vernacular utterance. This allows it to properly treat heightened subjects and not the mere quotidian, or the merely vulgar.

Now comes the most essential point regarding the difference between oral narratives, or literature, and the stage: *tragedy, and we might venture to say any theatrical production, must be enacted, and not merely narrated.* This was not at all to dismiss narration, or oral storytelling. Nor was it to dismiss, by extension, the tales that we find on the page.[17] The call for enactment constitutes a generic distinction or differentiation, which is once again what a categorizer or scientist will set out to provide.

Finally, and most importantly, tragedy leads to two sensations. The first of these is the sensation of pity, for the undeserved suffering of the virtuous, or at least those that are striving toward virtue. The second is fear, which comes of our identification with this striving main character, as well as our knowledge that what could so arbitrarily fall upon him might just as well fall upon us. Fear and pity, combined, will finally effect a catharsis, or a cleansing. This culmination represents the fulfilling of theater's, of imitative art's best destiny.[18]

One of the greatest differences between Plato's and Aristotle's attitudes is that the latter makes allowances for the spectator and includes her as part of the artistic and communicative equation.[19] The presence of the spectator, and the possibility that she might actively participate in and substantially contribute to the whole exchange of meaning and feeling, is one of the things most neglected by the media contrarians. It is also one of the very most important contributors to the edifying operation of enacted narratives.

In a theatrical performance, and just as easily in a film narrative, there is presentation, and then there is apprehension. Both intention and reception, semiotics and phenomenology, should be accounted for. The arguments that discuss and dismiss television as a mere straw man do not sufficiently allow for the effects of good programming or do not allow that individuals can view programs in a self-aware and substantial manner. "The excellence of the eye," says Aristotle, elsewhere, "makes both the eye and its work good; for it is by the excellence of the eye that we see well."[20]

Books and films, once again; Aristotle holds that an investigator should begin by considering the particularities of the medium of expression, then the content that is being communicated through that medium and by means of its basic characteristics, and finally the style or voice being utilized to make that communication. In the case of written or narrated stories and those stories enacted on stage or screen, this course will cause the investigator to understand that theatrical and cinematic narratives are fundamentally *different from*—not *better than*—oral or written traditions. Theater (as in Sophocles) must be enacted and not narrated (as in Homer). Allowing for passing time and changing circumstances, this is essentially the difference between literature and film. They are both narrative arts, but the first sets forth on a page the story that will be played out in the reader's mind. The second is closer to theater and adapts its primordial directive; it is and must be acted out.

How many books-good/films-bad discussions have been built on a lack of awareness or misunderstanding of this old, unexceptionable, incontrovertible idea? There are principles that can help us distinguish between and substantially enjoy both books and theater (the objects of Aristotle's original discussion), or films. In sum, while it is true that different media are sometimes, indeed, deeply different, those differences are actually reconcilable. In the end, if we are sufficiently open and active, they can even be complementary.

Adaptation

The Aristotelian impulse is to calmly consider, to methodically measure the object of study, and then to draw any moral conclusions that may be forthcoming. We might now apply this project more specifically to a particular part of the relationship between books and films and to the insistent prejudices that continue to inhibit our understanding and enjoyment thereof.

Stanley Kauffmann, the distinguished American film critic, once wrote that it was pointless for Hollywood, or the American commercial film industry, to adapt literary classics for the screen. It was inevitable "that Hollywood distorts and corrupts serious literature for the entertainment pleasures of a mass audience."[21] Kauffman's point is hard to deny, at least in terms of it being a frequent result of an industrial process that has inherent flaws. However in elaborating this difficulty, and even as a deeply informed advocate of the film medium, Kauffmann goes on to make the very negative assumption that we have been discussing. He compares "art and commerce, individual creativity and collaborative fabrication, culture and mass culture, the verbal and the visual."[22] The second term always belongs to commercial cinema, which in this formulation is inherently opposed to artistic enterprise and accomplishment.

Why is the visual downgraded here? This is not at all Neil Postman's media-hating polemical point; Kauffmann knows all about the numerous verbal accomplishments of the film medium. It is also no longer a matter of enacted narrative's moral dangers or the concerns of informed, though perhaps overly alarmed, commentators. Rather, this is an uninterrogated platitude, glancing in this otherwise knowledgeable source, but nearly epidemic as it flows out to the lay public. Among the lay public, it often appears or operates as an out-and-out prejudice. It is one of the most serious obstacles to an equal and abundant enjoyment of page and stage and screen.

As with chapter one's reference to a high school English curriculum's attitude toward film, here is another personal, local example to indicate how widely and commonly distributed the sentiment really is. At my university bookstore, next to a display of books that had been adapted or optioned for adaptation,[23] the promotional people placed the following sign: "Books to Movies. Read the Story Before the Film Release. Think the movie is going to be good? 99.99% of BYU Bookstore employees say the book is better." It is important to acknowledge that this promotional material was not placed among the textbooks, but in the general book section. That is to say, this is a commercial communication and not a scholarly one. As such, it can be taken with a sense of humor or a grain of salt. But still.

More than a half a century ago, George Bluestone's influential book-length study *Novels Into Film* put paid to this kind of careless dismissal. In fact, it has been some hundred years since Vachel Lindsay's pioneering study, *The Art of the Moving Picture*, first went beyond mere commercial boosterism or moralistic condemnation, endeavoring rather to calmly consider the respective characteristics of each medium. Sales promotions cannot be expected to reflect current scholarly conversations, nor can they be held to scientific, quantitative standards. But it is partly amusing, partly dispiriting to find such gleeful, unsubstantiatable bigotry at this very late date. Here is a dubious assertion, supported by dubious hyperbole, leading to the reaffirmation of a dubious, divisive myth.

My experience with sending our six children most of the way through the American public school system (as of the time of writing there are four down, and two more to go) is that film scholarship may as well not even exist, for all of its penetration into the grass roots of the culture. In these public schools, the most mediocre of innocuous, ostensible family programming is used to placate the children as they approach a holiday, or grapple with a heavy snowfall, or even discuss an actual curricular unit that deserves to be more substantially illustrated.

In the face of all this, the following ideas are offered in rebuttal, incorporating the narrative media that we have been discussing. The page and the screen are completely valid media for the transmission of story. They are also markedly, necessarily, distinct from one another. When adaptations occur, there may be continuities from the source, but there must also be changes. These changes must take into account the properties specific to the medium being utilized. Stubborn allegiance to a particular medium, or to a specific work created for that medium, will often make it difficult to accept any adaptation of that work and from that medium. The resultant dissatisfaction with the work in question may have little to do with the adaptation itself.

Reading books is pleasurable for any number of reasons. An especially satisfying one is that reading can approach a kind of comprehensiveness. A careful and patient reader can meditate deeply, envision multiply, make connections and cross-references, follow and weave any number of interpretive or contextual threads. Another kind of careful reader can pare and prune, choosing focus over completeness, establishing and following an interpretative through-line in the work. Similarly, that patient reader may also create a kind of performance, a visualization of the book that he is reading, in his head.

Individual film adaptations are often disappointing to these careful readers, who have a hard time letting go either of that multiplicity or of that particularity. It is true, of course, that film adaptations can fall short in all sorts of ways, but this particular kind of disappointment has little to do with the actual production. This problem is basically in the eye of the beholder.

Too often our critical disapproval relates to a wrong turn on the road we would have taken, or that we would like to have seen taken. Our disapproval has little to do with the particular journey taken by an artist not ourselves, or an ensemble not our own. That is to say that criticism often constitutes little more than an expression of pique, or petulant preference. In our concern for what should have been done, we often neglect or misinterpret the actual critical object, the network of choices and efforts that actually lies before us.

As familiar as these ways of responding may be, they are not ultimately very helpful in that they invite us to be dismissive and not like things. This need not be. Those inclined to complain will continue to find things to disapprove of in films, whether or not these films are adaptations of books. But it is just as true that with due sympathy and openness, this complaining could give way to approval, pleasure, and even gratitude.

The following ideas might be of assistance. A film production that tries to incorporate every nuance and possibility found in the literary source, or uncovered by the comprehensive reader, would almost certainly be unbearably busy, unfocused, even endless. An enacted production must select only a certain few out of an abundance of possibilities. To regret options not explored, especially when the actual interpretive of directorial choice is valid and viable, is profitless.

As for the paring and pruning reader, actual film productions will never be exactly the same as his original conception, or preference. This is even true when that reader is the director or designer; given the collaborative nature of film production, sensibilities must meet and, in some measure, meld. The results will inevitably reflect this process of negotiation and hybridization. This, not incidentally, is one of the main reasons that people love theater. It could just as easily contribute to a satisfying love for and enjoyment of films.

Traditional storytelling, and the traditional story, are multiple. This means that establishing the original, "real" version of Cinderella matters much less than the fact that there are many versions that figuratively converse across chronological and geographical axes. The evanescent nature of the theater is healthy in this respect: if the text is fixed, then the range of interpretive possibilities, the healthy appeal of continual production becomes practically infinite.

Movies participate in and enrich this healthy process. *Great Expectations* (David Lean, et al., 1946) complements *Great Expectations* (Mr. Dickens, 1861). Henry V (fighting at the Battle of Agincourt, 1415) informs *Henry V* (W.S., 1599), which informs *Henry V* (Olivier/1944, Branagh/1989). The production you saw at the British National Theatre in 2003, or at Shakespeare's Globe in 2012, enters this conversation, as does the one in which you participated in college, as well as every like incursion in real-life of beleaguered forces against an implacable, outnumbering foe.

What does it all mean? Is the current instance (what and when and wherever it might be) heroic, or dubious, or obscured by clouds of uncertainty and ambiguity and duplicity? Precisely: there are many sources to cite, to help us in our grappling. Art and life reflect upon and enrich one another.

For all this, as we have seen, some feel that film remains suspect. This is especially true when it is perceived that film has gone poaching in the preserves of some older, more legitimate art. There is at least one good reason for this guardedness, though it's less the fault of the medium itself, than of the industry or industries that has grown up around it. Since watching appears to be easier than reading, and film can preserve performances that in the Theater only remain, and that diminishingly, in memory, then film has in many ways become the default medium, the final destination to which texts from all media tend. One unfortunate result, inextricably linked to the megacorporate nature of contemporary media production, is that instead of a healthy conversation between multiple versions, there is a search for the definitive take. Disney's (excellent) 1940 version of *Pinocchio* leaves the electrifying original unread, leaves the contradictory and fascinating Roberto Benigni adaptation of 2002 unseen and even unconsidered, and the whole disheartening situation leaves us prescriptive and proscriptive and grumpy about the stories and enactments that might otherwise connect us.

What is to be done? The trends may not be reversible, or even addressable, but the individual correspondent can still read and watch and think, substantially and joyfully. Adaptations are often discussed, as Seymour Chatman has suggested, by using a lover's vocabulary.[24] Someone is faithful, or there is betrayal. These terms may be unduly, unhelpfully inflated. This is no marriage, and the stakes are not as high. Since that is true, it may also be that in the realm of story a form of dalliance, or rather a willingness to positively consider variations and alternatives, may actually be helpful and healthy.

Adaptation contains a range of possibilities, a spectrum from attempting absolute congruence with the source to complete revisions or reformulations. An adaptor can transpose (a handmaidenly attempt at exactitude), transcribe (fidelity, but allowing for differences in mode or medium), translate (a service of the spirit, but knowing languages are so different that equivalencies may not be available), or utterly transform a work. From a critical perspective, a reader can also do all these things. As for hierarchy or morality, it may be that each of these courses is, in the abstract, neutral. The good and ill is in the work, and in the understanding, and in the application.

Books Are Great

The disposition of this work will be obvious by now: it posits that literature can be wonderful and that it very often is. Is there anything like a book? Can words be matched for the way that they describe and measure, color and caress? Is there anything like the way that words allow or require the reader to meet them halfway? As she interacts with the book the reader visualizes its action, or its argument, and decorates described scenes in her own particular fashion. Not only that, but she also colors the whole assembly with her own experiences, intuitions, and aspirations. A book is a conversation with the world and all of the people in it. It is once upon a time, and I never knew that. It is just so, and what did you say, the most bracing opposition, and the most embracing familiarity and fellowship. However long ago and far away the tale, a reader, particularly when young, will find kindred spirits that reassure and envelop and embolden.

This point doesn't need proving, though one is tempted to multiply illustrations in order simply to savor the self-evident. For instance, it is difficult to resist quoting Norman Lindsay's irrefutable, irreplaceable 1918 children's classic *The Magic Pudding*. It describes one of its protagonists, Bill Barnacle, as having "one of those beef-and-thunder voices."[25]

The great Hans Christian Andersen very clearly demonstrates the particular qualities and contributions of literature, especially in the lives of children. One of the most direct, one of the sweetest of these can be summarized very simply. During the course of his life, Andersen oversaw numerous editions of his works. As an epigram on the frontispiece of his final assembly, completed in the year of his death, he states his intent and his accomplishment: "My gift to the world."[26]

Good books, of which there are so many kinds, are a gift, a boon and a delight. They are a pleasure to giver and receiver, to reader and read-to, alike. In "The Old Street Lamp," Andersen articulates the particulars and implications of this exchange.

> The old lamp shone more brightly than it ever had before. "That was a lovely gift!" exclaimed the lamp. "The brilliant stars above, whom I have always admired and who shine so much more clearly than I have ever done—even though I have striven, throughout my whole life, to do just that—have sent down to me—poor, dim street lamp that I am—a most wonderful gift! They have given me the power to make those whom I love see clearly anything that I can remember or imagine. What a marvelous present! For that happiness that cannot be shared with others is only half as valuable as the one that can."[27]

Of course this lamp represents the author himself. Andersen's idealistic expression is amply embodied in his collected works, and in the whole institution of children's literature. Good books share the burdens and subsequent insights of great minds and great souls. They create order out of chaos—or felicitous chaos out of oppressive order—and shine a light into the dark places of the earth. They can do this, regardless of geography or chronology. Erik Haugaard, a Danish-American children's writer who also fashioned the finest translation of Andersen's complete fairy tales, has it as follows:

> That a sonnet by Shakespeare was written 400 years ago is not important, nor is the age of the bronze charioteer standing in the little museum at Delphi. We read the poem or look at the statue, and something within us is touched, almost physically, by them. It is our soul, alive because blood is coursing through our veins, that recognizes another soul, as alive as our own, in the cold metal and the printed word.[28]

Literature is precious for its applicability, for all of the permeable relations between text and context. In Andersen's "A Story from the Dunes," we find a young protagonist traveling. "And truly, the boy felt that he was driving right into a fairy tale country, and yet it was real."[29] Andersen's "What the Whole Family Said" describes little Maria's birthday and the array of marvelous presents that she received: "But better than even the best of fairy tales was a birthday, and preferably, many of them."[30] As we will see in this book's second section, one of literature's greatest gifts is that it helps the young person to look forward, shoulder a happy burden, and embrace a defining opportunity. Literature helps her to grow up and to live bountifully beyond the storybook's page.

"'It is lovely to live,' said little Maria, and her godfather added that life was the best of all fairy tales ... 'for one is in it oneself.'"[31] Andersen's story proceeds as different familial branches on different floors of the familial home all consider this idea. They run it through their various individual circumstances, say it in their own way, and all come to an agreement. Stories distract, or console, or instruct. But after the stories—"Life is the best fairy tale of all."[32]

For all of this book's advocacy on behalf of films, sometimes books really are better than movies. The superiority is not inherent, but it clearly operates in many individual cases. For instance, many contemporary films for children and adolescents are way too noisy, and the noise goes on for way too long. Strident children's films come and go, but one of the pioneering exemplars of a current, very insistent spate is director Joe Johnston's film adaptation of Chris Van Allsburg's *Jumanji* (1995). Another adaptation of another Van Allsburg book, *Zathura* (2005), operates more or less identically.[33]

These films are, respectively, 104 and 101 minutes long. In contrast, their literary sources both contain sixteen two-page spreads, with one illustration and some brief text on each page. Each book portrays, or rather implies, a considerable amount of velocity and kinesis and collision. The striking thing is the droll, elliptical way in which all of this uproar is treated and rendered. This is partly a study in, a triumph of contrast. But there is a conceptual benefit as well. In these books Van Allsburg approaches violence—or mayhem, which we might say is violence with the training wheels still on—more or less as it was portrayed in Sophocles' *Oedipus*. Consider: the meeting at the crossroads, the death of Jocasta, Oedipus' climactic, atoning disfigurement. These are all essential to the plot, and to the theme, and they all occur offstage. That this is so reinforces the fact that in the original text violence is an idea, or a set of ideas. It is power and presumption, fate and a falling. It is an institution and an historical reality, and it is indirectly rendered so as to insure that ideas, not horror or the unseemly consumption thereof, prevail.

Whether or not he was thinking about Sophocles, Van Allsburg also contains or implies most of his mayhem between picture panels. "They'd been playing almost three hours," as one bit of text informs us. How efficient, and how elegant! The part is sufficient to the rendering of the whole as the author evokes, suggests, and leaves the applications and implications to the young reader. *Jumanji* features Van Allsburg's typically sure-handed illustrations, and worlds between them. For its part, the film, for all of its imaginative design and well-executed effects, fills it all in, cranks it all up, and simply will not be quiet.[34]

Sometimes books are better than films, or maybe an individual book is able to maintain a course that film industries so often refuse. Nicholas Roeg's creditable, even estimable, adaptation of Roald Dahl's *The Witches* (1990) cut, streamlined, elaborated, and generally interpreted its source. This is as it should be, as it must be even. As we have seen, media are different. Furthermore, enactors distill, and select, and interpret. An adaptation could and should never be all that a book contains or implies.

Thus far, so good. Then, at the end, writer-director Roeg, or perhaps the producers who wished to insure the film's profitability—and who can completely blame them for that?—changed everything. Both book and film begin with a fatal car accident, in which the protagonist's parents are killed. Midway through, this same protagonist is caught out by the eponymous witches and turned into a mouse. In the book the change is permanent. At the conclusion of the film, the main character is magically turned back into a human, which not only obscures, but obliterates what may be the novel's most powerful point: in many ways the death of the parents and the transformation of the protagonist are the same event. Accidents happen, some of them terrible, and the results may be irreparable. While most everyone else in Dahl's book goes into conniptions at the sight of a mouse, the boy's faithful grandmother at first mourns, deeply, and then stirs herself to action. More importantly, she retains and even increases an unfailing tenderness and loyalty toward her traumatized and altered charge. All of this both warns and reassures the reader. It confirms the protagonist's initial, healthy response to the previously unthinkable. It says that new opportunities, insights, and even abilities can accompany tragedy. Perhaps this relates to a child's native optimism. Or perhaps it is a bid to push the child toward an optimism that isn't necessarily native, and certainly not always easy, in the face of dire circumstance.

This tremendous children's book addresses the direst, potentially most debilitating of adult issues. It passes through the noble weariness of Samuel Beckett's mournful "You must go on, I can't go on, I'll go on"[35]— moving straight on to the paradoxically positive, insufficiently remarked conclusion to Sartre's drama of infernal banality. *No Exit*? Not necessarily. After disaster, and despair, one can always choose affirmation, as in the play's electrifying, unironic last line. "Well, let's get on with it."[36]

Films, of course, are also capable of this. The most moderately initiated film historian comes to realize that in this medium anything is possible, and everything has been accomplished. But there are certain material interests too, and the costs, not only of production, but of distribution and exhibition as well. And then there are the home rights. Nicholas Roeg's creditable, even estimable film version of Dahl's *The Witches* gleefully, exquisitely elaborates all sorts of things that are only hinted at in the original text. It is, in fact, that most desirable of adaptations: a gestalt, in which the whole, the tandem, is greater than the sum of the already excellent parts. But then there's that ending. The business of books, if not necessarily the medium entire, can sometimes hold more insistently to a principle. Sometimes books are better than films.[37]

Books Are Not Great

On the other hand, who says that books are always so sacred? The uncritical idealization of books and of the oral culture that leads up to and out of them need interrogating. Robert Burns' poem "The Cotter's Saturday Night" (1785) very famously and sweetly paints a picture of pre-industrial, pre-mediated plentitude.[38] Its simple characters gather together after a day's seemly occupation. They turn to a few small, remaining domestic tasks. They talk, together, reinforcing right teaching and strengthening the bonds of loving familial obligation. This is the subsistent, sufficient economy so lauded by Jean-Jacques Rousseau in his "Discourse on the Arts and the Sciences."

William Butler Yeats' *Fairy and Folk Tales of Ireland* (1888) gathers a number of absolute page-turners from a number of Irish sources, for the contemporary reader's instruction and, especially, delight.[39] Yeats' foreword informs the reader that many of these stories originated rurally, were fashioned and preserved and proliferated by people who were both plain and humble, sensitive and creative. His book *The Celtic Twilight* (1893) reminds us that many of these stories originated orally as well.[40]

Well and good, but not quite complete. The Western Scottish writer Ian Crichton-Smith gleefully conflates a Yeatsian image of Romantic tales told 'round the peat fire with modernity, technology, and the fact that most people may be unable to harness the imagination or summon the energy required to effectively spin their own yarns. This from his hilariously droll *Thoughts of Murdo* (1993): "The oral tradition? I remember that we used to sit around the fire in the *ceilidh* house reading *The Guns of Navarone* aloud. It took three weeks. Before that we had *Where Eagles Dare*."[41]

Crichton-Smith intentionally describes this scene with an oral-storyteller's presumed lilt, and what he describes is by no means unattractive, culturally, or emotionally insubstantial. How wonderful that Alastair MacLean, a modern Scottish writer of arrestingly violent thrillers, should so arrestingly occupy the humble occupants of a Scots Cotter's (or Crofter's) cottage. That he might do so, however, provides a bracing counter to too often idealized images of families in literary communion. The family in Crichton-Smith's fictional-comical interview is eclectic. It also hints at the possibility that family reading and reading-to-family can be inapt, and ineffective.

Ideal, real: the eleventh chapter of James Barrie's *Peter Pan*[42] is both amusing and exasperating as it renders a situation familiar to any parent who has attempted to regale living, breathing, actual youngsters with a story.

"Listen, then," said Wendy, settling down to her story, with Michael at her feet and seven boys in the bed. "There was once a gentleman—"

"I had rather he had been a lady," Curly said.
"I wish he had been a white rat," said Nibs.

Many of the most celebrated milestones of children's literature contain two tales. The fictional narrative is doubled by an explicit, multiply detailed account of how that narrative is being imparted to actual, diegetic listeners,[43] as well as to an implied readership out in the world.[44] This double articulation is the great hope and the great accomplishment of children's literature, properly imparted. The heartfelt tale touches the tender heart, and the mother who tells it takes her beloved child upon her lap. All are edified in the exchange. However, like those dual beacons of democracy, liberty and equality, the idea of reading and the experience of reading sometimes come into conflict. The children's tale is often obscured and even jeopardized when one tries to tell it to the actual children. Barrie describes this phenomenon with gleeful accuracy.

> "Quiet," their mother admonished them. "There was a lady also, and—"
> "Oh, mummy," cried the first twin, "you mean that there *is* a lady also, don't you? She is not dead, is she?"
> "Oh, no."
> "I am awfully glad she isn't dead," said Tootles. "Are you glad, John?"
> "Of course I am."
> "Are you glad, Nibs?"
> "Rather."
> "Are you glad, Twins?"
> "We are glad."
> "Oh dear," sighed Wendy.
> "Little less noise there," Peter called out, determined that she should have fair play, however beastly a story it might be in his opinion.[45]

Yeats' aforementioned fairy tale collection was a commercial bid and a successful commercial venture, chockablock with the most delightful, arresting yarns. His *Celtic Twilight* is a more reflective, scholarly collection, more committed to exploring truths than to distilling their most marketable essence. The book includes an important corrective to the overidealization of the oral tale. In "Dreams that have no moral,"[46] Yeats describes the dispiriting material condition of so many Western-Irish holdings, the perennial poverty, the lack of nutrition and education and, subsequently, ambition or opportunity. He observes that out of this deprivation almost inevitably comes a certain kind of story: tentative, meandering, distracted, petering-out. This is the objective correlative[47] set historically; the object, or the incident, evokes the very feelings that the author wishes to engender. Or more pointedly, absurdly futile tales testify to the absurd futility of the world in which so many have struggled and that so many have experienced.

We may not be peasants from the west of Ireland, but we may very well be subject to some of the same deprivations and their consequences. When we are, when the oral or literary exchange in which we are involved just doesn't measure up to expectation or idealization, it may just be that a well-nourished and executed cinematic assembly will provide us with the very best service.

This is not an isolated situation. It is often pointed out that the Brothers Grimm amended the tales that they collected.[48] It is usually mentioned that these amendments were censorious, which is to say that Jacob and Wilhelm cut the impropriety out of what had been previously been more spirited, unguarded, authentic recitations. There is truth to this, and much insight to be gained by contemplating it. But have we given sufficient thought to the fact that some of Jacob and Wilhelm's amendments were also literary, craft-related, and designed to make what must sometimes have been rough and ragged tales into something altogether more polished?

We can experience something of what might have been when reading the unedited, unimproved tales assembled by the American folklorist John Bierhorst.[49] Bierhorst's exemplary collections leave these Inuit or Central or South American tales as they were, which often means that they are extremely glancing, occasionally vague, generally semi- or unformed. They are gold, anthropologically speaking. Mythically too, and they bear a striking, beautiful resemblance to the raw dream material that Freud analyzes and elaborates in his inexhaustible *The Interpretation of Dreams* (1900). They are gold, but not full, or finished, or even conventionally satisfying.

Book-idealization serves publishers, but actual authors are occasionally more frank and forthcoming about the nature of story-telling in the beleaguered, over-programmed contemporary family. For instance, Allan Ahlberg's 1996 picture book, *Tell Us a Story*, turns a humorous and sympathetic eye on how pinched and poverty-struck parent narratives can sometimes be. A combination of weighty responsibility, sleep deprivation, pique, even and often their own imaginative shortfall mean, once again, that these oral or textual exchanges are not always the shining thing of myth and legend. Since this is true, it is also true that a fine film can sometimes serve both parent and child better than the spoken or read-aloud tale.

Films Are Great

Gillian Avery characterizes the beginnings of children's literature by quoting Sir Thomas North, who in 1579 had completed a translation of Plutarch's *Lives*. North rejoiced in these biographical tales, leading him to conclude that "stories are fit for euerie place, reach to all persons, serue for all times."[50] Avery observes that, for the most part, contemporary clerics felt similarly to scholars like North. "Stories were for everyone, young and old."[51] Could our film-fearing bibliophiles not consider this possibility, and expand it? Modern media had obviously not even been imagined in 1579. But the advent of film and television, and the formal and technological differences that distinguish the various media, do not really alter or weaken North's point, nor Avery's either. Stories are a pleasure and a benefit to all, and this is the case regardless of the medium through which they are transmitted. In fact, it could well be argued the proliferation of media technologies combined with inexhaustible repositories of both ancient and contemporary tales makes the happy reality even greater. This is permutation, abundance unto infinity, and cause for great gratitude.

Books are marvelous. Yet, they are not complete or comprehensive. As Aristotle suggested, narration is not the same as enactment. And in fact, narration, or the text on the page, can never quite match the plenitude provided by actors performing, by a facial expression, by the pitching of a voice, or the movement and disposition of a body. Hans Andersen's "The Emperor's New Clothes" is a story for the ages, full to bursting and most sufficient, in its own right. But why do literary partisans so infrequently fail to address the power of performance? For all of the story's good sense and boldness, it can never quite replicate, never quite approach, the effect of actor Dick Shawn's actual, surpassingly silly transports as he faux-dons his non-existent duds, and then cavorts with mad dignity before his gaping subjects.[52]

A later chapter in this book features a detailed analysis of Charlie Chaplin's 1924 film, *The Pilgrim*. The sequence in question features an infernally naughty child played by Dean or "Dinky Dean" Riesner, who was actually the young son of one of Chaplin's intimate friends. The scene proceeds precipitously, and very effectively. This child is a caution, and he generates all sorts of inappropriately aggressive impulses in the mind of the adult spectator.

But now there is the briefest fermata: very glancingly, and only if she concentrates, that adult spectator can see Chaplin seated, and the bad little boy standing quietly between his knees. His hands are placed lightly thereupon, while Chaplin's hands are placed with like gentleness around the child's waist. For this instant, and again at the very conclusion of the scene, we see the person beneath the part and the relationship beneath the roles. This man and this child know and love each other.

This is why films are sometimes much better than books. It is much more than a matter of actors performing—the cinema is an ontological, indexical medium, replete with layers and levels of rich documentation, physical and relational realities that predate, lie beneath, and transcend any fictional contrivance that may be at hand. This documentary component is capable of providing not only the physical facts but also all of the implications and emotions that go along with them.

Aristotle states that plays must be enacted, and we have applied that same assumption, and approbation, to films. Enactment, however, comprises much more than mere performance. Films are great in ways that books cannot be, because of all of the other superb things that they can imagine, fashion, and bring to light.

In 1941 the American writer Holling C. Holling published an estimable informational picture book called *Paddle to the Sea*. The book tells two fine stories, simultaneous and complementary. The first has to do with a young Native boy's carving of a little wooden Indian, and the little wooden canoe in which he sits. The wooden Indian and his little craft will subsequently journey from the child's upland home, all the way to the sea. It is an exciting odyssey. It is also the vehicle for Holling's second story, an educational narrative, in which the wooden Indian illustrates the workings of gravity, the downward flow of water, the interlocking, interdependent water tables and waterways and the complex relations between industry and environment, science and nature.

On his way to introducing and communicating all of these good things, Holling paints a pleasing little picture, through a single illustration and the following text:

> [The Indian boy] returned to his bear robe by the fire where he had sat for many days whittling a piece of pine. Now he worked on in silence. He bent over the fire to melt lead in an iron spoon, and poured it out to cool and harden in a hollow of the wood.... Then he brought out oil paints and worked carefully with a brush.[53]

This is very well described—"to cool and harden in a hollow of the wood"—and this is the whole of it. Now the long journey, and its environmental elaboration, begins.

We have seen great value in the way that illustrators like Chris Van Allsburg, in the way that the entire genre of the picture book can leave things unspoken, and unelaborated. On the other hand, sometimes filling in is better. In 1966, the Canadian filmmaker Bill Mason produced a film version of Holling's book for Canada's National Film Board (NFB). It seemed an unlikely subject, at least in terms of the usual mandates and motivations of the commercial cinema. The NFB, however, marches to the beat of a different drummer, and in service of a different set of civil and educational objectives. "Between what matters and what seems to matter...."[54] The film is a triumph in all sorts of ways,[55] but its accomplishment, which is typical of the entire medium, can be distilled and appreciated in the way that Mason renders the above-quoted scene.

Holling's version of the story is, frankly, a bit perfunctory. It may be that the picture book itself is somewhat prone to this problem. Its rich evocations can, in some circumstances, turn into sparse insufficiency. For his part, Mason undertakes to suggest and even document much more of this entire process and the contexts that inform it. Like Holling, he has utilized maps of North America to exactly situate the action that is about to unfold. Unlike Holling—or the lovely, productively de-limited, occasionally limited medium in which he is working—Mason has access to cinematic time, with its palpable passing. He has access to that time interacting with space, which in this case is a topographical space. He has utilized maps and an animation stand in order to trace the distance between the individual and the geographical, the cultural and the geological. He has, with all these things combined, not only the idea of expanse and distance, but something of its experience.

A towering, dissolving series of overhead views have brought us from the extremities of Canada's east coast all the way to the "north of Lake Superior, in the Nipigon country."[56] Here is an establishing shot of the boy's cabin. As in the book—this need never be a contest, or a battle; the book and the film, as is so often the case, finally and wonderfully complement each other—the film, through its narrator, reminds us of its scientific objective: "Now that cabin was not only far away from the sea, it was also far above the level of the sea."[57]

But here is the special, strictly cinematical elaboration. Having placed us geographically, Mason now situates us particularly: "And that's why the boy from the cabin got a cedar log from the woods and started to carve Paddle to the Sea."[58] Mason moves into the cabin's firelit interior. Here he selects and shows to the audience a representative few out of a whole array of homely appointments and implements. By doing these things, Mason makes many suggestions about the values and economics of this household, the occupations and dispositions of its inhabitants. One of the most important of these suggestions relates to the fact that Mason gives Holling's slightly generic Native protagonist an actual name. Where in 1966 many movie Indians were still being arrayed as nameless threats along overlooking ridges, this boy is named Kyle Apotegan.

Now Mason, and Apotegan, proceed to the carving of the canoe and its conductor. This task is set forth in a strategic series of extreme, extremely beautiful close-ups. Here is the partially fashioned piece of wood, and here the very tip of the knife blade. Here the knife blade scores the surface of the wood, repeatedly, so that the figure gradually emerges out of blank potentiality into increasing definition.

Mason makes of this process a powerful symbol that Holling had not himself imagined. The carving is the little boy himself, moving through activity and inquiry into increasing self-sufficiency. It is also impassive nature, or mere picturesqueness, resolving under the child's—or the viewer's—close and patient scrutiny into knowledge and experience. It turns out that sometimes you can't see the trees for the forest. But Mason knows, and shows, that intense and joyful concentration is not only the essence of wondrous childhood but also the road to productive and joyful adulthood.[59] He lingers especially on the fashioning of the little figure's eyes, which emerge out of the flat impassivity of the wood to become, literally, animated, life, or a leap of faith. With the workings of imagination, this mere block has become the figure of a man. With the workings of imagination, and with similar and sequential industry, this child's mere wood carving could very well resolve into forestry, ecology, hydrology, horticulture, or whatever he chooses to be in and contribute to the world.

These actions are portrayed visually, but they are also adeptly captured on the soundtrack. A soundtrack, obviously, is something that books do not have in common with films, as well as being something that literarily-biased film analysts far too often ignore. In *Paddle to the Sea*, the scoring and carving and shaping produce an equal variety of different sounds, pleasingly rhythmical, with their own deep tone and texture. Carefully enhancing this ensemble of diegetic sights and sounds is Louis Applebaum's flitting, bird-like score. The sound, along with the picture, reinforces the materiality of this whole process, its melding of time and place, of a task and the individual agency that takes it on and completes it. A normal kid might well get bored with this rather elaborate project and give up. This cinematical child, immersed in all of these richly rendered sights and sounds and sensations, wouldn't even think of doing so.[60]

Young Kyle continues with his project. Mason continues shooting in close-up. This means that his depth of field is narrow—in fact, very narrow.

We see mere centimeters, even millimeters in intense focus, while the background continues to be softly, impressionistically lit by that warm firelight. At one level, this is a photographic decision, leading to a pleasing photographic sensation. But the sensuous can also signify; the narrow depth of field also bespeaks this child's tremendous concentration and absorption. This is a cinematic, formal manifestation of dedicated play. Quite electrifyingly in this context, and given this implied audience, this is also a manifestation of dedicated work and its equally surpassing satisfactions.

The cinema is greatly benefited by its proclivity for substantial spectacle, for all manner of arresting audio-visual highlights that can so impress themselves upon the brain, and the soul. The Little Colonel's charge in *Birth of the Nation*, the Odessa Steps in *Battleship Potemkin*, the vision of Moloch in *Metropolis*, almost innumerable sequences in the cinema of Alfred Hitchcock—there is no end to the eye-popping, jaw-dropping images that cinema can create. It seems that this is what aficionados most celebrate, and what they come back to. However one of film's greatest abilities—and, in an o'er kinetical, supersensated time, one of its most valuable benefits—is that it is capable of fashioning highlights that are just as searing, just as affecting and moving, in a smaller register.

In the book quotation placed above, Holling C. Holling briefly described this electrifying action, though the action did not—and need not—register as such. For his part, Mason and his small crew of collaborators makes this glancing thing into one of the most memorable, indelible moments in all of children's cinema. While Kyle has been carving, a metal container that he had placed amidst the burning logs in the fireplace is melting lead into liquid. This metamorphosis completed, Kyle lifts the handle of his container with a wooden stick, and lays it on the flags just this side of the flame. He now dips an iron ladle into the molten. He turns the craft that he has fashioned upside down. He has burned these words into its keel.

> I AM PADDLE TO THE SEA
> PLEASE PUT ME BACK IN THE WATER

These scored capital letters are all placed straight and true, as is the narrow carved hollow toward which Kyle now lifts the steaming ladle, with its metamorphic contents. Continuing to shoot with a very narrow depth of field, Mason frames the canoe so that it cuts a diagonal from the lower left to the upper right of the film frame. Now Kyle, who is after all just a young boy, quickly and confidently tilts the ladle so that its fearsome contents flow into the trench that he has carved for them. As the lead runs, the soundtrack sizzles, steam and smoke rise, and the hollowed space is filled, exactly and perfectly. By the time the lead has reached the end of its trench, it moves out of focus and into an impressionistic, perhaps even archetypal or mythological indistinctness.

When, or perhaps just before all of this enormity has registered, Mason cuts slightly ahead in time to another shot of the canoe's keel, now stretching straight from left to right. The molten lead is now all set and hardened and firmly anchored. Kyle turns his creation over, and with the same care and craft and joy that had attended all of the previous stages of preparation, proceeds to paint it. This labor is also framed narrowly, and is firelit. After two minutes of elapsed screen time—and twelve rapturously unhurried, lingering shots—the whole job is done. Or at least the viewer feels that it is. In fact, this process has been elliptically assembled, giving the impression of completeness rather what might have been an agonizing totality. But what a sense of duration, and blessed difficulty, and sweet satisfaction this elliptical selection has given to its audience!

Its elements notwithstanding, these two processes, the child's precocious crafting and the small crew's sensitive cinematic capture are not really, not at all alchemical. No one has actually turned lead into gold. But they have done more, and better. They have turned lead into lead, liquid into solid, potential into kinetic, aspiration into action, idea into actuality. This isn't commercialism, or escapism, and it is certainly not the agonized, heartfelt, and ultimately untenable representations of the likes of Neil Postman. This is the cinema and what it can do, what it does all the time, for children and adults alike.

Now a question may arise, and quite fairly. Has this last description been overly enhanced? Perhaps or almost certainly so; but it may also be that this heightening is simply another emblem of the same basic transformative possibility. For all of its alleged mind-numbing qualities, for all of its allegedly inherent passivity, film is itself a craft—where each image can be and where so many of its images have been carefully and lovingly and beautifully fashioned to communicate information, emotion, conviction, education. It is for its viewers what Bill Mason fashioned for and with his Native protagonist, for and with any attentive viewer that internalizes his adventure. Here are craft, chemistry, science, industry, everything. Kyle, Mason's film, and the entire medium can just as easily take passivity and turn it to engagement and the most gainful employment.

This is what film can do, and what it does, all the time. Sound, nuances of design and direction, explorations and expressions of time and space, and especially the glories of performance repeatedly demonstrate that theater/film are neither superior nor subordinate, but sufficient, complete, and indeed, perfect on their own terms.

Both Are Great— The Reciprocal Influence of the Arts

A certain kind of commercial or competitive mindset operates exclusively in terms of victory and defeat. The winner triumphs, and opponents are vanquished. Melodrama, with its morally polarized characters and its conflicts resolved through violent physical confrontation, often proceeds similarly. In these and other scenarios, striving and strife seem always to take precedence over diplomacy or compromise.

Melodrama, or the jungle, can be countered by gentler alternatives. There are other options and approaches to all sorts of things, and they need not always be opposed or annihilated. The person willing to explore this course may combine confidence and partial self-certainty with curiosity, humility, and even gratitude. He investigates and equips himself with methodologies and sensitivities that allow him to analyze and understand what he had not previously encountered or even imagined. While continuing to nurture his own strong roots, he opens himself to new abundances, which he may come to own or share.

Richard Schickel records how the pioneering American film director D. W. Griffith drew upon Charles Dickens while developing his notion of parallel montage. To the objections of an unnamed Biograph executive, who claimed that audiences would only be confused by what seemed to be the random alternation of different story strands, Griffith replied that Dickens had always written that way. His readers were oriented not just through the elaboration of individual scenes but by the juxtaposition of multiple scenes. Their very proximity led the reader to connect and comprehend these parts on her own.[61]

Dickens was the inspiration for Griffith's most famous innovation, the thing that most distinguished film from its ancestor arts. Soviet cinema's most precocious figure,[62] the great filmmaker/theorist Sergei Eisenstein, elaborated on this relationship in his tremendous long essay "Dickens, Griffith, and the Film Today."[63]

In that essay, Eisenstein quotes from the twenty-first chapter of *Oliver Twist*, which describes the dawning of a new day and how that dawning physically and figuratively awakens an entire landscape and all who dwell therein. Eisenstein observes that Dickens accomplishes this effect through an accumulation of carefully chosen, exactly ordered details. These are, essentially, images, described physically, while adjectival glosses suggest something of the meaning or morality of each component part.

For Eisenstein this juxtaposition and accumulation of images, with which the traditional nineteenth-century novel is absolutely filled, clearly anticipates the cinema. In fact, Eisenstein goes so far as to suggest that the cinema will eventually perfect, and even surpass, Dickens's device. Committed as he was to affirming his new medium and to distancing himself from the bourgeois habits of the older arts, it may be that Eisenstein overstates this case. However he does not at all overstate or inflate what is basically a beautiful affiliation between the two arts.

The world is full of chaos and disorder. Societies, or the institutions that operate within them, are constituted to try to fend these things off. A carefully cared for child may be protected from the entropic extreme, and she will be spared much of the responsibility for combating it. Still, on its own scale, her life is also full of incompleteness, and the uncertainty that goes with it. The day's outfit is still in the bureau, breakfast is yet unmade, outside relationships with neighbors, with potential friends, remain unimproved. The child's parents will help her with all of this, but they will also guide her toward taking it all upon herself, to organizing her own life, and to making her own way. This is part of maturing and of maturity. We turn our hand to the unimproved opportunities that surround us, turn potential energies into actual kinesis, and begin to accomplish our lives.

Sergei Eisenstein saw descriptive, synthetic literature as an anticipation of the cinematic montage aesthetic to which he dedicated most of his artistic life. And for him, montage was not merely an aesthetic, but a perfect representation of the energies and conflicts that undergirded modern industrial life, that anticipated a great revolutionary change. We needn't share Eisenstein's political faith to see a profound correlation, one that applies most especially to the child.

Stories, fictions, art in general can quite validly be seen as an organization of life's chaos, a challenge to its insistent disorder. Each artist takes the materials of his or her medium and organizes and orders and arranges them. Each artist takes these materials and speaks to something, says something beyond mere physical assemblage. It may be that out of these organizations come entertainment and pleasure. Just as importantly, stories suggest, they are a striving for coherence, a making of meaning and of purpose.

2. From Confrontation to Conciliation

The 1948 Cineguild production of *Oliver Twist* opens with a superb extraliterary, invented-for-the-film prologue. A young woman makes her way through a terrible storm and the black night to a distant set of gates. She is, as it turns out, also in labor. The storm and her travails are folded together in a montage sequence linking and equating these two mighty upheavals. The rain and the thunder are an answer, a correlative to her agony, both bodily and spiritual. These physical pangs are perhaps exceeded by her solitude, which is mostly owing to her unmarried state.

This is Oliver's mother, of course, and she will not survive the night. It is uncertain whether director David Lean, screenwriter Ronald Neame, photographer Guy Green, or any other of Cineguild's tremendous team of collaborators were aware of Eisenstein's Dickens essay.[64] Whether or not they were, their assembly, though lacking any literary original, operates exactly like the compounded images in Dickens's twenty-first chapter. As Eisenstein had suggested, the technique works wonderfully in either medium, is essentially native to either medium, and, one might add, is another reason that we need not choose between either medium.

For those unburdened by partisan prejudice, film and literature form constant, constantly proliferating bonds of mutual sustenance. The first chapter of Leon Garfield's already cited *The Sound of Coaches* demonstrates the felicitous interpenetration and cross-fertilization that can be, and so often is, shared between literature and film. Its gripping account of a nameless girl making her agonizing way to a stranger's door, only to give birth and die, is clearly inspired by the opening of the 1948 film.[65] Garfield, as designated Dickensian,[66] is equally engaged in evoking the great master and in evoking masterful film adaptations of the great master's works.

The correlations continue, if we will. This is from Hans Christian Andersen's 1836 story, "The Traveling Companion":

> Next week his father was buried. Johannes walked behind the coffin. He could no longer see his father, whom he loved so much. He heard the earth fall on the coffin lid. He peered down into the grave. He could see the corner of the burial chest; another shovelful of earth and that, too, was out of sight. At that moment Johannes felt that his heart would break from sorrow. A psalm was sung and it sounded so beautiful that he burst out crying, and the tears relived his grief. The sunlight played on the leaves of the trees; it was as if the sun wanted to say, "Do not be sad Johannes! Can't you see how beautiful the blue sky is? Your father is up there and he is begging God to help, so that all may go well for you."[67]

Can the reader not see this as an implicit blueprint, a storyboard for a beautiful film sequence? Here are a number of very specific shots—the corner of the burial chest, and the earth falling upon it—as well as the opportunity to elaborate or add unto what is already here. How beautifully could one enhance and multiply the mournful walk behind the curtain or the playing of the sun on the leaves of the trees?[68] Here is *Oliver Twist*, chapter 21, all over again! Andersen is obviously as much engaged in the assembly of protocinematic images as was his erstwhile English friend. Film aficionados reading Andersen's description may also find it echoed in an early sequence of another David Lean film. In his 1965 adaptation of Boris Pasternak's *Dr. Zhivago*, a mourning child stands at his parent's graveside, where the tempests of his grief interact with the brightness of the awakening world. As he had in his 1948 film, Lean elaborates most lyrically, even rapturously. Is he also aware of another similar sequence at the beginning of Jacques Feyder's masterly French film from 1925, *The Faces of Children*? There, again, a boy mourns his mother's death as he stands, in dramatic physical surroundings, at her grave. At this juncture, Feyder's previously decorous compositions and shot juxtapositions leap into expressionism and lyricism, finding ways in which the medium can evoke, invoke, and express the racking emotion and exquisite beauty that are there intermingled.

This is just one point of literary-cinematic accord, though there are countless dear, and dark, and delightful manifestations thereof. There are many more parallels, if we'll have them. Erich von Stroheim (in)famously set out to film—design, decorate, populate, and enact—every single paragraph of Frank Norris's 1897 naturalist novel, *McTeague*. The result, *Greed* (1924), is a multiple milestone in film history, a landmark and a ruin, a tale of excess or integrity, depending on one's loyalties and ethical disposition. Regardless of what happened, however, or who was at fault, there is a tremendous, instructive literary-cinematic component to the story.

Von Stroheim went wildly over budget and over schedule. He stretched the studio's resources to the breaking point and paved the way for the destruction, or at least the evisceration of his own film. (His nine-hour cut was eventually reduced to 2¼, for all of Rick Schmidlin's later efforts.) But the director's obsessive detailing was not merely a provocation or a profligacy. Devoted as he was to Norris's naturalist tenets, von Stroheim knew that exactly arranged physical surroundings, that milieu, were the key to his source and to the adaptation that he was attempting. By completely decorating each scene, he was creating a visual, dramatic equivalent to Norris's naturalism, in which characters were completely determined through heredity and environment. By surrounding both his actors and his audiences with these very determining elements, von Stroheim both honored and effectively adapted, with spatial and temporal cinematic equivalents, his source. Here was a thorough, thoroughly thought out cinematic correlation to a literary concept.[69]

The fifteenth chapter of James Barrie's *Peter Pan*, entitled "Hook or Me This Time," features a stirring, exhaustive description of a climactic shipboard battle.[70] Much as in von Stroheim's film, director Hebert Wilcox and his collaborators designed, decorated, and filmed every bit of this literary conflict in their 1925 film version. James Barrie is not a naturalist— though his early, pointedly Scottish works *Auld Licht Idylls* (1888) and *A Window in Thrums* (1889) do bear a striking resemblance, or at least show definite traces of the form—but Wilcox's adaptation attempts a practically naturalistic exactitude. The significant thing is that the viewer will not realize any of this until she has read the book and seen the film, perhaps in very close proximity and with her eyes peeled. Could it be that our dissatisfactions with specific adaptations, and with the relationship between books and films in general, are partly owing to our own inattentiveness or insensitivity? Whether, as here, the parallels are scrupulously intentional or whether we connect through intuition and our own active reading, the fact remains that if we'll have it, books and films go together and multiply.

It might just be that we need both, or that we wouldn't want to and needn't do without either. Robert Browning paid homage to the troubled life and art of the poet Christopher Smart, who fervently sought to accomplish—and occasionally succeeded in accomplishing—a necessary, nigh on impossible thing. Smart "Pierced the screen/'Twixt thing and word, lit language straight from soul."[71] Could it be that the image, faithfully rendered, bravely captured, artfully transformed, is closer and truer to elusive reality than the word?

The first section of this study has portrayed a fierce, longstanding battle between the children's literature and what have often been perceived as its media foes. It began, however, by citing a conciliatory essay by André Bazin, who saw correlations between seemingly irreconcilable forms, and who had faith in their mutual strength and efficacy. If we'll have it, books and films can productively address, substantially help us with, a number of issues of interest to children and adults alike. But all of that is in the abstract. Another concept of Bazin's allows us to conclude this part of the discussion with something concrete and practical.

Bazin recognized the reasons for and regretted the pugnacity of critical discussions relating to the supposed superiority of the ancestral arts. He proposed an alternative, which in fact he also practiced. This was that participants in the conversation could acknowledge a profound and beneficial reciprocal influence of the arts, which would open a way to replace conflict and contention with a kind of communion.

As explored in a number of calm, thoughtfully argued essays, Bazin concluded that three productive and felicitous consequences attended many meetings between film and its forebears—literature and the theater, primarily. The first was that these familial arts—a kinship, mind you, that cannot be overly emphasized or appreciated—explored common themes and utilized common methods of approaching and articulating them. The second was that, though the various media were indeed different from one another in important ways, it was still true that differences could operate complementarily, distinct but sounding harmoniously together. The last possibility was that film adaptations could provide productive contrast from the originals, such that the complacency of ossified interpretations would be replaced by dynamic, engaging dialogue.[72]

This possibility obviously relates to books and films. It also extends beyond specialized explorations of medium and into to the arenas of scholarly and public discourse, into the mutual implication and interdependence of academic or administrative constituencies and the lay public who run the greatest risks, have the greatest need, and can potentially enjoy the greatest benefit from the civil and substantial exchange of ideas and experiences.

Part II: Defining Childhood—Evolving Representations and Realities

3

The Angel Child

Jesus, He loves one and all,
Jesus, He loves children small,
Their souls are waiting round His feet
On high, before His mercy-seat.

While He wandered here below
Children small to Him did go,
At His feet they knelt and prayed,
On their heads His hands He laid.

Came a Spirit on them then,
Better than of mighty men,
A Spirit faithful, pure and mild,
A Spirit fit for king and child.

Oh! that Spirit give to me,
Jesu Lord, where'er I be!

—Charles Kingsley, "Child Ballad"

I sigh that kiss you,
For I must own
That I shall miss you
When you have grown.

—W. B. Yeats, "A Cradle Song"

A Conciliatory Dialectic

The dimensions and durations of children's lives change through time, and vary according to geography and circumstance. Our concepts of childhood are similarly mutable. This evolving conversation has ranged from the short, sharp existence of the medieval serf to the burgeoning awareness of the rising merchant classes, from Original Sin to Émile, or Oliver Twist, from the devoted idealization of the Romantics to the dire sentimentalities and dismissals of post/modernity. Each historical period, each demographical formulation, is also, inevitably, a historical or demographical construct. Thus we have reality, and we have the shaping of reality's raw materials into numerous narratives. Out of all these settings and contexts arise important, challenging questions of a very basic kind: What is a child? What is childhood? Out of all of the hypotheses and histories, which one is correct, and when, and in what sense?

An appeal to the dialectical suggests an answer, or perhaps a method, which has already informed the last chapters' take on books and media. In his famous dialogues Socrates prevails against, practically obliterates, most all of his interlocutors. But the *Apology*, Socrates' stirring statement of principal and immovable integrity, does not so easily vanquish the contrary integrities of Confucius's roughly contemporary *Analects*, which so convincingly and inspiringly advocates opposite solutions to many of the challenges that Socrates addresses.[1] In terms of the present conversation, this means that even though children trail clouds of glory, as Wordsworth maintained,[2] they may also deserve the occasional spanking, as the Sorcerer demonstrated to his apprentice.

Marx's dialectical project was confrontational and combative. Hegel's was more conciliatory, in a sense more positive. My own approach to a number of key kid narratives is that each emerges out of real circumstances, or out of real perceptions thereof. Since this is the case, each basic position deserves a real, sympathetic hearing. This careful consideration will inevitably reveal flaws and failings, which of course provide the impetus that drives dialectical evolution. But flaws and failings in the basic position do not altogether invalidate it. Our careful consideration will also demonstrate that each position has real substance, and will have been applied to real, productive ends. The fact that an opposite, equally powerful position has similar provenance, substance, and (de)limitation leads to the supposition that each of the basic positions is true, though none is complete.

This combination of partiality and multiplicity informs the discussion that takes up the remainder of this book. This is the nature of childhood, and the ways that books and films have represented it. Though we may not agree that children are actually conceived in sin and that they are thus naturally and even dangerously inclined toward transgression, it cannot be disputed that many have felt and continue to feel that this is the case.[3] Those who have so believed have lived and grappled and written accordingly. As such, Original Sin has and deserves a place in any conversation on the subject of children.

At the same time, in the interests of thorough inquiry and balanced application, Reform and Enlightenment must also be brought to bear. John Locke's notion of the tabula rasa[4] constitutes a more hopeful, generous alternative to Original Sin. Locke held that the mind begins as something like a blank slate. This unscored surface is subsequently marked by experience, through which children develop into rationality and adulthood. They act, and through experiencing the painful or pleasurable consequences of action they learn, and become.

These two contrary notions are not juxtaposed in order to establish any kind of preeminence, nor necessarily to identify and eliminate error or falsehood. Rather, with regard to Adam's Fall and the Blank Slate, the immutability of the first is set against the navigability of the second. The catechism of the first is added unto, and may in the application be countered by, the curriculum of the second. After juxtaposition, even confrontation, each idea will still remain on the table.

This is the inclusive dialectical process aforementioned, and it would not stop here. Locke's faith in rational processes might lead us to Jean-Jacques Rousseau's contrary notions that feeling is more important than reason, especially with regard to the nurturing and educating of children.[5] More pointedly, Rousseau's ideas about human nature, about the basic goodness[6] of men—and children—would further reflect upon the not-only-Catholic notion of Original Sin, or inherent error.

What is a child? And once we have ascertained the answer to that question, what do we do with him? The dialectical process means that we continue to gather evidence and perspectives. Rousseau's *Social Contract* (1762), as read against, say, Locke's *Two Treatises on Government* (1690), brings us from abstractions about human nature, through the localities of educational policy and pedagogy, to political philosophy. Is it all a matter of inherent virtue, or of primordial vice? Do we legislate, regulate, and subsidize, or do we leave the whole process to its own development and self-correction?

This is not a work of philosophy or political theory. As seen in this book's first section, my method is to draw upon scholars in the arts and the humanities, and more particularly on a number of primary literary and cinematic texts that reflect various dialectical positions, and present an array of alternatives for the reader to consider and perhaps adopt. So, with regard to precept and pedagogy, to Adam and (Rousseau's) Émile, we will have less of Catholic commentary, or Rousseau's political writing, and more of the following:

> I was their plaything and their idol, and something better—their child, the innocent and helpless creature bestowed on them by heaven, whom to bring up to good, and whose future lot it was in their hands to direct to happiness or misery, according as they fulfilled their duties towards me. With this deep consciousness of what they owed towards the being to which they had given life, added to the active spirit of tenderness that animated both, it may be imagined that while during every hour of my infant life I received a lesson of patience, of charity, and of self-control, I was so guided by a silken cord that all seemed but one train of enjoyment to me.[7]

This stirring passage from Mary Shelley's *Frankenstein* reflects its time—and radiates well beyond it. As it happens, Shelley's book was profoundly influenced by Rousseau's thinking, which it reflects, replicates, and also critiques.[8] Thought leads to art, and art leads to, or back to, the thought that generated it. The beauty of the expression, and the conviction and devotion that gives it rise, complicates and even confuses the dialectical discussion. It also, quite immeasurably, enriches it.

This sensible contemporary statement illustrates the idea and suggests the manner in which my own arguments will be conducted:

> At different times, childhood has been perceived as a necessary stage from which to graduate into adulthood, where one could be considered "useful": it has also been regarded as the "golden age" of a person's life. It does, however, remain a varied experience, and the concept of "childhood" is effectively the product of a constantly changing, adult-led society as well as a personal experience.[9]

A number of notions inform our present day perceptions of childhood, and the ways in which we experience or cultivate it. The first of these, laid out in chapters three and four and then critiqued in chapter five, lovingly and sometimes quite strategically idealizes childhood, and the individual child.

Children and the Bible

The Bible contains a number of familiar and beloved passages about children. Many of them celebrate the child's sweetness and purity. Just as importantly, and just as memorably, they express these sentiments very purely, and very sweetly.

> At the same time came the disciples unto Jesus, saying, Who is the greatest in the kingdom of heaven? And Jesus called a little child unto him, and set him in the midst of them, And said, Verily I say unto you, Except

ye be converted, and become as little children, ye shall not enter into the kingdom of heaven. Whosoever therefore shall humble himself as this little child, the same is greatest in the kingdom of heaven. And whoso shall receive one such little child in my name receiveth me.[10]

The lesson is repeated, and reinforced, in the very next chapter of Matthew's record.

Then were there brought unto [Jesus] little children, that he should put his hands on them, and pray: and the disciples rebuked them. But Jesus said, Suffer little children, and forbid them not, to come unto me: for of such is the kingdom of heaven.[11]

Luke elaborates a little further in his account of the same incident, from the eighteenth chapter of his gospel:

And they brought unto him also infants, that he would touch them: but when *his* disciples saw *it*, they rebuked them. But Jesus called them *unto him*, and said, Suffer little children to come unto me, and forbid them not: for of such is the kingdom of God. Verily I say unto you, Whosoever shall not receive the kingdom of God as a little child shall in no wise enter therein.[12]

These lovely exchanges are extremely familiar, and they are so pretty that it is possible to key on sentiment at the expense of instruction. But there are important lessons here that are particularly relevant to the topic at hand. One of the most important of these also extends through the entirety of this study, and is particularly elaborated in its last chapter. Although children are the subject, adults are, at the very least, a structuring absence. Everything that we might say or learn about children implicates the adults that care for them.

This is nowhere more evident, or more important, than in these teachings about the nature and importance of childhood. In the foregoing exchanges Jesus places children at the very center of Christian precept and practice. He states in no uncertain terms that children are heirs of salvation. Even more, he declares that children are heavenly already. While the striving adult disciple will try to transcend earth's sinful bounds, the child has in many ways already done so. She represents a powerful, ever-available immanence, or God-among-us.[13]

In these passages, Jesus' disciples are careful and troubled about what were undoubtedly many good things. In the second incident, the disciples' care about pressing matters caused them to be too busy to attend to the children in their midst. This is not the only instance of adults forgetting to choose the better part, or not realizing that that better part naturally resides in the sweet humility of childhood. Not noticing children, or not appreciating their sufficiency and substance, is a problem of very long standing. From the Hebrew Bible, or the Old Testament:

> And Samuel said unto Jesse, Are here all *thy* children? And he said, There remaineth yet the youngest, and, behold, he keepeth the sheep. And Samuel said unto Jesse, Send and fetch him: for we will not sit down till he come hither. And he sent, and brought him in. Now he *was* ruddy, *and* withal of a beautiful countenance, and goodly to look to. And the Lord said, Arise, anoint him: for this *is* he. Then Samuel took the horn of oil, and anointed him in the midst of his brethren: and the Spirit of the Lord came upon David from that day forward.[14]

David had been dismissed because of his age, and perhaps because of the subordinate position, the less honored tasks associated with his birth order. Previously in this same chapter, Samuel had looked upon David's elder brethren. Upon stating his opinion that one of these splendid young men must be the chosen one, Samuel received an instruction of practically infinite application, most especially in the matter of the relation between a child's diminutive stature and his actual worth:

> But the Lord said unto Samuel, Look not on his countenance, or on the height of his stature; because I have refused him: for *the Lord seeth* not as man seeth; for man looketh on the outward appearance, but the Lord looketh on the heart.[15]

By most worldly or material measures there is nothing more unprepossessing than a child. In a heavenly economy, those measures do not matter at all.

David's case is complicated because of the fact that his anointing implies and prefigures his kingship, and the unusual power he will eventually assume. Does all or any of this apply to a poor man's child? Most all of human history attests that it does not, that in this matter the ideal and the actual hardly ever coincide. But the Bible, while demonstrating what is, also has an interest and confidence on what should and will be. David himself—if in fact he composed this Psalm—suggests how the principle stands, or should stand, regardless of worldly power or position:

> Lord, my heart is not haughty, nor mine eyes lofty: neither do I exercise myself in great matters, or in things too high for me. Surely I have behaved and quieted myself, as a child that is weaned of his mother: my soul *is* even as a weaned child. Let Israel hope in the Lord from henceforth and for ever.[16]

As the cases of Saul and David and Solomon demonstrate—even righteous Hezekiah, and Josiah, and certainly the rest of the mostly ill-behaved kings of Israel and Judah—kingship, even adulthood, will not necessarily bring joy, or salvation. Rather, as the Psalm suggests, the humility and pliability of the child are also proper for the man, and for the woman. In fact, if men and women could manage to cultivate these childlike qualities, they would hasten an end to enmity and ensure their own salvation.

Christians interpret the following verse as prophesying of Jesus:

> For unto us a child is born, unto us a son is given: and the government shall be upon his shoulder: and his name shall be called Wonderful, Counsellor, The mighty God, The everlasting Father, The Prince of Peace.[17]

As with the just-cited episode in the first book of Samuel, this verse also reflects the regenerative influence of a child, while looking forward to that child's eventual, exceptional adult influence. The sixth chapter of Isaiah describes the future advent of this great figure, as well as the mighty change that he will initiate. Again, for Christians, this is Jesus Christ, upon whom the Lord's spirit will rest, who will judge for the poor and the meek of the earth, smiting the earth and slaying the wicked. Righteousness and faithfulness will follow, as well as this extraordinary vision of a peaceable kingdom. "The wolf also shall dwell with the lamb, and the leopard shall lie down with the kid; and the calf and the young lion and the fatling together; and a little child shall lead them."[18] This millennial advent inverts and eliminates all of the customary enmities and is culminated by the most implausible, the greatest inversion of all. In the end the child, so frequently the least and the last in the eyes of the adult, emerges not only as exemplar, but as principal.

The passage from Isaiah continues to describe this transformed world, and the gloriously impossible[19] juxtapositions that will then obtain:

> And the cow and the bear shall feed; their young ones shall lie down together: and the lion shall eat straw like the ox. And the sucking child shall play on the hole of the asp, and the weaned child shall put his hand on the cockatrice' den. They shall not hurt nor destroy in all my holy mountain: for the earth shall be full of the knowledge of the Lord, as the waters cover the sea.[20]

As with previously cited New Testament passages featuring little children, this description is surpassingly impressive, combining tender delicacy with an expansive, almost tympanic grandeur. But while the Bible provides hopeful prefigurations of millennial plenitude, it also clearly places us here, still, down below. Until that hoped-for day, man is born to trouble, as the sparks fly upward.[21] And yet, even so, there are tremendous consolations. And in the end, as in the beginning of this conversation, some of the very greatest of these pertain to our little children: "A woman when she is in travail hath sorrow, because her hour is come: but as soon as she is delivered of the child, she remembereth no more the anguish, for joy that a man is born into the world."[22]

It is interesting and most significant that though its praises linger in the mind, and with very good reason, the Bible is actually somewhat more balanced, more multiple in what it has to say about children. It does not unanimously endorse them, or the childish way that they sometimes behave. The book of Second Kings contains a memorable account of the other side, as it were, as well as of the sharp responses to which long-suffering child-carers sometimes feel tempted:

> And [Elisha] went up from thence unto Beth-el: and as he was going up by the way, there came forth little children out of the city, and mocked him, and said unto him, Go up, thou bald head; go up, thou bald head. And he turned back, and looked on them, and cursed them in the name of the Lord. And there came forth two she bears out of the wood, and tare forty and two children of them.[23]

Apart from the appalling magnitude of their comeuppance, this passage reminds us how children are often disrespectful and disordered, ill-behaved and in need of correction. As with its expressions in praise of children, this is not an isolated biblical instance. In Genesis 8:21 the Lord recalls the just-ended deluge and, while promising there will never again be anything like it, observes that "the imagination of man's heart is evil from his youth." Proverbs counsels that "Foolishness *is* bound in the heart of a child; *but* the rod of correction shall drive it far from him."[24]

There are vast scientific, sociological, and aesthetical literatures that set forth the native foolishness of children, and the many ways in which that foolishness has been addressed, eliminated, or sometimes, inadvertently, propagated by correcting adults.[25] For now it is enough to point out that even exemplary, conscientious childhood falls short in important ways.

The most notable biblical expression of this important assertion comes from the apostle Paul, in his first epistle to the Corinthians:

> For we know in part, and we prophesy in part. But when that which is perfect is come, then that which is in part shall be done away. When I was a child, I spake as a child, I understood as a child, I thought as a child: but when I became a man, I put away childish things. For now we see through a glass, darkly; but then face to face: now I know in part; but then shall I know even as also I am known.[26]

Implicit in this passage is the simple and compelling assertion that childhood is insufficient, or incomplete. The marvelous image of the dark glass, of the obscure, opaque, possibly distorted vision it discloses, suggests all of the things that a little child cannot see, or know. The implications are obvious, especially in light of that chapter's preceding verses. Verses 1–8 famously, definitively, explicate the attributes of charity, which require amounts of concentration, consistency, and self-control of which sweet little children are simply not capable. Again, in addition to retaining the best of childhood's qualities and characteristics, the successful Christian adherent must also rise to the capacity of the adult.

The Bible honors and praises children, and it also acknowledges a child's insufficiency. It suggests that the ideal man will maintain the childlike and purge the childish. First Corinthians 14:20 reads: "Brethren, be not children in understanding: howbeit in malice be ye children, but in understanding be men." And, once again, Paul sets forth the manner and method by which this balance can be achieved:

> Now I say, *That* the heir, as long as he is a child, differeth nothing from a servant, though he be lord of all; But is under tutors and governors until the time appointed of the father. Even so we, when we were children, were in bondage under the elements of the world: But when the fulness of the time was come, God sent forth his Son, made of a woman, made under the law, To redeem them that were under the law, that we might receive the adoption of sons. And because ye are sons, God hath sent forth the Spirit of his Son into your hearts, crying, Abba, Father.[27]

The child is sweet, submissive, unwise—in need of instruction and even, purity notwithstanding, redemption. And it is only through adult or divine intervention that this redemption is effected.

These are all, in some way, sermonic communications. They are didactic statements that suggest realities at the same time they seek to shape that reality. In addition to precept, however, we must also consider how all of these things operate in the realm of real relations. This is the deep, resonating emotional experience of childhood, of which there are countless examples. One of the richest of these is the tale of Joseph in the book of Genesis. It powerfully demonstrates the virtues and limitations of childhood, and how they operate in a broader family and social context. To put it more feelingly, it also nears comprehensiveness in its portrayal of the joy and sorrow and unutterable complexity of children and families.

> Now Israel [or Jacob] loved Joseph more than all his children, because he *was* the son of his old age: and he made him a coat of *many* colours. And when his brethren saw that their father loved him more than all his brethren, they hated him, and could not speak peaceably unto him.[28]

Childlike and childish do not occur in a vacuum, but in the swirling counterpoint of family relations. Joseph, so beloved of his aged father, stirs the resentment of his older, still immature brethren.

> And Joseph dreamed a dream, and he told *it* his brethren: and they hated him yet the more. And he said unto them, Hear, I pray you, this dream which I have dreamed: For, behold, we *were* binding sheaves in the field, and, lo, my sheaf arose, and also stood upright; and, behold, your sheaves stood round about, and made obeisance to my sheaf. And his brethren said to him, Shalt thou indeed reign over us? or shalt thou indeed have dominion over us? And they hated him yet the more for his dreams, and for his words.[29]

In all of this lies a further childish wrinkle, patterned and repeated to the point of behavioral law. Joseph is like the child that Jesus set in the midst of his disciples. He is a model of virtue, the little child that leads, even before Isaiah's millennial day. Prophetic dreams come to him in the night to attest the fact. Unfortunately his brothers, perhaps less morally advanced, respond with hostility. But that is not the whole story. Joseph may also, as it were, have been asking for it. He presses his advantage overly, and his righteousness may border on the self-righteous. His brothers' responses are both blameworthy, and completely understandable.

In similar manner, Joseph goes on to provoke his prophetical father, Abraham's heir, the patriarch of the sands of the sea:

> And he dreamed yet another dream, and told it his brethren, and said, Behold, I have dreamed a dream more; and, behold, the sun and the moon and the eleven stars made obeisance to me. And he told *it* to his father, and to his brethren: and his father rebuked him, and said unto him, What *is* this dream that thou hast dreamed? Shall I and thy mother and thy brethren indeed come to bow down ourselves to thee to the earth? And his brethren envied him.[30]

In this definitive family story we see not only the principled substance of righteous childhood, but the disturbing way that it can operate within a family dynamic. The fact is that the paragon errs, and the sinners deserve sympathy. Cain reaped the whirlwind, and quite properly, but could Abel have provoked him, just a little? In the case of Israel's family a terrible crime is now committed, and a most blameworthy one—and a very small, very real portion of the blame might just have gone the other way.

This important motif—the possibility that righteousness can also be priggish, or worse—is often explored in both scriptural and secular discourse. It is the subject of Christ's tirade against the Pharisees in Matthew, chapters 23 and 24. John Steinbeck (1952) and José Saramago (2009) consider it in their accounts of Cain and Abel, while Thomas Mann figuratively elaborates almost every possible permutation in his massive tetralogy *Joseph and His Brothers* (1933–43). Nikos Kazantzakis goes so far as to turn this lens on the mission or myth of Christ himself in his celebrated/abominated *The Last Temptation of Christ* (1960).[31] Do believers, do anxious parents, want to countenance these revisions, at the expense of the conscientious and classic statements? Conversely, can they afford to ignore them or the certain complications that they investigate? At the very least, the ideal of the exemplary child contains ambiguities that need to be acknowledged.

Joseph's brethren go to water Jacob's flocks. Jacob sends his favored son to check upon them, but his brothers do not respond favorably.

> And when they saw him afar off, even before he came near unto them, they conspired against him to slay him. And they said one to another, Behold, this dreamer cometh. Come now therefore, and let us slay him, and cast him into some pit, and we will say, Some evil beast hath devoured him: and we shall see what will become of his dreams.[32]

As mentioned, the annals of didactic literature contain both the history and the complex necessity of sternly instructing children. On the other hand, mud-pie or cat-in-the-hat impulses will assert a contrary view, that naughtiness is not only natural, but necessary and frequently joyful. A closer and more concentrated look at superficially bad behavior, as well as the seemingly reckless narratives that so gleefully chronicle it, can reveal laudable high spirits just beneath, and the seeds for all sorts of adult autonomy and accomplishment.

Now, given all that, and in this particular setting, naughtiness—sin, in fact—assumes an unexpectedly poignant, overwhelmingly powerful aspect:

> And Reuben heard *it*, and he delivered him out of their hands; and said, Let us not kill him. And Reuben said unto them, Shed no blood, *but* cast him into this pit that *is* in the wilderness, and lay no hand upon him; that he might rid him out of their hands, to deliver him to his father again.[33]

Reuben, Jacob's eldest son, is perhaps most remembered for having transgressed greatly and for having lost his birthright as a result.[34] But here the sinner acts with heroic fraternal feeling, and with more maturity than the boy that will supersede him presently possesses.

Alas, though the little child will someday lead, at present he is still subject to unrighteous dominion. In this world ye shall find tribulation,[35] and perfidy often prevails. For all that Reuben can do, his brethren prevail upon Joseph. They strip him of his coat and cast him in a pit. Judah compounds their offense, as his enmity is succeeded by the sin of avarice. In him family feeling, and family duty are eclipsed by the love of money.

> And Judah said unto his brethren, What profit *is it* if we slay our brother, and conceal his blood? Come, and let us sell him to the Ishmeelites, and let not our hand be upon him; for he *is* our brother *and* our flesh. And his brethren were content. Then there passed by Midianites merchantmen; and they drew and lifted up Joseph out of the pit, and sold Joseph to the Ishmeelites for twenty *pieces* of silver: and they brought Joseph into Egypt.[36]

Or is Judah really at fault? Could it be that, like Reuben, he is also shamming, trying to distract his more wrathful brothers from their original intent by introducing the option of a much lesser sin?

The point is that, at some level, there is almost always a question, an uncertainty. By all of this we see that in the attributes and actual behavior of children good and bad, right and wrong, are not as clearly apportioned as we might think. What is clear, and incontrovertible, is the immeasurable depth of feeling that attends the complex interactions of parents and children and siblings. Once again, inconstant Reuben, ultimately powerless to prevent much of anything, shows us the way. "And Reuben returned unto the pit; and, behold, Joseph *was* not in the pit; and he rent his clothes. And he returned unto his brethren, and said, The child *is* not; and I, whither shall I go?"[37] Howl! This is sorrow, a soul cry of Shakespearean proportions.[38] And yet the die is cast; the brothers take Joseph's coat and dip it in the blood of a goat that they have killed, and return it to their father.

> And he knew it, and said, *It is* my son's coat; an evil beast hath devoured him; Joseph is without doubt rent in pieces. And Jacob rent his clothes, and put sackcloth upon his loins, and mourned for his son many days. And all his sons and all his daughters rose up to comfort him; but he refused to be comforted; and he said, For I will go down into the grave unto my son mourning. Thus his father wept for him.[39]

This discussion began with Jesus presenting a little child as an ideal for the instruction and edification of his adult followers. It also considered that child's moral sufficiency, as well as his simultaneous inadequacy. The story of Joseph goes far beyond these poles of possibility, or the mere teaching of precept. Significantly, it no longer exclusively concerns the very young. For one thing, given what followed soon after with Potiphar's wife, it is likely that Joseph was physically mature when these events took place. Similarly, the Hebrew source suggests that Elisha's victims were probably youths and not little children.[40] These facts are important, and still quite reconcilable with the subject at hand.

As suggested previously in this chapter, every biblical reference to children contains implicit instruction for the adults who care for them. Furthermore, the burden of biblical precept is that all of mankind sees through the glass darkly, all are children—precious, sufficient, and in constant need of instruction. We will now proceed to trace the development of these biblical child motifs in the discourse and literature of children. Even here, especially with the real interactions between reader and read-to that children's literature implies and depends on, the mutual implication continues. Morten Borgen, the patriarch in Carl Theodor Dreyer's sublime 1955 adaptation of Kaj Munk's play *Ordet*, observes his little granddaughter, seemingly distressed at the foot of her mother's coffin: "She doesn't understand any of this. She is too little. And the rest of us, we don't understand any of it either."[41]

Jesus was correct, and Paul also. The circumspect adult has a responsibility to help the child rise to his own moral potential, and the submissive, saintly child pulls the adult back from the abyss of his own insistent errors. Since this is the case our questions about the nature of children, and of childhood, are of utmost interest and ultimate concern to us all.[42]

Two Ideals in Classic Children's Literature

The Bible ranges widely on the subject of children, and it suggests any number of possibilities relating to their nature and potential. In the main, however, it alternates between the idea that the child is an exemplar, and that he is in need of constant instruction. These notions seem to be in opposition to each other, and it will be seen that they reflect two very distinct answers to the question of childhood's essence. However, if these answers are opposed, they are not necessarily in conflict. A survey of the literature and of the lives that generate it suggest that both these things are simultaneously and tremendously true.

As it begins to form in the late seventeenth and the eighteenth centuries, Western children's literature will often be didactic, full of catechism, moral indoctrination, and moralistic reproof. Indeed this strand continues into the present, and it is an important part of any what-is-childhood discussion. But the contrary idea of the exemplary child likewise continues on apace, being advanced by numerous deeply felt statements. There are too many of these statements to cite or to need citation. It is important, though, to take note of how this ideal evolves, and what that evolution reflects.

John Bunyan, one of the grand pioneers of children's literature, was unwavering and single-minded in his devotion to Puritan principle, and to the duty of imparting it in sermonic form. However this is not at all to say that his preachments were humorless, or without tenderness. Although he wrote of sin with great conviction and sternness,[43] his take on innocence was surpassingly mild and sweet.

In the second part of Bunyan's *The Pilgrim's Progress,* his protagonists, Christiana and Great-heart, come upon this pretty, pastoral scene.

> Now as they were going along and talking, they espied a boy feeding his father's sheep. The boy was in very mean clothes, but of a very fresh and well-favoured countenance; and as he sat by himself, he sang...
>
> > He that is down needs fear no fall,
> > He that is low no pride;
> > He that is humble ever shall
> > Have God to be his guide.
> >
> > I am content with what I have,
> > Little be it or much;
> > And, Lord, contentment still I crave,
> > Because thou savest such
> >
> > Fulness to such a burden is
> > That go on pilgrimage:
> > Here little, and hereafter bliss,
> > Is best from age to age.[44]

This little refrain, also commonly known as "The Shepherd Boy Sings in the Valley of Humiliation,"[45] is consistent with biblical precept. It echoes Christ's ideas about heavenly children, as well as the manner in which he communicated those ideas. Bunyan describes a child's natural state, proportion, and capacity. This description contains additionally a prescription for the adult, who learns that if he would be saved he must comport himself in like manner.

For all of these Christian echoes, there is also something of the Arcadian in the scene that Bunyan creates here. Though he might have been mortified by the parallel, his image suggests pagan scenes of similar prettiness. *The Heroes* (1856) is Charles Kingsley's collection of selected Greek myths, retold for young readers. In a lovely preface, Kingsley refers to the innocently credulous nature, the stormy, passing passions of the beloved ancients who first fashioned these tales:

3. The Angel Child

> For nations begin at first by being children like you, though they are made up of grown men. They are children at first like you—men and women with children's hearts; frank, and affectionate, and full of trust, and teachable, and loving to see and learn all the wonders round them; and greedy also, too often, and passionate and silly, as children are.[46]

Kingsley's meaning is obvious, just as his sincerity and affection are practically palpable. Are children naturally pagans, or are they more like heathens?[47] Christianity would generally proscribe against and even seek to destroy the wild old assumptions, but Kingsley is loath to do so. Why? It may be that the necessary disillusionment of Mr. Toad,[48] of Christopher Robin,[49] even and especially of Don Quixote[50] strikes us as nearly tragic, or at least unbearably poignant. Are we so anxious to have them grow up and put away their childhood? Are we so anxious for them to enter into dire, unmiraculous reality? It is this certain prospect that lends a degree of urgent indulgence to much children's discourse of this and every period. The concept of the angel child has much to do with the raptness with which her parent views her.

Though Talmud and Bible and Koran are unanimous in their stern monotheism,[51] it is certainly true that children's discourse, especially regarding the motif of child-as-angel, can border on the idolatrous.

G. K. Chesterton's "A Christmas Carol," from *The Wild Knight and Other Poems* (1900), concludes as follows.

> The Christ-child stood at Mary's knee,
> His hair was like a crown,
> And all the flowers looked up at him.
> And all the stars looked down.[52]

So far, so orthodox—there is nothing unseemly or unfamiliar here. As discussed the infant Jesus is both God-in-embryo, and God-already. In Chesterton's simple quatrain we find that all of creation waits upon this little child, while all of mankind holds its breath. What is interesting is that in this particular instance the staunchest non– or anti–Christian may also find himself able to subscribe to this scenario, and the sentiment that underpins it. So much of Christian precept combines Christ's power with the duty we owe him as a result. And, paradoxically, so much of that power and duty are contained, or perceived, in the image of the babe in the manger, or the infant in the temple, or the little one on his way to Egypt. Contrary to the grandeur of God or the daunting prospect of perfection that is required of us, this is divinity at its most accessible. We have all been, and we have all worshipped, babies.

Christians ask, in any number of ways, what Jesus would do.[53] Christian parents, perhaps partaking a bit of the pagan, also find the divine child in their own offspring.

> I'd watch his breath go in and out.
> His little clothes would all be white.
> I'd slip my finger in his hand
> To feel how he could hold it tight.
>
> And she would smile and say, "Take care,"
> The mother, Mary, would, "Take care"
> And I would kiss the little hand
> And touch his hair.
>
> While Mary put the blankets back
> The gentle talk would soon begin.
> And when I'd tiptoe softly out
> I'd meet the wise men going in.[54]

Innumerable witnesses[55] express this sentiment and affirm this testimony. The manger and the nursery are perceived similarly, equally. They are sacred spaces, and the kneeling, worshipful adult is utterly transformed by his experience there.[56] These holy precincts, with their holy contents, make the very world numinous. Every parent's child both embodies and brings peace on earth, and good will to all men.

If this is true during the untroubled, rapturous initiations of an ideal early infancy, how much more when time passes and relationships form and deepen, how much more when the prospect of harm or loss make their inevitable entry? From Mark Twain's *A Connecticut Yankee in King Arthur's Court*:

> Well, during two weeks and a half we watched by the crib, and in our deep solicitude we were unconscious of any world outside of that sickroom. Then our reward came: the center of the universe turned the corner and began to mend. Grateful? It isn't the term. There *isn't* any term for it. You know that yourself, if you've watched your child through the Valley of the Shadow and seen it come back to life and sweep night out of the earth with one all-illuminating smile that you could cover with your hand.[57]

The apostle James speaks of the tongue, its disproportionate power, and the necessity of governing it. He could just as well be describing the Connecticut Yankee's ailing little child (or Twain's own, beloved, lamented daughter Jean), or any of the tiny, helpless demi-gods in our lives. "Behold also the ships, which though *they be* so great, and *are* driven of fierce winds, yet are they turned about with a very small helm, whithersoever the governor listeth."[58] Children's literature—and, as we shall see in the next chapter, children's cinema—sounds a strong, Christ-derived motif of perfect, angelic, even salvific childhood. It includes a contradictory, barely blameworthy hint of child-worship: "Miss Honey was still gazing at the child in absolute wonderment, as though she were the Creation, The Beginning of The World, The First Morning."[59] The whole world revolves around this tiny axis, while both nature and culture obey.

Small Saviors

For Roald Dahl's Miss Honey and for every enchanted adult, this motif may have the force of law. But it also has a history, and a context. Here are a few more signal instances of this particular trope. Following chapters feature genealogies of other key and sometimes contrary kid motifs. Inasmuch as we are thinking about the nature of children and of childhood, these genealogies combine to demonstrate the strength and validity of each particular line. They also demonstrate their partiality, or that each possibility or perception has its valid, verifiable counter.

A powerful, much subscribed-to example of the angel child is that of the salvific female. It is very important to interrogate some of this figure's ideological implications. As has been well and almost infinitely documented, the idealization of women, whether devotedly sincere or darkly strategic, has led to all manner of dire objectifications and subjugations. Still, for all of that essential conversation, in the present brief instance we will consider the salvific female at face value, or we will at least consider some of the voices that have done so. If little children represent innocence and renewal, then little girls often represent salvation, and even serve as saviors.

The redemptive, saving female appears frequently in the works of Hans Christian Andersen. "The Philosopher's Stone" features four brothers, sent by their father to search, and to encounter the refining that goes with every fairy quest. Their younger, blind sister has remained at home. A combination of magical intuition and the Holy Spirit has apprised her of her brothers' experiences and sorrows. She dreams of having found the Stone, but awakes to find that she is merely holding the spindle of her spinning wheel. Merely? "Through the night she had spun a thread finer than that which spiders make. It was so thin that the human eye could not see it, and yet because it had been moistened by her tears it was as strong as the anchor tow of a ship."[60]

The limitation of blindness—and of being a little child—is balanced here by a vast figurative power. Where the young men have striven and failed, the sister has stood, and waited,[61] and prevailed. This thread will lead her much more directly to the Stone, or rather a modern Christian's equivalent thereto. It is faith, and charity, not to be accessed by the clamorings of masculine quest, but by the patient waiting of submissive girlhood. These, because of her efforts, will save her young men as well.

In Andersen's "Inchelina" the swallow has waited too long to migrate, and winter's blast appears to have killed him. Inchelina mourns. "She put her head on the bird's breast; then she jumped up! Something was ticking inside: it was the bird's heart, for the swallow was not really dead, and now the warmth had revived it."[62] Medical professionals can resuscitate, of course, but this is something else altogether. Inchelina is too small to fend for or save herself. Her female charity, however, ensures she doesn't have to. The swallow that she has saved will quite properly, quite proportionately, go on to save her.

Here are sentimentality and idealization. These are deepened and broadened in other narrative settings, by the lengths to which the female child must sometimes go, and to which she is willing to go. Andersen's "The Wild Swans" concerns eleven princely brothers who are dispossessed, disinherited, and enchanted by a malevolent fairy. She turns them into swans, and then turns to their younger sister Elisa: "'Your brothers can escape their fate,' began the fairy, 'if you have enough endurance.'" Elisa has already been subjected to a terrible series of trials. The fairy now sets forth a final task that requires of her a last appalling sacrifice: she can restore her brothers if she will tread on nettles until they become soft as flax, and if she will then twine the thread to knit for them eleven shirts. And if she does not say one single thing through the course of the entire ordeal.[63]

The Christ parallels in this scenario are obvious. This is distinct from Inchelina's virtuous passivity, the combination of righteousness and powerlessness that presses the chivalrous male (or male swallow) into virtuous action. Elisa has committed no fault and owes no debt on her own behalf. The work that she undertakes for her brothers is pure sacrifice, containing nothing of self-interest. It is also a sacrifice of the most painful, punitive, and consuming kind. The echoes are obvious: "He was oppressed, and he was afflicted, yet he opened not his mouth: he is brought as a lamb to the slaughter, and as a sheep before her shearers is dumb, so he openeth not his mouth."[64] For all of the excess and impossibility of this task Elisa, saviorlike, undertakes it willingly. She must complete it by a certain time or else be executed. That time draws near, and so we find her on the way to her execution. "Even on the way to her death she did not cease working."[65] Elisa is a fine and terrible example of this powerful trope, blameless child and ministering parent, Isaac and Abraham all in one. In the end she succeeds, vanquishing the enemy and restoring her brothers.

The Snow Queen constitutes Hans Christian Andersen's most continuous, comprehensive exploration of the idea of the salvific female. After an idyllic prologue, the lives of little Kaj and Gerda are turned upside down by the arrival of the Snow Queen. The Snow Queen takes Kaj with her, leaving Gerda both bereft and ignorant as to where he has gone.

In the novella's third story, Gerda discovers Kaj's whereabouts. Once again echoing the actions of Abraham,[66] she rises straightway and goes to his rescue. The particulars here are significant. Gerda's actions throughout the course of *The Snow Queen* have none of the passivity, none of the submitting to punishment/acceding to victimhood that we might find in "Inchelina," and certain parts of "The Wild Swans." She not only has faith, but her works follow immediately after. In fact, here the traditions/assumptions of womanly sacrifice and male chivalry are combined. Though as a child she must submit to the brigands in the fifth story,[67] on the whole we find Gerda to be active, decisive, and powerful.

A talking reindeer in the sixth story summarizes the power of both child, and girl child particularly. "'I can't give her any more power than she already has! Don't you understand how great it is? Don't you see how men and animals must serve her; how else could she have come so far, walking on her bare feet. But she must never learn of her power; it is in her heart, for she is a sweet and innocent child."[68]

At the novella's powerful conclusion we find little Gerda to be the equal of the formidable, elemental Snow Queen, whom she vanquishes.[69] But can she restore life, and soul, to her corrupted companion?

> Kaj sat still and cold; then little Gerda cried and her tears fell on Kaj's breast. The warmth penetrated to his heart and melted both the ice and the glass splinter in it. He looked at her and she sang the psalm they had once sung together.
>
> > Our roses bloom and fade away,
> > Our infant Lord abides always.
> > May we be blessed his face to see
> > And ever little children be.[70]

As before, Christ as a child, Christ and the child become emblems of hope and salvation. Such prospects would be especially powerful for any young reader. And yet in *The Snow Queen* these ministrations go beyond the merely reassuring conventions of child-centered protagonism:

> Kaj burst into tears and wept so much that the grains of glass in his eyes were washed away.... Gerda kissed him on his cheeks and the color came

back to them. She kissed his eyes and they became like hers. She kissed his hands and feet, and the blue color left them and the blood pulsed again through his veins. He was well and strong.[71]

Christ, mother, sister—and now, as Andersen's text so sweetly suggests, this archetypal array is being added unto by the roles of helpmeet, companion, and yes, lover. They are all of them so central, and yet so simultaneously secondary, and subordinate. Andersen is telling his tale, but moving beyond that fictional space we find, repeatedly and overwhelmingly, this same paradoxical perception, this same unreasonable, oft-accomplished expectation. The child, and the woman that she becomes, is the least and the greatest, center and circumference both.

Silas Marner and the Redemptive Child

This motif of the good child has many iterations, then. We have seen the exemplary child, the worshipped child, the sacrificial female. The following extended analysis of George Eliot's luminous *Silas Marner* (1861) combines and incorporates all of these traits, adding up to a powerful influence that is measurable, quite natural, and bordering on the mystical. While not a children's book, it still reflects the pattern we are tracing here. Indeed, it suggests how far this pattern transcends the generic and commercial limitations of kids' culture. It is an exemplary essay on the saving, almost supernatural influence of children.

Silas Marner is an eccentric, solitary weaver. Many years previous, he had been part of a community of believers, but a robbery occurred, and he had been unjustly accused of being the culprit and making off with the money. Having been removed from his community's fellowship, and having subsequently removed himself from the community, we find him embittered and alone, exclusively devoted to a constant round of dull industry. He is a miser, a successful hoarder, possessed of a formidable sum of gold. And then this too is stolen from him, leaving him inconsolable and seemingly irredeemable.

Among other things, Eliot's book contemplates the operations of religious faith. At first, in Silas' life, religious faith is not operating at all. Rather, he simply soldiers joylessly on, a woeful heir to Adam's curse—"In the sweat of thy face shalt thou eat bread, till thou return unto the ground."[72] However unexpectedly, miraculously, a deliverance is at hand. The great, blessed paradox of the novel is that this deliverance comes by means of that other postlapsarian, post–Edenic curse: "in sorrow thou shalt bring forth children."[73]

3. The Angel Child

Silas is still longing for his lost money when a little child toddles into his life. She is the product of a misalliance, and of a number of twisting story strands that need not be detailed here. She appears as follows. Coming out of a cataleptic fit, Silas sees a mass of gold lying by his fire, exactly resembling his lost treasure. In amazement he reaches toward it, only to find, to his greater amazement, that these are the golden curls of a sleeping little girl. Silas is astonished, and confused. This inexplicable child sets him to thinking:

> [He] sank into his chair powerless, under the double presence of an inexplicable surprise and a hurrying influx of memories. How and when had the child come in without his knowledge? ... But along with that question, and almost thrusting it away, there was a vision of [his] old home ... and within that vision another, of the thoughts which had been present with him in those far-off scenes. The thoughts were strange to him now, like old friendships impossible to revive; and yet he had a dreamy feeling that this child was somehow a message come to him from that far-off life: it stirred fibres that had never been moved in Raveloe—old quiverings of tenderness—old impressions of awe at the presentiment of some Power presiding over his life.[74]

This is the beginning of Silas's religious reclamation, his reconciliation with God and man. However there is some denominational ambiguity in this reclamation, consistent with the more ancient, more mythological religious motifs that we have just been tracing.

If Silas's Christian feelings are beginning to stir to life, there is still, perhaps, another kindly cosmology, another object of worship at hand. The child has awakened, and been afraid, and finally responded to Silas's uncertain attempts to comfort her.

> She was perfectly quiet now, but not asleep—only soothed by sweet porridge and warmth into that wide-gazing calm which makes us older human beings, with our inward turmoil, feel a certain awe in the presence of a little child, such as we feel before some quiet majesty or beauty in the earth or sky—before a steady glowing planet, or a full-flowered eglantine, or the bending trees over a silent pathway.[75]

This is a striking description. The child is herself, but as presently perceived by Silas, and still throughout the course of the novel, she is something else besides. She is a symbol, a mystery, an eminence. Here, she is even the Piper at the Gates of Dawn, or a Shinto emanation out of a Hiyao Miyazaki movie. This is true of so many literary children of this period,[76] of so many actual children in times and places where infant mortality rates are high, in times and places where the prospect of bright childish promise gives way to melancholy, diminished adulthood.

Judeo-Christian or not, the vision of this vulnerable child stirs Silas out of his longstanding torpor. Presently, with little sense of the implication of it, he makes a portentous decision:

> "You'll take the child to the parish to-morrow?" asked Godfrey, speaking as indifferently as he could.
> "Who says so?" said Marner, sharply. "Will they make me take her?"
> "Why, you wouldn't like to keep her, should you—an old bachelor like you?"
> "Till anybody shows they've a right to take her away from me," said Marner. "The mother's dead, and I reckon it's got no father: it's a lone thing—and I'm a lone thing. My money's gone, I don't know where—and this is come from I don't know where. I know nothing—I'm partly 'mazed."[77]

The second half of this short novel sets forth the gradual, glad process by which Silas is rejuvenated—"warming into joy because she had joy"[78]—the process by which he and the child, Eppie, become a family. Just as importantly, Eliot describes the manner in which this newly formed family becomes part of the wider community, the more surely and inextricably because of the unconscious ministrations of this child:

> Silas took her with him in most of his journeys to the farmhouses ... and little curly-headed Eppie, the weaver's child, became an object of interest at several outlying homesteads, as well as in the village. Hitherto he had been treated very much as ... a queer and unaccountable creature, who must necessarily be looked at with wondering curiosity and repulsion, and with whom one would be glad to make all greetings and bargains as brief as possible.... But now Silas met with open smiling faces and cheerful questioning, as a person whose satisfactions and difficulties could be understood. Everywhere he must sit a little and talk about the child, and words of interest were always ready for him.[79]

Silas and his neighbors begin to counsel on the craft of child-raising, its challenges and blessed satisfactions. This broad subject becomes a key that admits Silas into further familiarity and greater intimacy:

> No child was afraid of approaching Silas when Eppie was near him: there was no repulsion around him now, either for young or old; for the little child had come to link him once more with the whole world. There was love between him and the child that blent them into one, and there was love between the child and the world—from men and women with parental looks and tones, to the red lady-birds and the round pebbles.[80]

Eppie has quite matter-of-factly, quite miraculously drawn Silas back into meaningful intercourse with his fellows. As a natural part of that process, she has also provided the means for him to become reconciled with his past, to purge his own anger and sin and sorrow. As with Hans Christian Andersen's more fantastical salvific females, the echoes here are very striking, and very moving.

The twenty-first chapter of the Book of Numbers features a celebrated account in which erring Israel is assailed by flying fiery serpents. The serpents' bite is fatal, and many die as a result. But a remedy is also offered:

> And the Lord said unto Moses, Make thee a fiery serpent, and set it upon a pole: and it shall come to pass, that every one that is bitten, when he looketh upon it, shall live. And Moses made a serpent of brass, and put it upon a pole, and it came to pass, that if a serpent had bitten any man, when he beheld the serpent of brass, he lived.[81]

Once again, Christians tend to take this for a figure of Jesus Christ, lifted and offered up, bringing life and salvation to those who would simply look. There is no reason to think that Eliot was necessarily thinking of this incident while she composed her novel—especially given her mixed, or unmixed, feelings about organized religion—but a profound parallel can still be marked. Silas, hopeless and lost, looks to a child, and lives.

Silas Marner is a powerful, emblematic tale, so powerful that it registers as a kind of testament. The angel child is a myth, which also means that it comes out of ritual, and from the lives, the calculable realities, that ritual and myth always reflect. For all of the idealization of the Romantics and the sentimentalizing of the Victorians, this is surely a fact, understood by millions of parents who have undergone the refining fire and the healing balm of bearing and raising children.

> In old days there were angels who came and took men by the hand and led them away from the city of destruction. We see no white-winged angels now. But yet men are led away from threatening destruction: a hand is put into theirs, which leads them forth gently towards a calm and bright land, so that they look no more backward; and the hand may be a little child's.[82]

4.

Idealism, Sentimentality and the Advent of Film

The previous chapter sympathetically elaborated one half of a biblical binary, the angel child, and traced its appearance in some of children's literature's more stirring texts. But it is important to recognize that the other side of the binary can be advocated. There are great limitations to speaking as a child, and behaving like one too. Chapter 5 examines some of the ways that naughty has countered and balanced nice, both in children's literature and beyond. Before that, however, it would be well to bring film more firmly into the picture.

Regardless of origin, a good percentage of early films that have anything to do with children idealize, and often go so far as to subscribe to the angelic ideal. Many of these films express that ideal with great sincerity and power, adding to the authoritative literary affidavits that we have already considered. Others are less consistent, and less convincing. Where the testimonials of Hans Christian Andersen and George Eliot may still feel so indelible as to be nearly irrefutable, the seemingly superannuated methods of the early silent cinema, together with the tentative nature of some of its infant expressions, more clearly reveal gaps and ruptures that also exist in the record, and in the thinking that informs it.

Burgeoning visual technologies in the late nineteenth century quickly began to contribute to child-related conversations. A huge interest in children had already led to a correspondingly huge proliferation of child imagery in conventional media. The advent of cinema caught the crest of that wave, as it were, adding motion pictures to the paintings, illustrations, and photographs that had already been produced in such abundance.[1] Children were used both as spectacle and as subject in earliest films and throughout film history. Their mere images were a phenomenon at first, an especially dear manifestation of the oft-observed and celebrated miracle of the medium. It moved! It lived! Though distance and death were inevitable, the motion picture now ensured that after a certain fashion, the lives of the beloved would continue on. And what could be more beloved, what more loveable than a little child?

Many of the earliest narrative films were based on familiar sources from literature or from the stage. These preexisting properties had built-in appeal for audiences who might otherwise have resisted the new medium. Their familiarity also ensured that audiences would be able to navigate their way through the uncertainties of early cinematic syntax. If the film itself did not communicate with complete clarity, then the spectator's familiarity with the source allowed her to fill in the gaps and remain oriented.[2]

The English film scholar Vicky Lebeau suggests that the image of the child served a similar function at this time and that it was as effective in decoding film's infant speech as any celebrated novel or play. Just as importantly, and more strikingly, she argues that the "Child Picture" may actually have been the first fully constituted cinematic genre. Before the domestic melodrama or the problem play were effectively imported from the popular stages, before the *course comique* or the Western were developed into the natively cinematic spectacles that they would one day become, the child was the stable center around which early film narrative coalesced.[3]

Most all of the major production entities in the first years of film were involved in these child-centered productions: France's Lumiere brothers, Pathé, the Gaumont studios, Edison in the United States, and Vitascope. Together these organizations produced literally hundreds of films that featured children, in portrait, or decoratively, or rolled into simple little narratives.

As for the fictional treatment of children in early film, it would remain for some time limited to, and limited by, idealism. Modern audiences may be put off by the seemingly excessive sentimentality in this material. This must certainly be addressed, and attended to. Still, a closer look reveals that the ideal is much more nuanced than a distant or dismissive glance might suggest. The angel could carry some weight, as it turns out, informing a number of very interesting narratives and suggesting tremendously important things about the world beyond.

It might be said, in fact, that early cinema's portrayal of children was emblematic of early cinema itself, not to mention the earliest stages of childhood. There were natural, inherent developmental limits. Progress was marked in and by rudimentary steps. But what is more delightful than the child that rolls and creeps, crawls and stands upright, toddles and then takes off? For the careful and sympathetic observer these early, limited expressions contain an intensity of interest and hard-won, admirable accomplishment that is unmatched in the rest of film history.

D. W. Griffith at Biograph

In order to get a proper sense of how an idea operates in a particular time or place, it is important to have a sufficient volume of pertinent material. There is no better repository for early film's treatment of and attitude toward children than the work of the pioneering American director, D. W. Griffith. Griffith is most celebrated—and sometimes most vilified—for the groundbreaking and often grandiose feature films that he undertook from 1915 (*Birth of a Nation*) and onward. However, it is the work produced in Griffith's first years as a filmmaker that provides the greatest insight into our subject.

Between 1908 and 1913, Griffith directed nearly 400 short films for the American Mutoscope and Biograph Company. These ranged from a half-reel to two reels (from five to twenty minutes) in length, with some of the later films becoming longer and more elaborate. His output during this period is an astonishing feat of industry and productivity, by any measure. Though it is an exaggeration to say as it once was, that Griffith invented the modern narrative cinema,[4] it is true that he synthesized the preexisting strands like no other before him. His background, his talent, and the felicitous industrial and commercial circumstances in which he found himself made him a very important figure during a very important period. The result of all these things is that under Griffith, film as medium, as industry, and, increasingly, as art, leapt quite astonishingly forward.

D. W. Griffith had been steeped in film's ancestral arts, an exposure that had supplied him with a considerable grounding in the work of numerous writers and poets and playwrights, both contemporary and classic. He was also very much affected by the cultural centrality of children in the Victorian and Edwardian periods, and he carried that influence forward toward WWI and cinematic modernity. Scores of his Biograph films featured children in key roles. Even in productions where youngsters were peripheral, their participation was instructive, eloquent even, in revealing any number of child-related ideas and values.

In March of 1909, Biograph released a Griffith-directed film called

4. Idealism, Sentimentality and the Advent of Film 103

And a Little Child Shall Lead Them.[5] The *Biograph Bulletin* provided exhibitors with a synopsis of the film. The details, along with the tone in which they are communicated, are significant:

> This is one of the most pertinent proverbs ever propounded, for the tiny hand of the babe has power to turn the universe. Ever since the foundation of the world has the little child been the ruling potentiality. The child has stimulated our every action, spiritual and actual, since the night of Bethlehem. The house divided against itself has been united by the child, as is the case in this story.[6]

Another Griffith-directed release from 1909, *A Fair Exchange*, was advertised as a "free adaptation of George Eliot's *Silas Marner*."[7] Given the source, Biograph's promotional literature is predictably effusive about children's inherent, irresistible leavening influence.

> After all, God's most precious gift is the little child. Our darkest moments are brightened by the child's advent. Their presence dissipates all sorrow, and sheds sunshine where clouds shaded, for the mantle of darkness that shadowed the world in the beginning was dispelled by the Child of Bethlehem.[8]

These invocations of the infant Jesus suggest the exalted and even inflated esteem in which children, or the concept of the child, was held at this time. Though Charlie Keil describes a prevalent attitude toward women in Griffith's films, he could just as well be describing the convictions that motivate Griffith's very frequent portrayals of children: "Insistence on their inherent frailty is balanced by conviction of their moral superiority."[9]

The Biograph films will continue the fashion, will affirm the demitheology by portraying children as heavenly, and as angels. They illustrate this idealistic abstraction in a wide range of narrative and situational settings. In urban milieus and in pastorals, in Westerns and in protogangster pictures, in the melodramatic spirit that so dominated during this period, as well as in the subtle stirrings of a more nuanced psychological cinema, children possess a disproportionate regenerative power.

Griffith's Biograph films contain an extraordinary number of examples:

In the aforementioned *"And a Little Child Shall Lead Them"* (March, 1909, Biograph No. 115) a married couple's first child dies. In time, another child is born. Still later the pair has decided to divorce. Their little daughter holds up the favorite doll of her deceased sister. "Who will keep this?" The parents, heart-stricken, reconcile.

In *A Child's Impulse* (June 1910, Biograph No. 265) a young man is faced with a choice between two young women; one is worldly and sophisticated, while the other is wholesome and virtuous. He chooses the former. A younger sister of the thrown-over woman pursues the man. "The child enters into the midst of a Bohemian gathering. One look into the child's sweet face, so much in contrast to the features around him, and but the sound of one word of her pleading, is enough to decide him, so picking up the child in his arms he dashes from the place."[10]

In *The Modern Prodigal* (August 1910, Biograph No. 282), a wastrel saves the life of the young son of the sheriff who pursues him. As a result of this experience, the wastrel reforms and the sheriff relents.

In *The Iconoclast* (October 1910, Biograph No. 289) a printer is found drinking on the job and is fired. He vows revenge on his former employer. As he prepares to strike, however, he sees the man's tender interactions with his crippled child. The child's patience under this constraint is inspiringly balanced by her father's loyalty and love. The printer, reproved, turns over a new leaf. He is subsequently reinstated.

In *A Child's Stratagem* (December 1910, Biograph No. 303) a child pretends to have been kidnapped in order to bring together her bickering parents. The mother has been especially at fault. Her worry, followed by the realization of what has motivated her child's ploy, brings her to her senses, and to a reconciliation with her husband.

In the period piece *The Smile of a Child* (June 1911, Biograph No. 342; a lost film), an unjust prince is taken aback by his coming into contact with a sweet child, who engages him frankly and disarmingly. His reclamation is completed when his mother, whom he had intended to rape, treats him with similar courtesy.

In *The Voice of the Child* (December 1911, Biograph No. 383) a cherub's plaintive cry of "Mamma, Mamma" effects a reconciliation between estranged spouses.

In *The God Within* (December 1912, Biograph No. 445) Blanche Sweet plays a young woman who, partly as a result of the broken promises of her former fiancé, has fallen into dishonor and dissolution. She bears a child out of wedlock, and it dies. Another woman, a pillar of the community, has also just given birth. She does not survive. The fallen woman takes on the surviving baby and is, as a result, rehabilitated.

As we have just seen, children run rampant in Griffith's Biograph films, or at least they circulate in virtuous ubiquity. In doing so they serve as much more than mere pretty ornaments. Scott Simmon observes that "this reformation by a child of the brutal or heartless man is the single most pervasive narrative pattern in Griffith's Biographs."[11] This pattern is not only significant at the level of plot. Simmon further observes that the Biograph films reflect a key, even epochal shift in the perception of children. This shift was first elaborated by the likes of Jean-Jacques Rousseau (*Émile, The New Heloise*), William Blake (*Songs of Innocence, Songs of Experience*), and William Wordsworth ("Intimations...," the Lucy Poems, "Michael," etc.). This shift saw original sin give way to inherent innocence, and it turned out to have an affect almost as diffusive as its stern predecessor. Although that literary and cultural change had been initiated more than a century previous, Griffith's films demonstrate its continuing currency, and potency.

The desert-set *The Female of the Species* (April 1912, Biograph No. 401) is another powerful case in point. It features a murderous, *McTeague*-like scenario in which an apparently wronged woman and her prodding sister prepare to wreak revenge on the perceived temptress. Their enmity, however, is diverted by the cry of a helpless, abandoned baby. In the face of the child's greater need, all three of the women decide to turn from their strife, devoting themselves instead to its care.

Plot synopses can fail to do justice to the ways in which plots are actually enacted. What might sound implausible or even preposterous in the recounting often plays out quite credibly, and creditably. The same can be true of the morals that such tales espouse. *The Female of the Species'* portentous climax conflates the nature of women and of children, such they become in important ways nearly identical. The child is virtuous, and she naturally calls adults to virtue. Here and elsewhere in the Biograph films women are presented as the most childlike of adults, the most willing to heed that call, and the most able as a result of their own inherent sweetness to fulfill its directives.

It might well be argued that this scenario infantilizes women or denies the rightful reality of their passion, anger, and agency.[12] And yet, in addition to this undoubted difficulty, such scenarios also have important applications, even for the most autonomous adult. Would that we were all this humble, and tractable! The lamb would lie down with the lion. The Old Testament/Hebrew Bible's bloodily Heroic Book of Judges would give way to the Book of Ruth's gentle womanly sublimity, its gentle disciple's modesty and circumspection. The moral and theological implication of these narratives is that they opt out of the confrontational, often violent manner in which melodrama tends to resolve plot conflict. In doing so they invert and then, still, echo the story of Abraham and Isaac. The vulnerable infant who lies on the altar of adult strife simultaneously plays the part of the angel that stays strife's hand.[13]

This omnipresent cinematic child, like her literary predecessors, descends directly from the little one set forth by Jesus in the New Testament. By her very nature she acts as a reproof to erring adults. Even the upstanding adult is stirred by the sight of her, aware of and awed by her simultaneous vulnerability and sufficiency. The little child moves the adult world from inertia to action, from disengagement to diligent, ethical interaction.

Preachment and Ideology

In most of the foregoing films, children serve as a general, generic leaven. They are inherently good, and their goodness infuses the settings and situations in which they find themselves. In some Biograph titles a child's benevolence, or vulnerability, operates more pointedly, explicitly serving as part of a sermon on any number of specific subjects.

One of the most important of these subjects was alcohol. Temperance dramas, with children as missionaries for the cause, were distributed throughout the run of Griffith's Biograph productions. *As In a Looking Glass* (December 1911, Biograph No. 378) features a drunken father and a child who is amused by his antics. The next day, Father sees his son imitating last night's inebriation, amongst his small friends. He is appalled, and repents, and reforms.

In *A Father's Lesson* (February 1913, Biograph No. 453), a drunken man storms about, menacing his children as he does so. After becoming increasingly enraged he locks one of the children in a trunk and then sets fire to the house. After nearly killing everyone, himself included, the father finally comes to his senses. Again, remorse and reform follow.[14]

Modern viewers can be struck and even put off by the apparent artlessness, the out-and-out obviousness of so many early film narratives. The modern viewers' perceptions are partly valid: dramatic motion pictures in these comparatively early days could be quite glaring. Griffith's temperance dramas, however, suggest that at times this obviousness might actually have been intentional. Films of the period were quite capable of subtlety and psychological nuance,[15] but these qualities would not necessarily have been sought in didactic settings where more forceful techniques were both called for and quite customary.

The child's role in Griffith's *A Drunkard's Reformation* (March 1909, Biograph No. 118) is a case in point. The *Biograph Bulletin* summarizes its extraordinarily blatant message and manner:

4. Idealism, Sentimentality and the Advent of Film

A temperance drama. A working man is led by bad companions to drink and frightens his wife and daughter by coming home intoxicated. The little girl persuades him to take her to see a stage performance of Zola's *L'Assommoir*.[16]

Unlikely reading matter for an exemplary infant; today this film's heavy hand comes across as shocking, if not hilarious. But today's scoffing dismissal may also be misguided, owing to a misreading of the original text and context. It is quite possible that what seems implausible to modern viewers may also have seemed implausible at the time of the film's release. Dramatically implausible, but not morally so. Given the then preponderance of temperance literature and also of much, much higher levels of church going and church affiliation, the filmgoer of 1909 is very likely to have recognized Griffith's film as a sermon. The sermon constituted a genre, and narrative—story—would have been a very familiar, very important component thereof. If in the early twentieth century Anton Chekhov and Konstantin Stanislavsky had pioneered methods through which the theater could replicate the infinite subtlety and multiplicity of human interaction,[17] then the institution of the religious parable also operated, quite distinctly, to provide a more irreducible kind of admonition.

In a parable, the communication of moral precept takes precedence over plausibility or verisimilitude. In Griffith's time at Biograph from 1908 to 1913, and in a very high percentage of the literature that informed and led up to the advent of film, parables would have been pervasive—delivered and heard with equal frequency, willingness and even alacrity. Even leaving religious denominations and observances aside, a viewer at the time of Griffith's Biograph films may well have enjoyed the current stylings, stories and poems of O. Henry, of Edgar Guest, of Henry van Dyke. They are likely to have remembered the unashamed and immensely popular literary preachments of *Oliver Twist* (1838) or *A Tale of Two Cities* (1859), of *Uncle Tom's Cabin* (1852) or *Ben-Hur* (1880), or even *The Picture of Dorian Gray* (1890). As for contemporary writing for and about children, moderns may think of this period as belonging to Baum and Barrie and Frances Hodgson Burnett, to Anne Shirley and Mole and Mr. Toad. They would be right to do so, but also present, or precedent, were the formative preachments of John Bunyan, Isaac Watts, or Ann and Jane Taylor, the more recent and varyingly didactic writings of Anna Laetitia Barbauld, Mary Mapes Dodge, Maria Edgeworth, Juliana Ewing, Hannah More, Anna Sewell, Mary Martha Sherwood, Johanna Spyri, Hesba Stretton and Sarah Trimmer, not to mention the complicatedly, demonstrably didactic works of the Brothers Grimm and Hans Christian Andersen and even Mark Twain.

Preaching in the literature and film of this period was pervasive, and very often effective. But the substance and validity of the didactic impulse does not mean that there were not instances in which specific sermons went badly off the rails. In *What Drink Did* (May 1909, Biograph No. 144), once again, a hard-working father is waylaid by his workmates. Together they turn to drink, and the father becomes increasingly unreliable.

> Night after night he comes home more the beast than human, until one evening he is later than usual and the oldest of [his] two girls [8 years old] goes in search of him. From tavern to tavern she goes until at last she finds him, but her pleading is in vain, and she is driven out by the drunken father. However, she returns and makes her last pleas, for the father crazed by drink hurls her aside, and the poor little child falls against the bar. This arouses the sympathy of the waiter, who reproaches the father for the brutal assault. The father resents his interference with a blow, and the waiter retaliates with a pistol, firing it just as the little one has arose [sic] and run to her father, receiving the bullet in the head, and drops lifeless to the floor.[18]

This is appalling contrivance, and a horrifically punitive conclusion. This particular temperance sermon indicates the lengths to which moral storytellers were willing to go in order to proselyte their subscribers. It shows how the often benevolent institution of the moral tale could also, quite easily, become a bully. For all of these pages' sympathetic discussion of idealized children and didactic narrative, texts like these are a reminder that such narratives also require our most critical, even skeptical attention.

The shortcomings of sermonic sensibility and method remind us of a further cause for caution and productive attention. Drink was not only a spiritual ill, but a social one as well. The Biograph films frequently held forth on any number of important contemporary issues. Inevitably, as with most any modern communication, their explicit social messages were often accompanied by unsuspected ideological undercurrents and contradictions. For all of their effacement at the level of ideology, these films are not ahistorical. Tom Gunning reminds us of the ways in which these child films, which were so prevalent as to constitute their own genre, also told tales that went beyond their intended settings.

> *A Salutary Lesson* [August 1910] is typical of a number of Griffith's domestic dramas in which the fabric of a middle-class family becomes frayed by family members who ignore their responsibilities. Sometimes this takes the form of a temptation to an adulterous affair, but just as frequently neglect of children serves as the source of tension. The importance of children to a family, and to a plot, highlights the domestic ideals

4. Idealism, Sentimentality and the Advent of Film 109

of Griffith's Biograph films and the films' ties to middle-class sentimental literature, as well as being a possible acknowledgment of the popularity of nickelodeon programs with children and women, obvious audiences for what the industry would eventually call "kid pictures."[19]

As Gunning suggests, Griffith's salvific children were not just articles of faith, or of hope. They were also part of a calculated, rational commercial strategy. And they were a central part of a broader ideological conversation, one that usually reflected and reinforced a certain set of values, as well as serving as a vehicle for the exploration and exorcism of various social anxieties.

Race and class were two of the most important and pressing of these anxieties. Children in D. W. Griffith's films reveal three major attitudes or approaches to these subjects. The first two of these reflect malice or ignorance, or a combination of the two. They are unkind, unduly fearful, and/or aggressively exclusionary.

Before becoming a director, Griffith wrote the scenario for a Biograph film entitled *The Valet's Wife*, directed by Wallace McCutcheon, Sr., and released in December 1908. A rascal is charged with acquiring a baby in order to deceive a philanthropist and dupe him out of his cash. The climax of the film arrives when said rascal inadvertently brings home a black baby—"Great Jupiter, it's a coon!"—at which point the deception is uncovered.[20]

A similar gag appears in *Mixed Babies*, an earlier Griffith-written, McCutcheon-directed film released in June 1908. The local department store has a checking service. A mischievous boy switches the numbers there, such that Mrs. Jones arrives home with a black child. Predictably, zany consternation ensues.[21]

This is unequivocal, unapologetic racism, where race functions as a joke or part of a punchline. Films like these may have been manifestations of outright race hatred. They may also, less reproachably perhaps, simply have reflected inherited and uninterrogated cultural attitudes.[22] This latter, somewhat unconscious kind of discrimination informs the second major social-anxiety motif in the films of D. W. Griffith, and in the literature and cinema of his period. This motif demonstrates how early cinema's insensitivity was often fueled by fear, and informed by real relations that existed outside of the confines of the theater.

Biograph films consistently address racial anxieties in stories concerning children, and white children in particular, endangered by a racial Other. The *Biograph Bulletin* describes *The Adventures of Dollie* (July 1908, Biograph No. 27), Griffith's very first film as director: "One of the most remarkable cases of child-stealing is depicted in this Biograph picture, showing the thwarting by a kind Providence of the attempt to kidnap for revenge a pretty little girl by a Gypsy."[23]

As with many narratives of this period, *The Adventures of Dollie* places ethnicity completely on the antagonistic side of its conflict-based plot. The *Bulletin* continues: "There has come into the neighborhood a band of peripatetic Nomads of the Zingani type, whose ostensible occupation is selling baskets and reed ware, but their real motive is pillage."[24] Contemporary fears and suspicion are reflected by the *Bulletin*'s generalizations and capital letters. In the film "they" are a collective, an unambiguous uniformity, and "their" united aims are unremittingly nefarious. Since this is the case—in the film and, often, in the perceptions that spectators carried away from it, or from others like it—then harsh expressions and actions must somehow have seemed more justified. When one of the gypsies is about to make off with the mother's purse: "The husband, hearing her cries of alarm, rushes down to her aid, and with a heavy snakewhip lashes the Gypsy unmercifully, leaving great welts upon his swarthy body, at the same time arousing the venom of his black heart."[25]

This is vivid advertising copy, designed to sell an exciting film. It is also hateful. Here is racism's pugnacious, unapologetic violence, and something of the fear that motivated and, for some, justified it. All these things together inform and energize many of Griffith's Biograph films, which in turn reflect common contemporary attitudes. In *The Adventures of Dollie*, Gypsies pose the threat. Later, in *Birth of a Nation*, it would be African Americans, though only those not loyal to the Confederacy and its ethnic hierarchies. A nefarious Sicilian couple snatches the baby in *One Touch of Nature* (January 1909, Biograph No. 74), while in *The Baby and the Stork* (January 1912, Biograph No. 382), the child is jeopardized by a passel of Black Hand Italian immigrants. *The Inner Circle* (August 1912, Biograph No. 424) finds its two vulnerable young principles endangered by a less specific, more generic Italian secret society, which resides in the heart of the city's Italian quarter. *In Fighting Blood* (June 1911, Biograph No. 349) reflects what would become one of American film's most familiar generic standbys, portraying Native Americans as a threatening horde. *Billy's Stratagem* (February 1912, Biograph No. 38) is a comic melodrama in which similarly undifferentiated Natives menace a doughty lad and his pretty little sister.

Other ethnicities were pressed into comparable antagonistic service in Griffith's films and in other productions of the period.[26] The immediate, intended result was that audiences became even more involved, even more sympathetic to the films' protagonists, as well as to the ideas that emerged out of their activities. A further consequence was not necessarily conscious. These constant ethnic villainies also had a negative effect on actual social discourse, inhibiting attempts by individuals and communities to replace strife with a measure of understanding and accord.

All of these dynamics also apply to matters of class, power, poverty, and the distribution of wealth. Film melodramas of this period frequently pitted tramps or convicts against their imperiled, innocent protagonists. Predictably, as with the race-related pictures, many of these protagonists were children, or women, or both together. Just as predictably jeopardized innocence raised narrative stakes, heightened spectator interest, and inadvertently contributed to harmful social misperceptions.

Two of Griffith's most celebrated, most wonderful Biograph films depend upon this underconsidered and problematic opposition. In *An Unseen Enemy* (September 1912, Biograph No. 426) Dorothy and Lillian Gish, respectively 14 and 18 years old, make their luminous Biograph debuts. They are menaced by the household's disgruntled servants and by their unsavory friends. The resulting confrontation is most involving and entertaining. However, as with most all of Griffith's melodramas—though not necessarily with some of his more searching, socially sympathetic films—*An Unseen Enemy* does not to consider what actual inequity might have set the servants off, nor what perpetual disadvantage might have so soured their companions. The same goes for the tremendous *A Girl and Her Trust* (March 28 1912, Biograph No. 398) and for its disadvantaged antagonists. An abrupt intertitle—"Tramps!"—signals their arrival and dispenses with any explanation of or curiosity about what might have brought them to this actual extremity.[27]

Was D. W. Griffith, or the society that his work reflects and in many ways inflects, simply a thorough and multiple racist or classist? Perhaps, partly. And further, the Black Hand actually did exist, and there had been actual strife with some Italian immigrants as well as not-so-distant and highly charged interactions with any number of Native nations. All of this means that insensitive melodramatic bluster could reflect real, nuanced, often understandable social tensions.

There is the baby, and then there is its bathwater. These films, and this filmmaker, cannot simply be dismissed. To speak only of the most celebratedly sinful of Griffith's films, *Birth of a Nation* also features innumerable cinematic innovations, and it is full of exquisite emotional and dramatic insights.[28] Similarly, Griffith's Biograph melodramas are much more than the sum of their insensitivities, whether aggressive or inadvertent. In fact, it is often true that their seeming or actual transgressions are also the flip side of some heartening advance.[29] *A Girl and Her Trust* is dismissive of its antagonists. On the other hand, its heroine, played by the delightful Dorothy Bernard, is wonderfully active and autonomous, pushing through the chivalrous straightjacket of idealized and sometimes infantilized female passivity to actually save the day, though with more than a little help from numerous male friends.

This is not to apologize for the indefensible, but it is to say that there is hardly a life, or a film, that can simply be reduced to its unseemly or inappropriate parts. Another extenuating, mitigating circumstance should also be acknowledged. If Griffith is now most remembered for his attitudes toward race, then the Biograph films demonstrate that many of his now-offensive attitudes belonged to a complex set of conventions he had inherited. It must be more pointedly stated that these were conventions to which he was in some ways beholden, in a professional sense. For instance, baby-stealing stories were common in the films of this period.[30] The *Bulletin*'s objectionable language and attitude are also consistent with the requirements of melodrama, which thrives on formidable, outsized antagonists, and on the vivid conflict that they engender.

In a sense, some of Griffith's race and class films have no more real animosity toward ethnicity or poverty than a fairy tale populated with menacing giants and malevolent dwarves would have toward individuals that grapple with growth anomalies.[31] In the Biograph films, the good and the ill are often intermingled, sometimes inextricably. Further, these unseemly perceptions and enactments were often rooted in the real, such that subsequent missteps often had their reasons. They may even have felt irresistible. These complexities, and the sympathy that follows upon encountering them, underpins a third important pattern in Griffith's issue films.

Griffith's children were sometimes used to both portray and increase suspicions toward racial and social Others. But just as frequently these children brought Griffith and his audiences in touch with their own better angels. The children motivated him, his characters, and his subscribers to resist prejudicial temptation and reach for a better accord. With some power and plausibility, with palpable and most creditable conviction, the angel child in this period increased understanding and sympathy, even going so far as to effect reconciliations between race or class constituencies that been previously sundered.

As an example, Griffith tended to be very sympathetic in his treatment of Native Americans. *The Redman and the Child* was released in July 1908,

4. Idealism, Sentimentality and the Advent of Film 113

and it roughly replicates the plot *of The Adventures of Dollie*. This time the culprits are not gypsies or tramps, but "a couple of low-down human coyotes, who would rather steal than work."[32] In contrast stands the eponymous Indian, who will eventually and most heroically go on to rescue the endangered infant. He is introduced to us as follows: "Alongside of a beautiful mountain stream in the foothills of Colorado there camped a Sioux Indian, who besides being a magnificent type of the aboriginal American, is a most noble creature, as kind-hearted as a woman and as brave as a lion."[33]

The idea of noble savagery,[34] tinged perhaps by postconquest remorse, helps to shape this particular cinematic statue. These, plus sentimentality, and especially the semireligious regard we have already observed, serve to paint a much more affecting picture when a native child now comes upon the scene.

The Broken Doll (October 1910, Biograph No. 292) is the story of nineteenth-century settlers in the western United States. The Caucasian protagonist's wife and daughter encounter a neglected Native child, played by the seminal cinematic angel (and non–Native) Gladys Egan. The settlers treat her kindly, going so far as to give her a doll. Meanwhile, in contrast, adult Natives are being very badly treated by the Caucasian folk in town. These Natives plan to rise up in response. There is some evident sympathy from the filmmakers in portraying their plight. For all that, the Native child seeks to dissuade them. In response the adult Natives take away and destroy her doll, being an emblem of Caucasian culture and the injustice with which they associate it. The child proceeds to bury her discarded doll with solemnly observed—and respectfully portrayed—traditional tribal rites. Then she overhears the noise of a War dance. She runs to warn her Caucasian friends, and succeeds in doing so. The Native attack is warded off, but not before the child is struck by an errant bullet. She returns to the doll's grave and dies there.

The death of the Gladys Egan character signifies that no accord has been accomplished between the film's adversaries, and that historically factual enmity still prevails. But tragedy, or at least an important interpretation of Aristotle's description thereof, filters diegetic disaster through the sympathies of the receptive spectator; the result is fear, and pity, and a cleansing catharsis.[35] It was hoped that the contemporary viewer of *The Broken Doll* would view the senseless death of this innocent and transform her own attitude toward or treatment of her benighted people.

This strategy was versatile. *The Two Sides* (May 1911, Biograph No. 334) is the story of a ranch owner's daughter who befriends a poor Mexican laborer, his wife, and their sick baby. The innocent, ailing Mexican infant and the loyal, morally exemplary Caucasian child are able to effect a narrative reconciliation that has both ethnic and class-related ramifications. A number of unjust hierarchies, unjust practices, and dismissive attitudes are portrayed and challenged as the busy plot strands move toward resolution. Typically, it is the little child (Gladys Egan again) who does the morally needful work while heedless adulthood is temperamentally and ideologically disinclined. Notwithstanding her efforts, the workers are dismissed, which eventually leads to a fire that threatens the rancher's own child. The film's last-minute rescue is conventional, but the issues remain. *The Two Sides* avers that Labor, and especially migrant Labor, is powerless. It must be left to the privilege, and even racially preeminence, to put things right.

There are, quite obviously, condescending and naïve strands among these partly Progressive sentiments. The films reflect, perhaps even understand very little of the work that is really required—justice, legislation, representation, and not just fickle or underfunded charity—to address these inequities and to right these wrongs. Nevertheless, in their inadequacies these old films are still most instructive, and full of real and affirmative substance. As before, as ever, the child is at the heart of a great many of their generous impulses, and she is the exemplar in many of their generous enactments.

Confusions will ever remain, and inadequacies as well. The point is that D. W. Griffith and D. W. Griffith's times, in addition to holding some demonstrably inflammatory attitudes on the subject of race, and conventionally insensitive attitudes on the subject of class, meant and often did well. But at this point it is fair to suggest that speaking generally, and also more particularly with regard to his portrayal of children, Griffith and his times might not have meant or done well enough.

5

The Problem with Perfection and Ways Forward

As we have seen, the child productions of D. W. Griffith contain a number of ideological contradictions. On the subjects of race and class, for instance, they could be plainly hostile, or even hateful. They could also reflect real social tensions in ways that were simultaneously anxious and insensitive. They could be generous too, voicing and acting upon any number of kindlier, more progressive impulses. And they were frequently an instructively muddled combination of all of these things.[1]

Through a glass, darkly. In the midst of all of this puzzlement, the institution of angelic childhood begins to look as vulnerable as the oft-imperiled angel child himself. It is instructive to compare all of this problematic idealization with the moral-literary root, with the exemplary child as seen in the Bible, in the *New Testament* particularly, as well as in the previous chapter of this study. Though they may have seemed identical, the two constructs are actually quite distinct. The biblical notion is fairly unexceptionable, because it is really quite modest. Little children really do tend to be submissive and meek and loving, in addition to a few other simultaneous and slightly more contrary characteristics, which the Bible also acknowledges. In this, its position is tasteful and seemly, both in approving and in reproach.

Griffith and much of the late nineteenth- and early twentieth-century children's discourse falls short when it favors one side of the equation at the expense and near exclusion of the other. It fetishizes, taking a part to be the whole, and therefore gives an incomplete and even distorted sense of what the whole actually is. Now it is well, once again, to remember that Victorian Sentimentality and its various constituent conventions often reflected the experiences and deepest convictions of the people that subscribed to it. Despite lapses in taste and sensitivity, many, many texts of the period are redolent of real feeling, and still capable of contributing to substantial conversations about real issues.[2]

And yet, after a certain point, enough can be enough. The foregoing conversation about idealized children has been critical, but respectful, and often affirmative. But not everyone feels so sympathetically.

Screwball Squirrel, a Tex Avery–directed MGM cartoon released in April 1944, begins with an outlandishly cute, Disney-derived little squirrel named Sammy. Sammy, a little basket hung over his little arm, is skipping through the forest in an affected manner. He is accompanied on the soundtrack by the saccharinized strains of Felix Mendelssohn's "Spring Song,"[3] which quickly morphs into "Here We Go Gathering Nuts in May." The camera tracks right, following Sammy until he suddenly runs into another, much less likely-looking squirrel. This is Screwy, who is leaning impudently against that tree, and who stops Sammy in his tracks. "Say!" sniffs Screwy, "what kind of cartoon is this going to be, anyway?" "Well you see," pipes the poppet, "I play the lead in this picture and my name is Sammy Squirrel and the story is all about me and my cute little furry friends in the forest." Sammy reels off a ream of alliterations: "Billy Beaver, Wallace Woodchuck, Buster Badger, Horace Hedgehog, Scott Skunk, Barney Bear, Donny Monkey, Dorothy the Duck…"

"Oh!" cries Screwy, in some agony. In a way that is markedly distinct from the pretty, patient, long-suffering film-child of whom we have been reading and to whom we have become accustomed, Screwy takes aggressive action. He leads this lisping paragon to just behind yon tree, where he pummels him right out of the picture. "You wouldn't have liked the story anyway," says Screwy, not evincing the least bit of remorse. "The funny stuff will start as soon as the phone rings."

The phone rings directly—it hangs, somehow, in the hollow of that other tree there—and there follows an awesome effusion of the kind of perfectly calculated, exquisitely executed cartoon violence for which director Avery is quite justifiably celebrated (and quite justifiably criticized for as well).[4] In the present discussion, however, it becomes clear that Avery's wicked glee does not occur in a vacuum. *Screwball Squirrel*, like so many of the Merry Melodies and Looney Tunes being produced just across town[5]—not to mention pictures featuring the harlequinesque Mickey Mouse, in the days before he became a buttoned-down corporate spokesman, and the sputtering, self-centered Donald Duck, or Felix and Oswald, Bosko and Ko-Ko, Betty Boop and Bluto, and Tom and Jerry and all the rest—is as much a reaction as an assertion. Sweet little children are one thing, but eventually all that implausible, oppressive wholesomeness just makes you want to hit somebody.

It may have been a bit of just this feeling—plus God, working in mysterious ways—that got Joseph sent to the land of Egypt. And this side of antiquity and archetype, in the modern realms of entertainment and commerce and ideology, this also hints at a near fatal limitation of excessively idealized childhood. Griffith's pretty *Pippa Passes* (October 1909, Biograph No. 189), is an adaptation of Robert Browning's long 1841 poem. Its young heroine awakens on New Year's Day, her only day off in the whole year.[6] For all the privation and injustice that this fact implies, she nevertheless goes out cheerfully, circulating widely and singing all the while. As she makes her way, Pippa passes by a number of individuals who find themselves in varying difficulties, or funks. Though they are unaware of her, their lives become brightened and leavened by her mere, glancing presence.

Eileen Bowser notes that in the film "Pippa is a moral voice that ... stays outside the diegesis."[7] This glancing observation has portentous implications. What is true here is actually, in a sense, operative in so many of Griffith's child films, and with the idealized child generally. Though the children participate in the plot and are certainly subject to its dangers, they are often immune to the core conflict that fuels and carries the plot forward. In other words, they function as moral voices that somehow remain outside of the diegetic space of unseemly desires and temptation and succumbing. There may well be some didactic advantage in this. But nondiegetic characters—consider the discourse of women, film, and scopophilia—are easily objectified, reduced, and utterly removed from the contradictory complexities and potential satisfactions of actual reality. What of agency, autonomy, even the precious right to err?

The dear and durable notion of idealized childhood will always have a place when urged in a seemly, sensible manner.[8] Some, blessed to have had a portion of the ideal realized in their own lives, may articulate it in insistent, heightened fashion.[9] Others have insisted too much, and gone too far.[10] In such discourse, the dear and durable notion of idealized childhood is also a distortion, and even a deception. In fact, this notion is so idealized, so selective, so denying of certain central realities, that it is basically untrue.

Tex Avery and the like object to excessive idealization, and film historians can do so as well. Russell Merritt, a distinguished Griffith scholar and, often, defender, cuts through the excess with a matter-of-fact, surgical, cynical eye: "Among the sub-genres that emerge from Griffith's increasing enthusiasm for family melodramas, the Child-Centered Family Reconciliation Romance was threatening to eclipse all rival variations." Merritt points out that "marriages saved by children—especially dead children"—were a particular Griffith specialty. "[He] had tried other ways to reunite estranged husbands and wives, pressing into service such agents as the blind mother, the Bible, and the resourceful kid sister. But nothing could compete with distraught, dying or dead children for emotional impact."[11]

Outmoded, overdetermined idealism, and all of the manipulation and poor taste that goes with it: Is there nothing to salvage from these generations' worth of perception and narrative practice? Fortunately, and quite frequently, there are a number of alternatives that fix idealization more firmly, foreground the affections on which it is based, and put the resultant combination on a more plausible and pleasing footing.

This book's remaining chapters will explore some of this other, often antical side of the child equation, concluding with the product of the two terms, or the rich syntheses that result when the conceptual poles are combined and reconciled. And it is only fair to acknowledge that childhood is not completely a garden of virtues in the films of D. W. Griffith (chapter 7 touches upon an earthier, more developmental tenable childstrand in the Biograph films). At the present juncture, however, the exemplary side of the naughty and nice binary requires some elaboration, and some helpful rumpling.

There are three main limitations to the Victorian concept of the angel child. The first is that it does not square with the real but partial perfections of actual children. Actual children cannot measure up to idealist abstraction. They may not even want to do so. And yet even as they fall short they are still, so often, exemplary.

The second limitation is that the idealist abstraction can only be maintained at the expense of normative, healthy cognitive and emotional development. As they learn and grow, children attempt and experience things. When they do so, inevitably, they err. And in erring they potentially, hopefully, learn and grow even more. The cinematic/literary angel child does not sufficiently provide or allow for this fact.

The last limitation of the angel child is that however perfect she may be in isolation, in the broad context of human society, she cannot survive, at least not without becoming a permanent ward of that society, which is to say a permanent project and a permanent drain. Individuals, as well as some political and economic philosophies, gladly take on the obligation to protect the vulnerable and care for the unfortunate. However, these individuals and political and economic philosophies maintain the expectation that the fatherless—as in James 1:27—will eventually grow to effectual fatherhood, as it were, and take on the caregiving role by which they themselves benefited.

Isaiah echoes, or rather, anticipates James' stirring call for permanent, systematic charity in the first chapter of his record: "Learn to do well; seek judgment, relieve the oppressed, judge the fatherless, plead for the widow."[12]

Learning and well-doing, judging and relieving oppression, pleading and empowering are largely within the purview of adults. In other words, childhood is a miracle, and a marvel, and a cloud-trailing glory. But it is also a stage, an impermanence, and an inherent insufficiency. It is well to treasure it, celebrate it, and then to pass happily on to further challenges, satisfactions, and accomplishments.

Perfectly Imperfect

These are the main challenges. Can idealization survive them, or should it even attempt to do so? Yes, and yes, if reasonable alterations are made. Christ's Sermon on the Mount is found in chapters 5 through 7 of the gospel of Matthew in the New Testament. The first of these chapters concludes with this daunting instruction, and expectation: "Be ye therefore perfect, even as your Father which is in heaven is perfect."[13]

To many readers—including many compliant Christians—perfection may sound impossible, and the expectation to become perfect, unreasonable. But a biblical footnote suggests an alternative reading to this verse in Matthew, and a reason for mere mortals to maintain hope. "Perfect," here, comes from the Greek word for "complete," which might also be rendered as finished, or fully developed.[14] It would not be productive at this point to enter into an etymological debate, let alone a theological one. Suffice it to say, or hypothesize, that an imperfect but practicing, striving Christian can still fulfill Christ's commandment of perfection by becoming whole, or consistent, or complete, which is different from being expected to completely eliminate all error.

And what of children? How does Christ's instruction apply to them? A number of exemplary texts chime in on these important questions, and in doing so add up to a kind of figurative, qualitative consensus.

Carl Bloch (1834–1890) was a Danish painter, devoted both to his craft and to his chosen project of representing the life of Christ. These broadly distributed images, so familiar to Western Protestantism,[15] are overwhelmingly affirmative, practically proselytizing. They also provide some valuable perspective on the nature of a perfect, which is to say exemplary, complete, childhood.

Bloch's *Healing of the Blind Man* (1871)[16] draws the spectator's eye to the miracle in question, but it also fills in the margins with complementary and interestingly contrasting material. Look, for instance, at that naked boy, who is holding an orange, or perhaps an orange ball, there on the left side of the painting. The child is being restrained, gently, by a disciple. The child is also looking mischievous, or maybe just energetic. The same goes for a second, slightly older boy, the one standing just behind, picking for some reason at the first child's head.

This first child, who stands in the shadow and may just have red hair, is not being mindful of Christ's ministrations. He may not even be aware of them. In fact, alone among the sixteen figures composed in the tableaux, he is looking beyond the frame, beyond what mostly constitutes a fourth wall, at the viewer. It is hard to be sure exactly what is intended here, or what meaning we are to derive. It is possible though, given how broadly beaming the child, that he is merely happy and that that is message enough.

Bloch's *Sermon on the Mount* (also 1871)[17] gives further credence to this interpretation. It centers on Christ's miraculous preaching, once again skillfully leading the spectator's gaze by line and look and gesture to the Messenger, and by extension to his Message. As near as can be calculated, the painting features twenty-seven attentive adult figures, in addition to Jesus himself, as well as another adult who appears to be looking toward one of her fellows. And there is also that kid over there, on the left again. This one is reaching for the brightly colored butterfly that has landed on the shawl or veil or headpiece of the reverently attentive woman who sits, head bowed, in the foreground.

The child in the first painting might well be a Caution, though there doesn't seem to be any censure attached to the fact. This second child seems a quieter sort. He reaches out with his index finger, curiously, but very quietly and gently. This proper, plausible paragon is not really, not remotely attending to Christianity's most thorough, far-reaching statement of purpose, principle, and moral expectation. Bloch, forbidding him not at all, does not seem to mind. This is not, after all, a bad boy. Far from it. In fact he is a lily of the field, and the time for toiling or spinning has not yet come. Still, for all that, he is glorious.[18]

D. W. Griffith's child films are tremendous, but a great many of them do rather protest too much. How much more pleasing, credible, and

5. The Problem with Perfection and Ways Forward   121

organic the developmentally normative, semi-minding child in Bloch's images and in countless other concurring narratives.

In Hiyao Miyazaki's rip-roaring adventure film *Porco Rosso* (Japan, 1992), airborne pirates pursue a vessel that for some reason is carrying a big shipment of gold and a whole bunch of little children—or little girls, to be exact.[19] The pirates soon catch up with the ship, remove both of its precious cargos, and make off with them. The children are at first excited. "Wow, Pirates!" They are even appreciative. They catch sight of the pirates' notorious, fear-inducing standard: "Look at the skull. And very well drawn!"

The adults on the ship are terrified, and communicate as much to another incoming pilot, Porco Rosso: "They took the girls and the money! Bring them back for us!" Imperiled innocents and outsized villains: these are the dimensions and conflict structures of classic melodrama. Now Miyazaki undertakes to undermine them.

We return to the marauding pirates, who are now addressing their clamoring captives with some impatience. Like the girls' parents, they are getting a little bit anxious themselves, though not at all for the same reason. The little children have spread out over and covered the surface of the pirates' aircraft. They are exultant. "We're flying!" they exclaim. The pirates are less happy, and are edging into recrimination. "You're the one who said to bring them all," grumbles one, to another. These children are not as tractable as they hoped they would be. Far from it: "Will you all shut up?!"

While Porco Rosso covers the distance between them, the children have made their way to the gunner's turret. The gunner begins shooting, and the children cheer. Porco has come into view and is approaching in his airplane. He too starts blasting away. He takes out the pirates' primary engine, despite the fact that the children that he is supposed to rescue are in the open all the while. The children do not seem to be remotely alarmed by the fact.

The pirates are having trouble defending themselves, partly because the children are hanging on to their gun mount and keeping it from rotating properly. "You missed!" the children taunt. Eventually, because of Porco's attacks and the children's interference, the pirate plane is brought down and then scuppered. The pirates are terrified: "We crashed! We're going to sink!" For their part the children, again, are elated. They are also unworried. "No we're not. This is a sea-plane." But now Porco blasts the pirates' craft once again, and the tail drops off. The pirates are certain now. "Help!" they say. "We're going to sink!" say the little girls, excited, in reply.

Now these unconcerned infants simply open the door and jump into the water. The pirates, feeling all manner of contradictory feelings, remonstrate. "Don't worry," say the girls, reassuringly. "We're all on the swim team."

The pirates are about to lose their collateral, having lost the upper hand, their adult preeminence, and their dignity some time since. They attempt to salvage something out of the situation. They try to bargain with Porco. "Give [us] half of the money and the kids. You can have the rest."

No dice; the pirates are utterly defeated and the rescue is finally, fully effected. Porco extricates the little children from their terrible predicament, such as it was. "Bye-bye! Bye-bye Pirates!" the children cry. A few of the pirate underlings wave back, warmly.

The little girls are now distributed across the surface of Porco's plane, as he undertakes some repairs of his own. There, on the surface of the wine-dark open sea, the children doff their pinafores. For them it is in the end as it was in the beginning. They continue on in innocent half nakedness—as angels or, perhaps, as *putti*—cheerful and abiding and eternal.

Could this be why the disciples once forbade the little children? For the reason that though they may be of the kingdom of heaven—Matthew 18:1–4—they are also a handful, and a headache?

This sequence in Miyazaki's film is both fanciful and avowedly comical. What of more realistic narrative settings, and more problematic behaviors? Can a normative, plausible angel child act in a more aggressively contrary fashion and still remain angelic?

The Italian writer-director Ermanno Olmi's 1983 film *Cammina, Cammina* (*Keep Walking*) is an unusually indirect, extended portrayal of the journey of the Magi to Bethlehem, concentrating particularly on the travails and the faith—"help thou my unbelief!"[20]—of one of the wise men. With regard to the present discussion, the film's most significant sequence occurs near its beginning, and features its faithful protagonist, Mel(chior). Mel is a Jewish astronomer-priest, preparing lambs for sacrifice as required by Moses' Law, and by his own priestly duties, and by his own willing inclination. In addition this sequence just as pointedly features the protagonist's equally devout young servant, Rupo, who has become very fond of these lambs, and is very upset at the prospect of their impending demise.

On its surface, Olmi plays the scene for quiet comedy. Mel proceeds patiently, and then long-sufferingly, while Rupo becomes increasingly agitated, and angry. In fact he begins to shout and carry on, throwing things and generally making a mockery of what is, after all—and as usual, this most gently reverent of film directors concurs—a sacred rite and a sacred obligation.

Beneath the surface, Olmi is enacting something altogether deeper and more merciful than mere comedy. The tender thing is that Mel holds and reconciles two very contrary things. As an initiate, as one anointed to perform sacred rites, he is proceeding with pious resolve and concentration. But as a mature and loving adult, he is also mindful of his young charge. Rupo has not been fully instructed or ordained. He doesn't fully understand the reason and implication of this observance, nor does he really have a way or reason to do so. Given this misunderstanding, and the perspective that informs it, Rupo is actually acting upon a most creditable sentiment. Such behavior from a consecrated person would border on blasphemy. Such behavior from a developmentally normative and liturgically limited child only reflects his love, loyalty, and courage. Rupo is not quite an angel, nor is he perfect in behavior. He is, however, whole, or sufficient, perfect in innocence and sweetness, courage and faithfulness.

This is a point that cannot be overemphasized. It transforms our experience with and attitude toward children both literary/cinematic, and actual. We have been concentrating on cinema, but children's literature also provides ample testimony on this point. In *Anne of Green Gables* (1908), Lucy Maud Montgomery's carrot-topped creation, whom Mark Twain famously described as "the dearest and most loveable child in fiction since the immortal Alice,"[21] wishes to be called Cordelia, though her name is Anne Shirley. She positively will not stop talking and often speaks the most utter nonsense. She is disrespectful toward divinity, simply because divinity is responsible for her regrettable red hair. She is most impertinent to Mrs. Rachel Lynde, who is her elder and her better. She wears a wreath of wildflowers to church. She does not appreciate the minister or the Sunday school teacher and finds their ministrations to be boring. She confesses to illicitly borrowing and then losing Marilla Cuthbert's prized amethyst brooch. It later turns out that this confession was, in fact, a lie. She breaks a slate over Gilbert Blythe's head, then refuses to talk to him for a whole five years. She allows a mouse to drown in the plum pudding sauce. She gets her bosom friend and kindred spirit, Diana Barry, drunk on currant wine, though she claims to have thought that it was merely raspberry cordial. She leaps recklessly into beds in guest bedrooms, causing harm to the crotchety old maiden aunts that lie there. She puts anodyne liniment in the cake, though the recipe called for vanilla. She walks recklessly upon ridgepole roofs, which results in her falling and breaking her ankle. She dyes her hair green, without having received or even sought permission to do so. She sinks her neighbors' watercraft, then causes her devoted friends to think that she has perished as a result. She even goes so far as to neglect her studies and indulge in the reading of novels in class.

Anne Shirley causes no end of trouble, and she is at fault in almost every instance. Her transgressions, however, are almost always a consequence of her lack of experience, of fine impulses just slightly misdirected or misapplied, of the fact that she is, after all, only a child. The important thing is that most every error leads to incremental, believable, and eventually transformative improvements. And the greatest transformation, ultimately, takes place in the hearts of those whom Anne most inconvenienced.[22]

Felix Culpa

The positive, productive nature of Anne Shirley's errors relates to and refutes the second great limitation of the idealized literary child. This is that perfection, or the idea of perfection, is not consistent with the norms of emotional, intellectual, and moral development. In other words, perfection is not natural.

Inert idealism has its place in a didactic or an activist setting, where childish vulnerability operates to spur the reader toward improvement or action. This is the case with Tiny Tim, or the Little Match Girl, or Cosette; with CBS Reports/Edward R. Murrow's *Harvest of Shame* (1960), or the National Film Board of Canada/UNICEF's *Every Child* (1979). But if child narrative is to have any compelling tension or dramatic interest of its own, if it is to have anything to do with reality or praxis, then at some point this strategic inertia has to give way to actual movement. Whether dramatically or developmentally, children must venture out, take risks, and reap the rewards thereof. Further, when children venture out, when they attempt to do things, they make mistakes. Often, and repeatedly. This is also normative and, within certain rather broad limits, very healthy.

It is customary to think of error as running counter to truth, just as light is the opposite of darkness, and right of wrong. This is correct, and in countless ways. But there are important exceptions, and mitigations: Socratic and Platonic dialogue, or Socratic/Confucian dialogue[23]; the comprehensive psychological expanse of Shakespeare's characters, or Don

5. The Problem with Perfection and Ways Forward   125

Quixote's wise foolishness; the scientific method, Hume's kindly skepticism, and Hegel's capaciously generous dialectical project; political pluralism, diplomacy, marriage; empathy and charity; "existence precedes essence,"[24] the Imaginary giving way to the Symbolic, and reaching for the Real, ideological interrogation and philosophical deconstruction, curriculum and curricular pedagogies; the way that infants who parallel play subsequently squabble and start to have to account for the existence of a life other than their own—all of these are encounters that cannot be reduced to Christian soldiery nor to facile binaries or melodramatic oppositions.[25] Sometimes, as in a child's long journey toward maturation and effectual adulthood, it is well to see error as a necessary part of a more positive process.

Narrative art and theory often concurs. Aristotle contends that plot was the first and most important of the elements of drama and that character followed afterwards. This may seem counterintuitive, or even inappropriate. Aren't people more important than the circumstances in which we find them? Perhaps, or certainly. But not in a(n Aristotelian) narrative.[26] Plot is primary because without it, without action, without an objective or a challenge and the resourcefulness required to address it, character does not register. In fact, it does not even exist.

Aristotle introduced his hierarchy of elements in the context of a discussion about tragedy in the *Poetics*.[27] Tragic plots, fueled by conflict, lead to complications and crises. These in turn cause reflection and instruction for the protagonist of the play, and by extension and just as importantly, for its spectators.

Do these ideas apply to children or to children's narratives? The loss of a child is unutterably tragic, but with regard to the theatrical medium, Aristotle's theory did not allow children a place in the tragic equation. Tragedies were to have such magnitude, to occur among such exalted personages that everyone would be affected by the repercussions. This was something that the fall of a mere sparrow, however beloved, could never do.

We may recall that Plato, as discussed in the first chapter of this book, was even more proscriptive when it came to enacted narratives. He agreed that tragic plots were fueled by conflict, but maintained that conflict could only take spectators further and further away from virtue. His solution, of course, was to simply outlaw the theater. Either way, the Greeks were not hospitable to children in theatrical settings.

For all that, Aristotle's hierarchy of elements can still be profitably applied to children's contexts. For one thing, as children move toward their majority, they may well be exposed to malice and even harm, if only through the powerful proxy of vivid and occasionally troubling stories. Holocausts occur, in part because of the actions and the inactions of people. Youth on the brink of exercising their franchise should begin to face that fact.

There is another, even more immediate and palatable way for Aristotle and his hierarchy to be applied to child settings. The hierarchy of elements does not only relate to tragedy, or the contentious strivings of conventional plot. It can also operate within a scenario that involves choices, their consequences, and the things that can be learned from the combination thereof. It can apply to stories about real or plausible children who strive, fail, and then prevail.

"*O felix culpa quae talem et tantum meruit habere redemptorem!*" ("O happy fault that merited such and so great a Redeemer!")[28] Writing in the thirteenth century, Thomas Aquinas speaks against the grain of Catholic theology, or at least against the Augustinian view of Original Sin. Far from being the primordial curse, or mankind's fatal error, Aquinas finds the Fall of Adam to be the joyful inciting incident of mankind's triumphant saga. Adam's transgression prefigures Christ's atonement, the thing that not only made it necessary, but possible.

John Milton concurred. After its manifold and multiple agonies, his *Paradise Lost* concludes with a ringing affirmation of the necessity, the happy consequences of man's first error, of woman's brave, perceptive part in it, and of the incalculable greater good that would follow, for all.[29]

There are also stirring illustrations for moderns who may be skeptical about Judeo-Christianity's core myths. In the realm of rapturous cinema, the theme is figuratively, beautifully played out in Wim Wenders' epochal *Wings of Desire* (1987), as well as its sequel *Faraway, So Close* (1993). Wenders arrays a host of attentively ministering angels who go about doing much good in the world. One of them falls, voluntarily, and he is followed by his colleague in the following film. In the first film the angels had been witness to error, sin, and terrible sorrow. In the second, the angel himself receives a full measure of all of these things. But there are also, paradoxically, participatory transports, much sweeter than the loving vigils that had gone before.[30]

All of these narratives are united by the assertions that Eden's bounty is in fact a pale partiality and that it is only through bitterness that sweetness can be properly savored. More, all of them hold that sweetness does not only come in contrast to error, but that it is actually contained therein. "But at least I tried," says Randall Patrick McMurphy, when laughed to scorn after a conspicuous failure.[31] "Now life is beginning for us,"[32] says Mikkel Borgen, so recently bereft, so suddenly restored to "Life ... Yes ... Life ... Life."[33] "And the Lord turned the captivity of Job ... [and] the Lord gave Job twice as much as he had before. So the Lord blessed the latter end of Job more than his beginning."[34]

There has been much debate about Aristotle's use, in the *Poetics*, of the term *hamartia*.[35] It has long been understood as referring to a character's fatal flaw, which precipitated the dire resolution of a particular tragedy or of tragedy in general. Now, and for some time since, scholars understand that "flaw" might more properly be rendered as "error."[36] A mistake is less blameworthy than a deep moral demerit. Rather than sitting in judgment of the ambitious or the jealous or the credulous, the spectator who witnesses an error and its dire dividends is more likely to feel the fear and pity that lead to catharsis, or cleansing, and to empathetic epiphany as well.[37]

All of this and then, once again: children who strive, who fail, and who then prevail. The distinguished British biographer Ann Thwaite credits Frances Hodgson Burnett, particularly in her novel *The Secret Garden* (1911), with breaking important ground in applying these essential concepts to children's literature.[38] The novel's adult characters are, for the most part, of three distinct and distinctly unhelpful varieties: distant and disengaged (Mary's parents, Colin's father), overweening and condescending (Mrs. Medlock), or merely peripheral (the scurrying, subordinated staff).[39] Hans Christian Andersen and Charles Dickens, among many others, have turned this kind of broad-based and diverse neglect into an emblem of the sinfulness of man. For her part, according to Thwaite, Hodgson Burnett takes another refreshing, productive tack, quite distinct from then-contemporary practice.[40]

In *The Secret Garden* the seeming disadvantage of ineffectual adulthood is turned to a very particular, pleasing kind of profit. This is that the children undertake and accomplish things all on their own. It is precisely here, and thus, that mere idealism becomes something more, something better. It is not enough to merely celebrate childlike qualities, whether they be abstract or actual. Qualities, in praxis, translate into capacities. Virtue, when combined with agency and opportunity, leads to autonomy and usefulness. Children's literature and film accomplished an enormous advance and deepening when they began to incorporate these developments into the record.

For all the mere sentimentality or virtue of early kid films and early film kids, Edwardian-era films and filmmakers also hinted at just this kind of advance. *A Four-Year-Old Hero*, a 1907 production by the pioneering French directress Alice Guy, is a tremendous case in point. The plot is simple. A nursemaid takes her four-year-old charge to the park, and loses her. However, far from being frightened or menaced, this child sets out to explore, and to act.

To reiterate: Griffith's angels are usually conceits, or abstractions. They embody prevalent perceptions, which also correspond with profound realities. Children are innocent and pure. They are also, always, vulnerable. This combination both reproves and saves the adult, who is shown his or her failings, and then provided with a mandate of care, or a means to overcome self-absorption and even adult-sized sinfulness. Very good. But there is a deep sentimentality in this, and if it is not completely untrue then it is certainly incomplete. It is not only that one has to add childish to childlike in order to paint a more thorough picture. Just as importantly, one has to consider that children have inner lives, and real perceptions, and, most importantly, the potential for growth.

Guy's film has bourgeois interior bookends, beginning and ending with comfortable and prosperous surroundings, with parents and a child and, very significantly, that servant. Ideological contradiction and caricature lurk here, vis-à-vis the working class. More positive is an ideological assertion that the film also makes about children. The servant may have lost the child, to a degree, but only to allow for an important discovery. Not only is this little one a paragon of virtue, but that virtue is expressed by the fact that she is also a paragon of resourcefulness, which is a virtue in itself.

This idea is developed in the film's three episodes. In the first, signaled by the intertitle "Apaches!," the little girl foils an attempted assault by tying her jump rope across a gateway. The perpetrators trip and stay tripped while the child fetches the policemen.

In the second episode, an unfortunate blind man is on the brink of falling into a canal. The child saves him by quite cleverly manipulating a moveable hydraulic platform, so that instead of lying parallel with the water and on the side opposite to the one the blind man is approaching, it now rotates to cross it perpendicularly, and form a bridge. A sweet elaboration of this situation is that the blind man now crosses that bridge without any knowledge of what has just happened, or what the child has just done for him. The four-year-old hero does not inform him either, thus making her more than just a generic angel, but rather placing her and her intervention in the much more particular, active and autonomous category of the guardian angel.

5. The Problem with Perfection and Ways Forward 129

In the last episode, our little hero encounters some "drunkards in danger," and extricates them with similarly decisive, matter-of-fact resourcefulness. *A Four-Year-Old Hero* approaches a kind of climax as the housemaid wakes up and finds the child gone. The actual climax, however, will end up being wonderfully anti-climactic, at least as compared to the often or obligatory last-minute rescues so typical of that time. How distinct, in surface and substance, from Griffith's *The Adventures of Dollie*! The child has made her way to the police station, quite calmly, and on her own. The police receive her with underplayed admiration and matter-of-fact affection—after all, this four-year-old character is played by an actual, flesh-and-blood four year old—and then they escort her quite calmly back home.

Decades later, and with similar sweet simplicity, the English author Shirley Hughes' *Alfie* series demonstrates the substance and continuity of this key literary and developmental motif. From 1981 to 1984, Hughes published four superb, developmentally attuned picture books about a little boy who encounters difficult challenges. In the first, *Alfie Gets In*, Alfie and Mum and little Rose come home from the shops. Mum turns the key and opens the door, takes the groceries inside, and then goes back out to get the baby and her push-chair. Just as she does so, Alfie enters and closes the door shut. Now he is inside, with the key, and everyone else is outside, without it.

Hughes stages this crisis and its resolution very beautifully, with the neighborhood street on the left side of the two-page spread, and Alfie, alone, on the right. The reader looks from one to the other, seeing the neighbors mobilize, hurrying to help, unstintingly pooling their ideas and resources. On the other side Alfie manages to move through surprise, the sudden awareness of his own insufficiency—he is all of three years old and he can't reach the door catch, nor the letter chute either—the distraught feelings that result, all the way through recovering and resolve to the finding of his very own solution to his own problem. While the adults encourage, console, counsel and then go clambering up on ladders, Alfie goes and gets his little chair, and places it next to the door, and climbs up, and opens it, and lets them all in.

This is a very dear assembly. It features what might seem a surpassingly small problem, though it is more than sufficiently large for a little child with limited capacities and experience. Solutions to that problem come untidily, and in pieces. The adults, though very anxiously engaged, are not quite successful. This is both disconcerting and liberating. Alfie, and of course the little child who shares this adventure with him, learns that he will eventually have to solve his own problems. Further, he learns that he can actually do so. And why not now? At the same time that he considers these solemn and exhilarating prospects, the child also feels abundant and reliable reserves of affection and loyalty from those around him. All these things together add up to self-reliance, sufficiency, emotional, intellectual and moral advance. I can be adequate to any challenge!

Here are realism—plausible complication and contradiction, interest in and sensitivity to process, a degree of duration—and reassurance both. This bracingly effective pattern continues through the next three Alfie books.

In the third installment, *Alfie Gives a Hand* (1983), Alfie attends a birthday party for the first time, and feels very nervous. He brings his favorite blanket along and withdraws himself, until the birthday boy's— brief, not especially blameworthy—misbehavior upsets another little guest, not to mention the birthday boy's mother. This discomfited guest looks to Alfie, who discovers that he can't help her and hold his blanket both. So he puts away another childish thing and succeeds in taking on a bit more of big-boy responsibility, and benevolence.

With regard to the present subject, the Alfie books demonstrate the continuity of Frances Hodgson Burnett's important innovation. First, they show us that children cause problems and that they are a problem. As ever, this is natural and expected. No one much minds or cares. But then the Alfie books, in parallel to the realities that we experience, or the realist ideal toward which we might well aspire, also demonstrate the processes by which the child ceases only to be the cause of those problems, and starts to find her own solutions.

This is not just, not only the great Christian paradox of finding oneself by losing oneself in service to others.[41] More basically and immediately, it is the developmental dictum that one finds herself precisely by learning to sustain herself, thus freeing everyone else to help the next dear, little, still-helpless child.

A similar, similarly moving development occurs in Tove Jansson's beautiful coming-of-age novella for children, *Moominland Midwinter* (1957). In the deepest winter, with its deepest cold, Jansson's fantastic, utterly invented Moomin-creatures are hibernating. Suddenly, prematurely, young Moomintroll wakes up. He does so just as all of the small non-hibernating creatures start to arrive in Moomin Valley, hoping to find food and warmth there. For some time Moomintroll resists their requests, anxious as he is about his mother's stores and her things, anxious, as he ever is, to be obedient and behave properly. But as the cold deepens and the small creatures' discomforts actually become dangerous, Moomintroll realizes that obedience is not merely a passive principle, and certainly not an inert one. Obedience is also active, evolving, a key to the acquisition of knowledge, skill, and wisdom. Obedient children, when they obey nurturing parents who gently nudge them forward, become autonomous, confident, wise, and able to act independently for themselves. Moomintroll opens up the house and the family's stores, invites everyone in, even goes so far as to let the more enterprising guests burn up some of the furniture. Presently, Mamma wakes up. Immediately, upon seeing what her son has done, and what everyone else has done as a consequence, she approves.[42]

Tove Jansson's work contains multitudes, and offers rich rewards for every kind of reader. Alice Guy and Shirley Hughes' tremendous creations are intentionally less expansive, less comprehensive. They prettily portray the benefits of burgeoning self-reliance, and properly forego some of the tremendous risks than come with the territory. Still, that territory, and the risk that goes along with it, needs exploring. One of the most evident, immediate, and ubiquitous of these risks is that the imperfectly perfect child, the child sent forth from shelter to experience challenges and develop self-reliance, just might become contrary, even ill-behaved. This may be quite natural, and healthy. Or, it can lead to the whirlwind.[43] A second, more troubling component of self-reliance is that risk doesn't always lead to reward, or only to error; in fact, sometimes risk means jeopardy and the possibility, the certainty, of harm.

Wards of the State

As we have seen, exemplary children can easily be upgraded or inflated to the superstitious, almost idolatrous rank of savior child. This frequent kid-culture refrain ascribes exceeding, implausible power to mere youngsters. The *Biograph Bulletin*, promoting D. W. Griffith's *In the Border States* (June 1910, Biograph No. 262): "There is no more powerful agency to stem the tide of affairs than the hand of the child. It has even smoothed the wrinkled front of grim-visaged war."[44]

Not so, or not barely. John Ford directed Shirley Temple in *Wee Willie Winkie* (1937), an immense expansion of Rudyard Kipling's glancing, modestly proportioned short story, first published in 1888.[45] In the original, a six-year-old English boy, the son of the regimental Colonel, faces down a group of twenty ill-intentioned Afghan insurgents. The story is a bit of a stretch, but it still lies within the realm of plausibility. The Afghan "bad men" relent, but not because of anything so magical or mythical in the child; rather, they do so because they know who Winkie is, and who his father is as well, and what the child means to the regiment, and what might happen if they were to harm him.

Some of the outlines of this story are retained in the 1937 film version. Some are not; the six-year-old boy is replaced by a curly-headed female cultural phenomenon, the glancing skirmish turns into a full mustering of troops, and a prudently strategic withdrawal becomes two lions, led by a little child, laying down together. Ford's film is a marvel, actually, the very best and most plausible utilization of Miss Temple's very particular talents. But it is a fable, and a fairy tale, and it knows it. Smoothing the wrinkled front of grim-visaged war?

William Shakespeare's Lady MacDuff has been conversing with her very precocious little boy. He has demonstrated remarkable penetration and wit in considering the ways of men and women, the instability of the local political landscape, and their possible effects on his family. The formidable Lady MacDuff is jousting a bit with this precocious child. She is gratified by his vast potential, coming so palpably to fruition before her eyes. She is also preoccupied, because there is danger in the air.

A servant enters, suddenly, warning Lady MacDuff of Macbeth's approaching assassins. "Be not found here; hence, with your little ones."[46] But the murderers follow hard upon, and arrive before the family can escape.

"Where is your husband?" demands the first assailant. Even in this extremity, Lady MacDuff replies in courageous, spirited fashion: "I hope in no place so unsanctified / Where such as thou mayst find him." "He's a traitor!" says the murderer. The child, who had just now been making genial mock of his father, leaps doughtily to his defense: "Thou liest, thou shag-eared villain." Brave, indomitable of spirit, fatally diminutive. "What! you egg," says the murderer, and stabs the boy to death.[47]

Children, smoothing the wrinkled front of grim-visaged war? *The Oxford Research Group*, 24 November of 2013:

> Based on the [published] data on children ... our principal findings are that: [b]y the end of August 2013, 11,420 children aged 17 years and younger had been recorded killed in the Syrian conflict, out of a total of 113,735 civilians and combatants killed. By far the primary cause of death reported for children was explosive weapons, killing 7,557 (71%) of the 10,586 children whose specific cause of death was recorded. Air bombardment was given as the cause of death for 2,008 of the children reported killed by explosive weapons. Small-arms fire was reported as the cause of death for 2,806 (26.5%) of the 10,586 children for whom cause of death was recorded, including 764 cases of summary execution

5. The Problem with Perfection and Ways Forward 133

and 389 cases of sniper fire with clear evidence of children being specifically targeted.... [F]our databases between them reported 128 children killed in the chemical attacks in Ghouta on 21 August 2013.

At least 112 cases of children tortured and killed were reported, including some of infant age.[48]

The last great flaw of the angelic myth is that it can become morbidly devoted to children's poignant weakness, and then mistake it for actual, practicable strength. The fact is that large-scale adult conflicts result in the annihilation of children. And in the absence of large-scale conflict, another sort of annihilation has still been all too common. The memoirs of the great Ukrainian film director Alexander Dovzhenko reflect a reality all too common throughout the history of children and families: "My parents had many children—fourteen in all, a variable group of whom two survived."[49]

A last facet of this same phenomenon is illustrated in the aptly scaled, heartbreaking climax to King Vidor's 1927 film, *The Crowd*. Even in the midst of seeming peace and prosperity, children also perish, for all of the care and keeping of those who love them, while the world carries heedlessly on.[50]

Myths have purpose, and power. Ideals and idealization can be and very often are rooted in realities. Millions and millions and millions have known blessing and bounty in their relations with children. And yet, though it might be well to withhold the actual statistics from the children themselves, at least for a while, dire reality demands its due.

Children's literature often bears the traces. James Barrie:

> The first to pass is Tootles, not the least brave but the most unfortunate of all that gallant band. He had been in fewer adventures than any of them, because the big things constantly happened just when he had stepped round the corner; all would be quiet, he would take the opportunity of going off to gather a few sticks for firewood, and then when he returned the others would be sweeping up the blood.[51]

This is indirect, and somewhat facetious, and possible to chalk up to high spirits. The adult record cannot be shrugged off so easily.

> "Alas," said the mouse, "the world is growing smaller every day. At the beginning it was so big that I was afraid. I kept running and running, and I was glad when at last I saw walls far away to the right and left. But these long walls have narrowed so quickly that I am in the last chamber already, and there in the corner stands the trap that I must run into."
> "You only need change your direction," said the cat, and ate it up.[52]

This is piquant, Aesop-like, fabulously removed from any concrete referent or measurable harm. Elsewhere, Kafka doesn't beat around the bush so much.

> The sun is already setting, but down below you see it lighting up the face of the little girl who strolls along looking about her, and at the same time you see her eclipsed by the shadow of the man behind overtaking her.[53]

As excerpted, this appalling Düsseldorfian fragment is profoundly inappropriate for child consumption; at the same time, it corresponds exactly to the way that children have so often been consumed.[54] Here, too, is the world as so many children have experienced it—stripped of sentimentality, or mercy, or any kind of reassurance. Its place in the record destabilizes the bright hopeful ideal, which we continue to present to our children with fear, and with trembling.

Modernity, with its dire, documentable realities and its ample narrative testimonies, no longer blathers so idolatrously on the subject of children. There is advantage to this, but surely a loss as well. Here is Modernity, not blathering: "Across the track on a long, low tin building, someone had painted 'The meek shall inherit the earth.' The letters sloped every which way so that the message seemed to have been painted by a child or an idiot."[55] Help thou my unbelief!

Numerous texts in children's literature and film acknowledge and incorporate these terrible things. Though they generally do so with a measure of love and hope and humor, there is nevertheless a solemn tinge to the recounting.

In Tove Jansson's *Moominsummer Madness* (1955) the utterly indomitable, outlandishly minute Little My has gone missing, washed down the river in a sewing basket. She meets this mischance as unflappably, as impertinently as ever. Jansson's description whispers, however, that she is actually in danger. Eventually the ever calm and reliable Snufkin finds and retrieves her, puts her in his pocket and brings her back. He reassures her, all the while. As ever, she scorns such softness. But what a slim chance![56]

Near the beginning of Laura Ingalls Wilder's *Little House on the Prairie* (1935), the Ingalls family is crossing a creek when the water suddenly rises. Young Mary and Laura and Carrie Ingalls are in the back of their covered wagon, frightened, only dimly aware of the danger or of its magnitude. They are frightened, but also somewhat reassured, in that they are being overseen and protected by their beloved, capable parents. But

Wilder's artful descriptions give us to understand that Ma and Pa Ingalls are equally as, even more anxious than their children. This is because, unlike the children, they fully understand the risk at hand and that sometimes in the face of fire or flood the young and old are ultimately equally powerless.[57]

The Ingalls family manages to make it through this misadventure, and any number of subsequent near-disasters. But it is with more than a little privation that they do so, and often at considerable cost. Even at that, they are very fortunate. Sonali Deraniyagala was holding the hand of one of her sons when she fled from the onrushing Indonesian Tsunami on 26 December 2004. It caught her up, though, and she never saw anything of the child, or of her other child, or of her husband, or of her parents, again.[58]

Warner Bros.' *Tweetie Pie* (1947), the first film in which Tweety and Sylvester appear together, begins in a freezing, snow-filled yard at night, with Tweety trying to warm himself over a cigar butt. The cat who would soon become Sylvester is lurking nearby. Later, the woman who would become Granny brings them both inside. She tries to make the cat kiss the bird. He eats him instead. Moralists and sentimentalists should take note: for all that Androcles or Aesop's mouse may claim to the contrary, it is generally true that when Sunday School uplift meets naturalism, naturalism brings out the bludgeon, and prevails.

Gathering and Synthesizing the Strands of Idealism

We have been asking ourselves about the nature of childhood and the essence of children. We have learned that children are heavenly, as Jesus stated. We have seen (and will see further, in chapter 6) that children are a problem—maybe even *the* problem, as Paul suggested. Books and films have very effectively illustrated these ideas, and have also twisted them into all sorts of pretzels.

This is an extraordinarily rich subject, and there are so many more wonderful, contradictory, invaluable voices that inform it. L. M. Montgomery's Anne Shirley, referenced briefly above, was no outlier, but rather a member of a very important sorority. She was a Glad Girl, a personage, and a phenomenon, that could at times exemplify the most extreme degrees of infantilizing, objectifying idealization.[59] However, what could be so was not necessarily so; Anne Shirley also represents the best of the glad impulse, and was instrumental in establishing new plausibilities, nuance and substance in the portrayal of children.

An extremely important part of this sorority is film's own Mary Pickford. Pickford, or the Pickford persona, was first formed at the Ground Zero of D. W. Griffith's childish menagerie at Biograph. But she soon struck out on her own, playing child characters in a remarkable number of films that went out of their way to remember, incorporate, and honor the healthy contrariness of real children. For all the skillful calculation of her films, Pickford strove for and very often succeeded in striking a balance between the sweetness and the spiritedness of actual children. Not excessive, nor defective: allowing, of course, for changes in custom and sensibility, an impressive number Pickford's feature films elucidate Aristotle's mean as it pertains to children.

Her contributions are far from glancing or incidental. Pickford entertained, inspired, and indoctrinated millions with a really remarkable number of wonderfully layered child-performances: *Tess of the Storm Country* (March 1914), *Fanchon, the Cricket* (May 1915), *The Dawn of Tomorrow* (June 1915), *Rags* (August 1915), *The Foundling* (January 1916), *The Poor Little Rich Girl* (March 1917), *Rebecca of Sunnybrook Farm* (September 1917), *The Little Princess* (November 1917), *M'liss* (May 1918), *The Hoodlum* (September 1919), *Heart o' the Hills* (November 1919), *Pollyanna* (January 1920), *Little Lord Fauntleroy* (September 1921) and the remake of *Tess of the Storm Country* (November 1922).

After Mary Pickford comes Shirley Temple and a fascinating return to pre-war idealistic platitudes, to Griffithian appeals to adult conscience and calls for adult action: *Little Miss Marker, Baby Takes a Bow, Now and Forever, Bright Eyes* (all 1934), *Our Little Girl* (a classic child-centered family reconciliation romance), *Curly Top, The Littlest Rebel* (all 1935), *Stowaway* (1936), *Heidi* (1937), *Rebecca of Sunnybrook Farm, Little Miss Broadway* (both 1938), *The Little Princess,* and *Susannah of the Mounties* (both 1939).

And this is saying nothing of the indomitable Deanna Durbin! If brave little Shirley Temple could do little for herself, then Durbin (starting with *Three Smart Girls*, 1936), entering into her adolescence, was instrumental in exploring the place of self-reliance in this whole equation. The oft-derided, as oft-condemned Stratemeyer Literary Syndicate[60] may have churned 'em out like sausage, but the artless formulae of its Rover Boys and Bobbsey Twins, its Tom Swift and Hardy Boys and Nancy Drew franchises also hinted to millions of enraptured young readers that they too could take on, take measure of and solve their own problems. Though

5. The Problem with Perfection and Ways Forward 137

scoffers may further deride, the same goes, and most productively, for Mickey and Judy in *Babes in Arms* (1939), *Strike Up the Band* (1940), *Babes on Broadway* (1941), not to mention the sublime *Muppets Take Manhattan* (1984). Ms. Durbin also contributes her delightful determination to this conversation, as do Erich Kästner's epochal Weimar-threatened, kid-resilient novels *Emil and the Detectives* (1929) and *Emil and the Three Twins* (1934), or the Ealing Studio's jaw-dropping post-war paean to child sovereignty, *Hue and Cry* (1947).

And harm? As Siegfried Kracauer suggests,[61] Gerhard Lamprecht and Billy Wilder's 1931 film version of Kästner's first Emil novel is aware of and hints at the malice and the menace of Hitler's Brownshirts. Its bravely optimistic conclusion would, of course, be no match for history. What can we make of this intractable, impenetrable mystery, as we conclude this chapter?

One possibility, partaking of dialectical impulse and optimism, is to combine terms, or hybridize. When a reasonable measure of perfection and self-reliance and an awareness of what the lone world really has in store are mixed together, inadequacies can be replaced by plenitudes.

Tweety Bird was not consciously created as an heir to film history's previous angelic innocents. Nor, for all the savor of his occasional and sometimes considerable mischievousness, was he intended as a counter to them. Still, as a matter of more or less spontaneous genetic descent, Tweety quite nicely, quite sweetly synthesizes the child-motifs that we have thus far surveyed. *All a Bir-r-r-d* (June 1950), the fifth of the Tweety films directed by Friz Freleng, beautifully illustrates this balance.

As with most every entry in this tremendous series, the initial setting and the accompanying scenario are superbly simple, an involving mixture of the absurd—the situation is a correlative to the idea that the situation invokes and the emotions that it generates—and the archetypal. A cat and a bird are enclosed in their respective cages, immediately adjacent to each other in the baggage car of a train.

We have just seen how the hard world can impinge upon children's narratives. Outside of the confines of children's discourse, there is often a dispiriting, even frightening sense of constant, terminal unease. Were it an exclusively adult franchise, we might find echoes in this film and its setting of the cataclysmic conclusion to Emile Zola's *La Bête Humaine*, of Jean-Paul Sartre's *No Exit*, or Luis Buñuel's *The Exterminating Angel*. We would certainly hear the strains of Aesop's more dog-eat-dog, the-strong-devour-the-weak sensibilities, not to mention Jack London's often annihilating Arctic tales. Here is a parallel, in metaphorical or fabulous form, of August Strindberg's agonizing assertion from *The Father*: "It's man versus woman [birds and cats, predator and prey, commanding and commanded], all the day long, endlessly."[62] Were this an exclusively adult franchise we would have enmity, only the fittest surviving, all adding up to a very hard world for the little ones.

That may well be the world of adult discourse, and the way of much of the world itself. It is not the way here, or in the wonderfully frequent occasions in which children's discourse harmonizes the various tensions that exist in its many contexts. Somehow, Sylvester gets loose, and starts stacking up the luggage to try to get at Tweety. He fails to do so. In fact, he repeatedly fails to do so, for a number of wonderfully staged, wonderfully varied reasons. *All a Bir-r-r-d* features a practically scientific series of momentum jokes, relating to some of the different velocities and trajectories, the different operations of the laws of physics as they relate to a cat in a series of precarious positions and to a train that keeps on starting and stopping and then starting again.

Of course *All a Bir-r-r-d* features one further law, as yet undiscovered by physicists, but of incalculable significance and reassurance for young viewers, and for very young viewers in particular. Sylvester is relentless in his designs to eat this tiny, (seemingly) defenseless creature. As he attempts to do so, he is repeatedly and quite punishingly foiled, and thrown back and forth besides. Meanwhile, and on the other hand, Tweety seems to be immune to these natural or physical forces, as well as being impervious to what would otherwise be Sylvester's evolutionarily determined actions and their evolutionary inevitable result.

As with the idealized, sentimentalized, and often jeopardized child of Victorian discourse and of early film, Tweety is vastly vulnerable. This vulnerability is forcefully established from the start and is evident in the great disproportion between his stature and the stature of his nemesis, and in the severe containment and immobility that are imposed upon him. These things will be constants throughout the course of the entire series. But unlike didacticism's calls-to-action, or sentimentality's bathos, Tweety's vulnerability turns out to only one of his attributes, and quite possibly the least of them.

Tweety is innocent, as a dove. But he is also as wise as a serpent.[63] He is well aware of the ways of men, or of cats. This makes him wary, and helps him to survive. Strangely enough, his wariness doesn't make him fearful. This is partly because beloved, sheltered, privileged children have less to fear. Tweety is all of those things. Just as importantly, and more to the point in the present context, self-reliant children have less to fear as well. While he is quite frequently preserved because of the intervention of a variety of protectors, it turns out that Tweety can also hold his own.

We have already considered some of the dire components of 1947's *Tweetie Pie*, that inaugural entry in the Tweety/Sylvester/Freleng series.[64] After its hazardous opening, Tweety goes on to find himself in any number of difficult predicaments. He is not in the least bit phased. Here, as elsewhere, Tweety proves himself to be a veritable dynamo of invention and resourcefulness. Where did he get that blow torch? Where did that pin come from? How did he learn to be such an effective demolitions man?

This narrative template, this array of patterns, structures the entire series and typifies how well films have served, cared for and cultivated the myth of the good child. *Puddy Tat Trouble* (1951) finds Tweety outside in the wintertime, perched like some avian pillar saint on a post between two very urban apartment buildings, in which dwell *two* cats who will soon be bent on his annihilation. It is a superb setting, elemental and, again, somehow primordial. It evokes Samuel Beckett—*"A country road. A tree. Evening."*[65]—or perhaps a New Testament parable. This setting, with Tweety so exposed, so surrounded by implacable antagonists, powerfully communicates the usual idea. The vulnerability of children! Except for this particular child. In a happy combination of reassurance and reversal, the meek inherit the earth. And in the same way that perfect children (like those essayed by Bloch, Miyazaki, Olmi, Montgomery) are not actually perfect, Tweety is not particularly meek.

Tweety's eventual triumph is not very consistent with the setting—Naked City, Asphalt Jungle, Mean Streets—nor with the urban naturalism that tended to emerge from it. In this way, the film functions like other Warner Bros. cartoons that domesticated the horror film and the deep fears that horror films reflect and address. Whether it be *Puddy Tat Trouble* or the mad scientist and his split-ended monster in *Hair Raising Hare*, the voracious but inept vampire in *Transylvania 6-5000* or *Birth of a Notion*'s delightfully not-quite-threatening, Peter Lorre–resembling medical experimenter, many of these cartoons were able to address deep anxiety with the efficiency and effectiveness of an actual fairy tale. These films are partly, and very centrally, commercial products. They are also gifts of regard and reassurance and fond encouragement. Here are the realities, kids. And you'll be all right.

Once again, and in summary: if Tweety is a synthesis of child types, then what does all this have to do with D. W. Griffith's sentimentally angelic children? Well, Warner Bros. cartoons were not especially interested in sentimentality, and they were hardly angelic. But allowing for distinct sensibilities and the changing of perspectives over the course of a few decades, Tweety actually slots into this lineage very nicely. He is the constantly menaced, always vulnerable, never vanquished child. He is surrounded by danger, but also, always, by advocates (Granny, the conductor, the bulldog, laws of nature and his at-will circumvention thereof). In this way, he is that common literary/cinematic catalyst for adult improvement, the focus of the adult's generous and socially constructive impulses. More importantly, and because your minders will not always be mindful of you, Tweety also and always has himself to rely on, his own considerable intelligence and initiative and courage. With all of these resources at hand he gets out of every scrape.

Griffith's children often operated as part of a didactic communication. Warner Bros. cartoons tended overwhelmingly to be antididactic, and yet here they contain a clear lesson. This is a positive message for youngsters, growing and learning about the world and its challenges as well as its opportunities. It is a positive message even as the youngster learns about all of the things from which he might not be able to extricate himself. Reassuring fantasy or fable must eventually give way to often intractable reality. And yet, even at the child's stickiest actual impasse, the likes of courageous, constant Tweety will continue to offer perspective and reassurance.

The second possibility, and conclusion to this chapter and this discussion of idealized childhood, is not to worry about strategizing, or synthesizing, or arguments. The second possibility is to observe, and to absorb, and to understand.

Jacques Tati's exquisite *M. Hulot's Holiday* (1953) features an isolated, solitary jewel of a sequence that very nicely encapsulates the truth, the beauty, and the future of the angelic child. An ice cream cart sits in the middle of the frame, which it nearly fills. Its proprietor sits on this side of the wagon, on the right, turned three-quarters to the audience and absently reading a magazine. We are at a beach, in Normandy, in the summertime. In a moment, a little hand reaches over from the other side of the cart. The little boy, whom we can't quite see, holds up two fingers, and a coin. Barely taking notice the desultory ice cream man takes the money and dispenses the ice cream. Continuing to read, and without ever looking at his small patron, he holds the cones out to him. They are barely within the little boy's reach.

Two little hands strain upwards and take tentative hold. The boy, all of three or maybe four years old, comes cheerfully out from behind the cart, turns and begins to walk in the opposite direction, out toward the back of the frame. He is a stout, doughty little lad, handsomely attired in a rather brief, accidentally if slightly revealing pair of swimming trunks. He comes to the foot of a steep flight of stairs, the top of which rises out of the upper part of the frame. Still holding tightly and a bit uncertainly to the ice cream cones, he steps up. The stair is too high to for him to comfortably navigate, and he falters momentarily. The spectator, who has observed with patient interest this previously unknown little personage, may find himself gasping slightly. The easy and conventional delights of pretty little children on film take on a new aspect when jeopardy is introduced.

Unfazed, however, the little boy rights himself, and up-stop, up-stop, begins to climb up out of the frame. Tati cuts to the top of the stairs as the child reaches them. He is still a little bit unsteady on his pins, though this being how well he can walk, and having never walked any more certainly, the child does not seem to be aware of his vulnerability. Crossing a small expanse of pavement the child now comes to a closed door, with a doorknob that is, like the ice cream wagon down below, barely within his reach. The suspense that attended the child's uncertain passage up the stairs now increases markedly as he reaches his left hand up to turn the handle, all the while continuing to hold one of the ice cream cones in that same hand.

He grasps the handle, turns it downward, slowly, as the cone tips inexorably downward as well. The spectator's discomfiture increases. Relieved that the child has safely navigated this perilous flight of stairs, he is now in agonies in case the ice cream doesn't survive the journey. But at last the handle releases, and the door opens. The ice cream cones are safe. The child walks forward into the room, where he finds another fresh-faced little three-or-four-year old boy, seated on a bench waiting for him. The first little boy steps up to his smiling friend, reaches out his hand, and passes him one of the ice cream cones. Then he climbs up on the bench himself, still a bit unsteadily, and turns around to seat himself. They partake, together.

Much of the appeal of this sequence is simple and completely conventional. A protagonist has set and reached his objective, after having surmounted obstacles on the way to doing so. This is the essence of linear narrative, which provides the structure to a great majority of the films that have ever been made. Of course this seemingly gratuitous seventy seconds of screen time, devoted to a leisurely paced digressive trifle, is also and actually a masterful bit of duration and suspense. The extra *frisson* here comes from the child's simultaneous vulnerability and indomitability.

He is uncertain, inadequate, insufficiently scaled, such that when he actually prevails, the tympani thunders.

We have seen this before, in Griffith and most everywhere else. The familiar truth and beauty of this sequence, and of so many more like it, lies in its perfect, exquisite illustration of fraternity, of dauntless courage in the face of the void, of the second Great Commandment,[66] not to mention of how a little child shall lead us. The aforementioned future is that, like Frances Hodgson Burnett's Mary Lennox, these children are doing something for themselves. A child's sweetness is sufficient for a while, but he must also move forward.

Children and childhood are precious, but to refuse maturity, whether developmentally or literarily, is to embrace an unhealthy arrest. As we shall see in this book's last chapter, seminal publications and a number of contemporary commercial films (*The Little Prince, The Polar Express*) will try to deny this developmental commonplace, but the best of the films and of the books will affirm and illustrate that it is good to grow up, in part so that we can treasure and help our own children as they begin their own journeys.

6

Bad Boys and Demon Seeds

"My goodness!" Mary said. "I couldn't be as mean as that Nellie Oleson."
Laura thought: "I could. I could be meaner to her than she is to us, if Ma and Pa would let me."[1]

Laura and Carrie Ingalls, upon being warned about the crews of rough men with their rough language, and upon being told, unequivocally, to stay away:

"Yes, Pa," Laura promised, and Carrie almost whispered, "Yes, Pa," Carrie's eyes were large and frightened. She did not want to hear rough language, whatever rough language might be. Laura would have liked to hear some, just once, but of course she must obey Pa.[2]

Naughtiness as Corrective, and as Threat, in the Discourse of Children

The Angel Child is prevalent, even dominant, in the annals of classic children's literature and film. Dominant, but not uncontested: George Bernard Shaw, for one, offers a corrective, contrary view: "'I must have been an insufferable child; all children are.'"[3]

Shaw's sentiment is also an important part of the record and reality of childhood. The English poet Charles Causley has a superb poetic counter to the customary, too often uncritical idealization of children. In "Infant Song" a grandmother has been invited to praise her daughter's new child, but finds it difficult to unreservedly do so. She cannot help but wonder why he burns "with brimstone heat." She hesitates over his cloven hooves and fish-hook hands, and she feels outright concern about his sharp teeth, pointed ears, and "eyes that flicker in the dark."[4]

Causley's witty verse articulates a contrary view, a strong minority voice. It may not be universal, but it is ubiquitous. The notion of naughty children crosses every border and culture, is rooted in the past, and radiates into the future. It can be merely glancing, as when Plato holds that to act hypocritically, even inconsistently, is to be "no better than children."[5] It can also be summative, as when gentle Blaise Pascal states the following: "*Mine, thine*—'This dog is mine,' said those poor children; 'that is my place in the sun.' Here is the beginning and the image of the usurpation of all the earth."[6] The concept of original sin further underscores and extends this sentiment. Childish urges and selfishness are not only the root of strife and inequity, but of iniquity as well.

It is for reasons like these that so much of children's discourse in early modern times is devoted to the child's instruction. This particular strain can have something of the rod about it, and certainly much of correction. The English Romantics, as well as their successors, more consistently praised children, in part as a response to the puritanical, even punitive sternness of that which went before. But the puritanical impulse runs deep, as do the biblical precepts that inform it. And even when the precept is not being urged by some beetle-browed, bible-black religious authoritarian, there is still plenty of convincing, often gleeful testimony as to the deep, durable naughtiness of children.

A Caution and a Corrective: Charlie Chaplin Wages Battle with a Brat

Charlie Chaplin's *The Pilgrim* (1923) features an audacious sequence in which an admirably awful child wreaks utter, unsentimentalized havoc on all that he surveys. For reasons that need not be detailed here, Charlie is impersonating a minister of the gospel, and in that capacity he visits his new lodgings, where dwell a faithful widow and her pretty daughter. They are presently joined by a trio of Sunday callers: a family comprised of a loquacious, strategically neglectful mother (Mai Wells), a bland, ineffectual father (Chaplin's half-brother, Sydney), and their four- or five-year-old son (Dean "Dinky" Riesner).

They settle in for a visit. Mother sits down, screen right, and begins engaging the widow in conversation. Charlie and the father sit together on a pair of straight-backed chairs, facing the spectator at screen left. There is a chest of drawers behind them. There is a fishbowl sitting on top of the chest of drawers, and a strip of flypaper lies beside it. It will

6. Bad Boys and Demon Seeds 145

emerge that these two objects contain a dire inevitability like unto Hedda Gabler's loaded gun.[7] The little boy, dressed in a neat sailor's jumpsuit, Mary Jane shoes, and a straw Gondolier's hat with a long ribbon trailing from the back, will turn out to be even more dangerous, Hedda and Løvborg all in one.

This young prodigy begins his ministrations by running up to his just-seated mother and squeezing her bosom, which is to say her breasts, and that none too gently. He then puts his hands on her cheeks and slaps them both, twice. The mother, unfazed, and evidently quite accustomed, shoos the child in the direction of the gentlemen. Charlie the faux–Minister, wishing to play his part convincingly, lifts the child up on his lap. The child makes two fists and strikes Charlie with a quick left and a right and a left. Charlie precipitously hands the child over to his father.

The young man now hits his father with a right roundhouse, at which point the father pushes the child back in Charlie's direction. The child throws a wild right, which connects. Charlie looks at his counterpart incredulously. His counterpart does not respond. Charlie receives a left jab to the nose. He pushes the child gently away, slightly to his left. The child steps upon a footstool that stands beside the chair and renews his attack. From the side he delivers two quick right hooks.

As mentioned, "Dinky" Dean Riesner portrayed this young hellion. At the time of filming he was a small child, and his most forceful efforts could never have done the damage that the script requires of him. It is Chaplin that enhances the effect of Riesner's barrage through effective pantomime, through a superbly variegated array of exaggerated starts and head snaps and curly-haired flourishes. This convincing pantomime is a pantomime nevertheless.

Now the infant throws a left hook, and Charlie, or the Minister, finally responds. This is to raise an index finger in remonstrance. He also shoots an appealing, interrogatory glance at the child's still not-intervening father. The father continues to not intervene. Now comes another left hook, and another, and a fourth, and a right jab. Charlie passes the child back again, and the father takes a left of his own. Meanwhile, mother chatters on.

Father pushes his alleged issue back in front of Charlie. The child swings, and misses for the first time. This causes his hat to fall to the floor, and the gentlemen exchange indulgent smiles, perhaps like the ones that typically attended more conventional, sentimental child-featuring films of the time. They help the child with his hat. They place it back upon the child's head, for the which service Charlie receives a ringing left-handed slap. The child jumps back on that stool and immediately connects with a rather devastating right, right across Charlie's nose, from the side. A right jab. A right jab. A left hook. A left roundhouse. Jab. Hook. Cross. Charlie sits and takes his punishment, like Marlon Brando at the end of *On the Waterfront*, or in the finger-smashing sequence in *One-Eyed Jacks*, or through the whole brutal, battering conclusion of *The Chase*.

The child is now ushered back toward Father, who receives a right jab, right to the spectacles. As Father bends down to look for this pair of glasses, the little scamp runs back to mother, who wastes no time in sending him back from whence he came. "Go play with the gentleman," urges the intertitle. After pausing briefly to give his mother another affectionate slap in the face, the child exits the frame, enters the contiguous diegetic space, and slugs Charlie right on the jaw. Back he goes, onto the stool, from which he throws another right. At this point Charlie pushes the child back, just a little. Another right hand is met with another, slightly firmer push. Father is, after all, now looking for his spectacles. A man, even a minister of the Gospel, can only take so much.

Not at all nonplussed, the fiendish imp actually feints now, pretending to hit high, then driving low, right into Charlie's throat. Now the child retreats, leaves this frame, and enters the next. Here is a chair, upon which sits a knitting basket, which contains a ball of yarn and a sharp needle. The child touches the needle, then looks speculatively at the gentlemen. He extricates the needle and positions it in both hands. He runs out of the present frame, and then back into the previous one, and behind those straight-backed chairs upon which the long-suffering gentlemen are seated. Suddenly Charlie leaps up, recoiling now as if his curls, or perhaps his posterior, were all aflame. Now we cut back and, for the very first time, get a hint of reproof from mother. But the dark cloud of her censorious glance is quickly succeeded by the sunshine of her indulgent and approving smile. So Father gets skewed next.

This causes Charlie, or perhaps the minister that he is impersonating, to lead the child out from behind the chairs. He gives the child a corrective look that comes close to nearly bordering on sternness, and then tells him to go play with his mama. The child goes, but of course comes immediately back. Film director Chaplin, ever the master of the evolving gag or the compounding comic situation,[8] now has his small adversary climb up on the dresser, where he finds a convenient cup, dips it in the fishbowl, and throws four facefuls at the unsuspecting adults below.

In doing this, the child has inadvertently knelt on the flypaper, sticking himself firmly thereto. The gentlemen immediately rise to his aid, perhaps because we are enjoined to suffer the little children, however

6. Bad Boys and Demon Seeds 147

hellacious they may be. The result is that the child with admirable resourcefulness contrives to transfer the flypaper from his own shins to all over his father's face. After a brief and furious struggle father removes the flypaper, which reveals him, finally, to be angry. This means that he runs over and tattles on the child to his mother.

Most of this extended, distended sequence has been covered by medium and two-and three-shots. Now we remove to a shot of the entire room, like the one that established this space and initiated this whole routine. The kindly widow/hostess leads father away to clean himself. Now, finally, Mother springs into action. She grasps the child, sits down, places him very firmly upon her lap, and very firmly scolds him. She then rises and turns, revealing that the piece of flypaper is now stuck to her bottom—shades of Ibsen, once again, not to mention Chaplin's customarily exquisite comic economy; at his frequent best, nothing is ever wasted, squandered or left behind. Off she storms, leaving the faux–Minister alone with this most contrary and recalcitrant congregant.

This beautifully distributed sequence lasts all of four minutes and thirty-six seconds. Within that time, by this referee's count, the child landed twenty-four scoring blows on Chaplin alone. There have been flurries of violent action, with respites and cut-aways and editorial, almost Greek-choral pauses that allow the audience to consider and savor and be amazed. This sequence is a tremendous comic construction, and a tremendous comic accomplishment. Now it resolves with a twice-tremendous, positively Beethovenian cadence that not only satisfyingly concludes the business at hand, but also makes a ringing statement about the other, awful side of the childish equation that we have been considering.

Again, it is Charlie, with the child. What would Jesus do in this situation, especially considering his clear instructions about the nature of children, and of the adult's responsibility toward them? This particular child is very pleased with himself. He has a very pleased expression on his face. Charlie decides to drop his charade of circumspection and take leave of his erstwhile charge. He stands up and moves to leave the frame. The child stands up and grabs his coattails, leaving the frame with him.

Charlie and the child enter into the next shot and then come to a stop. They are standing, full frame. Charlie dexterously removes the child's hand from his skirt. He dexterously places his foot in the center of the child's chest, and, without a harsh word or angry expression, firmly and fully and dexterously extends his leg. The child tumbles to the ground— no performance this—tips back on his bottom, his legs all tapsalteerie.[9] It may be said that at this outlandish affront to the Inherent Innocence of

Childhood, Chaplin, the fly-papered father, and most every incredulous member of the delighted audience feels not a pang. Charlie raises one last amonestary finger, gives the child a last amonestary look, and exits the scene.

In his autobiography, Chaplin covers *The Pilgrim* in a mere couple of paragraphs.[10] He simply states that it was the means by which he satisfied the terms of his contract with the First National film company. He has nothing to say about the story, about any technical considerations, or possible significance. He certainly has nothing to say about the sequence that we have just considered at such length. Chaplin biographer David Robinson likewise passes by the sequence in question, pausing only to praise it as an admirable bit of sustained comedy and to confirm that the little Dean Riesner was in fact a very nice child, who had to be coached very considerably in order to have him play so effectively against type and disposition.[11]

And yet, for all of this comparative inattention, *The Pilgrim* remains a great milestone in the portrayal of childhood, especially in film. It was released just prior to the generally acknowledged end of the golden age of children's literature. Although many of that period's milestones were quite radically ambivalent about the nature and, more specifically, the unmitigated purity of the child, the fact remains that sentimentality and idealization still tended to inform the image and narrative of childhood. As we have seen, film overwhelmingly tended to place itself in the middle of this broad, sweet main stream.

The Kid (1921) is quite justifiably Chaplin's most celebrated contribution to this whole conversation. It is profoundly accomplished, in a Classical, conservative way. What it says about children, and their effects on the adults that care for them, is quite familiar. *The Pilgrim*, on the other hand, anticipates a real sea change. In 1929 Jean de Brunhoff's pioneering picture book *The Story of Babar* will begin with the sudden, violent death of the protagonist's parent. More troublingly, in films like Carl Laemmle, Jr., and James Whale's *Frankenstein* (1931), Fritz Lang's *M* (1931), and Alfred Hitchcock's *Sabotage* (1936), violent death will begin to be visited upon children themselves.

These are not the moralistic or manipulative demises so often imputed to—and too often dismissed because of—the Victorian era. They are not at all like the satirically comic demises featured in Heinrich Hoffmann's properly celebrated *Der Struwwelpeter/Shockheaded Peter* (1845), or in Hilaire Belloc's elaborations thereof.[12] In part because of the often troubling power of image, as opposed to the often indirectness of literary description, the deaths in these films are quite viscerally shocking, the more so because their causes cannot quite be remedied. The culprits will be caught, but with this kind of loss, the world remains forever out of joint.

The difference in Chaplin is that he is not exploring the idea that children are subject to terrible danger, or even that this danger is often irremediable. Neither is he saying that the world is corrupt, or that children can fall victim to and eventually grow into that corruption. The great difference, after Alice and Jo and Meg and the Piper at the Gates and Winnie the Pooh, is that children are actually a part of that danger, and that it is quite possible that corruption lies at the very, childish root.

There were, of course, precedents to this notion. We have touched upon original sin, and the sometimes fierceness of preceptual communication for children.[13] Even the Golden Age of children's literature—from Carroll and Kingsley to A. A. Milne—is not so straightforwardly celebrative about them. The Panto promotions and the latest stage revival of *Peter Pan* may not be sufficiently aware of the positively chilling note that James Barrie injects at the introduction of his creature:

> [Wendy] started up with a cry, and saw the boy, and somehow she knew at once that he was Peter Pan. If you or I or Wendy had been there we should have seen that he was very like Mrs. Darling's kiss. He was a lovely boy, clad in skeleton leaves and the juices that ooze out of trees but the most entrancing thing about him was that he had all his first teeth. When he saw she was a grown-up, he gnashed the little pearls at her.[14]

There is an infernal frisson to this, and these dental details hint at all of the unnatural and arrested that Barrie will explore throughout his great and troubling novel. On the face of it, Peter Pan is childhood triumphant. But the resonance, the brilliance of Barrie's creation, is that Pan's triumph is so tinged with tragedy. Angels like George Eliot's Little Eppie aside, it may not be seemly for children to carry the day.

Peter Pan articulates the idea that unchecked childhood can be dangerous, even demonic. Carlo Collodi is more matter-of-fact about the problem, and at the same time more marvelously Catholic. Pinocchio's literary advent is very different from the one portrayed at the beginning of Walt Disney's more familiar film version. In Collodi's original, Geppetto starts making his puppet by fashioning its frame. Then he works on the hair, then the forehead and the eyes, which immediately begin to move and to look. "When Geppetto saw those two wooden eyes looking at him, he did not like it at all, and he said angrily, 'Naughty wooden eyes, why are you staring at me?'"[15] The animation or birth of Disney's Pinocchio is fairy-generated, attended by the divine signifiers of what Paul Schrader has referred to as the abundant style.[16] The abundant style uses heightened techniques—shots and cuts, music and effects that surge and soar—to portray the sacred, or the miraculous, on film. Collodi's character also comes to life quite miraculously, or maybe magically. But there is nothing divine in its sudden animation, and certainly not in the way that it immediately starts behaving.

> After the eyes, [Geppetto] made the nose; but as soon as it was finished, it began to grow. It grew, and it grew, and in a few minutes' time it was as long as if there was no end to it.
> Poor Geppetto worked fast to shorten it; but the more he cut it off, the longer that insolent nose became.
> After the nose, he made the mouth; but before he had finished it, it began to laugh and poke fun at him.[17]

Of course Disney places this nasal incident much, much later in his story, and in doing so takes a very fundamental, meaningful liberty with the original text. In Collodi, there isn't a star or wish or beautiful song. There is no angel or fairy—at least not yet. As a result there is no causation, no rational explanation for this breath of life. Furthermore, Geppetto is in attendance the whole time. He may not understand what has happened, but he has witnessed, has participated in, the whole thing.

As for the puppet, Disney's limpid-eyed infant does not transgress, his nose doesn't begin to grow, until scoundrels enter in to tempt him. He has previously been blameless, and for all of his later errors—he is too easily influenced and he embellishes—he is still, always, dispositionally innocent. Collodi's infant is obviously an entirely different, fallen, even phallic case.

As the literary episode proceeds, Pinocchio continues to behave badly. "This cheeky, mocking behavior made Geppetto feel sadder than ever before in his life. He turned to Pinocchio, and said, 'You scoundrel of a son! You are not even finished, and you already disobey your father! That's bad, my boy—very bad!' And he wiped away a tear."[18]

Things get worse: "There were still the legs and feet to make. When Geppetto had finished [them], he received a kick on the nose."[19] This is not restlessness, or the croup, or fear in the night. Collodi's child is wildly, willfully impertinent from the first. There is no infant grace period, no hint at all of the film's more familiar, idealized angelic behavior. From the first, as well, the parent is left to wonder if all this trouble is worth it: "'It serves me right,' [Geppetto] said to himself. 'I should have thought of it before. Now it is too late.'"[20]

Mark Twain hilariously and quite devastatingly punctures the notion of perfect childhood—and of the propagandistic nature of good child stories—in short satirical pieces like "The Story of the Good Little Boy" and "The Story of the Bad Little Boy."[21] He is famous for celebrating the healthy inconsistency and contrariness of children with the character of Tom Sawyer, especially in *Tom Sawyer* itself. Huckleberry Finn, too, is taken to represent some kind of salutary waywardness that is native to children. Twain, however, is far from being simply celebratory. Tom Sawyer's ministrations during the last third of *The Adventures of Huckleberry Finn*, in which he jeopardizes Jim's liberation for the sake of a number of purely selfish and extremely dangerous fancies, present a sober alternative to too often mindless celebration. Children are not only a mess of trouble, but they can and quite often do a heap of harm.

These literary testimonies are all vivid and convincing. They do not, however, get to the heart of the matter. Or, rather, they do not assert that a different matter lies at the very heart. We allow that children have an inclination to err and even, if we subscribe to the terminology, to sin. Going further, we will allow that a few children attain a deep and even dedicated naughtiness. These inclinations may well be problematic, but they will ultimately do little to jeopardize our devotion to children or our faith in their inherent decency. But there is something worse than waywardness, a fearful suspicion about children that probably does not belong in children's actual bookshelves. And yet there is testimony of this too, and it needs to be heard.

Case Study: Richard Hughes's *A High Wind in Jamaica*

It is not that far from Tom Sawyer's unconscionable conduct toward poor Jim to the fearsome ambiguities of Henry James's *A Turn of the Screw* (1898). There are many competing interpretations of this intentionally, epochally enigmatic novella. The unnamed governess at the center of the story may actually have seen the apparitions of her late predecessor and the sinful serving man, of Miss Jessel and Mr. Quint. Alternatively, these may have been manifestations of the governess's own neurosis, or sexual repression. Either way, her young charges, Miles and Flora, seem to be fertile ground for the seeds of corruption. In this book James raises once again the question of whether children are corruptible, or whether they are not, in fact, fundamentally corrupt.[22]

The English novelist William Golding is responsible for one of the most celebrated and familiar explorations of this idea. *The Lord of the Flies* (1954) raises, and goes a long way toward proving, an evolutionary, primordial possibility:

> And in front of Simon, the Lord of the Flies hung on his stick and grinned. At last Simon gave up and looked back; saw the white teeth and dim eyes, the blood—and his gaze was held by that ancient, inescapable recognition. In Simon's right temple, a pulse began to beat on the brain.[23]

This dread recognition, this answering heartbeat is distinct from traditional Catholic notions of our natural proclivities toward error. It is deeper than the insistence of didactic communication. There is a dread here that is nearly H. P. Lovecraftian, however infrequently that name may be associated with children's discourse.

As a last presentation of evidence, here is a book, less familiar to most readers, that quite definitively makes the case. *A High Wind in Jamaica* (1928), by the Welsh writer Richard Hughes, consciously counters the Romantic idealization that sees children as a perfect balance of innocence and wisdom. So thorough is this counter that the idealistic commonplace sustains some very serious damage. Indeed, by the time Hughes gets through with it, the ideal is barely still standing.

In Hughes' novel children are not bright angels, and they inhabit no peaceable kingdom. *A High Wind in Jamaica* is an illustration of the second law of thermodynamics, or the law of increasing universal disorder. The illustrations is made by means of the devolution of its child protagonists, particularly of the girl Emily Bas-Thornton. This descent into entropy and disorder is contained in two major set pieces. The first of these occurs toward the beginning of the novel, in a hurricane that destroys the Bas-Thornton family's Caribbean home, as well as the colonial and patriarchal pretensions that had until then made them feel so safe and secure and preeminent.

The hurricane episode is introduced by the family's near feral-cat, which is clearly compared to its soon to be feral children. They are all of them liminal creatures, either unformed, or so inchoate as to be unformable. Tabby is a perverse and a provocative creature. Because of this she is eventually, literally torn apart by a dozen wild cats who actually chase her into the Bas-Thornton's house, into what is supposed to be the protected, sanctified domestic space.[24] The children see the whole thing, and are deeply traumatized by the sight. In fact Hughes shapes the incident into another, alternative primal scene. Contrary to the classic scenario however, this is not a procreative prospect, but rather a dire foundational vision of dismemberment and unmaking.[25]

The hurricane that destroys the family's home and eventually separates children from parents is the cat's unmaking, writ large. It is exhaustively, electrifyingly described. Hughes outlines the exertions made by all of the Bas-Thorntons to survive it. The adults are not equal to the task, and the fact that none of the family is killed has little to do with them. For their part, the children have made use of the resources available to them. "While what was left of the house was blown away over their heads ... John, Emily, Edward, Rachel, and Laura, blind drunk, slept in a heap on the cellar floor: a sleep over which the appalling fate of Tabby, torn to pieces by those fiends almost under their very eyes, dominated with the easy empire of nightmare."[26]

After the hurricane, the parents send the children on a ship back to England. This is where the second entropic episode comes in, and it unfolds throughout the remainder of the book. Soon after they embark, the children are captured by pirates, at which point the same prospect previously presented by the hurricane comes back into play. The children, vulnerable innocents that they are, would seem to be doomed. Were this a historical account, perhaps they would be. In this case, though, the children defeat the inevitable. Against reality's odds, and in the seeming spirit of the adventurous yarn—for example, Robert Louis Stevenson's *Treasure Island* (1883) or J. Meade Falkner's *Moonfleet* (1898)—they survive. Troublingly, terminally, they survive by devolving, unless this seeming devolution is, in fact, a return to their native, natural savagery.

One of the most electrifying things about Hughes' multiply electrifying novel is the extent and implication of its central thesis. If the notion of the angel child is jeopardized, then literally everything is in danger of being knocked in the hazard. Children's literature is only one, only the least of things that are jeopardized. *A High Wind in Jamaica* expresses a chillingly offhand skepticism not only about the reassuring bromides of children's literature but about the very bonds of family. Here is the children's ineffectual mother, and her negligible influence:

> If it would have surprised the mother, it would undoubtedly have surprised the children also to be told how little their parents meant to them. Children seldom have any power of quantitative self-analysis: whatever the fact, they believe as an article of faith that they love Father and Mother first and equally. Actually, the Thornton children had loved Tabby first and foremost in all the world, some of each other second, and hardly noticed their mother's existence more than once a week. Their

father they loved a little more: partly owing to the ceremony of riding home on his stirrups.[27]

At first these fickle affections may seem like adaptability and resilience. The children are thrilled by an earthquake[28] and unbowed by a hurricane. Soon, however, their resilience becomes troubling. Father brings an old servant's dead body out of the storm and into the house: "Emily and John, who had slipped unbeknownst into the passage, were thrilled beyond measure at the way he dangled."[29]

The prospect only get worse. After their capture, the children gloss over the violent accidental death of their elder brother and then, finally, out-pirate the pirates. In the popular imagination the direness of actual piracy had, has largely given way to romance, or at least an acknowledged Panto-like artificiality.[30] But while Rafael Sabatini or Errol Flynn might portray high spirits and blithe, melodramatic derring-do, Hughes conveys something quite different.[31] For one thing, we have complex psychology in unexpected places. It is the pirates in particular that have contradictions, have their own reasons, even their justifications. It is in the matter of the children that a salutary reconsidering of the nature of antagonism assumes a darker aspect. In their fall from the angel grace of childhood, and in their blithe unconcern about that fall, these children raise a darker possibility: could it be that they already, natively had these black hearts?

A High Wind in Jamaica reflects some of the scientific discourse of the last hundred years. Unlike the Christian catechizers or the exultant Romantics, Hughes places his children upon an evolutionary continuum. They are marked by genetics and instinct, by the incalculable duration of their species' long history. He illustrates this idea in his description of Laura Bas-Thornton, who is almost four:

> The inside of Laura was different indeed: something vast, complicated, and nebulous that can hardly be put into language. To take a metaphor from tadpoles, though legs were growing her gills had not yet dropped off. Being nearly four years old, she was certainly a child: and children are human (if one allows the term "human" a wide sense): but she had not altogether ceased to be a baby: and babies of course are not human— they are animals, and have a very ancient and ramified culture, as cats have, and fishes, and even snakes: the same in kind as these, but much more complicated and vivid, since babies are, after all, one of the most developed species of the lower vertebrates.[32]

The discourse of childhood has always concerned itself with the child growing into adulthood. There are many perspectives on the subject and on its various components. Hughes offers a shocking new viewpoint:

6. Bad Boys and Demon Seeds

> Possibly a case might be made out that children are not human either: but I should not accept it. Agreed that their minds are not just more ignorant and stupider than ours, but differ in kind of thinking (are *mad*, in fact): but one can, by an effort of will and imagination, think like a child, at least in a partial degree—and even if one's success is infinitesimal it invalidates the case: while one can no more think like a baby, in the smallest respect, than one can think like a bee.

Alternatively, as he moves from scientific analogy to more fanciful metaphors, it may be that Hughes is elaborating a stylized, Swiftian vision that is utterly convinced not only of man's fundamental perfidy, but of the child's: "How then can one begin to describe the inside of Laura, where the child-mind lived in the midst of the familiar relics of the baby-mind, like a Fascist in Rome?"[33]

Much later in the book, the pirates overtake a Dutch vessel, and they remove its captain onto their own ship. He is bound and placed in a closed cabin, with Emily Bas-Thornton to guard him. The Dutch captain is in fear for his life, here at the hands of these brigands. Thinking that their mutual captivity would incline her toward him, he tries to get Emily to hand him that knife. She refuses to do so. He tries to get it himself. She misunderstands, thinking that the captain means her harm. Her confusion is natural. Her response, perhaps, is not. She stabs and slashes him a dozen times.

An alarm is raised, and the pirates come upon the dreadful prospect: "The Dutch Captain they could see on the floor, stretched in a pool of blood. 'But, Gentlemen, I have a wife and children!' he suddenly said in Dutch, in a surprised and gentle tone: then died, not so much of any mortal wound as of the number of superficial gashes he had received."[34]

This last is a marvelous and terrible image. It is also a portentous one.[35] Literature—and life—affirm that the little actions of little children can accumulate into benevolent enormity. The same is true, of course, when adults join the cause. Their incremental acts of Christian kindness or nondenominational moral courage[36] fend off the darkness, if they don't actually save the world.

George Eliot concludes her great novel *Middlemarch* with a sublime expression of this comforting, not remotely reductive or sentimental platitude. Its protagonist, Dorothea Brooke, has failed to fulfill her great personal potential and has likewise failed to realize so many of the bright and benevolent projects that she had hoped to accomplish. However, as we have seen before with the seemingly limited capacities and inconsequential actions of literary women and children, inherent virtue turns out to have enormous, cumulative consequence. "But the effect of [Dorothea's] being on those around her was incalculably diffusive: for the growing good of the world is partly dependent on unhistoric acts; and that things are not so ill with you and me as they might have been, is half owing to the number who lived faithfully a hidden life, and rest in unvisited tombs."[37]

Emily Bas-Thornton's fatal sticking of the innocent Dutch Captain effects an infernal inversion of this sublime, even saving commonplace. And it doesn't stop there. The pirates think that Margaret, the Bas-Thornton's servant whom they had also taken captive, had committed this murder. Appalled by its inhumanity and by Margaret's seemingly utter lack of remorse, they summarily toss her overboard. Emily, the actual man-slaughterer, closes her eyes, goes away to hide beneath the covers, and never says a thing.

It is difficult to overemphasize the power and significance of this extended episode with the Dutch captain. Film and the operations of popular commercial culture have made the expiring cry of Joseph Conrad's Mr. Kurtz into a proverb, even an empty lampoon. But "The horror!"[38] is nothing to laugh at. Adult literature is rife with these kind of excoriating moments. Frank Norris, from *McTeague* (1899):

> Beside herself with terror, Trina turned and fought him back; fought for her miserable life with the exasperation and strength of a harassed cat; and with such energy and such wild, unnatural force, that even McTeague for the moment drew back from her. But her resistance was the one thing to drive him to the top of his fury. He came back at her again, his eyes drawn to two fine twinkling points, and his enormous fists, clenched till the knuckles whitened, raised in the air.
> Then it became abominable.[39]

As with the long-ago rending of the children's tabby cat, this is a different kind of primal scene. Instead of loving union, or a consummation with promise, this is a localized, individualized playing out of the previously cited second law of thermodynamics. Whether it is the child growing or the race evolving, this is, in Tennyson's famous phrase, "nature, red in tooth and claw."[40] It is Hughes' dread and signal accomplishment to have placed one of the direst of these scenes in the midst of this erstwhile children's adventure.

Primal scenes, of course, not only illuminate our origins but point the way to our futures. Emily wonders why she has to grow up:

> Most children have something of this feeling. With most children it is outweighed: still, they will generally hesitate before telling you they prefer to grow up. But then, most children live secure lives, and have an at

least apparently secure future to grow up to. To have already murdered a full-sized man, and to have to keep it for ever a secret, is not a normal background for a child of ten: to have a Margaret one could not altogether banish from one's thoughts: to see every ordinary avenue of life locked against one, only a violent road, leading to Hell, open.[41]

Later at the pirates' trial, Emily turns Judas, or perhaps simply betrays by her silence regarding the things that she knows, or has done. She leaves the innocent and, more, the affectionate and mindful pirate captain to be put wrongfully to death.[42] Now, with the death of the novel's real innocents—the pirates—any notion of Judeo-Christian justice departs as well.

As the foregoing block quotation demonstrated, Emily had experienced Dostoyevskian agonies within her tender conscience. But these now cease as the scruples of conscience give way to the satisfaction of having gotten away with it all. Emily Bas-Thornton is not a dear child subject to sin, as in Ken Russell's lovely, contemplatively Catholic film *Amelia and the Angel* (1959). Neither is she an age-adjusted Raskolnikov, willfully transgressing and wildly rationalizing before coming to accept the magnitude of her offence, and the sweet, sure promise of forgiveness and redemption. Rather, Emily Bas-Thornton prefigures Patricia Highsmith's exquisitely sociopathological Tom Ripley, who kills, and understands, and regrets it not at all.

The import and meaning of all of this is contained in the exquisite, earlier episode of the baby alligator, to which Emily is drawn, and which she takes to herself, in bed. The baby alligator and the little girl look at each other.

> Presently the beast opened his mouth and hissed again gently. Emily lifted a finger and began to rub the corner of his jaw. The hiss changed to a sound almost like a purr. A thin filmy lid first covered his eye from the front backwards, then the outer lid closed up from below.
> Suddenly he opened his eyes again, and snapped on her finger: then turned and wormed his way into the neck of her night-gown, and crawled down inside, cool and rough against her skin, till he found a place to rest. It is surprising that she could stand it as she did, without flinching.
> Alligators are utterly untamable.[43]

Epple, Inchelina, Elisa, and Gerda[44] are nurturing, Marian children. If Wordsworth's child is the father to the man, then a certain, very dominant kind of literary female child is, in many ways, already the woman, even the savior. In the face of all of this compelling, exalting, bedeviling evidence, Richard Hughes' Emily is utterly Other, and she makes us wonder about all that has gone before. The alligator episode quite intentionally suggests suckling, and of a terrifyingly intra-species variety. It brings a dread precedent to mind:

> I have given suck, and know
> How tender 'tis to love the babe that milks me;
> I would, while it was smiling in my face,
> Have pluck'd my nipple from his boneless gums
> And dash'd the brains out, had I so sworn as you
> Have done to this.[45]

Emily Bas-Thornton echoes Lady Macbeth, or Medea, or even Grendel's mother. Another variation of Hughes' dire question arises: In this alligator scene does Emily betray her kind? Or is she herself a reptilian, autochthonous, primordially cold-blooded creature?

Near the end of *A High Wind in Jamaica*, the children, against all hope, are reunited with their parents. In children's literature this prospect, this frequent plot resolution has been Eden, or Bethlehem, or heaven, all rolled up into one. The usual reflection upon this happy scenario might bring adults and children alike to think of home, the end of all wandering, the consummation most devoutly to be wished. We are reminded of Dorothy, or Wendy and Peter and Michael returned to the bosom of their family, or "Little Gidding," which provides the transcendentally reassuring conclusion to Eliot's *Four Quartets*.

> We shall not cease from exploration
> And the end of all our exploring
> Will be to arrive where we started
> And know the place for the first time.[46]

For his part, Hughes describes the tender scene thusly:

> "Mother!" cried Emily. She had not known she could be so glad to see her. As for Mrs. Thornton, she was far beyond the bounds of hysteria. The little ones held back at first, but soon followed Emily's example, leaping on her and shouting: indeed it looked more like Actaeon with his hounds than a mother: their monkey-like little hands tore her clothes in pieces.[47]

The children's rescue and its aftermath are portrayed elliptically, and with a troubling partiality. It has been so with the book's portrayal of children, which gives us a glimpse into the heart of darkness and then gives way to something worse. And what does it all mean? At the book's conclusion, we find Emily, seemingly untouched by all this tragedy and ruin, moving blithely on and being reabsorbed into the company of the young women at her boarding school. The school's officials have been apprised of what has happened to her.

"Poor little thing," said the mistress, "I hope she will soon forget the terrible things she has been through. I think our girls will have an especially kind corner in their hearts for her."

In another room, Emily with the other new girls was making friends with the older pupils. Looking at that gentle, happy throng of clean innocent faces and soft graceful limbs, listening to the ceaseless, artless babble of chatter rising, perhaps God could have picked out from among them which was Emily: but I am sure that I could not.[48]

This dread conclusion flies in the face of the moral conventions of children's literature, as well as the norms of developmental psychology. Emily Bas-Thornton is no angel, or little princess, and she will not progress from innocence to productive, initiated adulthood. For the duration of Richard Hughes' vividly terrifying book, and echoing through the impending abattoir of the 1930s and '40s, Emily illustrates and embodies the law of increasing and potentially, eventually annihilating entropy. In fact, Emily cries, Emily is, Havoc.[49] Phyllis Nirdlinger[50] closes in for the kill. Hannibal Lecter melts into the crowd.[51] The fresh-faced young females run gabbling off to amuse themselves, and to ripen, and rise to their dire and uncontested supremacy.

The Roots of That Branch: Literary Naturalism

> For there is no creature whose inward being is so strong that it is not greatly determined by what lies outside it.— George Eliot

The angel child and the bad seed are essentialist notions, marking the extreme ends of the debate on the subject of children. In addition to essence, however, the discourse of children is also concerned with causes, and effects. The literature, and the lives that inform it, has much to say about how children's souls are marked and determined by the physical, material conditions in which they are raised.

"Forgive me if I am not justified in what I ask," said Scrooge, looking intently at the Spirit's robe, "but I see something strange, and not belonging to yourself, protruding from your skirts. Is it a foot or a claw?"

"It might be a claw, for the flesh there is upon it," was the Spirit's sorrowful reply. "Look here."[52]

Ebenezer Scrooge is about to part company with the Spirit of Christmas Present. They have just been to visit the Cratchit family. Scrooge has seen severe privation there, and he has understood for the first time that he is essentially the author thereof. He has also seen how this privation is countered and balanced by the deep love that the Cratchits feel for one another. And he has become aware that if all of these shadows remain unaltered by the future, this great family affection will not be sufficient to save Tiny Tim Cratchit.

The Cratchits are poverty made presentable, but Dickens knew it had also a fiercer, more intractable countenance. Once again, Scrooge, has seen something protruding from beneath the skirts of his companion.

> From the foldings of its robe, [the Spirit] brought two children; wretched, abject, frightful, hideous, miserable.... They were a boy and girl. Yellow, meagre, ragged, scowling, wolfish; but prostrate, too, in their humility. Where graceful youth should have filled their features out, and touched them with its freshest tints, a stale and shrivelled hand, like that of age, had pinched, and twisted them, and pulled them into shreds. Where angels might have sat enthroned, devils lurked, and glared out menacing. No change, no degradation, no perversion of humanity, in any grade, through all the mysteries of wonderful creation, has monsters half so horrible and dread.

For all that sentimentality and idealism can claim or accomplish, this is the real face of poverty. The powerless and disadvantaged child is most particularly determined and marked by it. Dickens' reference to angels and devils is very significant, and carries with it a plain and powerful point. It submits that angelic and demonic qualities are not inherent parts of childhood, or of the child. Nor are they necessarily the consequences of choices and the actions that attach to them. As we have already seen in the films of D. W. Griffith, Tiny Tim and Little Nell and their like are the picture of the saintly, suffering child. In the didactic, sermonic setting of Dickens' story, these two attributes impel the erring or simply inadequate adult to stir himself and provide needed succor, and to reclaim his own life as he does so. On the Bowery, however, or deep in the East End of London, things are not likely to be so tidy. "Scrooge started back, appalled. Having them shown to him in this way, he tried to say they were fine children, but the words choked themselves, rather than be parties to a lie of such enormous magnitude."

These two prodigies are, of course, Ignorance and Want, and in the story they foretell and even prefigure mankind's doom. Like Tiny Tim, they are heavily symbolic. But they also show how Dickens could balance the sentimentality for which he is often remembered with a much more aggressive kind of characterization. As King Lear stated in the face of his own extremity, this is the thing itself, children as poor, bare and forked beasts, brute products of their brutalizing nurture.[53]

In praxis these matters are addressed and attended to by journalists, activists, social scientists, legislators, and any number of other devoted professionals. In the narrative arts, the susceptibility of the organism to its environment has primarily been the province of the naturalist.

Speaking generally, a naturalist studies nature. She concerns herself with material reality—not the immaterial or the metaphysical—as a first principle.[54] At its first appearance, literary naturalism was the result of a positivist ferment in the nineteenth century, a general trend toward classification and taxonomy. It was informed by a faith that all phenomena could be measured and then, eventually, comprehended by scientific explanation. The result was not only a general movement toward scientific inquiry, but the extension of that inquiry into other discourses.

Hippolyte Taine, the great French positivist and historian, established the terms of this conversation in the area of literature.

> No matter if the facts be physical or moral, they all have their causes; there is a cause for ambition, for courage, for truth, as there is for digestion, for muscular movement, for animal heat. Vice and virtue are products, like vitriol and sugar; and every complex phenomenon has its springs from other more simple phenomena on which it hangs. Let us then seek the simple phenomena for moral qualities, as we seek them for physical qualities.[55]

Taine sets forth the basic tenets of his influential argument in the introduction to his *History of English Literature* (1863–64). Here he states that individuals and collectives both are ultimately determined by the influences of race, milieu, and moment.[56] Single sensibilities can never fully transcend the totality of genetic and cultural inheritance, or of material determinants like climate, geography and topography, or want. All of these things together create a basically irresistible context, a historical and cultural frame that sets and inflects everything that lies within it.[57]

The novelist Émile Zola articulated and elaborated upon Taine's notion, at first with his 1867 novel, *Thérèse Raquin*, and subsequently in the Rougon-Macquart cycle, his enormous 20 volume sequence of linked novels portraying the French Second Empire through the history of one benighted extended family. Zola's characters are, as Taine would have had it, largely and sometimes utterly determined by their heredity, and by the milieu in which it operates.

An artist's intentions evolve, as does his work, and his attitude to the theories that inform it. There is a great deal of this evolution over the course of Zola's project, from the semi-scandalous partly-provocations of *Thérèse Raquin* to the deepening insight and empathy of the later novels. Still, a number of notions inform the whole and illuminate the present conversation.

For Zola, the task of the naturalist novelist was similar to that of a scientist. He was to consider his characters objectively, as a scientist might do with a cross-section under a microscope.[58] By doing so he could observe the effects of environment and of each individual component thereof, upon the organism. Zola eschewed sympathy, and did not try to create for his readers a conventional identification with his characters. This was because human interest and the adoption of a particular, personal point of view were bad science, obstacles to objectivity and dispassion.

This denial of human interest, however, was not the same as a lack of human interest entire. In fact, it may be that this counterintuitive delimitation was the paradoxical source of one of naturalism's greatest moral benefits. The emphasis on milieu, as manifest in its almost obsessive rendering of physical environments, may have inhibited the reader's sympathetic engagement. But it could also inhibit her natural or socially determined impulses toward dismissive moral judgment.

Naturalism has a firm place in the history of literary and cinematic storytelling.[59] A common consequence of every contribution, however, is that it has become difficult to simply dismiss, to unequivocally condemn the drunk, the prostitute, the murderer. As André Bazin's especial favorite, the great French film director Jean Renoir would later demonstrate in his film *Rules of the Game* (1939), and, in fact, in his entire deeply compassionate oeuvre, "the terrible thing is that everyone has his reasons."[60]

With regard to the present discussion about children's literature, the naturalists have, to some degree, portrayed all of their variously impoverished protagonists as poor children, or as unfortunate innocents. "Father, forgive them, for they know not what they do."[61]

D. W. Griffith's essentialism on the subject of children leads to sweet and often questionable generalizations. Richard Hughes' cataclysmic contrary vote is similarly across-the-board, and discourages any kind of negotiation or even ministration. In contrast to these essences, the naturalists say that there are always causes, and that those that are subject or subject/ed to these causes are always determined by them. For this reason it is wrong to be reductive or gleefully judgmental. It is wrong to say that Othello was merely jealous, that Macbeth merely ambitious, or Hamlet merely indecisive. And it is not at all wrong to observe that Oliver Twist's prospects were almost fatally blighted by the orphanage, or Amy Dorrit's by the Marshalsea specifically and debtors' prisons in general, or Esther and Richard and Ada's, as wards to the suit of Jarndyce vs. Jarndyce, by the abuses of the Chancery Court.[62]

The present work is eclectic, which is to say that it is inclined to seek and appreciate the merit that exists in most every reasonably constituted philosophical formulation. Something can always be extricated, though the original source may not be fully subscribed to.[63] The present work is also committed to the concept of the mean, which is to say that with regard to the nature of childhood, idealism and the horror! are both marked by excess and defect. Naturalism is not generally considered a conciliatory movement, but in this case it mediates between these two binaries, and finds for them a productive midpoint.

Zola's novel *La Bête Humaine* (1890) features this significant description of a block of flats built just above its primary setting, a train yard in Le Havre, France.

> The flats on the right had windows overlooking the station yard, planted with old elms above which opened out the wonderful view of the Ingouville hills; while those to the left had low, arched windows which looked straight out at the station roof, the steep pitch of which, with its ridge of zinc and dirty glass skylights, shut out the horizon. Nothing was more cheerful than the one side, with the continual bustle of the station yard, the green trees and the distant view of the country, while you could die of boredom on the other side, in which you could hardly see, and the bit of sky was walled round like a prison.[64]

One can argue about whether children have angelic essences or demonic ones. But it is difficult to dispute the profound effect of heredity and milieu on the ultimate prospects of any child, regardless of its native disposition. Again, naturalism affirms that setting and origin are everything, and that the difference between a well and an ill-favored child could be one of mere degrees, of a slightly shifted angle of vision, or of access.

Case Study: Émile Zola's *L'Assommoir*

Zola's *L'Assommoir* (1877) is one of the greatest of all naturalist novels, a superlative dissertation upon the disastrous effects that environment and heredity can have. Its main characters are adults, but the children at hand are some of its most irrefutable witnesses and provide some of its most searing testimony. In his introduction to the book, translator Leonard Tancock discusses the "left-wing mythology" of the noble working class, ever bedeviled by the iniquitous rich. The myth is nourished by the "great romantic illusion" (forever enshrined by Victor Hugo's *Les Misérables*) that the noble working class remains largely unaffected by this vast disadvantage. For Tancock, Zola's work offers a necessary corrective, distinguishing as it does between "well-founded pity and blind idealization."[65]

Blind idealization does not fully acknowledge, and cannot remotely remedy, intractable material reality. Remedies require accurate descriptions and diagnoses of the problems at hand. Prescriptions and cures are a whole other matter, and naturalism largely leaves those to legislation or the agency of the engaged and outraged reader. Tancock summarizes Zola's diagnosis, which is "that life in mean and depressing surroundings without the money ever to escape, even for a few days, leads to a dreary existence from which the only relief is drink and promiscuity, a vicious spiral leading down to degradation."[66]

Zola himself responded to attacks directed at him and his book by making the following observation: "It is a work of truth, the first novel about the common people which does not tell lies but has the authentic smell of the people. And it must not be concluded that the masses as a whole are bad, for my characters are not bad, but only ignorant and spoilt by the environment of grinding toil and poverty in which they live."[67]

This is the setting, then, and the situation: Zola's protagonist, the washerwoman Gervaise Macquart, has come to Paris with her two sons and their no-account father, Lantier. He quickly absents himself, and leaves the woman and her small children to make their own way. The prospects are bleak. "[Gervaise] cast her eyes up and down the outer boulevards to left and right, stopping at each end with a dull terror as if life itself from now on was going to live itself out in this place, between a slaughterhouse and a hospital."[68]

This hopelessly overdetermined prospect is similar to the one described in the earlier quotation from *La Bête Humaine*, except that in this case neither alternative is very hopeful. Gervaise does manage to find her feet, for a while at least. She meets a reasonably steady man and marries him. She even manages to establish a temporarily thriving laundry. However bad luck, bad impulses, and especially an overpoweringly bad milieu eventually restore things to the dire status quo. The once bustling wash house, and its once prospering proprietress, are eventually reduced to this:

> It goes without saying that as laziness and poverty came in, so did squalor....
> The woodwork and windows of the shop front were now never cleaned and were splashed from top to bottom with mud from passing vehicles. In the shop window, hanging on the brass rod, were three grey rags that had belonged to customers who had died in hospital.... [I]nside ... the damp from drying washing had loosened the paper on the ceiling ... in its corner the broken stove ... looked like some old iron in a junk-shop; the work-table ... [was] stained with coffee and wine, plastered with jam and greasy with the remains of Monday blow-outs. Add to all that a reek of stale starch and a stench made up of mildew, burnt fat and dirt. But Gervaise felt nice and cosy in the middle of all this.[69]

Gervaise began with promise and a measure of virtue, if broadly defined. And for all of Zola's interest in tainted blood (as particularly explored through the character of Jacques Lantier, Gervaise's son and the eventual protagonist of the later novel, *La Bête Humaine*), the same could be said of her children. But in Zola's version of naturalism, the potential of the poor is almost always spoiled by their poverty. Gervaise will not turn out at all like Victor Hugo's ruined, martyred, and yet morally unbesmirched Fantine. Nor will her daughter, Nana, or their tiny neighbor, Lalie, escape degenerate circumstance as did Cosette There will be no superhumanly devoted benefactor, Valjean, no thrillingly impossible familial deus ex machina. Rather, Gervaise will fall, and fail. Her daughter, Nana, will be quite quickly, inevitably, and completely corrupted, if by degrees. And Lalie, who actually manages to preserve her original promise and purity, is only able to do so because death intervenes before these qualities can be extinguished.

Zola's children are not bad, until their environment makes them so. Gervaise has just given birth to Nana. Her husband, Coupeau, arrives, grateful:

> She gave him a weak smile, and murmured:
>
> "It's a girl."
> "Quite correct!" he said, joking to cheer her up. "I ordered a girl and, lo and behold, a girl it is! You do everything I want, don't you?"

Taking up the baby he goes on: "Let's have a look at you, you little slut. You've got a black little mug. Oh, it'll get lighter, never you fear. You must be a good girl and not go running after the boys."[70] This is a most inapt thing to say to one's infant daughter. Whether or not there was any intention or expectation attached to this comment, a process soon begins that culminates in having it all come to pass.

A little later we encounter Nana, now aged six, "and by way of becoming a perfect terror." She attends a little school, contriving "[un]savoury schemes that couldn't be mentioned." At home she runs in and around a tenement full of swarms of unwashed, unattended, practically unraised children, "noisy thieving sparrows" all.[71] "Hordes of them came out of every room. In this milling throng of pink-nosed vermin, never washed except by the rain, there were big ones, very artful-looking ones, fat ones, pot-bellied ones like little old men."[72] In the midst of this positively Boschian assemblage, Nana quickly rises to a position of childish preeminence and asserts her will in a very particular, unseemly manner. "The little hussy was forever suggesting playing mother, undressing the little ones and dressing them up again, and she insisted on examining the others everywhere, playing about with their bodies with the tyranny and inventiveness of a grown-up with a dirty mind."[73]

Presently Lantier, Gervaise's first, long-ago lover and the father of Nana's two half-brothers, returns to the scene. Nana is now ten years of age. Lantier takes the measure of her. "They were bringing her up bloody badly in his opinion. Neither was he wrong over this, for when her father went for her, her mother stuck up for her, and when her mother hit her, her father made a scene. Nana, delighted to see her parents falling out over her, felt she was excused in advance and had a high old time."

Nana is described tearing around with a gang of local guttersnipes. "Lantier was the only one who could tell her off, and even then she knew how to get round him. This dirty little bitch of ten sailed past him like a lady, swinging her hips and looking at him out of the corners of her already vicious eyes."[74]

These are appalling descriptions of an appalling situation. But Zola would not have us simply condemn, or dismiss. His settings determine the courses of the characters that live within them: "I wanted to depict the inevitable downfall of a working-class family in the polluted atmosphere of our urban areas. The logical sequel to drunkenness and indolence is the loosening of family ties, the filth of promiscuity, the progressive loss of decent feelings and, as the climax, shame and death."[75]

Nana is a horribly behaved, hellacious child. It was not ever thus, at least at first. Could her degradation have started here? Coupeau, Nana's father, is a roofer.

> "Daddy, Daddy!" [Nana] yelled at the top of her voice. "Daddy, look at me!"
> He went to lean forward but his foot slipped. Suddenly, stupidly, like a cat whose feet have got mixed up, he slid down the gentle slope of the roof and couldn't stop.

"Christ!" he muttered in a choking voice.

Then he fell. His body came down in a sagging curve, turned over twice and flopped into the middle of the road with the dull thud of a bundle of washing dropped from a great height.[76]

Nana saw the whole thing, of course. Coupeau is terribly injured, and during his long convalescence he starts to drink. Meanwhile, as mentioned, the no-account Lantier has returned and has even taken up residence in their rooms. He has designs on his former companion, which she has intended to resist. There comes an evening when they have been out together. They come back and ring the bell. There is no answer. They manage to get inside.

> Gervaise, groping for a box of matches, realized she was walking in something wet. When she had managed to light a candle a pretty sight met her eyes. Coupeau had thrown up the lot: it was all over the room, the bed was coated with it and so was the carpet, and even the chest was splashed. And he had fallen off the bed ... and was lying snoring in the middle of his own filth. He was lying at full length, wallowing in it like a pig, one cheek covered with it and breathing foul breath out of his open mouth, soaking up with his already grey hair the puddle spreading round his head.[77]

Gervaise is horrified. But this is her husband, and this is the bed that they share. She tries to climb over Coupeau, to get to the little surface that remains unsoiled. Lantier sees his chance, and begins to draw her away. She resists his urging, at which point, in the midst of all of this reeking filth, he begins to kiss her. At this point Gervaise feels ancient stirrings, which vie with her desperately rising nausea. She looks at her insensible husband. "Coupeau, knocked right out by drink, was sleeping it off with limbs dead and mouth askey, slumbering as though on a feather bed. The whole street could have come in and had his wife and not a hair of his body would have stirred."[78]

Caught between the devil and the deep blue sea, Gervaise succumbs.

> And as Lantier was guiding her into his room Nana's face appeared behind one of the panes in the glass door of the slip-room. She had just awakened and got quietly out of bed in her nightdress, pale with sleep. She had a look at her father wallowing in his own vomit and then, glueing her face to the glass, she stood there watching for her mother's petticoat to disappear into the other man's room opposite. She concentrated attentively, and the child's vicious eyes, staring wide, were lit up with a lubricious curiosity.[79]

A High Wind in Jamaica contains a counter–Freudian Primal Scene, one in which violence and entropy emerge as the origin and destiny of man.

Here Nana has witnessed another awful alternative to the standard story. Again: instead of stumbling upon a seemly and circumspect, authorized and affectionate exchange, she is initiated into incontinence, predation, and an almost irresistible degradation. This is not George Eliot, and it is also far from Richard Hughes. Zola's point once again, and the purpose of detailing this distressing account in the context of children's literature, is that naughtiness, or immorality, or criminality, or depravity, actually spring from bad genes proliferating in a milieu of filth and brutality.[80]

So much for innocence, or even moral neutrality, and its eventual loss and corruption. But what of virtue, or Christ's exemplary child? Zola also makes room for this phenomenon and even for its post-biblical possibility. But as with Nana's case, the reality of exemplary childhood, as well as the literary elaboration thereof, is eventually unable to overcome the crushing weight of poverty and moral chaos.

Gervaise's neighbor, little Lalie, serves as a foil to Nana. She is eight years old and in sole charge of a three- and five-year-old brother and sister. "Since [her father] Bijard had killed his missis with a kick in the belly, Lalie had taken on the job of being little mother to the lot of them.... Without a word she had taken the dead woman's place, even to the extent that her brute of a father, no doubt to complete the resemblance, now hit the daughter as he used to hit the mother."[81]

Nana is spirited, and resourceful, and she at least makes something of the limited possibilities that are presented to her. Lalie is much milder, and she does not really have any opportunities of which she can take advantage. We see her being thrashed and kicked, tied up not just for the sake of restriction but for the mere pleasure her father takes in inflicting pain. He heats coins in the fire and then tells her to go and fetch a loaf of bread with them. When she drops the hot coins, he whips her to within an inch of her life.[82]

Zola stages another poignant parallel to the adulterous primal scene that Nana had witnessed. Gervaise has been succumbing, steadily, to all sorts of temptations, which are gathering in force to the point of her absolute degradation. She is now, as usual, in her cups. Lalie hears and recognizes her step. As Gervaise had always been kind to her, she rushes out.

> "Madame Gervaise, Daddy isn't in, come along and see my babies asleep. Oh, they do look sweet!"
> But catching sight of Gervaise's fuddled expression she drew back and trembled. She knew that smell of spirits, those bleary eyes that contorted

mouth. Gervaise staggered on without a word, and the child stood at her door watching her with her dark eyes, silent and solemn.[83]

Lalie demonstrates Dickensian constancy and patience in the face of all of this abuse and entropy. Unlike Little Nell, however, she cannot even maintain herself over the course of the entire novel.

Gervaise, now fifty pages worse off, visits Lalie and her children again. She finds their dwelling bare, but as always, swept clean. Lalie is in bed, dying. Her father comes raging in, and then realizes what is actually happening. Gervaise rushes to Lalie, displacing the ragged sheet that covers her.

> The very stones would have wept. Lalie was quite naked ... the bleeding, agonizing nakedness of a martyr. She had no flesh left, the bones looked as though they were coming through the skin. Thin purple weals striped her ribs and right down to her thighs—recent lashes of the whip. A livid mark went round the left arm as if this delicate limb, no thicker than a matchstick, had been crushed in a vice. The right leg had a still unhealed gash.... From head to foot she was one black bruise. Oh, what a massacre of the innocents.[84]

In *La Bete Humaine* Zola considers the prospects of his protagonist Jacques Lantier, who is, once again, Nana's half-brother. Jacques scrupulously avoids drink, and does his best to avoid situations that will inflame other, related dark impulses that bedevil him. But still, always there, is a family flaw, a hereditary taint.

> He did not drink, not even allowing himself a single tot of spirits, having seen that the least drop of alcohol drove him out of his mind. He was coming to think that he was paying for others, fathers, grandfathers who had drunk, generations of drunkards, that he had their blood, tainted with a slow poison and a bestiality that dragged him back to the woman-devouring savages in the forest.[85]

The idealization of childhood has had a dominant place in the literature of the last 200 years, and a similarly prevalent place in film since its advent. As we have just seen, however, idealization has also been powerfully opposed. The two tropes here outlined—that of Naturalism, and the inherent corruption of Man—again suggest the vivid range of discussion relating to the nature of children.

To end, however, it is time to bring the ideal and the cautionary hyper-real together. The penultimate chapter of this study outlines how the extremes of the argument can be reconciled by a conciliatory or dialectical compromise. Children, like books and films, combine conventions and mitigate both excess and defect. The results constitute a wonderful compromise, or synthesis, in addition to suggesting the way forward into the possible apotheoses of adulthood.

7

Reconciling and Synthesizing Polar Positions

> No mere mortal has a right
> To carry that exalted air;
> Best people are not angels quite:
> While—not the worst of people's doings scare
> The devil; so there's that proud look to spare!
> —Robert Browning, *Pippa Passes*

The naturalists discussed in chapter 6 demonstrate that deep disadvantage is as harmful to a child as any inherent soul-darkness, and it is much more likely to entangle him. The experience of innumerable people and the preponderance of literary and film artifacts affirm that these two important and ponderous extremes, the angel and the demon child, can be overly emphasized. We have been discussing the nature of children and, just as much, the nature of the representation of children. We have seen how classic statements in formative years defined the poles of possibility and that these outer edges have frayed, sometimes. There are limitations and outright weaknesses in the concepts of angel and demon, and there are important mitigations that help us to more securely situate and balance them.

Once again these mitigations emerge after dialectical inquiry of the sort that doesn't so much contest as correlate. As further informed and even inspired by Aristotelian moderation and the conciliatory mean, the remainder of this study turns to how books and films have cultivated an expansive and wonderfully fertile middle ground.

In the 1890s the pioneering French filmmakers Auguste and Louis Lumière helped to inaugurate the entire film medium with the invention

7. Reconciling and Synthesizing Polar Positions

of their superb Cinematograph. This compact and extremely mobile miracle photographed, developed, and projected strips of film, and enabled the Lumières, or more particularly the many cameramen in their employ, to travel throughout the world gathering images. As they did so, they occasionally ventured into the fictional, and many, many of their films were arranged or directed, in one way or other. Still, for the most part, the Lumières made and distributed documentaries.

It is a now a commonplace to point out that these documentary images also contained much of ideology, hierarchy, colonialism, and so on. This is certain. But for all of that, the Lumière films also have a direct, uninflected, indexical relationship to their subjects. Much of what they show is simply true.

Scores of Lumière titles featured children, and the truth that they demonstrate is an edifyingly untidy one. These films reveal children that are energetic and curious, sociable and tractable, resourceful and irrepressible and tender. The ideal and its counter are in evidence, but there is so much more besides!

Because of technical limitations, the Lumière films lasted no longer than forty or fifty seconds. How can we read all of this abundance into films that were so brief, and silent besides? It is because for these few seconds the children are not constrained by scenarios or scripts or directorial edict. They are not contained by philosophical predisposition or preconception. It is true that they feel freed or restrained by their clothing, by the event being recorded, by the presence of adults—depending on which adults are present—or by their absence, by the fact that they are in their own milieu, or perhaps abroad and on holiday. They are freed or restrained by their company or their comparative solitude, by work or by play, by social custom or by the resisting thereof. Though restricted in all sorts of ways, the mercurial and multiple dispositions of these children are still clearly in evidence. And the world is as multiple as they are! Essences can be distilled, or forced, on the stage and on a page. On the streets and the lanes, however, in the fields and in the forests, essence and existence intermingle with dizzying abundance.

Fervent testimony and overwhelming evidence attests that children are angels. And that children are devils. *Peter Pan*, which has offered compelling testimony in support of the latter assertion, also has something more mediatory to say on this matter:

> Tink was not all bad; or, rather, she was all bad just now, but, on the other hand, sometimes she was all good. Fairies have to be one thing or the other, because being so small they unfortunately have room for one

feeling only at a time. They are, however, allowed to change, only it must be a complete change.¹

In this passage James Barrie very nicely gets the measure of a child's mutable emotional makeup. She is passionate, deeply feeling, and prone to being either this or that. But in addition to offering an apt psychological observation, Barrie might also be lampooning the literary and cinematic extremes that we have been surveying. At the time of his writing, they constituted a still predominant bifurcation in children's literature. This may, in turn, have contributed to an untenable perception and division with regard to real life children. One or the other is good for defining properties or for establishing boundaries. One or the other can definitely contribute to the vivid telling of a compelling story. And in the trenches, on the tarmacs of family and community life, one or the other cedes to a more reasonable combination of views: children are almost always a complicated, recoupable combination of the two.

Save for certain unusual and distressing clinical extremes (scrupulosity, sociopathology), the designation of angel or devil, whether applied to the child or the adult, is almost always inflated. Dante speaks of the

> three dispositions
> That strike at Heaven's will: incontinence
> and malice and mad bestiality [;]
> And how the fault that is the least condemned
> And least offends God is incontinence [.]²

The episode of the woman taken in adultery, as recorded in the eighth chapter of the Gospel of John, suggests that Jesus might have felt similarly. She had erred, greatly, and he had reproved her in no uncertain terms. But he had reproved her would-be executioners much more strongly, and after having dispensed with them, he chose encouragement over condemnation. "Sin no more" must have included "do better," which certainly implied that better was well within the woman's capacities and perhaps even in her nature.³ Similarly, and even more relevant to the present subject, Jesus's evidently cheerful contributions to the wedding at Cana demonstrate that his definition of continence was not Draconian, or extreme.⁴ We might combine these two incidents and imagine that the children that Jesus placed in the midst of his disciples and presented as examples to be emulated were perfect in the aggregate, but naturally or appropriately spirited in fact. If they were, then it had to be that they occasionally went too far, or acted incontinently. If they did, then divinity was surely not overly offended.

Dante's sentiment applies very nicely to children. Seminal books like those by George Eliot or Richard Hughes vividly mark the outer edges of this argument. Contemporary children's books tend to take a more conciliatory approach, where naughty and nice are unproblematically combined. Here a very few examples among a very many possibilities.

American writer/illustrator David Small's *Eulalie and the Hopping Head* (2003) demonstrates to the reader that imperfect children are fun, and naturally occurring, and proper. *When Findus Was Little and Disappeared* (2007), by Sweden's Sven Nordqvist, features a clamorous infant who causes considerable consternation when he gets himself lost. Disorder multiplies in a subsequent search. None of this is put to the child's account, however, as he is so precious, and so little too.

In John Burningham's English kids' classic, *Mr. Gumpy's Outing* (1970), kindly Mr. Gumpy tells the youngsters accompanying him that they must do this thing, and that they must not do that other. They all disobey, after a fashion. Mild disasters ensue. No great harm results. Mr. Gumpy does not become impatient or angry, because he knows that at their age the children can't quite help themselves. In *Trubloff* (1965) we find another of Burningham's young protagonists disobeying in a way that is both profitable and necessary. Mindful parents are sometimes overmindful. Mistakes can turn to instruction and profit. Family commitment ensures that all of these small difficulties and misunderstandings can be reconciled.

Contrarily, the Netherlandish writer Max Velthuijs's *Frog and the Wild World* (2000) features a youngster who isn't ready to venture out, but who insists on doing so anyway. As everyone said would happen, Frog gets into difficulty, and in doing so frustrates the plans of a better-prepared, more mature companion. We learn that better-prepared people anticipate and understand this kind of thing. Next time the child should listen. Or next time he might just be ready.

Velthuijs's Frog is self-aware, or at least is on his way to becoming so. In *Stuck* (2011), Oliver Jeffers, of Northern Ireland, gives us a protagonist who is blithely oblivious to the inconvenience he causes the rest of the world. Floyd gets his kite stuck in a tree and then proceeds to throw everything and then everyone else at hand in order to dislodge it. First a cat, then a duck, and a chair, a bicycle, the kitchen sink, the front door, the family car, the milkman, the orangutan, a small and a big boat, a rhinoceros, a lorry, a house, a lighthouse and a very surprised whale. The firemen in their fire truck arrive. Floyd makes use of them, and they get stuck as well.

By small and surprising means, Floyd finally succeeds in getting his kite loose. Then he goes blithely off, "enjoying the rest of his day very much."[5] He doesn't notice, never even considers that all of the things and the people he exploited are still stuck in the tree. "That night Floyd fell asleep exhausted, though before he did he could have sworn there was something he'd forgotten."[6] There is an implicit caution in Jeffers' story, but its explicit and gleeful narcissism may obscure it. And where's the harm? Self-absorption, developmentally normative and even appropriate, all most amusingly and affectionately presented.

Amusement and affection are possible because self-absorption is almost never isolated, exclusive, or unmitigated. Barbara Reid's joyful *Perfect Snow* (2009) features a whole schoolyard full of Canadian kids, making something of a wintertime mess during recess and the lunch hour. As they disarrange and build up last night's massive snow drifts, their high spirits, resourcefulness and irrepressible optimism completely outpace any mild childish impropriety. Neither their teachers nor their creator even remotely consider reproving them.

These sweet picture books, with their bracing bits of savor, are all in fun. The place and status of seemingly bad behavior, however, is really of profoundest import. We have discussed how Sunday School divisions might distract us from the developmental, psychological, therapeutic fact that there is much more to naughtiness than conventional poles and perceptions may suggest. The natural and proper contrariness of children takes on different dimensions when removed from the nursery and placed in a more elemental, evolutionary setting. The principle, though, remains basically the same. Jack London, *White Fang* (1906):

> But there were other forces at work in the cub, the greatest of which was growth. Instinct and law demanded of him obedience. But growth demanded disobedience. His mother and fear impelled him to keep away from the white wall. Growth is life, and life is forever destined to make for light. So there was no damming up the tide of life that was rising within him—rising with every mouthful of meat he swallowed, with every breath he drew. In the end, one day, fear and obedience were swept away by the rush of life, and the cub straddled and sprawled toward the entrance.[7]

Here we find that though authority may try to contain, youth will out. London further states that a less seemly situation is also healthy and necessary:

> White Fang knew the law well: *to oppress the weak and obey the strong*. He ate his share of meat as rapidly as he could. And then woe the dog that had not yet finished! A snarl and a flash of fangs, and that dog

7. Reconciling and Synthesizing Polar Positions 175

would wail his indignation to the uncomforting stars while White Fang finished his portion for him.[8]

A wolf is a wolf, but young readers and their affectionate adult minders may perceive that this is analogous to human competition and striving, in any number of settings and circumstances. Further, and perhaps more poignantly, both of these quotations suggest the natural and often painful processes of separation and individuation. By some models, and to some degree, growing up will always involve a degree of conflict and discomfort. By almost any measure, this kind of discomfort is necessary and carries with it the possibility of independence, expansion, and greater happiness.

Young readers treasure Jack London for his vivid way with an adventurous tale. We have already discussed some of the tenets of naturalism, which also very much inform London's writing. But one need not be committed to the depredations of environment and heredity in order to subscribe to this larger idea. Even outside of such elemental settings, aggressive or unseemly behavior can often be a very good thing.

The following episode occurs near the end of Tove Jansson's beautiful short story "The Invisible Child." Everyone has gone to the seashore. Moominmamma looks out to appreciate the prospect that greets them there. Moominpappa pretends that he is going to push her into the water, though it is clearly evident to almost everybody that he is only joking. However,

> Before he reached her a pink streak shot over the landing stage, and Moominpappa let out a scream and drooped his hat into the water. Ninny had sunk her small ... teeth in Moominpappa's tail, and they were sharp....
> Ninny was standing on the landing stage. She had a small, snub-nosed, angry face below a red tangle of hair.[9]

By most measures Ninny has behaved inappropriately. In most every imaginable circumstance one should not bite one's kindly host on the tail, especially when one is a little child.

By most measures, but not by all: preachment depends upon principle, and text can be inflected and even overturned by context. Ninny is the invisible child referred to in the story's title. The tale begins with her being so worried, so belittled by the scornful criticism and outright dismissal of a careless adult that she has positively, literally disappeared. At this point, tiny, insignificant Ninny is introduced to the healingly nurturing Moomin family. She stays with them, and as she does so, she slowly, incrementally begins to fade back into view. This is a tremendous advance, but it is not without its wrinkles and complications. As Ninny re-emerges it becomes clear that her habitual deprivation has had its serious effects. She has not learned to play properly, she is prone to get angry, and she never laughs.

Despite all this Ninny's loving hosts bear with her, encourage her, draw her out. Moominmamma is especially instrumental, especially faithful in the performance of her challenging and irrefutable moral duty to this little charge.

It is in this context that the previously described behavioral indiscretion takes place. Seconds before Ninny had been frightened by the vast expanses stretched before her. She has, after all, been inconsequential all of her life. How much more so before the infinite and heedless ocean? As usual, Moominmamma reassures her. This is why, when a seeming threat presents itself, Ninny is able to put away her feelings of insecurity and insignificance. For the first time she asserts herself, her physique, her personality. This is why, for the first time, she becomes fully visible. As we have seen, then:

> Ninny was standing on the landing stage. She had a small, snub-nosed, angry face below a red tangle of hair.
> "Good work!" cried My. "I couldn't have done it better myself!"
> "Don't you dare push her into the big horrible sea!" [Ninny] hissed [at Moominpappa].
> "I see her; I see her!" shouted Moomintroll. "She's sweet."
> "Sweet my eye," said Moominpappa. "She's the silliest, nastiest, badly brought-uppest child I've ever seen, with or with-out a head."[10]

Little My, whom we have already met, is the Moomin clan's infinitesimal, infinitely/wonderfully contrary adopted child. She always says things like that, and she is rarely opposed when she does so. She is, it might be said, in the middle of a developmental a stage, which can only be left to work itself out. Meanwhile, she still and always belongs.[11]

For his part Moomintroll is, to mix our cosmological metaphors, very much like Christ's exemplary child, unwaveringly submissive and meek, unremittingly generous and loving. And as sweet as he or any ideal/ized child might be, Moomintroll is right in saying that Ninny's seeming ill behavior is sweeter. Her bad temper and patent disrespect have replaced her previous non-entity, and are far preferable to it. What are Disney doe-eyes to the thriving, contrary healthiness of flaming red hair and a snub nose?[12]

As for angry Moominpappa, he far overestimates the gravity of the offense, and far overstates the guilt of the offender. Are not these words that leave permanent wounds? Has Ninny made all this progress only to fall all the way back to her brutalized beginning?

Well, no. If kids can err, then so can, and so will, adults. Strong personalities in healthy relationships can make mistakes, make up, and move on. In other words, and at the end of all of these illustrations, bad is good! All the way across the board! And good can be a little less circumspect than it tries, or sometimes makes itself out to be. Cardinal points are essential for all sorts of important orientation and orienteering, but literature, and life even more, must allow for the diagonal, or the hybrid.

So it is that in this instance Ninny's temper and disrespect are also tenders of love and loyalty, emblems of her emerging self-esteem. They may even lead to her eventual autonomy. Marx can be martial, or melodramatic, but Hegel's dialectical project describes *internal* contradictions, simultaneously intractable and capable of reconciliation. Faithful Martha, careful and troubled about so many good things, is blind to the better part represented by Jesus's visit, and his ministrations.[13] Could it be that sensitive Mary, fully justified as she sits at Christ's feet, has in the past run out on a chore or two? A child's best qualities can and do occasionally present less ideally. Her less seemly traits can be useful, even exemplary, in certain situations.

The Mean, Between Extremes, with a Little Bit of Dominance and Recession Thrown In

We have been moving from polarization to the layered, complex rendering of character. This kind of psychological nuance is a commonplace in the adult record. More than that, this kind of nuance is who and what people are. This is both the knottiest problem and the greatest satisfaction of what we might presume to call real life. It is certainly the frequent concern, one of the greatest appeals of adult discourse in the social sciences, as well as in theatre and literature and film. And it has been applied to and very much increased our understanding of the subject of children.

Anthony Trollope's 1855 novel *The Warden* features a number of microscopically detailed, infinitesimally perceptive descriptions of its central characters, and of the narrative currents in which they find themselves. One of the most concentrated of these descriptions occur in the eighth chapter, "Plumstead Episcopi," in which we are introduced to Dr. Grantly's three sons.

They were called, respectively, Charles James, Henry, and Samuel.... The boys were all clever, and gave good promise of being well able to meet the cares and trials of the world; and yet they were not alike in their dispositions, and each had his individual character, and each his separate admirers among the doctor's friends.

Dr. Grantly's eldest is a plain and dutiful soul:

> Charles James was an exact and careful boy; he never committed himself; he well knew how much was expected from the eldest son of the Archdeacon of Barchester, and was therefore mindful not to mix too freely with other boys. He had not the great talents of his younger brothers, but he exceeded them in judgment and propriety of demeanour.[14]

A lack of spontaneity, a possible excess in caution or reserve, also makes Charles James the most reliable of the brothers. A want of conspicuous talent is compensated for by an abundance of virtue, or discretion. This virtuous discretion, however, has another aspect: "His fault, if he had one, was an over-attention to words instead of things; there was a thought too much finesses about him, and, as even his father sometimes told him, he was too fond of a compromise."[15]

The doctor's second son is a lad o' parts, his gifts inextricably intertwined with clear, related defects: "The second was the archdeacon's favourite son, and Henry was indeed a brilliant boy. The versatility of his genius was surprising.... He was a most courageous lad, game to the backbone."[16] Abstract qualities like these become particular, and sometimes problematic, in specific settings and interactions:

> It was soon known ... that young Henry could box well and would never own himself beat; other boys would fight while they had a leg to stand on, but he would fight with no leg at all. The ring was the only element in which he seemed to enjoy himself; and while other boys were happy in the number of their friends, [Henry] rejoiced most in the multitude of his foes.[17]

As encountered on the playing field, we might well admire the young man who becomes bloodied but remains unbowed, who is assailed, but never yields. But steadfastness in principle can be intransigence in fact, and athletic resolve falls far short in the more diplomatic precincts of family and community.

> [Henry's] relations could not but admire his pluck, but they sometimes were forced to regret that he was inclined to be a bully; and those not so partial to him as his father was, observed with pain that, though he could fawn to the masters and the archdeacon's friends, he was imperious and masterful to the servants and the poor.[18]

7. Reconciling and Synthesizing Polar Positions

How often do we admire the strong-willed, and how often decry the bully? How often do we realize that these two qualities often operate in tandem? Do we consider that a possible, frequent consequence of resolute leadership is partial, even rank insensitivity to the rights and reasons of those being led?

Trollope continues with Samuel, or Soapy, his mother's pet, and his brothers' nemesis.

> He was soft and gentle in his manners, and attractive in his speech; the tone of his voice was melody, and every action was a grace; unlike his brothers, he was courteous to all, he was affable to the lowly, and meek even to the very scullery-maid. He was a boy of great promise, minding his books and delighting the hearts of his masters. His brothers, however, were not particularly fond of him; they would complain to their mother that Soapy's civility all meant something.... Henry declared that he was a false, cunning creature; and Charles James, though he always spoke of him as his dear brother Samuel, was not slow to say a word against him when opportunity offered. To speak the truth, Samuel was a cunning boy, and those even who loved him best could not but own that for one so young, he was too adroit in choosing his words, and too skilled in modulating his voice.[19]

With each of these three boys, what seemed at first to be unalloyed virtue turns into a muddle of the positive and the near-perfidious. And yet, can we be sure of this? In introducing the boys our narrator suggested that they "gave good promise of being well able to meet the cares and trials of the world." With all of the uncertainty and mixed motives that every child is sure to encounter, these Machiavellian muddles might well be necessary.

This mixing of merit and shortcoming is also, unsurprisingly, manifest outside of the bounds of narrative. The superbly perceptive and expansive Anthony Trollope has this to say about Dr. Grantly's two daughters:

> The two little girls Florinda and Grizzel were nice little girls enough, but they did not possess the strong sterling qualities of their brothers; their voices were not often heard at Plumstead Episcopi; they were bashful and timid by nature, slow to speak before company even when asked to do so; and though they looked very nice in their clean white muslin frocks and pink sashes, they were but little noticed by the archdeacon's visitors.[20]

There have been and will continue to be many inconsequential young women in the world. Their image could well and fairly be applied to a literary project like this. While accounting for the lives of his male creations, an author need not necessarily or always perform like service to his women. In other settings Trollope shows himself to be capable of doing justice to his female characters.[21] And yet, for all of that, we might venture to say that in this particular instance Trollope has fallen short. In the midst of his abundant, even shocking, psychological penetration is this clear, gender-related paucity.[22]

Good writers have blind spots and are still good writers. Adults err, sometimes egregiously, and yet are not to be utterly dismissed for all their erring. And, as illustrated, children stumble and stray and still qualify, more than anyone, for our continued patience and forbearance.

As a psychologist, Bruno Bettelheim understands and affirms these complexities. As a literary critic, and especially as a literary critic considering the therapeutic value of folk and fairy literature in the lives of children, he strongly disagrees with the notion of introducing these complexities into the nursery.

> The juxtaposition of opposite characters [in the folktale] is not for the purpose of stressing right behaviour, as would be true for cautionary tales.... Presenting the polarities of character permits the child to comprehend easily the difference between the two, which he could not do as readily were the figures drawn more true to life, with all the complexities that characterize real people. Ambiguities must wait until a relatively firm personality has been established on the basis of positive identifications.[23]

For Bettelheim, ambiguities are confusing to the developing child, and may even do him a measure of harm. So he addresses complexity from another direction and in doing so provides a wonderfully productive elaboration of the good and bad child dynamic. In one of his most elegant analyses, Bettelheim illuminates the common fairy tale motif where kindly Mother dies and is succeeded by a wicked stepmother, or Grandmother seems to have been transformed into a ravening wolf. Bettelheim suggests that these dramatic, traumatic story events can have deep psychological significance. They relate to and cope with a very distressing, confusing challenge in every child's life: what does she do with the parent or caregiver who is loving at one moment, then threatening or punitive in the next? It is in this common circumstance that

> the typical fairy-tale splitting of the mother into the good (usually dead) mother and an evil stepmother serves the child well. It is not only a means of preserving an internal all-good mother when the real mother is not all-good, but it also permits anger at this bad "stepmother" without endangering the goodwill of the true mother, who is viewed as a different person. Thus, the fairy tale suggests how the child may manage the contradictory feelings which would otherwise overwhelm him at this stage of his barely beginning ability to integrate contradictory emotions.[24]

7. Reconciling and Synthesizing Polar Positions

So it is that the ineffectually loving father and the powerfully punitive stepmother in "Hansel and Gretel" also represent a single, actual parent. The same goes for the parental cottage and the fatal witch's abode, not to mention the dark forest that lies between.[25]

It is not only the adult who is inconsistent or in conflict with himself. Bettelheim discusses how this same splitting operation also applies to the child himself: "When he experiences the emotional need to do so, the child not only splits a parent into two figures, but he may also split himself into two people who, he wishes to believe, have nothing in common with each other."[26]

Adults and children both have dual natures, at the very least. Bettelheim demonstrates how folktales conflate and distribute this duality in a number of ways that are helpful to the child's psychological and emotional development. This symbolic, therapeutic splitting serves the child through the course of her journey toward maturity. Eventually her subordination to parents will be succeeded by a degree of autonomy, and then by adulthood, and finally, perhaps, by the child becoming a parent herself. In parallel, the female figures of the stepmother and the witch in "Hansel and Gretel" give way to the male figures in "Little Red Riding Hood," the ravening wolf and the rescuing hunter, the seeming seducer and the nurturing protector/breadwinner.[27] This is also true of Madame De Villeneuve's Beast, whose terrifying physicality—read sexuality—evolves until it is perceived and welcomed as loving and life-enhancing.[28]

These are fascinating, affirmative insights. Bettelheim's split or polarized characters are quite distinct from the idealistic and melodramatic sorts already considered. His oppositions are not facile, or frightened, or self-satisfied. He applies them in a very particular way, but the juxtaposition of opposites can also operate in nontherapeutic contexts and independent of Bettelheim's prescriptions. Delineated or separated characters form a kind of figurative aggregate in a number of other settings, with a number of productive results.

Splitting can also contribute to the portrayal and understanding of idealized good children, as well as to our graduation to a more realistically integrated notion of children's actual goodness. Cecil B. DeMille's *King of Kings* (1927) is an intensive study and celebration of Christ's ministry, sacrificial death, and triumphant resurrection. Predictably, given Christ's teaching on the subject, children play an important part in the narrative. At the beginning of the film, DeMille and scenarist Jeannie MacPherson create an effectively suspenseful anticipation in the audience by withholding the Divine Presence for some time. As they do so, they lay out in convincing detail the conditions that necessitate his coming and his saving intervention.

A prologue features a resplendent and utterly unrepentant Mary Magdalene, surrounded by Roman revelers, exulting in her iniquity and in the material abundance that supports and sweetens it. But today Mary is missing one of her favorites, one Judas Iscariot. She wonders where he has been of late.[29] She is informed that Judas has abandoned brazen pomp in order to follow a remarkable carpenter, lately come from Nazareth. Mary is taken aback, but in her surprise she is equal parts scornful and confident. She will go to see this carpenter, and confront him, and again take possession of her lover.

Mary Magdalene and all that she represents is about to be countered and defeated. It is not Jesus, however, who strikes the first blow, but rather an unexpected pair of his most perfect followers. From this first excess, DeMille turns to excess of another kind, a broad courtyard before a much more humble dwelling place. The space is filled with aspirants and communicants, a multitude clamoring for attention or relief. Here is another kind of abundance, of poverty and pain, of the halt and the lame. Like Mary Magdalene's patrons, these individuals also seek a boon, but of an altogether more fundamental, desperate kind. It has been noised about that Jesus is in the house.

Out of the press emerges a little boy, alone and in rags, reaching out uncertainly. He is seven or eight years old, and he is blind. The blind boy accosts the nearest adult: "Take me to Him, please—I cannot find Him!" This adult, in rags and holding a crutch himself, cannot help. But now another child appears, a boy of 11 or 12 years. DeMille and MacPherson are elaborating, once again. An intertitle tells us that this is "Young Mark ... healed by the Great Physician; and destined to be one of the FOUR to write the immortal Gospels." There is no scriptural or historical authority for this elaboration. Be that as it may, Mark is also holding a crutch, but it turns out that he no longer needs it. He is lifting and shaking and kicking his right leg, until just lately useless to him. The leg has just been restored, by Jesus, to wholeness.

These two children, combined, constitute an affecting, effective composite. The gentle little blind boy will presently lead the spectator to Jesus, who will be most artfully and movingly introduced by means of the child's sight being restored. This will happen by degrees, and the gradual illumination will resolve into the very first image that the child has ever seen, which is the kindly face of his divine benefactor.

For his part, Mark is much more hale, and assertive, and efficacious.

7. Reconciling and Synthesizing Polar Positions 183

But he is not yet an adult, and for now we are still dealing with the early formation of the impending Evangelist. Now an intertitle—"Spies of the High Priest—PHARISEE, SCRIBE, and TEMPLE GUARD"—alerts us to the presence of the Jewish clergy, and the villains of the piece. Mark has just brained one of these eminences with the crutch that he had just tossed away. The Pharisee confronts Mark as a reckless, disrespectful scamp. In fact, DeMille, as director, would seem to concur with this assessment. Mark will appear intermittently throughout the film and will sometimes act in a manner that is unconsidered and nearly unbecoming.

But DeMille also makes it clear that this young scamp has still, quite properly, been deemed worthy of divine favor. The Pharisee tells Mark that this man, Jesus, is not of God. Once again departing from the standard Gospel Concordance, MacPherson gives Mark the mighty rejoinder: "This I know—that I was lame before, and now I WALK!"[30] Here is a declaration, and a celebration. It is also an impropriety. Mark laughs impertinently at the man, who after all is an adult and an authorized official. And if Mark knew better, he would be in the wrong. But at the stage of development at which he finds himself, and knowing what he does, and especially in comparison to the whited wall that confronts him,[31] DeMille's brave boy has little to repent of. And again, this is even more the case if we consider these two boys as a kind of composite, the tender heart and the brave spirit of perfect childhood. Appearing together in the narrative itself, or figuratively conflated in a psychoanalytical reading, this is the child that Jesus so joyfully and lovingly suffers.[32]

A similarly bright aggregation operates more variably, which is to say with a greater expanse, in D. W. Griffith's *The Sunbeam* (February 1912, Biograph No. 391). Here is one of Griffith's most perfect productions, and one of the most exemplary and productive films in the entire children's genre. Little Inez Seabury, not yet five years old, plays the lead. She is angelic, as per usual with Griffith. She circulates, however, in the midst of a broader, unmelodramatic array of personality types. None of these are vilified or condemned, so that the collective ends up providing a whole spectrum of viable, laudable behavioral and dispositional options.

Little Inez, the eponymous sunbeam, lives in a tenement, and her mother lies ailing in their flat upstairs. Inez goes below to find someone to play with or something to do. But the other bright children are too rambunctious for her, so she approaches first a flinty spinster, and then the lonely bachelor who lives across the hall. They interact, very prettily. But now the spinster thinks that the child has made off with her "hair puff." She follows her into the man's flat to retrieve it. Just as she does so those older, more rambunctious children stick a Scarlet Fever quarantine sign to the bachelor's door. The police arrive immediately and refuse to let anybody out until the emergency has passed. Forced into close quarters, and with the child to draw them together, the lonely people warm to each other. The scamps' prank is soon exposed, and the captives are released. Together the spinster and the bachelor take the child back upstairs to her own place. The little girl's mother has died in the interim. Stirred by the call of duty and by their newly awakened tender feelings, they resolve to wed, and adopt, and form a family.

Because she is a child, the Inez Seabury character successfully performs the same saving work as George Eliot's Eppie. And, as with Eppie, she is framed by a social and child-psychological diversity. The setting, and the details with which it is rendered, situates her sweetness and vulnerability in a plausible and productive way.

The Sunbeam takes place in just three rooms and two hallways, but these are fairly bursting with "playful romps, the practical jokes, and the unfolding of the gentle love story."[33] Russell Merritt quotes a perceptive contemporary review from *The Moving Picture World*:

> The picture is a picture of vivid life, centered on the child with all her special needs and budding ideas. And how true a picture of life it is. In the foreground, there are plenty of children, just 'kids' of the tenement, brim full of life and up to all kinds of pranks. In the middle distance are the two middle-aged lovers, and in the background, there is death … a wonderfully, but calmly quietly, suggestive picture of death. It isn't at all tragic and in this lies its remarkable freshness. As for that, this picture of death is something new. We don't know what to call it. The producer doesn't comment on this death or criticize it in any way; he merely shows it to us simply.[34]

Merritt points out that it is not just death, but that the scarlet fever quarantine—an actual epidemic would break out in New York City that very summer—police wielding their clubs, and three lonely people being mocked and excluded make for a real bleakness in the midst of the film's prevailing positivity. As was so often the case with these films, there is a context that both grounds and deepens what might otherwise be dismissed as mere sentimentality.

More to the point, however, Bettelheim's composite has here been expanded and enriched, coming to form a broader anthology of possibilities. Mocked and excluded? "People of distinction gathered in his house. Some had noble blood, others noble spirits; and a few had both, and a number had neither. But now there was a children's party, and children

7. Reconciling and Synthesizing Polar Positions 185

have a habit of saying what they think."[35] This is Hans Andersen's "Children's Prattle," and during the course of the gathering it describes its young characters will say a number of unkind and judgmental and insufferable things. In this case, Andersen, who knew much of incomprehension and unkindness in his life, chooses not to respond in kind:

> What happened to the other children: the offspring of good family, wealth, and intellectual arrogance?—None of them could point a finger at any of the others; they had all been equally silly—they had become decent and kind human beings, for they were, in truth, not evil. What they had thought and said then had only been children's prattle.[36]

Apart from the Sunbeam herself, none of the children in Griffith's film, and in fact none of its characters of any age, is without flaw or failing. And yet despite and because of this, and because of the generous attitude that is applied to their shortcomings, each character ends up being recoupable, justified, and even plausibly ideal.[37]

In some ways, Bruno Bettelheim's admirable equations echo the moral geometries of Aristotle's mean. Both apply in any number of narrative settings. In the second act and third scene of *Romeo and Juliet*, Shakespeare's Friar Laurence holds forth on the subtle, contradictory, reconcilable powers of "baleful weeds and precious-juiced flowers…"

> For naught so vile that on the earth doth live
> But to the earth some special good doth give,
> Nor aught so good but strain'd from that fair use
> Revolts from true birth, stumbling on abuse:
> Virtue itself turns vice, being misapplied;
> And vice sometimes by action dignified.[38]

Friar Laurence is talking to his impulsive and passionate young charge, Romeo. He is relating the mean to Romeo's impending relations with ardent, innocent Juliet.

> Within the infant rind of this small flower
> Poison hath residence and medicine power:
> For this, being smelt, with that part cheers each part;
> Being tasted, slays all senses with the heart.
> Two such opposed kings encamp them still
> In man as well as herbs, grace and rude will;
> And where the worser is predominant,
> Full soon the canker death eats up that plant.[39]

This herbological discourse of course doubles as a sermon on the blessed necessities and the potential pitfalls of sexual desire. It seems to describe an exact midpoint, with cold abstention and dire incontinence equidistant on either side. Moderation, says the Friar. This is seemly and sensible advice, generously and joyfully given.

Virtue is the midpoint between excess and defect, and this notion applies in romantic and reproductive settings. And the issue? Lynne Reid Banks' children's novel *Angela and Diabola* (1977) echoes Bettelheim's good and bad child bifurcation at the same time that it provocatively illustrates the Mean. Published six years after William Peter Blatty's *The Exorcist* (1971), Banks' novel seems to be aware of its literary predecessor—or at least of Blatty and Friedkin's film adaptation, released in 1973. This surprising source, or echo, raises the stakes of the conversation, and ensures that that conversation go beyond mere idealization or stereotype.

Banks' book is quite beautifully conceived and executed. A pair of female twins is born to an English mother and father. Angela is the Angel Child and a shining light. Diabola is the Bad Seed, an agent of convincingly escalating malice. At first the sisters behave and misbehave in a manner consistent with their stature and role. Soon, they graduate. Angela becomes a convincing, quite moving minister of grace. Diabola devolves, and quite monstrously. Property is damaged, then property is destroyed. The escalation continues. Fathers depart, ministers lose their sense of calling and then their belief in God. Diabola breaks things, then hurts things, badly. Eventually there is a shocking, quite apocalyptic portrayal of death.

As with, say, the Grimms' "The Fisherman and his Wife," these ministrations even start to affect the elements themselves. The results are unusually powerful and frightening. Beyond affect, it seems that the point of the book is that either extreme, in literature or in life, is unnatural. As the girls further separate, they discover that they can't continue separately and that either extreme is untenable. This is unusual, and unexpected, at least in a competitive, victor/vanquished setting. Conventional morality, or at least melodrama, would seem to suggest that Diabola must be dispensed with, not appeased or absorbed. Nevertheless, Reid Banks' solution is to have the children eventually meld. It appears that Diabola has been eliminated, but the Angela that remains is a paragon no more. Idealistic impulse might blanch, but it is not at all dystopian or nihilistic to conclude with a child that both shines and tarnishes.

The mean is almost geometrical, and its dimensions can be mapped almost exactly. "With regard to feelings of fear and confidence courage is the mean; ... [he who] exceeds in confidence is rash, and he who exceeds in fear and falls short in confidence is a coward."[40] This geometrical exactitude coincides, in some ways, with the strict separations of Socrates and Plato, as previously discussed.[41] We have suggested that with regard to stories and young people Socrates and Plato might have gone too far. The same may be true of geometry. Childhood, domesticity, recreation, and moral development itself tend not to be this tidy. Even the sublime Aristotle does not always apply, at least not to these dear subjects in these dear settings.

Mathematical calculations seek exactitude, while chemical equations seek reasonable predictability. Organic and reproductive exchanges are more subject to variables and indeterminacies. In the eventual issue, parental traits can emerge either dominantly or recessively. Or, to leave aside metaphors, outside of fairy tale and didactic settings, in more realistic stories, opposites will continue to meet in numerous ways. The product of that union will not always be as tidy or as predictable as Aristotle, or Bettelheim, would have it. And yet, when dealing with children and children's narrative, there must be a way to recognize and reward virtue, even in the presence of a little excess and defect.

André Bazin found continuities between silent and sound cinema, and this study charts similar correlations between literature and film for children and families. More, it hints at productive, necessary correlations between the arts and the actualities of family life. Regardless of initial intent or manner of distribution, children's film and literature always concerns real childhoods, real struggles and strategies of child-raising, and real family life. A certain kind of story tidies and reconciles contradictions, as may the striving psychological subject. In a scholarly survey such effacement is not necessary. And ultimately in the literature entire, and in the way it impinges upon and implicates actual lives, it may not be possible or desirable.

Ideally Balanced: Grahame, Collodi and Anne Frank

Contra (or in addition to) Bettelheim, the juxtaposition of opposites can operate in nontherapeutic contexts. The meeting or melding of opposites can also be productively untidy. Numerous literary and cinematic benchmarks illustrate the rich results. Kenneth Grahame's children's classic, *The Wind in the Willows* (1908), is a case in point. In the same way that Bettelheim reads folktale characters as figurative composites, so might Grahame's Toad and Mole constitute a superb compound of childish possibility, just as Rat and Badger represent a happy range of adult actuality. The many episodes and adventures in this particularly lovely book stand alone for their narrative interest and pleasure. In addition, however, if the reader would care to attend, she will also find a very expansive portrait of what young and old people are, and particularly what they can be as they combine their forces and their lives in mutual commitment and affection.

Quite early in the book we read of Mole's failed attempt to row Ratty's boat, which leads to a capsizing in which they nearly lose of all of their precious cargo. Mole had been impatient and impulsive, which has led to some considerable inconvenience and has even done some damage. So far, so childish. But there is another part to this equation. Mole is in the wrong and is mortified as a result, and he apologizes without pride or reservation. Better, sweeter: not only does Ratty forgive him freely, but he willingly goes two extra miles: "look here! I really think you had better come and stop with me for a little time…. And I'll teach you to row, and to swim, and you'll soon be as handy on the water as any of us."[42]

Mole learns from his errors, but he also learns from the way that Ratty responds to those errors. Ratty will occasionally take time to offer correction, but he also accepts and loves Mole unconditionally. Mole responds in kind, according to his capacities. These capacities are limited, as befits a little child. Mole will fall short again. But Mole's capacities, in terms of tractability and tender affection, are also practically inexhaustible.

Rat and Mole go on to visit Mr. Toad. Ratty lays the groundwork for what will be a complicated acquaintance and then, ultimately, a complicated and satisfying friendship.

> "Early or late he's always the same fellow. Always good tempered, always glad to see you, always sorry when you go!"
> "He must be a very nice animal," observed the Mole.

Having been judged gently in the face of his own errors and failings, Mole has learned to deal in a kindly fashion with his fellows. In this, as in so much else, Rat is ever the exemplar, both for Mole and for the young reader. Most readers will remember Toad's prodigious appetite and aptitude for mischief. For Rat, though this may be the most impressive point about Mr. Toad, it is not the most pertinent one: "'He is indeed the best of animals,' replied Rat. 'So simple, so good-natured, and so affectionate. Perhaps he's not very clever—we can't all be geniuses; and it may be that he is both boastful and conceited. But he has got some great qualities, has Toady.'"[43]

Previous to this last conversation, Rat had been discussing Toad with the Otter. They had discovered that, after a number of conspicuous unsuccesses—Toad had been unable to sail successfully, and had failed at punt-

7. Reconciling and Synthesizing Polar Positions

ing, and had practically scuppered his houseboat—Toad was back out on the water. In some consternation, given that his friends have had to extricate him from his tight spots—they now discuss Toad's flightiness. Their bemusement is leavened by deep affection: "'It's all the same whatever he takes up; he gets tired of it, and starts something fresh.' "'Such a good fellow, too,' remarked the Otter reflectively: 'But no stability—especially in a boat!'" Then they spot him: "a wager-boat flashed into view, the rower—a short, stout figure—splashing badly and rolling a good deal, but working his hardest."[44]

Mole and Toad are a compound child, which is to say that they are a literary conceit with a number of therapeutic benefits attached. This last exchange brings to mind another of Bettelheim's observations, and the idea toward which his literary analyses were tending. It is not just Mole and Toad together. Toad himself constitutes his very own compound. As Anthony Trollope had demonstrated, and as our lives affirm when we avoid hasty or melodramatic judgment, everyone is, with good and bad intermingled, with good and bad not always easily distinguishable. What a muddle, and a puzzlement! What an encouragement, and an optimism. It is such scene-setting, pointedness and kindness intermingled, that allows stories like these to help us understand, bear with, and love one another.

As with the child, so too the adult. Mr. Toad has caused another disaster, and his friend the Badger steps in:

> You've disregarded all the warnings we've given you ... and you're getting us animals a bad name in the district by your furious driving and your smashes and your rows with the police. Independence is all very well, but we animals never allow our friends to make fools of themselves beyond a certain limit; and that limit you've reached. Now, you're a good fellow in many respects, and I don't want to be too hard on you. I'll make one more effort to bring you to reason. You will come with me into the smoking-room, and there you will hear some facts about yourself; and we'll see whether you come out of that room the same Toad that you went in.[45]

This is the kind of thing that adults do, and the kind of thing that adults are for. It is easy, and often proper, to lampoon or even decry the way that grown-ups are always taking youngsters in hand, or taking their hands to the youngsters. And yet, imperfect execution does not necessarily invalidate the thing being attempted. The cruelties of Mr. Murdstone have nothing to do with the kindly (if extremely eccentric) corrections of Miss Betsy Trotwood, nor do they in any way jeopardize the right and reason that she has to correct.[46]

Badger is the necessarily, benevolently admonishing yin to Ratty's faithfully nurturing yang, his complementary, unconflicted opposite. He is an essential component of the compounded adult. He carries on.

> Through the closed door they could just hear the long continuous drone of the Badger's voice, rising and falling in waves of oratory; and presently they noticed that the sermon began to be punctuated at intervals by long-drawn sobs, evidently proceeding from the bosom of Toad, who was a soft-hearted and affectionate fellow, very easily converted—for the time being—to any point of view.[47]

Ratty and Badger are two parts of the same adult, Toad and Mole two parts of the same child. Toad's wailings, and the shortcomings that they reflect, bring to mind a similar incident connected with his more delicate counterpart. Here is Mole, confronted with a formidable, though not unsolvable, problem:

> The Mole subsided forlornly on a tree-stump and tried to control himself, for he felt it surely coming. The sob he had fought with so long refused to be beaten. Up and up, it forced its way to the air, and then another, and another, and others thick and fast; till poor Mole at last gave up the struggle, and cried freely and helplessly and openly, now that he knew it was all over and he had lost what he could hardly be said to have found.[48]

Mole had been on his way home, and had caught a glimpse of it, but lost his way again. This is an exquisite, poignant childish typicality—remember Shirley Hughes' Alfie, just home from the shops; the challenge that Mole faces is actually surmountable, but the stakes are so high, and his vulnerability on this subject is so great, that he is unable to surmount it. A crisis that the adult might consider simple or silly can be practically crippling to the child. As such, it deserves to be respected. After all, in the spirit of the Widow's mite,[49] a seeming little taken out of great privation or limitation can add up to be very much indeed.

Such glimpses of the sweet and childlike core prepare the adult for the more disordered manifestations of the compound. Later on in Grahame's book, as part of its virtuosically extended climax, Toad is dressed most memorably and hilariously as a washerwoman and is being overtaken by the vehicle that he had previously stolen, which is being driven by the people from whom he had stolen it.

> The terrible motor-car drew slowly nearer and nearer, till at last he heard it stop just short of him. Two gentlemen got out and walked round the trembling heap of crumpled misery lying in the road, and one of them said, "O dear! This is very sad! Here is a poor old thing—a washer-

woman apparently—who has fainted in the road! Perhaps she is overcome by the heat, poor creature; or possibly she has not had any food today. Let us lift her into the car and take her to the nearest village, where doubtless she has friends."

The affronted, now twice-deceived men tenderly lift Toad into the motorcar, prop him up with soft cushions, and proceed on their way.[50] In a few moments, of course, Toad will steal this vehicle once again and then immediately drive it into the horse pond.

As with the earlier, more idyllic episode with Mole and the capsized craft, there is an important, inspiring subtext to these exchanges. We have Toad, seeming to be in constant breach. Relatedly, we have numerous personages whom Toad has offended. And everywhere, eventually, we have the offended, forgiving freely. We cannot be sure of Grahame's intentions, just as we need not always appeal to what these might have been. Intended or not, this is a moral admonition to the adults who might be reading this book, especially when they are reading to or with their undoubtedly untidy and erring child. Similarly, since in Grahame the quality of mercy is not strained, the listening child cannot help but be stirred to similar liberality.

Toad is a real boy, which is to say that we ought to take warning. It is also to say that we ought not to overreact. Mole, after all, is a real boy as well. This phrase of course summons Carlo Collodi and his creation. With regard to the present conversation, *Pinocchio* quite definitively sets forth the whole contradictory, contrary, ultimately reconcilable and redeemable muddle.

We have already considered Pinocchio's spirited literary advent, and unlike Walt Disney's rendering, Pinocchio is a real problem for his overmatched parent, right from the very beginning. This episode illustrates how literature has countered idealization with what may appear to be uncomplimentary portraits of children. But *Pinocchio* is far from being uncomplimentary. It is, in fact, a very moving celebration. And yet it calmly considers all the contradictory points before arriving at that happy conclusion.

Collodi's novel begins with a very sensible take on the essence of childhood:

> Once upon a time there was a piece of wood.
> It was not the best, but just a common piece of wood, such as is used in stoves and fireplaces to kindle the fire and warm the rooms in winter.[51]

At first we merely have the raw material, and the promise or possibility of it being productively shaped. The piece of wood is not exceptional, and it is certainly not execrable. It is sufficient. At this point in the book, Geppetto fashions his creature, and immediately regrets it. Pinocchio has been disrespectful. He has kicked his creator, right on the nose. Notwithstanding, and because a naughty child is never just naughty, this follows: "[Geppetto] took the puppet in his hands, and put him down on the floor to see if he could walk; but Pinocchio's legs were stiff, and he did not know how to move them. So Geppetto led him by the hand, and showed him how to put one foot before the other."[52]

In *The Pilgrim*[53] Charlie Chaplin capped a superb bit of childish diablerie by kicking the little devil over onto the ground. Collodi's conclusion to his own scene of generative comic knockabout is even better. This very sweet, moving resolution accomplishes something that its more celebrated American film counterpart cannot approach. Disney's adaptation of *Pinocchio* is basically a Sunday School film, a moral tale with didactic elements. It is very efficient and effective in this, single-mindedly pruning the digressive, picaresque original until its unambiguous lesson stands clear and unopposed.

Collodi's original contains lessons as well, but they are bound up in something more contradictory, more complex, and ultimately, much richer. Collodi's concept is fantastic, and his scene is stylized. But underneath all that, he has fashioned a strikingly verisimilar view of family life and especially, in light of our present conversation, the nature of children.

So it is that beneath the magical, comical exchange that we have just been considering, we find a run-of-the-mill family squabble. This registers emotionally because of the scene's plausibility, and accuracy. There is aggression and pique, out of which emerge resentment and discouragement. But then, always, there is also help, loyalty, love.

The later, very affecting episode of Pinocchio's burnt feet operates similarly. Collodi stages what are basically comical slapstick scenes, and his characters respond with petulance. In this he grounds deep feeling in filial (or, in other settings, fraternal) reality. In other words, he avoids sentimentality. But he does express sentiment, and that very powerfully. The result of these combinations of sweet and savory is that family life is given to us in and as a muddle. Its precepts, the values that the individual family may hope to uphold and enact, are clear. But the communication and reception and application of these values are in a constant disarray. For all of the conceptual binaries, or Sunday School hierarchies, the fact is that Apollo and Dionysus, super-ego and id and plain ego, grapple, strive,

7. Reconciling and Synthesizing Polar Positions

and simply try to cope. Out of this there is also the possibility, perhaps the inevitability, of glancing, vivid, frequent accord.[54]

Pinocchio is so powerful a fictional creation as to approach archetype. We have seen how the poles are useful for the establishing of terms and for the telling of tales. We have also seen how the aggregate contains and combines opposites and paradoxes. As might be expected, all of these alternatives come into play in the historical and the contemporary world as well.

In the realm of the real, Anne Frank parallels Pinocchio's happy complexity. Thirteen-year-old Anne writes the following entry near the beginning of her diary:

> I have loving parents and a sixteen-year-old sister, and there are about thirty people I can call friends. I have a throng of admirers who can't keep their adoring eyes off me and who sometimes have to resort to using a broken pocket mirror to try and catch a glimpse of me in the classroom. I have a family, loving aunts and a good home.[55]

This child is vain, or insecure, or almost certainly both at the same time. She is decidedly frivolous, though there are intimations of profundity. This is who Anne Frank is, or appears to be, at the beginning of her chronicle.

In the public imagination, Anne Frank is a lionized martyr. This is right and as it should be. But that is only part of a more complicated, more wonderful reality. The diary itself reveals that Anne possesses a humanizing pettiness, as displayed in the incident of Mrs. Van Daan's china.[56] She often laughs people to scorn.[57] She is inappropriately impertinent, and often more than a little pleased about it: "More than once the air has been filled with the van Daans' admonitions and my saucy replies. Father and Mother ... keep telling me I should talk less, mind my own business and be more modest, but I seem doomed to failure. If Father weren't so patient, I'd have long ago given up hope of ever meeting my parents' quite moderate expectations."[58]

Anne is melodramatic in her rendering of family conflicts. She declares that she loves her mother and sister, but only because they are Mother and Margot: "I don't give a darn about them as people."[59] Through the course of the diary, we see some rather remarkable steps forward and also the inevitable backsliding as the impending adult reverts momentarily to the petulance and self-absorption of the child.[60]

We have been thinking of Anne Frank as a nonfictional parallel to the complex creations of classic children's literature. The truth is, though, that she is also something of a fiction, or at least a contrivance. As a writer she puts her best foot forward, or, sometimes, the most confrontational one. She gives her reader what she wants her reader to have or, alternatively, miscalculates and still leads us to different aspects of the truth.

In addition to Anne's self-creating, history and Holocaust have added a sheen of almost unbearable poignancy to this unexceptional, incalculable emotional account. This is an added complication, either an impediment to our clear understanding or a contextual component of all real relations. All of these things together mean that we find truth between the lines. It is a rich combination, and universal: self-perception and misrecognition, the apparatus, her own petulant immaturity, her family members' often shortcomings, the real flaws with their actual dimensions, the real deep feelings beneath the childish gloss.

Film Weighs In: Stan Laurel and Oliver Hardy

We have held throughout this long discussion that literature and film are both capable of richly elaborating many deeply patterned perceptions about the nature of childhood. One of the best and most beautiful cinematic examples of whole childhood is contained in the collected works of Stan Laurel and Oliver Hardy. *Brats* (1930), seems the most concentrated, most obvious place to begin when exploring Laurel and Hardy's contributions to the discourse of children. Randy Skretvedt synopsizes:

> Laurel and Hardy spend an exasperating evening at home with their sons, who look exactly like their respective fathers. The grown-up boys' attempts at recreation are thwarted by the noisy antics of the little boys. The children manage to leave the water running in the bathroom as the grown-ups attempt to put them to sleep; the kids agree to settle down if they can have a glass of water. Stan starts for the bathroom, but Ollie stops him: "Just a moment—you might spill it!' The apartment, as well as Ollie's dignity, is dampened in the ensuing flood.[61]

What actually happens at this conclusion is not so much dampening as a deluge, quite similar to the one following the opening of the elevator doors in that famous clip from Stanley Kubrick's adaptation of *The Shining* (1980). *Brats* ends in a cinematic tsunami, but the conclusion only differs from what preceded it in scale and comprehensiveness. Destruction, entropy even, is the essence of this world, even and especially in its domestic manifestations.[62]

As mentioned, this noted film features its principles performing as both parents and children. The latter roles allow both Laurel and Hardy to demonstrate how so many of their mannerisms, their moods and motivations, are actually derived from childish pique, self-absorption, and intractability. The fact that the boys' fathers—also known to their millions of devotees as simply "the boys"—do not seem to comport themselves with any more maturity than do their offspring, further elaborates a secondary theme that we have been developing: Childhood and adulthood are not as sharply delineated as we would sometimes have it. If the adult is sometimes concerned about inappropriately modeling grown-up behaviors unsuitable for children's eyes, then he might also consider how much that is unseemly in his manner is also an example of the childish things that are hard for him to put away.

But children don't just behave badly. Many missteps are simply a result of their imperfect understanding, or incomplete capacities. This is just as true when the boys are playing (ostensible) adults. In *Blotto* (1930) they are, as so often, infantilized husbands attempting to escape from their ubiquitous wives, upon whom they also, absolutely, depend. As they scheme and trip themselves up they get upset and impatient. Just as importantly, they quickly, almost immediately, make their way out of their bad moods. In this they are much like children, or men of sorrows and acquainted with grief, or even admirably long-suffering pilgrims in an absurd universe.[63] More pointedly, they are afraid of the waiter, afraid of everyone in uniform, afraid of every adult and authority figure. They are often unsure of themselves, always pre- or post-naughty, often unaware of the complications they have caused. Stan and Ollie always try very hard to explain and negotiate, through their own inadequate understanding, through their basic powerlessness.

But for all their naughtiness, and for all of the ways in which their worlds tend to externalize and make flesh that very naughtiness, the childish in Laurel and Hardy is inextricably linked with the childlike. Despite, or even because of, its misbehaving and silliness, this is an oeuvre thoroughly infused with vulnerability and with a very deep, unforced sweetness.

On this subject, Laurel and Hardy chronicler John McCabe cites David Robinson: "[Laurel] is not ... perhaps so much a fool as a child.... This child's innocence is a quality which Hardy shares with him, and which is, perhaps, the leading distinction of their comedy work. They are the most innocent of all the clowns."[64]

As McCabe concludes his important appreciation, a more or less scholarly book that is also a partisan endorsement of a previously undervalued filmography, this is the point that he most emphasizes. He sees this childlike innocence as the team's fundamental core.

> Innocence and blessed ignorance, out of tune with the sins and follies of the world. This is their artistic essence: no comedians in history were ever so innocent so funnily, so endearingly. "Where ignorance is bliss, 'tis folly to be wise," goes the old saw. This is exactly the state of existence of Laurel and Hardy. Their innocent ignorance makes them the epitome of all the Babes in all the Woods. The world is against them, and they care—but they do not mind. They are too eternally young to hold grudges, so they face the world with hope renewed daily, hourly. Their optimism is indestructible. Their ignorance is truly invincible because it is the angelic armor of perpetual childhood.[65]

This idea of a childlike core is also central in the analyses of Randy Skretvedt, the next of Laurel and Hardy's systematic apologists. Skretvedt finds the motif in a very wide variety of places: "Stan wore a flat-brimmed Irish children's derby—appropriate for his childlike character."[66] Such externals were part of a more thoroughgoing effort to establish a conceptual, moral core to these characters. Frank Butler, head for a time of Roach's scenario department, recalls that Leo McCarey, production supervisor for many of the early, formative films, found something beyond the obvious contrast of the boys' sizes. The team started to take off when its various contributors identified and nurtured a more abiding, reconcilable contrast. It was "dumbness combined with invincible innocence."[67]

In *Do Detectives Think?* (filmed May, released November 1927), an early entry in the series, there is already "a glimmer of something deeper; at one point, faced with a dangerous task, Stan holds onto Ollie's hand for reassurance, and there's no special attention called to it—it's the natural expression of two little boys lost in a grown-up world."[68]

Of *The Second 100 Years* (filmed June, released October 1927) Skretvedt states that "they're well on their way to becoming the two little boys who never grew up, united in innocence and braving the terrors of a hostile world."[69] There are numerous, even innumerable examples of this kind of thing in Laurel and Hardy's films. They argue, they bicker, they come to blows. They also, always, remember and reaffirm their loyalty to one another, as informed by the deepest and most immoveable fraternal feeling.

Blockheads, a feature film released in 1938, is one of the last great Laurel and Hardy films. World War I has ended, but no one told Stan about it. He has been patrolling the European trenches, all alone, for twenty years. He is finally discovered and repatriated. Ollie reads about it in the newspaper and undertakes to visit his old friend, now recuperating in a veteran's hospital.

Stan, who is untroubled by reversals like this, is actually in the pink of health. At the moment, however, he is rather restless. He is out on the hospital grounds, trying to get comfortable in a wheelchair that he has commandeered. After endlessly fidgeting he has finally found the right position, which is to fold his leg up underneath him. The chair's leg support remains extended straight in front of him. With the wheelchair, and the setting, it looks just like his leg has been amputated.

So far, so funny. At this point Laurel—the more-or-less mastermind behind all of the Laurel and Hardy films—decides to take a very unusual tack, which is to let the incipient sentiment of the whole series shine out uninhibitedly, if only for a moment. Ollie comes around a corner, searching for his long-lost friend. Presently he spots him, and beams, and approaches. Just before arriving, though, he looks down and sees that Stan has been dismembered, and is now disabled. He stops for the briefest moment, not to register disgust or horror, but real, actual sorrow. Then he rouses himself, smiles, and goes to greet his best beloved. A series of complications follow, and multiply, and compound, the final result somehow being that Stan releases a dump truck's full load on his friend, and on his car, in which he is sitting. After which Ollie, with a full heart, takes Stan home with him.

Love, impatience, consternation, love. Skretvedt quotes an anonymous Roach public relations man, "who wrote [*Double Whoopee*'s] press sheet [and] had a wonderful grasp of the Laurel and Hardy characters.... 'In their child-like eagerness to serve the hotel's guests, they create a hilarious havoc of destruction. From this the two grown-up children emerge, jobless but undaunted.... Together they depart for new fields, facing the rigors of the world with the naïve wonder and eagerness of their child hearts.'"[70]

Skretvedt enthuses: "Somebody give that man a medal!" Such encomiums might not seem quite critical, but they clearly and quite prettily make a very important point. John McCabe and Randy Skretvedt are both amateurs, in the best, most loving sense of the word. Their early exposure to Laurel and Hardy generated permanent feelings of affection and gratitude, which they sought to preserve and elaborate as they graduated to adult comprehension and to the adult's power to get his message out.

There is a bigger issue at hand. "A publicity release like this may not seem important, but it shows how Laurel and Hardy's characters were affectionately thought of as 'grown-up-children' at the Roach lot."[71]

Skretvedt then contrasts this tender favor with a harsher, more dismissive set of descriptors utilized by the machinery at MGM, to which the boys would later go, and where they would later languish. Instead of innocence and affection, Laurel and Hardy would later be attended and superannuated by cynicism, materialism, and incipient cruelty. At MGM they were discussed and publicized as "idiots."[72]

Later scripts for the dubious Laurel and Hardy films produced by 20th Century–Fox refer to the boys as "Jerks," "dopes," "Half-wits." "This shows how the Fox writers perceived Laurel and Hardy as two idiots who get in the way of the real hero—the romantic lead. Our sympathies are supposed to go toward the 'normal' characters for having to put up with Stan and Ollie's stupidity—the exact opposite of the philosophy in the Roach films."[73]

In a manner that might not seem quite rigorous, or even scholarly, these chroniclers bemoan the ill-treatment of their obviously beloved subjects. This choice emerges in another light, however, when considered in view of our present topic. Is this not a kind of parental delight, and regard, and fierceness? The real issue here is what is most appropriate for our children, or our children's thoughts, however much we may have graduated to adulthood. What are the attitudes and methods that should inform the production and exhibition and absorption of such movies? The pique, the seeming violence of such systematic slapstick, is merely a thin cover for the real heart of the matter: what seems naïve wonder is in fact loving regard and constant care—those same qualities which we anticipate in the kingdom of heaven, or despair of, in their absence, here below.

Though the nominal subject here is children, and the specific point the boys' childish characters, a larger light makes itself felt. Roy Seawright, head of Roach's optical effects department:

> I always remember the humor and love that developed in working with these two beautiful men.... It could be windy, rainy, dull outside; you'd walk through the stage door—and it was warm. It wasn't the temperature; it was a human element. You knew that you were participating in something unique. You'd walk on the stage, and everybody's smiling. It was vastly different from other studios—I've worked at them all. No comparison. The minute you walked onto the Laurel and Hardy stage, you were happy. You were grateful to be there.[74]

Without being in any way reductive, this bespeaks a possibility, a lived certainty that is manifest across artistic media and throughout times and places—literary and cinematic, fictional or actual, adults and children. They shine, and they fall short. They quite often and even mostly do both of these things one right after the other, or simultaneously. And as they do so, together, they are loving and beloved, forgiving and forgiven.

For all the valuable substance of the particular poles, this is the broad substance of childhood. To conclude, we will now and finally touch upon how this integration of attributes leads to, finds further attribution in the integration and union of actors. It is not only perfection and shortcoming that come together so sweetly and so feelingly, but finally, surpassingly, it is the child and the adult that come together as well.

8

Adults and Children, Mutually Implicated

"Why can't you fly now, mother?"
"Because I am grown up, dearest. When people grow up they forget the way."
"Why do they forget the way?"
"Because they are no longer gay and innocent and heartless. It is only the gay and innocent and heartless who can fly."
"What is gay and innocent and heartless? I do wish I were gay and innocent and heartless."
—J. M. Barrie, *Peter Pan*

"Listen, listen, the wind's talking," said John, tilting his head on one side. "Do you really mean we won't be able to hear *that* when we're older, Mary Poppins?"
"You'll hear all right," said Mary Poppins, "but you won't understand." At that Barbara began to weep gently. There were tears in John's eyes too. "Well, it can't be helped. It's how things happen," said Mary Poppins sensibly.
—P. L. Travers, *Mary Poppins*

We have just surveyed a range of ideas about the nature of children, and we have considered some of the ways that books and films have contributed to that conversation. Adults are obviously central to and mostly responsible for the terms and parameters thereof.[1] This is inevitable and, at least to some degree, necessary. It is true that adults often err in caring and then accounting for the young. But if adult error is frequent, and children most seriously affected by it, then adults still deserve a prominent and even honored place at this particular table. This is because the story of childhood is also, always, the story of the adults—and not just for the ways they complicate the lives of their charges.

So much of adult ministration toward children is well-meant. More than that, though the contrary cases might sometimes receive more attention, so much of that ministration is also well-done. Children may well be an adult's greatest stewardship, and the adult's faltering, faithful execution of that stewardship one of the world's most stirring stories. This is partly because that stewardship is actually reciprocal, though our younger ministers may not think of it that way. The fact is that parents and children raise each other, and that story inevitably becomes the larger tale of the family, and then of the community. As before, books and film are eloquent in recounting the trouble and the tremendous heights incident to this narrative. Though individual texts adhere only to certain points of the tale, when considered as a collective they demonstrate that what we have learned about the sweetness and contrariness and exquisite balance of children is really true of all people, great and small.

There is a great impediment to the proper understanding and implementation of this key concept. It is succinctly stated in the following standard sentiment, which is not, by the way, without its merits: "Grown-up people find it very difficult to believe really wonderful things, unless they have what they call proof."[2]

The great English children's writer E. Nesbit makes a fair point here, at least as part of a more complex reality. But this oft and overly subscribed-to sentiment, this almost stereotypically critical characterization does not account for the whole of adulthood, nor of adult interaction with children. For all of the numerous claims to the contrary, the idea of the earthbound adult is merely a small part of a bigger, more complicated picture:

> Now there are diversities of gifts, but the same Spirit. And there are differences of administrations, but the same Lord. And there are diversities of operations, but it is the same God which worketh all in all.... For to one is given by the Spirit the word of wisdom; to another the word of knowledge by the same Spirit; To another faith by the same Spirit.[3]

People possess a diversity of attributes. For all of her seeking, no individual attains to every gift, and each lacks a very great deal. Still, when formed into an affirmative community the individual's particular deficiencies diminish in importance. In tandem, together, individuals will manage to lick the platter clean. And what of E. Nesbit's generalized sentiment about earthbound adulthood? It is true: some grown-ups are joyless skeptics.

Others are rational, and work knowledge unto wisdom. This operation is most portentous and greatly productive, and it quite properly constitutes the core of adult power and preeminence. And other adults, it would seem, simply believe, and in doing so they are possessed of a spiritual gift that is equally as precious as the others.

Not every reader will appreciate the assertion that God is the author and grantor of these gifts, nor will she necessarily subscribe to Paul, his epistle, or the text in which it is found. But this is a conflict and a potential reconciliation that is basic to most any mythological formulation. If we wish to extrapolate, Paul is also reconciling Locke and Rousseau with regard, for instance, to the education of children. As with most every issue considered in this book thus far, this is mean and multiplicity, Aristotle and Blaise Pascal—"there are then a great number of truths, both of faith and of morality, which seem contradictory and which all hold good together in a wonderful system"[4]—to boot. Each end of the binary has its substance and justification, just as it has its limitations. So, adults often do the figuring. They often figure to the point of joylessness or oppression. But they are also eminently and most demonstrably able to have faith, feel wonder, and even hear the ringing of the bell on the Polar Express.

A Pretty Problem: Antoine de Saint-Exupéry's *The Little Prince*

Melodrama can be so easy, and reassuring, in the face of reality's intractable contradictions. A protagonist's objectives, and her nature too, stand in clearer relief when a vivid antagonist stands opposite. That is why in a very particular setting E. Nesbit states a possibility as a universality. And there are uses beyond the polarized, violent conflicts of melodrama. As we have seen, Bruno Bettelheim and others have shown us the great psychological substance of this fairy tale configuration of good and bad. Even fairy tales have their limits, however, and fairy tale polarization, as applied in non–fairy tale settings, is a notion in need of a ringing challenge.

Antoine de Saint-Exupéry's *The Little Prince* is the contemporary epicenter of this particular disturbance. Once again, as with Ms. Nesbit, Saint-Exupéry begins by making a fair point, and he makes it very vividly. We have been told how the pilot narrator of this little book was misunderstood as a child and how the adults around him managed to squelch his creativity and individuality:

8. Adults and Children, Mutually Implicated 203

> The grown-ups advised me to put away my drawings of boa constrictors, outside or inside, and apply myself instead to geography, history, arithmetic, and grammar. That is why I abandoned, at the age of six, a magnificent career as an artist.... Grown-ups never understand anything by themselves, and it is exhausting for children to have to provide explanations over and over again.[5]

"Never" and "always" are like vivid, primary colors. They are bright and saturated and powerful. They help us, especially in our youth, to survey the field and establish our position thereupon, to establish our allegiances and aspirations as well. Saint-Exupéry presses his advantage:

> Grown-ups like numbers. When you tell them about a new friend, they never ask questions about what really matters. They never ask: "What does his voice sound like?" "What games does he like best?" "Does he collect butterflies?" They ask: "How old is he?" "How many brothers does he have?" "How much does he weigh?" "How much money does his father make?" Only then do they think they know him. If you tell grown-ups, "I saw a beautiful red brick house, with geraniums at the windows and doves on the roof...," they won't be able to imagine such a house. You have to tell them, "I saw a house worth a hundred thousand francs." Then they exclaim, "What a pretty house."[6]

Here is a real problem, and a valid point. Hans Christian Andersen had likewise urged it, and most powerfully:

> Later, when [Gerda] came inside with the picture book, [Kai] told her that picture books were for babies. And when Grandmother told stories he would argue with her or—which was much worse—stand behind her chair with a pair of glasses on his nose and imitate her most cruelly. He did it so accurately that people laughed. Soon he learned to mimic everyone in the whole street. He had a good eye for their little peculiarities and knew how to copy them.

Andersen's Kai suggests that Saint-Exupéry's characterizations are not exclusive to grown-ups. Even before reaching the cares of adulthood, even as we make our ways out of the gardens of childhood, our growth is often marked by a kind of dire moral, emotional diminution.

> It is not now as it hath been of yore;—
> Turn wheresoe'er I may,
>   By night or day,
> The things which I have seen I now can see no more.
> The rainbow comes and goes,
> And lovely is the rose;
> The moon doth with delight
> Look round her when the heavens are bare;
> Waters on a starry night

Are beautiful and fair;
The sunshine is a glorious birth;
But yet I know, where'er I go,
That there hath pass'd away a glory from the earth.[7]

Saint-Exupéry's narrator grows up to become a pilot, as did Saint-Exupéry himself. The narrator (and pilot, once again, in December 1936) crashes in the North African desert and despairs for his life. It is at this point that he meets the eponymous Little Prince. On the fifth day of their shared extremity, the two companions are engaged in a conversation about flowers and thorns and such. The little prince is insistent to the point of relentlessness, and the pilot lashes out a little bit, fearing for their life and all. He tells the little prince that he is busy with something serious. "Something serious?" The prince now reproves the pilot, tells him that he is talking like a grown-up, compares him to a red-faced gentleman he once knew who never did anything but add up numbers.[8]

The narrator is reproved, and we are reproved with him. There is no sense, in the book at least, that it should be otherwise. And yet, is this situation really the same as crushing a child's creativity? It may be that in certain aeronautico-didactic fantasies, concerns like the pilot's are not necessary or productive. But in realist literature, not to mention in real life, it is possible that the adult engaged in life saving, or even in mere sweat-of-thy-brow breadwinning, may very well be engaged in something more serious, and more important, than childish prattle.

At the beginning of his book, and at certain points throughout, Saint-Exupéry is effective and just in urging his convictions about the visionary child and about his being subject to joyless, unpoetic adulthood. But just as often he misses the mark. The fox: "Here is my secret. It's quite simple: One sees clearly only with the heart. Anything essential is invisible to the eyes."[9] To a degree this is a valid notion, echoing such enormous expressions as "Now faith is the substance of things hoped for, the evidence of things not seen."[10] But in another sense, Saint-Exupéry's pretty, bumper-sticker sentiment does not really stand up to interrogation or analysis. In fact, it borders on the nonsensical. Anything essential is invisible to the eyes? What of experience, knowledge, and wisdom, or of faith that is combined with our most charitable works? What about the tactile, deeply material setting in which we found the Shepherd Boy, there in the Valley of Humiliation? And with regard to the subject of the present study, what about movies?

Saint-Exupéry similarly misses the mark in his account of the railway switchman, who "sorts travelers into bundles of a thousand."[11] These trav-

8. Adults and Children, Mutually Implicated   205

elers are in a constant hurry, going and coming, constantly looking for something that they never find. Inside the trains, on their way to and from nothing, the grown-ups yawn or sleep. "Only the children are pressing their noses against the windowpanes." "Only the children know what they're looking for," said the little prince. "They spend their time on a rag doll and it becomes very important, and if it's taken away from them, they cry...." "'They're lucky,' the switchman said."[12] In a sense this is more affectionate idealization, more mostly harmless sentimentality. In fact, when viewed from another angle, this will become an essential, transcendental motif in children's literature and film.[13] But you don't have to be a strip miner or a clear-cutter to see holes in this characterization. Yes, children are sensitive to the beauty of the earth and to the substance of small things. Yes, they are immune from Christ's third temptation, free from aspiring after substance and supremacy instead of yokes that are easy and burdens that are light.[14] But the railway switchman episode unfairly favors children at the expense of their most ardent admirers. It presents adulthood as a straw man, one that bears little resemblance to the real thing, or things.

It is not necessary, or just, to microscopically dismantle or dismiss Saint-Exupéry's very pretty, understandably beloved tale. But its central thesis is expressed melodramatically, and problematically. And it would be taken up, too uncritically, by any number of subsequent stories. It informs and energizes Steven Spielberg's faceless child-and-alien-hating government hordes in *E.T.*, the overdetermination of Chris Van Allsburg's *The Polar Express*, the smugly impertinent adult-baiting of *Home Alone*. And it continues to exert its influence on any number of other mediated texts and actual, social settings.

The prospects are affecting, but they do not stand up to more thorough scrutiny, or more specific contextualization. Toward the end of Saint-Exupéry's brief book the little prince begins to fail, precisely for the want of those inessential practicalities, of the sustenance that so-called soulless grown-ups and beleaguered, anxious parents gladly weary themselves to provide.[15] He dies, as did Harriet Beecher Stowe's Little Eva, for our reproof and our reclamation. The book concludes, after considering all that the prince knew and said and did: "And no grown-up will ever understand how such a thing could be so important."[16] Can this really be so? No grown-up, not even a pair of parents, reading sympathetically and in affectionate proximity with their own precious child?

Nostalgia, Morbidity, and Moving Forward

Although Saint-Exupéry may not have recognized the correlation, there is much of D. W. Griffith in *The Little Prince*. And as we have seen, the values or assumptions that these two estimable authors share have a very long and distinguished lineage. Humphrey Carpenter observes that many books at the core of the golden age of (primarily) British children's literature (1860–1930) "seem to be set in a distant era when things were better than they are now. And childhood itself seemed a Golden Age to many of these writers, as they set out to recapture its sensations."[17] Edward Lear states that the basic theme of this golden age, when informed by this particular premise, is "the search for the mysterious, elusive Good Place."[18] Here is childhood as garden. Implicit in this vision, though not always directly stated, is the related idea that the adult world is fallen and irredeemable.

The gardens of this golden literary period could be Edenic, derived from Judeo-Christianity and its assumptions. They could also be pagan/Arcadian, reflective of other historic or mythological templates. They could even combine these two otherwise irreconcilable cosmologies. Regardless of origins, the idea that childhood is a lost garden is very thoroughly established and elaborated by some of children's culture's most celebrated, celebratable texts. It was further fleshed out by countless children's books that followed after. All of this presents contemporary readers with a notion that is dramatic, poetic, and very compelling. It is the classic view, in more than one sense of the term, and as such it can easily be taken for granted. Further, if the reader takes the trouble to inquire, a closer look at so many of these actual texts will reveal how deep and dear they really are. Since this is the case, it becomes difficult to question or counter the standard view.

The Wind in the Willows is the most powerfully Arcadian of the golden age's classic texts. Its vision of a sheltered, paradisiacal place is quite exquisite, and it is very, very powerful. However, to its great credit *The Wind in the Willows* also takes its protagonists, together with the enraptured young reader, to the edge of the garden and beyond. As we have seen,[19] Rat is something of an adult figure, selfless and generous and always reliable. At the novel's beginning, though, he seems unwilling to fully embrace the implications of this role:

> "Beyond the Wild Wood comes the Wide World," said the Rat. "And that's something that doesn't matter, either to you or me. I've never been there, and I'm never going, nor you either, if you've got any sense at all. Don't ever refer to it again, please."[20]

8. Adults and Children, Mutually Implicated

This view bespeaks and, in its most powerful articulations, embodies safety, shelter, loving security. But that is only one part of the picture, one part of any life, and it must not completely prevail. Rat will both realize and represent this, as will Badger. Knowing that Shelter is only productive up to a point, they will eventually help Mole, Toad, and young reader alike move appropriately into the wider spaces, and on to the greater challenges and attainments that they proffer.

The standard, sheltered view has its roots and reasons. Humphrey Carpenter points out that throughout this period a decline in the fortunes of the British Empire, even as it coincided with the Empire's ongoing expansion, brought an air of uncertainty and anxiety to British life and letters.[21] More particularly, many of the key children's writers had gone through particularly traumatic experiences, from which they bore deep psychic scars.[22]

The result was a turn inward and a turn away. This phenomenon was not unique to children's discourse, and it is in many ways understandable. But being understandable is not quite the same as being healthful. In its proper place the Garden is a reassuring, nurturing concept. As such, it has often formed one end of a binary opposition, the opposite of which was that everything outside was lost and fallen, lone, and dreary. This is not so, and to insist otherwise is to court all manner of difficulty. The fact is that the Garden, unmitigated, becomes backwards-looking, arrested, and potentially crippling.[23]

The Little Prince indirectly endorses these morbid notions. Some contemporary voices, derived from classic statements or proceeding on their own recognizance, continue to reflect them.[24] In doing so they may not be noting the seminal texts' so often ambivalent attitude toward seemingly triumphant childhood.

> "Second [star] to the right, and straight on till morning."
> That, Peter had told Wendy, was the way to the Neverland; but even birds, carrying maps and consulting them at windy corners, could not have sighted it with these instructions. Peter, you see, just said anything that came into his head.[25]

Peter Pan's stirring navigational instruction is very famous and often quoted. The bemused critique that immediately follows is much less often remarked. Many film adaptations (1924—tremendous!—1953, 2003), not to mention innumerable pantomime adaptations of Barrie's original play, have effaced or even utterly excised *Peter Pan*'s dark undercurrents. But as before, Barrie frequently takes pains to point out that Peter Pan is a very unreliable model and childhood a most incomplete, most insufficient institution.²⁶ *The Little Prince* notwithstanding, much kids' culture has pursued this point, resisting uncritical and undue idealization while considering some of its troublesome consequences.

J. R. R. Tolkien's celebrated essay "On Fairy-Stories" discusses how poorly, how inaptly some fairy stories have been fitted for the actual needs or natures of children.²⁷ He holds that these adapted tales have, more often than not, been cut off from their adult roots and realities. In being so sundered they have in many ways been rendered ineffective, even ruined. For Tolkien, the best fairy stories are expressions of the full human experience, which they contain and comprehend, and toward which they lead. If these stories have been part of the purview of childhood then it is only because a child is properly destined to mature, graduate, and enter into his full franchise.

> If we use *child* in a good sense (it has also legitimately a bad one) we must not allow that to push us into the sentimentality of only using *adult* or *grown-up* in a bad sense (it has also legitimately a good one). The process of growing older is not necessarily allied to growing wickeder though the two do often happen together. Children are meant to grow up, and not to become Peter Pans. Not to lose innocence and wonder, but to proceed on the appointed journey: that journey upon which it is certainly not better to travel hopefully than to arrive, though we must travel hopefully if we are to arrive. But it is one of the lessons of fairy-stories … that on callow, lumpish and selfish youth peril, sorrow, and the shadow of death can bestow dignity, and even sometimes wisdom.²⁸

Maurice Sendak urges a similar point in a practical discussion about children and the visual arts:

> It isn't a work of art just because it arises from a genuine creative emotion; everyone has that. And that's why I object to people saying: "Children are wonderful artists, everything they do is gorgeous." It's true, but they can't take the next step, which is to give it form. And why should they? They're children, and experience and age are necessary. You get the idea, there's this wonderful palpitating thing, and then you construct a form—words, pictures, the shape of the book, the bind. Everything.²⁹

As Sendak suggests, we need not be reluctant about taking that next step, nor be so smotheringly sentimental about the children that have not yet done so. Bruno Bettelheim says that fairy tales frequently feature and importantly prefigure a trauma that is essential to and universal in a healthily developing child: "Self-realization requires leaving the orbit of the home, an excruciatingly painful experience fraught with many psychological dangers."³⁰ But Bettelheim reminds us that "trauma" does not always relate to injury, nor to the wound that results from it. A trauma can be much more neutral, a major change or upheaval that could just as easily lead to advance and increase.

As an example, Bettelheim finds that the Grimms' "Brother and Sister" demonstrates the potential or implicit positivity that lies beneath the anxious conflicts of the fairy tale. The story represents "the two great upheavals in life: leaving the parental home, and creating one's own family."[31] However, fearful as these upheavals may be, they also conduct protagonist and reader alike to a great insight, an even greater blessing: "What redeems us as human beings ... is solicitude for those whom we love."[32]

This is not at all to suggest that there is nothing to regret as little children grow and pass into adulthood. The older siblings in E. Nesbit's 1902 novel *The Five Children and It* are often inconvenienced by their baby brother, somewhat ironically known as the Lamb. At one point in this cleverly didactic wish-fulfillment fantasy they wish that someone, that anyone might want this child enough so as to take him off their hands. Their wish is fulfilled; suddenly, immediately, everyone starts trying to steal him. The farcical consequences of this ill-advised wish are effectively executed, and then resolved in a powerful, tender conclusion. Babies are indeed terrible trouble, which is exactly what makes them, paradoxically and incontrovertibly, so terribly precious.[33]

Precious, that is, until the next time they cause us inconvenience. Later in the novel an exasperated older brother wishes that their "original little tiresome beloved Lamb"[34] would just grow up. He does, of course, and instantly, to the great and even wrenching distress of the rest of the siblings. This is perhaps the most poignant and pointed part of Nesbit's novel, addressing as it does one of family life's most fearsome prospects. The wish transforms "their own dear tiresome baby brother"[35] into a supercilious, condescending young adult.

> "Look here," said Cyril, "if you're our elder brother, why not behave as such and take us over to Maidstone and give us a jolly good blow-out, and we'll go on the river afterwards?"
> "I'm infinitely obliged to you," said the Lamb courteously, "but I should prefer solitude. Go home to your lunch—I mean your dinner. Perhaps I may look in about tea-time—or I may not be home till after you are in your beds."[36]

Earlier in the novel the children almost lost their baby brother. Here, in a chilling combination of tragedy and banality, they lose him even more definitively, and heartbreakingly. Outside of the figurative narratives of classic children's literature, this is so much of what we fear from the wide world: estrangement from parents, the sundering of siblings, our love waxed cold,[37] our first, dearest, deepest affections dampened and then utterly disappearing.

Must it be thus? In the face of such dire developments, more sensibly balanced sentiments from the classic children's works come both as relief and reassurance. Rudyard Kipling's Mowgli has just routed the fearsome tiger, Shere Khan, and is scattering the recalcitrant wolves that had sought his ouster from their community.

> Mowgli struck right and left round the circle, and the wolves ran howling with the sparks burning their fur. At last there were only Akela, Bagheera, and perhaps ten wolves that had taken Mowgli's part. Then something began to hurt Mowgli inside him, as he had never been hurt in his life before, and he caught his breath and sobbed, and the tears ran down his face.
> "What is it? What is it?" he said. "I do not wish to leave the jungle, and I do not know what this is. Am I dying, Bagheera?"
> "No, Little Brother. That is only tears such as men use," said Bagheera. "Now I know thou art a man, and a man's cub no longer. The jungle is shut indeed to thee henceforward. Let them fall, Mowgli. They are only tears." So Mowgli sat and cried as though his heart would break; and he had never cried in all his life before.[38]

The communions of well-favored childhood are deep, and incalculably dear, for child and loving adult minder alike. That is why the prospect of their conclusion can be so wrenching. But the prospect is not always mournful, any more than adults are always joyless.

> "And the old wooden Pinocchio, where is he?"
> "There he is," answered Geppetto, pointing to a large puppet that was leaning against a chair with his head on one side, his arms hanging loosely, and his legs bent and crossed, so that it was a miracle that he could stand there.
> Pinocchio turned and looked at him for a moment, and then said to himself, contentedly, "How ridiculous I was when I was a puppet! And how happy I am to have become a real boy!"[39]

There is an undercurrent of melancholy at the conclusion of Carlo Collodi's great novel, but that melancholy is balanced by a bracing, outgoing countercurrent. *Pinocchio* renders perfectly the great paradox of childhood, which is that brat and angel so frustratingly and exaltingly intermingle. This paradox may sometimes seem, may often be experienced as an impossible impasse. But the impasse will be broken, healthily, and by the most natural means. The child becomes a man, or a woman! And it may be that after that comes another bright prospect, which is the possibility of another mild and tenderhearted Mole, another dearly impossible Toad, coming down the pike.

It's Good to Grow Up

We have discussed Bruno Bettelheim's notion of character splitting.[40] The fairy tale will sometimes divide actual parents into a sympathetic and an antagonistic half. These halved personages correspond with the fact that real parents both praise and scold, to the child's confusion and frustration. Folkloric splitting provides a therapeutic space in which the child can consider the reasons for this situation, and the options available to him as he negotiates his way through it.

We have also seen how this splitting device operates in any number of scenarios, many relating to the child himself. One of the most important of these finds the child at a crossroads, where the challenge and opportunity at hand is actually the putting away of childish things. Bettelheim observes that in the story of Sindbad the Seaman and Sindbad the Porter, there is a person who "escape[s] into a faraway world of adventure and fantasy, and [another] bound to common practicality."[41] Similarly in the Grimms' "The Two Brothers," the siblings represent "the striving for independence and self-assertion, and the opposite tendency to remain safely home, tied to the parents."[42]

Eventually, though, the wide world must be accounted for, and taken on. "The Rat looked very grave, and stood in deep thought for a minute or two. Then he re-entered the house, strapped a belt round his waist, shoved a brace of pistols into it, took up a stout cudgel that stood in a corner of the hall, and set off for the Wild Wood at a smart pace."[43]

Bettelheim talks about the kingdom gained at the end of the fairy tale by its heroes. Its nature is never elaborated, nor is the life that the protagonists, and the child who identifies with them, will come to inherit. This is because these details do not really matter. "To have become a king or queen at the conclusion of the story symbolizes a state of true *independence*, in which the hero feels as secure, satisfied, and happy as the infant felt in his most *dependent* state, when they were truly well taken care of in the kingdom of the cradle."[44]

This necessary, happy independence has a number of components, and they are all hard-won. Bettelheim details the traumas that the child must experience on the way to her majority. The fairy story, properly constituted, can aid in both traumatization and in ultimate graduation.

If, as we tell the story, the agonies of sibling rivalry do not reverberate in us, as well as the desperate feeling of rejection the child has when he doesn't feel he is thought the best; his feelings of inferiority when his body fails him; his dismal sense of inadequacy if he or others expect the performance of tasks that seem Herculean; his anxiety about the "animal" aspects of sex; and how all this and so much more can be transcended—then we fail the child. In this failure we also fail to give the child the conviction that after all his labors a wonderful future is awaiting him—and only this belief can give him the strength to grow up well, securely, with self-confidence and self-respect.[45]

We have already seen at the beginning of *The Wind in the Willows* how Mole makes a mistake, and it leads to a bit of a disaster. Rat forgives him for it, frankly and fully. He then goes even further and invites Mole to live with him. He promises that he will teach Mole to row, a promise that subsequently leads to so many other gladly rendered services. Coming where it does in the novel, this sweet episode suggests a potential and eventuality that is not only narrative but also moral. This is the simultaneous resourcefulness and other-awareness that constitutes the successful passage from sweet, insufficient childhood to conscientious adulthood. As Rat's ministrations accumulate, they come to resemble the kind of care associated with parenting and the kind of constant warmth that any child would most desire, and thrive under. For all its apparent and partial neuroses, in the end the golden age also comes down to this devout, desirable consummation: "At any age a child interprets becoming king or queen as having gained mature adulthood."[46]

Although this process begins abundantly, characterized at first by the parent's reliable, nurturing affection, at some point it must multiply and encounter confusing contradictions.

> For the process of individuation to become possible and necessary—and unless it becomes unavoidable we do not engage in it, for it is much too painful—the good parents have to appear for a period as bad, persecuting ones who send the child out to wander for years in his personal desert, demanding seemingly "without respite" and without consideration for the child's comfort.[47]

Kenneth Grahame subjects Mr. Toad to this very ordeal:

> Pressing his handkerchief to his face, he left the room, with faltering footsteps.
> "Badger," said the Rat, "*I* feel like a brute; I wonder what YOU feel like?"
> "O, I know, I know," said the Badger gloomily. "But the thing had to be done. This good fellow has got to live here, and hold his own, and be

8. Adults and Children, Mutually Implicated

respected. Would you have him a common laughing-stock, mocked and jeered at by stoats and weasels?"

"Of course not," said the Rat.[48]

Here is a central part of the didactic narrative. Loving parents will reprove their beloved offspring, and that reproof is one of the surest signs of their commitment and devotion.[49] We have to grow up.

> But if the child responds to these hardships by developing himself in an independent way, then as if by miracle the good parents reappear. This is similar to the parent who does not make any sense to the adolescent child until after the adolescent has achieved maturity.[50]

This is the graduation from childhood. And what of Ever After? The formative fairy tales are just a part of the bigger picture, just the start of a whole series of challenges and potential attainments. Many fairy tales concentrate on beginnings, with childhood struggle and early advancing. Others—like the animal groom cycles[51]—effectively address these next stages, with all of their challenges and opportunities. Much of the contemporary material—teen literature, of course, is a whole other matter—stop short of taking on the long term.

The ultimate object is not just to attain emotional maturity but to form adult relationships as well. There are two components to the formation of such relationships. First, "the message of these fairy stories is that we must give up childish attitudes and achieve mature ones if we wish to establish that intimate bond with the other which promises permanent happiness for both."[52]

The second objective has several components, a few of which lie at the root of the golden age's original psychological disturbance. It is certainly the thing that the censors and film-fearers[53] most suspect, condemn, and avoid at all costs.

> Fairy tales suggest that eventually there comes a time when we must learn what we have not known before—or to put it psychoanalytically, to undo the repression of sex. What we had experienced as dangerous, loathsome, something to be shunned, must change its appearance so that it is experienced as truly beautiful. It is love which permits this to happen.[54]

The danger and value of the fairy tale is that it enacts a process by which the child recognizes something beyond, something above his natural and even (age) appropriate self-absorption. The danger and value is that this glimpse impels the child past the boundaries of nursery and garden and fortress walls. With the mastering of self and the encountering of the other, the tales must even bring the child, now growing, now grown, to the point where her appropriate, precious purity confronts a new, natural set of alternatives and values. This is not the choice between safety and the men who plunder and murder. It is not a matter of salvation, and the degradation of sin. It is refusing frigidity for the sake of fecundity, isolation for the sake of blessed, permanent communion.

> After a month the snow vanished. After two months everything turned green. After three months the flowers sprouted from the ground. After four months all the trees in the woods grew more solid, and the green branches became intertwined. The birds began to sing.[55]

This is nature, and natural increase. This is the child, grown and now with child herself.

Children's culture is rife with didactic tales that lay out all of the parameters and instruct on every particular. Its anarchic tales leave a space for spontaneity and joy, amidst all of the duty and learning. There are wondrous perspectives and sensibilities, making a space for serenity, spaciousness, and the luminous revelations of childhood's stages and childhood's interrelations. But then comes the child's majority, which is partly attained through stories that hint and call forward and promise. This kind of tale does not offer flattery, endless recreation (as in Pinocchio's Boys' Town, which knows how dangerous it is, or in *The Polar Express*, which does not), and arrest. They play, at least on the surface. At the same time, they suggest bigger and better things: the acquisition of knowledge, the undertaking of needful, gainful tasks, and the willing entry onto the next challenging, soul-expanding developmental stage.

Kenneth Grahame charts this course in his semi-autobiographical diptych, *The Golden Age* and *Dream Days*. The first of these begins with a tremendous prologue, entitled "The Olympians." In it, the elusive, multiple narrator of these stories—an adult's perception and some of his ironic distance; the child's interests and concentration, his intensity and depth of feeling—compares grown-ups with the Greek gods. They are powerful, and yet not omnipotent. They are distant—except when they are suddenly, nerve-rackingly, not. They are paragons, and yet prone to tremendous, unaccountable lapses in judgment and behavior. The child-sympathizing narrator suggests that these demigods are, indeed, exemplars or perhaps inevitabilities—however the child may resist, and however regrettable it may be, he will arrive here someday.[56]

The stories in Grahame's collections are in some conflict with each other, and a very productive conflict, too. They move us forward to the child's eventual graduation to adulthood, plotting the little reversals, the sudden perceptual or emotional surging forward that marks every child's developmental passage. And they resist that move as well, relishing the adults' comparative neglect and the endless, quite Arcadian gambols that remain available as a result. The much more famous *The Wind in the Willows* is clearly prefigured here. Mr. Toad's apotheosis is echoed by the final story in *The Golden Age*, the spectacular "The Roman Road."

"The Roman Road" features a sense-perceptive, world-aware young boy out on a jaunt. Out in the country he encounters a painter, painting. The man is middle-aged, modest, warmly wise, poignantly diminished, perhaps. The two of them talk, about the road ahead and all of humanity behind. The child refers to things that he has heard and learned. The painter quietly replies that he has lived and experienced some of these things. He hints at disappointment and of the smallness of adult attainment. More pressingly, he evokes the pleasure and wonder of even making the effort and of those glancing, indelible moments when the effort pays off.

The painter has referred to Marcus Aurelius, reflecting not only his stoicism but some of his fatalism as well. But the painter has also been to Rome, which contains much more than just this one stoical classical reference. In fact, he paints there every year. He hopes that the boy will visit him there, one day. The boy, simultaneously sobered and shining around the eyes, thinks that he shall. They separate and evoke between them almost all of human experience and possibility.[57]

Expansion and increase: in addition to, after all of the childish things, this is the proper end of children's literature, or at least of each child who has been served and taught and made joyful by it. In *The Wind in the Willows*, all of Mr. Toad's wild adventures come to an amusing and unexpectedly poignant conclusion. After singing a last, surpassingly self-regarding song, Toad puts away his childish things once and for all.

> He sang this very loud, with great unction and expression; and when he had done, he sang it all over again.
> Then he heaved a deep sigh; a long, long, long sigh.
> Then he dipped his hairbrush in the water-jug, parted his hair in the middle, and plastered it down very straight and sleek on each side of his face; and, unlocking the door, went quietly down the stairs to greet his guests, who he knew must be assembling in the drawing-room.[58]

Beyond the hilarious prospect of a toad with his hair parted in the middle, we have here a final, permanent transformation similar to the one in *A House at Pooh Corner* and even Cervantes' *Don Quixote*. At the subsequent celebration of their great victory (Toad Hall had been breached and invaded, and then its invaders had been ignominiously defeated), Toad deflects praise and attention, refuses to be drawn into any kind of inappropriate behavior, and generally puts away all the maddening and childish things that have so dominated and complicated his life. This is right, and it is also very sad. Or at least it would be if it were not for another, brighter prospect.

In "Wonderful Afternoon," the tenth chapter of Laura Ingalls Wilder's *By the Shores of Silver Lake*, Laura spends an entire afternoon watching the railway crews that are plowing and scraping, dragging and dumping, cutting and filling near her family's holding. By her close observation Laura learns how all of these individual tasks are overseen and integrated into a great whole. She learns that each component is imagined then refined, planned and prepared for, undertaken and, finally, accomplished. She realizes for the first time that it all requires the utmost concentration and constancy. She also realizes that this is the greatest thing she has ever seen, or that has ever been. This is adulthood, with all of its power and purpose and glory.[59]

It is very important to add that Laura not only learns through and by her own ardent interest and close observation. She also learns because her exemplary, constantly and happily hard-working father stands by her side for the entire afternoon. He directs her attention, explains and interprets every single or compound action. He shares in and adds to her joy, and to her series-long assurance that the delights of a nurtured childhood will not only be superseded, but even eclipsed by the abundance of adulthood.

During the course of Laura Ingalls Wilder's *Little House* books, Charles Ingalls is a constant marvel of cheerful, coordinated, constant industry. He never stops, because indeed there is no end of work to do. Since this is the case it is especially significant, especially lovely, that on this particular day he fulfills the most challenging, irreducible, and joyful of his duties by doing nothing, with his beloved daughter, for an entire afternoon. Antoine de Saint-Exupéry's child-squelching adults would not understand. Indeed, neither do Laura's alternatively exemplary mother and older sister.[60] But that's as may be, and nothing to worry or feel badly about. Pa is contented with all of his manifold labors, as well as with the diversity of his fellow laborers. "It's pretty work," he says simply, and with all his heart.[61]

This is how continents are conquered, but the Wilder books devote much more time and space to adulthood's smaller, quieter satisfactions.

8. Adults and Children, Mutually Implicated 217

Earlier in *By the Shores of Silver Lake*, Laura has been sent out early to fetch water from the well. As she does so she pauses to watch the sun rise over the eastern shore. The prospect is very beautiful, and she pauses over it at some length. Then she returns home.

"'We have been waiting for the water, Laura,' Ma said when Laura went in."[62] Laura explains the reason for her delay. "She began quickly to help Ma get breakfast, and while she hurried she told how the sun came up beyond Silver Lake."[63] Laura's description continues, rendered most gladly and not at all exclusively of the labors that are quite properly being required of her. In this episode, and throughout the course of her remarkable multi-volume memoir, the reader sees Laura Ingalls develop into Mary and Martha both, careful about many things and troubled not at all. Laura's own sister Mary, recently blinded after a bout of scarlet fever, listens attentively and then expresses her gratitude: "Now I see it all. You make pictures when you talk, Laura."[64] Ma is appreciative as well, after a fashion. "Ma smiled at Laura too, but she only said, 'Well, girls, we have a busy day before us,' and laid out their work."[65]

Laura Ingalls' account of her progressive passage from childhood dependence to the joyful self-reliance of productive adulthood is paralleled in the story of her eventual husband, and of his own similarly arduous and abundant childhood. *Farmer Boy* finds Almanzo Wilder in a self-sustaining agricultural economy similar to that of the Ingalls family. Also similar is the book's bracingly positive attitude to the work of the hands and the sweat of the face. Far from being unwelcome, Almanzo comes to find that his seemingly endless labors are actually, quietly, leading him to a wonderfully attainable ever-after, to the actual fulfillment of his fondest dreams.

> All winter long, on stormy days, there would be threshing to do. When the wheat was threshed, there would be the oats, the beans, the Canada peas. There was plenty of grain to feed the stock, plenty of wheat and rye to take to the mill for flour. Almanzo had harrowed the fields, he had helped in the harvest, and now he was threshing.
>
> He helped to feed the patient cows, and the horses eagerly whinnying over the bars of their stalls, and the hungrily bleating sheep, and the grunting pigs. And he felt like saying to them all: "You can depend on me. I'm big enough to take care of you all."
>
> Then he shut the door snugly behind him, leaving them all fed and warm and comfortable for the night, and he went trudging through the storm to the good supper waiting in the kitchen.[66]

Conclusion

This last section has concentrated on the literary side of the ledger. Let us return to, and conclude with, movies. Films, produced through the decades and across the world, reflect all of the contradiction, occasional arrest, and ultimate abundance of the literary record. As discussed in the first two chapters of this study, books and films are complementary in almost every meaningful respect when it comes to exploring and illustrating the most important ideas, as well as their most bracing counters. And for all of the material differences between them, books and films are also eminently able to do justice to each argument's every turn and nuance.

With regard to the happy graduation of youth to maturity, film sounds this particular motif in an expansive, even comprehensive manner. It has a number of key aspects. Chapter 3 featured an extended discussion of George Eliot's *Silas Marner*, and the notion that the pure child and the adult that cares for her can bless and even save one another. Without necessarily being mindful of that specific source, films have most stirringly illustrated, even demonstrated, this hypothesis.

This is Charlie Chaplin's miraculous *The Kid* (1921), which so beautifully renders the typicality and tenderness of family life. Chaplin's character matter-of-factly takes on the care of a foundling baby. He learns of his responsibilities and then, gladly, fulfills them. Later, after the elliptical passage of a few years, we find that the child is returning that favor. The genial domesticity of these two characters is thoroughly and even excessively detailed. And then it is interrupted and jeopardized, subsequently leading to some of the most satisfyingly, cathartically emotional material in all of cinema. But it is that genial domesticity that fuels those fireworks, and its seemingly excessive detailing that make them so much more than merely spectacular.

Though we may not credit it, this is Chuck Jones and Warner Bros.' beloved cartoon, *Feed the Kitty*, in which—among several other possible interpretations—masculine strength, which can tend to dire displays of bravado and even brute force, is disarmed by a child's vulnerability and gentleness. And a child of another species, mind! Like Chaplin, Warner Bros.' ensemble of animators combines virtuosic gag comedy with the deepest sentiment, once again in support of the counterintuitive idea that to subordinate one's self to the care of a little one is also, surely, to save one's self.

The idea is endemic, even epidemic. It is the root of Wim Wenders' luminous milestone of New German Cinema, *Alice in the Cities*, the core

8. Adults and Children, Mutually Implicated 219

of screen gangster Hideshi Kitano's self-satirizing, then self-reproving *Kikujiro*. It is the slender, shimmering thread in arch-misanthropist Henri-Georges Clouzot's uncharacteristically tender *Quai des Orfevres*.[67] This is *Bachelor Mother, Paper Moon, Central Station, Être et Avoir, School of Rock, Tokyo Godfathers*.

It is not just individual adults that benefit from the care of children. Another refrain, repeatedly sounded throughout the history of world cinema, is that communities entire are simultaneous grounded and raised when they properly attend to their young. Here are Yasujirō Ozu's *I Was Born, but...* and *Good Morning*. Here are *A Tree Grows in Brooklyn* and *In the Street* and *Children Learning by Experience*. Here is a vast assembly, the world tree growing out of the world root: *The Sons of Ingmar, Nanook of the North, The Navigator, Faces of Children, Sparrows, The Crowd, One Hundred Men and a Girl, Bringing Up Baby, The Wizard of Oz* and *The Bluebird, Children from Overseas, How Green Was My Valley, The Jungle Book, Meet Me in St. Louis, A Diary for Timothy, The Southerner, The Yearling, Louisiana Story, The 3 Godfathers, The River, All My Babies, The Great Adventure, Mon Oncle, The 400 Blows, Patinoire, Tom Jones, The Hutterites, Sammy Going South, One Potato, Two Potato, The Children of Fogo Island, The Wild Child, The Traveler, Killer of Sheep, The Black Stallion, Heartland, In the Labyrinth, The Hockey Sweater, Crac!, Life, and Nothing More..., Lorenzo's Oil, Crooklyn, Searching for Bobby Fisher, The Secret of Roan Inish, The Mirror*, the best and the rest of Pixar's collected works, *The Iron Giant, Not One Less, Tzaritza, Please Vote for Me, Kung Fu Panda, How to Train Your Dragon, I Wish, Le Havre, The Kid with a Bike*.

There is a necessary complement, an activist or even prosecutorial parallel to this last broad theme. It is that the moral viability of the community or society, the ideology or the value system is finally measured by whether or not its children are adequately cared for. Films exploring this notion add up to an extraordinarily expansive, urgent and penetrating conversation. Indeed, again, although the following list is glancingly selective, films exploring this notion add up to world cinema, or even the world itself: *Ingeborg Holm, Frankenstein, Las Hurdes, Young America, Housing Problems, Dead End, Boys Town, The Childhood of Maxim Gorky, Angels with Dirty Faces, The Grapes of Wrath, Rome, Open City, Shoeshine, Great Expectations, Oliver Twist, Bicycle Thieves, Germany, Year Zero, Los Olividados, The Quiet One, Intruder in the Dust, Bellissima, Forbidden Games, Mandy, White Mane, The Red Balloon, Pather Panchali, Harvest of Shame, A Child Is Waiting, My Name Is Ivan, Vidas Secas, To Kill a Mockingbird, Hud, The War Game, Warrendale, Mouchette, Kes, My Home Is Copaca-*

bana, *The Green Wall, Mon Oncle Antoine, My Childhood* and *My Ain Folk, The Spirit of the Beehive, Taxi Driver, Every Child, Pixote, Testament, Foster Child,* the *Up* films, *Au Revoir, les Enfants, Distant Voices, Still Lives, Grave of the Fireflies, Landscape in the Mist, Salaam Bombay!, Homework, Burnt by the Sun* and *Anna from 6 to 18, The White Balloon, The Butcher Boy, The Apple, Babe: Pig in the City, The Color of Paradise, Gasman* and *Ratcatcher, The Little Girl Who Sold the Sun, The Day I Became a Woman, Baran, Afghan Alphabet, The Return, Born into Brothels, Nobody Knows, Oliver Twist* again, *Happy Feet, Last Train Home, The White Ribbon; Hoop Dreams* and *Stevie* and *The Interrupters; Rosetta, The Son,* and *L'Enfant.*

Commerce has contributed to these expansive conversations, as have the most dedicated and rigorous film artists, and the craftsmen, and the public servants besides. They have told this expansive, enormous story, often in small increments. The cumulative effect, however, is vast unto incalculable. And yet, as addressed above, this is only one part of the grand narrative.

And graduation? Like the great forward-looking books from children's literature's golden age, films can do, have done much more than merely entertain. In addition to the rest and release and plain pleasure that they provide, they also guide and counsel, giving perspective and courage as they bring their bright, attentive, lovingly shepherded viewers up to a thrilling brink. *My Grandmother Ironed the King's Shirts, The Girl Who Hated Books, Big Drive, Flawed, The Danish Poet, Ballet Adagio, Uncle Bob's Hospital Visit*—the young reader or viewer who synthesizes, who likens the lessons unto herself, finds affirmation and encouragement as she prepares for that happy step forward.

The 5,000 Fingers of Dr. T. and *The Little Fugitive, Jason and the Argonauts* and *Bye-Bye Birdie; The Yearling, Aparajito, Amelia and the Angel* and *Il Posto; Ponyo* and *The Secret World of Arietty; Spirited Away, Kiki's Delivery Service, Howl's Moving Castle* and *From Up on Poppy Hill; Where Is My Friend's House?* and *Lassie; Rushmore* and *Speed Racer; 2001: A Space Odyssey* and *The Tree of Life*—the array of treatments seems to approach the infinite, and each one affirms and encourages as its subscribers approach that brink.

Although it is natural to pause before crossing the threshold and into one's majority, the most seemly of these stories do so only briefly. After a fond and grateful backward look, they push bravely forward. Rudyard Kipling has the proper measure of the thing, striking a chord of admirable unsentimentality:

8. Adults and Children, Mutually Implicated 221

"Man-Pack and Wolf-Pack have cast me out," said Mowgli. "Now I will hunt alone in the jungle."

"And we will hunt with thee," said the four cubs.

So Mowgli went away and hunted with the four cubs in the jungle from that day on. But he was not always alone, because, years afterward, he became a man and married.

But that is a story for grown-ups.[68]

A story for grown-ups, in which children promise and are likely to play one of the profoundest parts. *Il Giornate del Cinema Muto* is a longstanding annual celebration of silent film, held annually in Pordenone, Friuli, Italy. This festival includes the work of various archives, artists, commercial institutions and national cinemas. In 1999, as part of a program of Scandinavian films, the festival's curators compiled a number of home movies shot by pioneering Swedish cinematographer Julius Jaenzon. Jaenzon is celebrated, among other things, for his mastery of the exterior scene. His powerful location work suggested both nature's vast magnitude, and the infinite, particular beauties of its smaller scale. Further, Jaenzon was able to situate his characters within the environment in which they found themselves, whether natural or cultural. Jaenzon's composition and blocking could communicate harmony or conflict, obliteration or reconciliation between the individual and his environment.[69]

Jaenzon's home movies were obviously shot in a different setting and context and for a different purpose. And yet these casually off-handed images, looser and more improvised than the majestic ones for which he is celebrated, achieve the same combination of magnitude and intimacy as the commercial films. The intimate part is obvious. Jaenzon shot footage of his family for ten straight years, from 1920 to 1929. The images glisten, revealing a *Wild Strawberries* fantasy come unfussily, *sans* vitriol, to life. In these films, we see their subjects recreating, relaxing, and loving each other. Of special interest, and most especially precious, are the growing children at the center of almost every frame. As they increase in stature and capacity we also see their affectionate parents, aging incrementally around the edges.

These images are domestic and undramatic. In this lies, paradoxically, their magnitude. Unlike a commercial release, or a sermon, these private films are too direct and unpremeditated to contain a theme or lesson. Rather, much more simply and directly, they contain a truth. It is a commonplace, and it can sound sanctimonious or bathetic in the stating. And yet: this compilation of old Swedish home movies says, as such innumerable witnesses have likewise done, that children are inexpressibly precious.

It says that to care for them is life's most sacred, satisfying task. The last section of the Jaenzon compilation jumps forward sixteen years. At the end of this long, leisurely assembly of films, the infant of the 1920s has a child of her own. In this light, and in relation to this setting, it can suddenly seem that commercial narrative and its various conventions are at best handmaids that bring us to life, and at worst utterly insignificant. The home movie is the only movie, or it is all movies.[70]

Not everyone can, not everyone will, not everyone wants to have children. That course is not universal, and multitudes of other options are available that enable every individual to make her mark. The child option, and its proper conclusion in the multigenerational repetition of the entire cycle, will only seem exclusive and all-consuming to the person who has opted through choice or circumstance to go down that road. But what an all-consuming, all-encompassing road it will become, for that person!

This whole great passage is not simply a matter of leaving our childhood behind, but of retaining the childlike virtues—meekness, humility, affection, joy—that will make us better as we do so. The duality that we have been tracing through the course of this study—children are heavenly, and childish things are to be put away—reminds us that the stages of childhood are glancing. Their briefness makes them all the more essential, all the more pleasing. They are to be fully and richly experienced with graduation gladly following, without mourning or morbidity.

This is so because of the way that the first snug plenitudes of childhood can be followed by adulthood's profoundly satisfying expanses. Confucius suggests something of their compass, and their comprehensiveness.

> At fifteen, I bent my mind on learning; at thirty, I was established; at forty, I was free from delusion; at fifty, I knew the decree of Heaven; at sixty, my ears became subtly perceptive; at seventy, I was able to follow my heart's desire without overstepping the rules of propriety.[71]

These are the adult's inner accomplishments, attained through adulthood's long course and many stages. And of course this internal refining is paralleled by a corresponding external advance, of which the care of children is so often, so profoundly a part. The consequences of this broad moral evolution are as sweeping as can be imagined, or articulated: he that findeth his life shall lose it: and he that loseth his life for my sake shall find it.[72]

In the face of all of this, books and films are merely handmaidens. And yet, what work they accomplish, and what a service they render!

Chapter Notes

Introduction

1. This essay is actually a "composite of three articles: the first written for a Venice Festival anniversary booklet, *Twenty Years of Film* (1952); the second 'Editing and Its Evolution,' *Age Nouveau*, No. 92, July 1955; and the third in *Cahiers du Cinéma*, No. 7, 1950." Bazin, *What Is Cinema*, 174.
2. Rudolf Arnheim was the primary proponent of this view, or at least remains the most anthologized of its proponents (i.e., his work appears in seven editions of Braudy and Cohen's *Film Theory and Criticism*). Arnheim's argument is laid out in his 1933 book, *Film as Art*, which develops the idea that the seeming limitations of silent cinema actually evolved into productive, artful delimitations. In four sections—"Film and Reality," "The Making of the Film," "The Content of the Film," and "The Complete Film"—Arnheim details the particulars of this paradox (8–160). The burgeoning of this melancholic celebration of silent film's greatness can be found in the Arnheim collection, *Film Essays and Criticism*, specifically in a number of early reviews and appreciations (11–39); in particular, see "For the First Time" (13–15), which is countered by "The Sad Future of Film" (11–13).
3. See also Bazin, *What Is Cinema*, 2:16–101.
4. Bazin, *Jean Renoir*.
5. Bazin, "The Evolution of the Language of Cinema," in *What Is Cinema*, 34.
6. Bazin, "The Evolution of the Language of Cinema," 28.
7. Bazin further elaborates on these questions in "The Myth of Total Cinema" and "The Ontology of the Cinematic Image," in *What Is Cinema*, 1:9–16, 17–22.
8. On the precipice of what would be an utterly transformative technological proliferation, Neil Postman's book *Technopoly* (1992) effectively represents and articulates this cautionary view. It holds that computers, with all of their platforms, formats and de facto narratives, are only operationally distinct from dreaded television. In the most fundamental respects, however, the various new technologies are all basically of a piece. For further elaborations and citations, see my second chapter.
9. Aristotle, *Eudemian Ethics*, Book III, VIII; Aristotle, *Nicomachean Ethics*, Book I–IV; see further elaboration in chapter 2, q.v.
10. Maltin and Bann, *Little Rascals*, 6.
11. In Butler and Cott, *Victorian Color Picture Books*, xvii.
12. Wood, *Museum of Childhood*, 91. Similarly, on a particularly elaborate doll's house in the Victoria and Albert Museum of Childhood collection, Wood states, "Dolls' houses were originally made by specialist craftsmen for the amusement of adults. This house would have been an extremely lavish plaything even for a wealthy family, not least because of its large size and high level of craftsmanship, and the hundreds of accessories it has been furnished with." Ibid., 17.
13. Zipes, "Once There Were Two Brothers Named Grimm," passim.
14. Schulz, *Peanuts Treasury*, n.p.
15. 1 Thessalonians 5:21.

Chapter 1

1. See Plato, *Republic*, trans. B. Jowett, 177–80.
2. Chris Marker makes a productive comparison between the Cave and the cinema in the ninth episode ("Cosmogony, or the Ways of the World") of his thirteen-part 1989 television series, *The Owl's Legacy*.
3. Plato, *Republic*, trans. B. Jowett, 178.

4. Plato, *Republic*, 179.
5. Plato, *Republic*, 177.
6. With regard to the use of the third person personal pronoun, this book will switch between "he" and "she," depending on the perceived sense or aptness of the situation.
7. Plato, *Republic*, trans. B. Jowett, 178.
8. Plato, *Republic*, 179.
9. E. C. Bentley, *Trent's Last Case*.
10. See Deuteronomy 30:3, Isaiah 5:26. For a few especially vivid accounts of this eternal enmity, see Jeremiah 50:23, 51:37, 47, and 60; Isaiah 13:19; Zechariah 2:7; and Revelation 14:8, 17:5. All biblical quotes and references herein are to the King James Version.
11. Isaiah 52:11.
12. Revelation 18:21.
13. *Techne*, in Plato, *Statesman*: 283b–285b, in Hofstadter and Kuhns, *Philosophies of Art and Beauty*, 5–8. For more on the mean see Aristotle, *Nicomachean Ethics*, ch. 1 and 2.
14. Aristotle, *Nicomachean Ethics*, in which he asserts that politics is the greatest of all of the arts, in that it is capable of doing the most good for the most people (1–2).
15. Plato, *Republic*, trans. B. Jowett, 51.
16. Plato, *Republic*, 67.
17. Plato, *Republic: Book III*, in Hofstadter and Kuhns, *Philosophies of Art and Beauty*, 20–21.
18. Plato, *Republic: Book II*, in Hofstadter and Kuhns, *Philosophies of Art and Beauty*, 11.
19. Plato, *Republic*, trans. B. Jowett, 64.
20. Plato, *Republic: Book III*, in Hofstadter and Kuhns, *Philosophies of Art and Beauty*, 22.
21. Plato, *Republic: Book III*, in Hofstadter and Kuhns, *Philosophies of Art and Beauty*, 19.
22. Plato, *Republic: Book X*, in Hofstadter and Kuhns, *Philosophies of Art and Beauty*, 31–33.
23. *Ibid.*, 33.
24. Plato, *Republic*, trans. B. Jowett, 69.
25. Plato, *Republic: Book X*, in Hofstadter and Kuhns, *Philosophies of Art and Beauty*, 30.
26. Aristotle, *Poetics*, 11–13.
27. See Aristotle's (admittedly elusive, much debated) commentary, which suggests a relationship between reasoning and character choice (*Poetics*, 12), as well as the subsequent understanding that choice and its ensuing consequence will bring. And with regard to reasoning, a subsequent reference to "rhetoric" (31)—and Aristotle's own *Rhetoric*—further suggests the moral landscape and the persuasive coinage of the entire exchange, or even institution. See Malcolm Heath's introduction (Aristotle, *Poetics*, xlvi). Marvin Carlson traces some of the twisting, uncertain path between Aristotle's lecture notes and an entire subsequent history of theatrical decorum, and adherence, in particular, to unities of space and time (Aristotle, *Poetics*, 12, 31); Carlson, *Theories of the Theatre*, 16–21, 39–50, 59–64, 72–84, 103–17.
28. Shakespeare, *Hamlet* 3.1.60–61.
29. Aristotle, *Poetics*, 13, 22.
30. Plato, *Republic: Book X*, in Hofstadter and Kuhns, *Philosophies of Art and Beauty*, 41–42. We might pause to note how many more images a filmmaker manufactures, and how much further from Socratic truth that might take him.
31. Plato, *Republic: Book III*, in Hofstadter and Kuhns, *Philosophies of Art and Beauty*, 23; Plato, *Republic*, trans. B. Jowett, 69.
32. Plato, *Republic: Book III*, in Hofstadter and Kuhns, *Philosophies of Art and Beauty*, 23.
33. Plato, *Republic: Book X*, in Hofstadter and Kuhns, *Philosophies of Art and Beauty*, 45; Plato, *Republic*, trans. B. Jowett, 265.
34. Plato, *Republic: Book III*, in Hofstadter and Kuhns, *Philosophies of Art and Beauty*, 27.
35. Mark 8:36.
36. In two parts, 1678, 1684.
37. Bunyan, *Pilgrim's Progress*, 78.
38. Bunyan, *Pilgrim's Progress*, 78–79.
39. Bunyan, *Pilgrim's Progress*, 79.
40. Bunyan, *Pilgrim's Progress*, ibid.
41. Bunyan, *Pilgrim's Progress*, ibid.
42. Bunyan, *Pilgrim's Progress*, ibid.
43. Bunyan, *Pilgrim's Progress*, ibid.
44. See Matthew 4:1–11.
45. Forman, *Our Movie Made Children*, 121.
46. Forman, *Our Movie Made Children*, 4, 108–9.
47. *Ibid.*
48. Plato, *Republic*, trans. B. Jowett, 50.
49. Maltby, "Censorship and Self-Regulation," 235.
50. Forman, *Our Movie Made Children*, 34–5.
51. Forman, *Our Movie Made Children*, 35.
52. Forman, *Our Movie Made Children*, 147.
53. Forman, *Our Movie Made Children*, 35.
54. Forman, *Our Movie Made Children*, 35–6.
55. Black, *Hollywood Censored*, 49–197, especially 154.
56. Maltby, "Censorship and Self-Regulation," 243.
57. Numerous other books contribute similarly or express similar concerns. Some do so without keying especially on children (e.g., Jerry Mander's *Four Arguments for the Elimination of Television*).
58. Postman, *Amusing Ourselves to Death*, 8.
59. Exodus 20:2–6; Matthew 22:34–40.
60. Postman, *Amusing Ourselves to Death*, 13.

61. Postman, *Amusing Ourselves to Death*, 70.
62. Postman, *Amusing Ourselves to Death*, 73-4.
63. Postman, *Amusing Ourselves to Death*, 71.
64. Postman, *Amusing Ourselves to Death*, 72.
65. Postman, *Amusing Ourselves to Death*, 92.
66. Ecclesiastes 1:14.
67. Buckingham, *After the Death of Childhood*, 38.
68. Plato, *Republic:* Book III, in Hofstadter and Kuhns, *Philosophies of Art and Beauty*, 24.
69. Plato, *Republic:* Book III, in Hofstadter and Kuhns, *Philosophies of Art and Beauty*, 25.
70. Plato, *Republic:* Book X, in Hofstadter and Kuhns, *Philosophies of Art and Beauty*, 43.
71. Plato, *Republic:* Book X, in Hofstadter and Kuhns, *Philosophies of Art and Beauty*, 41.
72. Buckingham, *After the Death of Childhood*, 13-15.
73. Signal contributions, among many examples: Aufderheide P. (1992), Hobbs, R. (1998 and 2010), Kellner, D., and J. Share (2007), National Association of Media Literacy Education (NAMLE) (2007).
74. Of course since Postman's writing speech, through the form of punditry, has increased exponentially. For some time, this proliferation has been subjected to a new wave of polemical attacks which are similarly motivated and may have some of the same salutary effects as Postman's original points.
75. Postman, *Amusing Ourselves to Death*, 71, 127.
76. De Saussure, *Course in General Linguistics*; Barthes, *Mythologies*; Metz, *Essays on the Semiotics of Film from 1964-67*.
77. Consider particularly the institutions of children's literature, with its sometimes implicit, sometimes quite open assumptions about the inherent dangers of media. This idea threads through the work of Huck and Trelease, Tunnell and Jacobs, Lukens, Kiefer, and others.
78. "A Teacher's Guide: *The Wretched Stone* by Chris Van Allsburg."
79. "A Teacher's Guide: *The Wretched Stone* by Chris Van Allsburg."
80. Van Allsburg's *Zathura* (2002) has a similar if more glancing view of television's meretricious effects. It also has a pleasingly emphatic way of dealing with the danger. "Then—KABOOM—a rock the size of a refrigerator fell through the ceiling and crushed the television" ("A Teacher's Guide: *Zathura* by Chris Van Allsburg").
81. "A Teacher's Guide: *The Wretched Stone* by Chris Van Allsburg."
82. Cai, "TV-Turnoff Week," 834.
83. Children's authors have frequently taken this course of opposing the enemy. A few among many in the United States: Stan Berenstain, *The Berenstain Bears and Too Much TV* (1984); Clive Dobson, *Fred's TV* (1989); and David McPhail, *Fix-It* (1992).
84. As elaborated, for instance, in Frances Flaherty's analysis and appreciation of her husband Robert Flaherty's films, *The Odyssey of a Filmmaker*.

Chapter 2

1. In Hofstadter and Kuhns, *Philosophies of Art and Beauty*, 94.
2. Aristotle, *Nicomachean Ethics*, trans. David Ross, 40, 42.
3. Bettleheim, *Uses of Enchantment*, 24.
4. Bettleheim, *Uses of Enchantment*, 107
5. Garfield, *Sound of Coaches*, 77.
6. History—and literary history—abound in these dialectical perspectives. As he creates his theatrical troupe, Garfield, who would later publish an acclaimed conclusion to Charles Dickens' unfinished novel, *The Mystery of Edwin Drood* (1870), is thinking about and drawing upon the Vincent Crummles Company in Dickens' novel *Nicholas Nickleby* (1838; see chapters 22 to 30). Dickens' portrayal of this troupe of actors is, as ever, full of caricature and satire. It is not without its implicit critique, at least of the foibles of individuals and of the way that individual foibles in likeminded people can multiply into institutional error. In the end, though, and all through this episode, Dickens sees the theater, playing, and collectives of artificiality as being benevolent, and, for Nicholas, positively life-saving.
7. See also the concluding chapter, "Children as Citizens," in David Buckingham's *After the Death of Childhood*, 168-88.
8. For more of the optimistic view, see Seymour Papert, *The Connected Family*; Douglas Rushkoff, *Playing the Future*; and Steven Johnson, *Everything Bad Is Good for You*.
9. Buckingham, *After the Death of Childhood*, 42.
10. Buckingham, *After the Death of Childhood*, 32, 45.
11. For a still-magisterial survey of the Soviets' pioneering film work see Leyda, *Kino*, 1960; also Schnitzer, Luda and Jean, *Cinema and Revolution*, 1973; for a more recent synthesis see Richard Taylor/Ian Christie, *The Film Factory*, 1988/1994 and Taylor/Christie, *Inside The Film Factory*, 1994; for individuals' contributions, see Eisenstein, 1949, 1958, 1970; Pudovkin, *Film Technique and Film Acting*, Trans. Montague, Grove, 1969; Vertov, *Kino-Eye*, Trans. O'Brien, Ed. Michelson, UC Press, 1984; *The Eisenstein Reader*, London, Bfi, 1998; etc.

12. As stated, for instance, in Hofstadter and Kuhns, *Philosophies of Art and Beauty*, 78.
13. Aristotle, *Poetics*, trans. Malcolm Heath, 3.
14. Aristotle, *Poetics*, trans. Malcolm Heath, 6–7.
15. Aristotle, *Poetics*, trans. Malcolm Heath, 10–13; see also 20–30.
16. Aristotle, *Poetics*, trans. Malcolm Heath, 10.
17. See, for example, Aristotle's strong endorsement of Homer in Aristotle, *Poetics*, trans. Heath, 1–8, 15, and especially 38–41.
18. Aristotle, *Poetics*, trans. Malcolm Heath, 10–17.
19. The German playwright and theoretician Bertolt Brecht will go on to criticize and even despise that cathartic equation, suggesting that it both requires and creates spectator passivity, that it allows too much ideological deception and even oppression (Brecht, *Brecht on Theater*, 33–42, 179–205, n276). This is an extraordinarily valid and important point. In response one might observe, again, that what might be need not inevitably or universally be.
20. Aristotle, *Nicomachean Ethics:* Book II, in Hofstadter and Kuhns, *Philosophies of Art and Beauty*, 93. C. S. Lewis's *An Experiment in Criticism* (1963) makes a similar assertion, suggesting that the quality or caliber of reading is just as important, just as powerful, as how well a book is written.
21. Quoted in Tibbets and Welsh, *The Encyclopedia of Novels into Film*, xvi.
22. Quoted in Tibbets and Welsh, *The Encyclopedia of Novels into Film*, xviii.
23. Books displayed included Tolkien's *Return of the King*, Card's *Ender's Game*, Martel's *Life of Pi*.
24. Braudy and Cohen, *Film Theory and Criticism*, 445–59.
25. Lindsay, *Magic Pudding*, 28.
26. Andersen, *Complete Fairy Tales*, frontispiece (n.p.).
27. Andersen, *Complete Fairy Tales*, 316.
28. Haugaard, *Portrait of a Poet*, 1.
29. Andersen, *Complete Fairy Tales*, 668.
30. Andersen, *Complete Fairy Tales*, 999.
31. *Ibid.*
32. Andersen, *Complete Fairy Tales*, 1001.
33. Other examples of this noisy trend in children's literature include *The Last Mimzy* (2007), *The Lion, the Witch and the Wardrobe* (2005), *The Voyage of the Dawn Treader* (2010), not to mention most everything out of the Marvel Comics stable.
34. It is important to note that the directors of these films, Joe Johnston and Jon Favreau, have also produced skillful, witty, even modest films in the blockbuster mode that we are now considering and criticizing. While *Jumanji* and *Zathura* may circumvent their sources—or, rather, are boldly transformative adaptations of those sources—they are, at the same time, eminent manifestations of a certain kind of much-desired, potentially profitable product. In many ways these directors are mostly responsible for doing exactly what was expected of them and what they were paid for.
35. See the conclusion to Beckett's 1958 novel, *The Unnamable*, in Beckett, *Three Novels*, 414.
36. Sartre, *No Exit and Three Other Plays*, 46.
37. Does this criticism of Roeg's film fail to take the advice so pointedly proffered earlier in this very same chapter? "Too often our critical disapproval relates to a wrong turn on the road we would have taken, or that we would like to have seen taken...." This is a very just question, and perhaps a very valid counter-criticism. Regardless of the particular case, or reading, however, the broader point about commercial film industries as they relate to individual books still stands.
38. Burns, *Works of Robert Burns*, 26–31.
39. Yeats, *Irish Fairy and Folk Tales*. (Yeats' collection, originally entitled *Fairy and Folk Tales of Ireland*, appears by this title in the Modern Library edition.)
40. Yeats, *Celtic Twilight*, in *Mythologies*. (*Mythologies* is an anthology of four distinct publications by Yeats, including *The Celtic Twilight*.)
41. Crichton-Smith, "Seordag's Interview with the BBC," 124–25.
42. Originally published as *Peter Pan and Wendy* (1911).
43. In the case of *Peter Pan* the diegetic listeners are the Lost Boys. In *Winnie the Pooh* the narrator, whom we might call "A.A. Milne," is asked by "Christopher Robin" to tell a story to Edward Bear.
44. As in the frequent extra-diegetic hailing in much of Hans Christian Andersen, or whoever Huck Finn is talking to, or all of the Milnes and Christopher-Robins who are at least figuratively inscribed within the Pooh books' actual, and mythical character dynamics.
45. Barrie, *Peter Pan*, 149. For a further example of this bracing corrective, see Ahlberg and Howard's *The Bravest Ever Bear* (1999).
46. Yeats, *Mythologies*, 125–37.
47. Eliot, "Hamlet and His Problems," in *The Sacred Wood*, 121.
48. Lang, introduction to *Blue Fairy Book*; Zipes, "Once There Were Two Brothers Named Grimm," in *Complete Fairytales*, xxiii–xxviii; Campbell, "Folkloristic Commentary," in *Complete Grimm's Fairy Tales*, 837–39, 857–64; Pullman, "Introduction," in *Grimm Tales: For Young and Old*, ix–xxii.

49. Bierhorst's books include *The Dancing Fox* (1997), *The Mythology of Mexico and Central America* (1990), and *Latin American Folktales: Stories from Hispanic and Indian Traditions* (2002).
50. North, quoted in Avery, 1994, 16.
51. *Ibid.*
52. Shelley Duvall, *Faerie Tale Theater.*
53. Holling, *Paddle to the Sea*, n.p.
54. Bentley, 1913, opp. cit.
55. A triumph is evidenced, for one thing, by its 2008 re-release by the distinguished American distributor of some of world cinema's most canonical films, the Criterion Collection. http://www.criterion.com/current/posts/657-paddle-to-the-sea
56. *Paddle to the Sea*, directed by William Mason.
57. *Ibid.*
58. *Ibid.*
59. The joy of self-sufficiency, for young and old alike, is one of several key motifs explored throughout the course of Mason's peripatetic career, manifest in the various titles that comprise his curious, searching oeuvre. See Ohayon, "Bill Mason: Beyond the Wild."
60. For another inspiring, physically detailed, and vivid example of this childish industry see *The Secret of Roan Inish*, American filmmaker John Sayles's 1994 paean to the resiliency and resourcefulness of children.
61. Schickel, *D. W. Griffith*, 66; Arvidson, *When the Movies Were Young*, 66.
62. Some may argue that the title for Soviet cinema's most precocious figure goes to Dziga Vertov.
63. Eisenstein, *Film Form*, 195–254.
64. Kevin Brownlow states that as an impressionable, film-fascinated youth, Lean had not been much exposed to the Soviets, and that throughout the course of his career he would generally eschew demonstrative "Russian cutting." He was, however, very much aware of and inspired by the similarly impressive, cumulative constructions of D. W. Griffith. See Brownlow, *David Lean*, 42, 60, 150, and 532.
65. Garfield, *Sound of Coaches*, 11–16, 162.
66. Sibert, "Leon Garfield," in Silvey, *Children's Books*, 264–67.
67. Andersen, *Complete Fairy Tales*, 40–41.
68. Other examples of these sorts of enhancement, see Jean Renoir's *A Day in the Country* (1936) or Peter Bogdanovich's *The Last Picture Show* (1971).
69. For more on literary naturalism and some of its specific relations to children's literature and film, see chapter six.
70. Barrie, *Peter Pan*, 204.
71. Philips, *Book of Children's Verse*, xxxvi.
72. Bazin, "In Defense of Mixed Cinema" and "Theater and Cinema," in *What Is Cinema?* 53–124; See also Edgerton, *Film and the Arts in Symbiosis.*

Chapter 3

1. Roughly, briefly, principled Socrates eschews the corruptions of official power and preeminence in favor of an independence and integrity that operates from without, to the point of being willing to pay for it with his life. (See "Apology," trans. Benjamin Jowett, in *The Dialogues of Plato.* New York, Bantam, 1986, 3–28.) Confucius, just as devoted to righteousness, pursues and exemplifies the same moral resolve but in a different register as he engages with and contributes to governance. See Confucius, *Analects*, 4:13–14 (69), 9:6–7 (102), 10:1, 10:3 (109–110), 12:1–24 (125–31), and most pointedly in the sequence of 8:7, 8:13–14 (97–98), 14:7 (144), and 18:6–7 (174–76).
2. Wordsworth, "Ode: Intimations of Immortality from Reflections of Early Childhood," in *William Wordsworth*, 282.
3. Romans 5:12–19 is often identified as the seed of this doctrine, or the root of this problem. St. Augustine articulated and even formulated its earliest and most influential elaboration. See Couenhoven, "St. Augustine's Doctrine of Original Sin."
4. The tabula rasa was introduced in *An Essay Concerning Human Understanding* (1690) and elaborated regarding its educational application in *Some Thoughts Concerning Education* (1693).
5. *Julie, or the New Héloïse* (1761); *Émile, or on Education* (1762).
6. See Rousseau, *Discourse on the Arts and Sciences* (1750); Rousseau, *Discourse on Inequality* (1754).
7. Shelley, *Frankenstein*, 35.
8. See Marshall, "Frankenstein, or Rousseau's Monster" 135–77; McWhir, "Teaching the Monster to Read," 73–82.
9. Wood, *Museum of Childhood*, 37.
10. Matthew 18:1.
11. Matthew 19:13.
12. Luke 18:15.
13. Of course not every individual, not every theological or moral formulation, will agree with this characterization.
14. 1 Samuel 16:11.
15. 1 Samuel 16:7.
16. Psalm 131:1.
17. Isaiah 9:6.
18. Isaiah 11:6.
19. L'Engle, *Glorious Impossible.*
20. Isaiah 11:7–9.
21. Job 5:7.
22. John 16:21.
23. 2 Kings 2:23.
24. Proverbs 22:15.

25. Consider, for instance, the pan-historical, transcontinental traditions of didactic or sermonic literature.
26. 1 Corinthians 13: 9.
27. Galatians 4:1.
28. Genesis 37:3.
29. Genesis 37:5–8.
30. Genesis 37:9–11.
31. See also Pullman, *The Good Man Jesus*.
32. Genesis 37:18–20.
33. Genesis 37:21–22.
34. Genesis 35:22, Genesis 49:3–4.
35. John 16: 33.
36. Genesis 37:26–28.
37. Genesis 37:29–30.
38. Cf. *King Lear*, act 3 scene 2 and act 5 scene 3.
39. Genesis 37:33–35.
40. In its Elisha entry the *Jewish Encyclopedia* states that "(t)he offenders were not children, but were called so ("ne'arim") because they lacked ("meno'arin") all religion (Soṭah 46b)." http://www.jewishencyclopedia.com/articles/5682-elisha
41. Dreyer, *Ordet*, 1955.
42. On "ultimate concern" see Paul Tillich, *The Dynamics of Faith*, 1–34.
43. Bunyan never wrote so unyieldingly as when he himself was at fault, as evidenced by the self-lacerating *Grace Abounding unto the Chief of Sinners* (1666).
44. Bunyan, *Pilgrim's Progress*, 212.
45. Bunyan, "The Shepherd Boy Sings in the Valley of Humiliation," in Quiller-Couch, 1919.
46. Kingsley, *Heroes*, Project Gutenberg.
47. Kenneth Grahame's *The Wind in the Willows* (1908) quite famously considers the possibility that children are naturally pagans (note especially the luminous chapter "The Piper at the Gates of Dawn"). His much less well-known, equally worthy *The Golden Age* (1895) and *Dream Days* (1898) offers a piquant take on the heathen side of the question. In the first chapter of his childhood memoir John Muir explicitly characterizes himself and his young Scots companions as pagans, while the remainder of the book is much occupied with his delightfully Calvinistic father's efforts to work and wallop that very quality out of him. Muir, *The Story of My Boyhood and Youth*, 1–25 (especially 6 and 12–18).
48. Grahame, *Wind in the Willows*, chapters 10–12.
49. Milne, 1928, chapter 10.
50. Cervantes, *Don Quixote*, chapters 71–73.
51. i.e., Exodus 20:2–5; "Come, I will tell you what your Lord has made binding on you: that you shall serve no other gods besides Him;" "This is the truth. There is no God but God;" "When your prayers are ended, remember God sitting, standing or lying down;" cf., also, the lovely story of Abraham, the stars and moon and sun, and his definitive turn from the idolaters. Dawood, *Koran*, 48, 72, 99, 107.
52. Chesterton, "A Christmas Carol," in *Wild Knight and Other Poems*, Project Gutenberg.
53. Sheldon, *In His Steps*, passim.
54. Elizabeth Madox Roberts, "Christmas Morning," in Philips, *New Oxford Book of Children's Verse*, 151.
55. As in Hans Christian Andersen's "The Wild Swans," in which nature and natural forces proclaim that which orthodoxy fears and resists. The firewood placed at the foot of an execution stake takes root and flowers to proclaim the innocence and godliness of a condemned child. See Andersen, *Complete Fairy Tales*, 130–31.
56. And the parent, not least of all. I use the male pronoun advisedly. In the just-quoted poem, the Catholic Chesterton's Mary is as central, as powerful, as irrefutable as the child. The biological matter-of-facts of maternity are very easily combined with mystery, myth, and worship, more or less. And, of course, from that profound and problematic idealization come feminisms, quite properly, of numerous varieties.
57. Twain, *A Connecticut Yankee in King Arthur's Court*, Project Gutenberg.
58. James 3:4.
59. Dahl, *Matilda*, 176. Similarly, *Oscar's Half Birthday* (2005), by the Australian children's author Bob Graham, is an especially sweet, felicitous exploration of the little child that leads. In this book, an infant, by simply being himself, reconciles race and class, even basic bigotries. Through the child, staid convention comes to countenance, even happily accept an interracial family, a long-haired dad, people with piercings and tattoos. External difference, together with the enmity it so often brings, simply disintegrates as a result of the child's transformative presence.
60. Andersen, *Complete Fairy Tales*, 511
61. Cf. John Milton, "Sonnet 19 (On His Blindness)."
62. Andersen, "Inchelina," in *Complete Fairy Tales*, 34; Cf. the Daisy toward the lark in "The Daisy," *Complete Fairy Tales*, 110.
63. Andersen, *Complete Fairy Tales*, 125.
64. Isaiah 53:7.
65. Andersen, *Complete Fairy Tales*, 130.
66. "And Abraham rose up early in the morning, and saddled his ass, and took two of his young men with him, and Isaac his son, and clave the wood for the burnt offering, and rose up, and went unto the place of which God had told him." Genesis 22:13.
67. And, most of all, Gerda must submit to

the brigands' stupendously ill-behaved young daughter. See Andersen, *Complete Fairy Tales*, 252–56.
68. Andersen, *Complete Fairy Tales*, 257.
69. Or, rather, the Snow Queen simply vacates the field. Andersen, *Complete Fairy Tales*, 259–60.
70. Andersen, *Complete Fairy Tales*, 260.
71. Andersen, *Complete Fairy Tales*, 260.
72. Genesis 3:19.
73. Genesis 3:16; Eliot, *Silas Marner*, 102.
74. Eliot, *Silas Marner*, 136–37.
75. Eliot, *Silas Marner*, 143.
76. Joanna Spyri's *Heidi* is both typical and tremendously influential in its thorough exploration of this idea. Heidi's bitter grandfather has turned over a new leaf: "Well you see, Heidi, I felt happy because I am on good terms with people and at peace with God and man; that does one good! The dear Lord was good to me when He sent you up on the Alm." Spyri, *Heidi*, trans. Helen B. Dole, 185.
77. Eliot, *Silas Marner*, 144.
78. Eliot, *Silas Marner*, 154.
79. Eliot, *Silas Marner*, 158–59.
80. Eliot, *Silas Marner*, 159.
81. Numbers 21:8.
82. Eliot, *Silas Marner*, 160.

Chapter 4

1. See, for example, Vicky Lebeau, *Childhood and Cinema*, 8–15. See also Roger Taylor and Edward Wakeling, *Lewis Carroll, Photographer*; Charles Darwin, *The Expressions of the Emotions in Man and Animals*; Eadweard Muybridge, *The Human Figure in Motion*; and Nancy Mowll Mathews, *Mary Cassatt: A Life*. The phenomenon entire is measured and critiqued in *The Politics of Focus: Women, Children and Nineteenth-Century Photography* by Lindsay Smith.
2. See Burch and Brewster, *Life to Those Shadows*, 1990; Elsaesser, *Early Cinema*, 1990.
3. Lebeau, *Childhood and Cinema*, 10, 28, 36.
4. Griffith seems over-credited, his contemporaries under-acknowledged in Jacobs, *Rise of the American Film*; Barrie, *American Film Master*.
5. Biograph No. 115.
6. *Biograph Bulletin*, March 22, 1909, in Usai, *Griffith Project 1*, 51.
7. *Biograph Bulletin*, No. 277. The film was also released in September 1909; Biograph No. 190.
8. In Usai, *Griffith Project 3*, 54.
9. Quoted in Keil's analysis of the April 1912 Biograph film release, *The Female of the Species* (April 1912, Biograph No. 401). Usai, *Griffith Project 6*, 28.
10. *Biograph Bulletin*, June 27, 1910, in Usai, *Griffith Project 4*, 102.
11. Simmon, *Films of D. W. Griffith*, 53.
12. Griffith's Biograph films feature a number of ambiguities, contradictions, and plain problems in their portrayal of women, young women, and female children. The difficulty can be simply that the conventions of sentimental idealism collide with the realities of so many actual women's dispositions, inclinations, and realities. As we will see in the fifth chapter of this book, being a paragon may not only be difficult, it may not even be desirable. A further difficulty is found in the frequent conflict between idealism and sentimentality, as well as the maturation or outright physical maturity of Griffith's female characters. Repeatedly—as seen in characters played by Blanche Sweet in *The White Rose of the Wilds* (a lost film, May 1911, Biograph No. 339), by Mary Pickford in *A Feud in the Kentucky Hills* and *The One She Loved* (October 1912, Biograph Nos. 430 and 432), by May Marsh in *The Little Tease* (April 1913, Biograph No. 468), *The Battle of Elderbush Gulch* (March 1914, Biograph No. 483), and *Birth of a Nation* (1915), by Dorothy Gish in *Her Mother's Oath* (June 1913, Biograph No. 481), by Lillian Gish in *Gold and Glitter* (November 1912, Biograph No. 436), *Broken Blossoms* (1919) and *Way Down East* (1920)—an asexual or infantilized female character will find herself to be both coddled and courted. Chronologically she has come of age. Conceptually, or contextually, she has not. The result is not only a confusing ambiguity but a real sense of actual impropriety. See Studlar, "Oh, 'Doll Divine'," 2001. These conflicts cannot all be laid at Griffith's door. Victorianism and melodrama, to name only two powerful contemporary institutions, often operated in this confusing register. Jean Webster's 1912 novel *Daddy-Long-Legs*, which was very successfully filmed with Mary Pickford in 1919, is a powerful non-Griffith case in point. In both the book and the film, the heroine is introduced in her infancy, followed through her disadvantaged and yet spirited childhood, then seen to her successful ascension to adulthood, and to the hand of the wealthy and now elderly male benefactor who has been taking care of her all the while. A bit of squeamishness might be inherent in the scenario itself; the child, and the mannerisms with which Pickford portrays her, are still present in the depiction of the ostensible adult. (See, and feel, a similar situation in Frank Borzage's 1925 film, *Lazybones*.) For her part the diminutive Pickford, so soon to become fully responsible for her own brand and her own career, continued to play just preadolescent girls until 1926, just short of her own 35th birthday. Victorian

mindsets, or nostalgia as Victorianism gave way to modernity, ensured that the woman/child conundrum maintained a presence and power for a very long time. This tension forms the core of a remarkable number of the features released during Pickford's remarkably prolific, profitable prime, including: *In the Bishop's Carriage* (1913), *Caprice* (November 1913), *A Good Little Devil* (March 1914; note that Mary is not the titular character), *The Dawn of Tomorrow* (June 1915), *Little Pal* (July 1915), *Esmeralda* (September 1915), *A Girl of Yesterday* (October 1915), *The Foundling* (January 1916), *Poor Little Peppina* (March 1916), *Hulda from Holland* (July 1916), *Less Than Dust* (November 1916), doubly, in *Stella Maris* (January 1918), *Amarilly of Clothes-Line Lane* (March 1918), *M'liss* (May 1918), *The Hoodlum* (September 1919), and *Heart o' the Hills* (November 1919). Sometimes, in addition to being part of contemporary convention, the woman/child scenario could be consciously and somewhat productively explored. For instance Griffith and Pickford's *Friends* (released September 1912, Biograph No. 428) has an echo, if distant, of Henrik Ibsen's Nora Helmer (*A Doll's House*, 1879). On the other hand, and probably for the most part, the uncomfortable prospect of these infantilized late adolescents is simply a problem. Another reason and a powerful emblem for this is Griffith's problematic and, in at least a few demonstrable cases, outright dubious dealings with some of his young ingénues. See Schickel, *D.W. Griffith*, 163–68.

13. See Genesis 22:10–12. It should be noted that Griffith's children cannot solve every problem, nor can they motivate every reprobate toward reform. To Biograph's credit, not every child-ministration in its films was miraculously effectual. The February 1913 release *Oil and Water* (Biograph No. 448) features a momentarily endangered youngster who brings an estranged couple to the point of considering reconciliation. In the end, however, the couple opts not to follow through. Here and elsewhere it can be seen that the child motif could be tinged with realist sensibilities and an acknowledgment of the realities operating outside of current film conventions. Another factor bears consideration here. In *Fate* (March 1913, Biograph No. 452), a group of villains are brought into contact with a number of bright little children. In this particular instance the children function solely as foils, to emphasize the perfidy of their adult antagonists. We should recall that melodrama had at least as much interest in involving conflict as in reformation or reconciliation; the adult/child contrast in this particular film serves to increase audience interest and concern as danger approaches and to increase audience satisfaction when the reprobates receive their comeuppance.

14. See also *Drink's Lure* (February 1913, Biograph No. 456). Griffith's final feature film, *The Struggle* (1931), is a subtle and sympathetic, decidedly non-didactic take on the travails of alcoholism. In an irony that does not invalidate his sermons on the subject, Griffith himself came to know much about this very struggle.

15. Griffith foremost: remembered as he may be for a variously heavy hand, Griffith's films were quite often surpassing subtle, and artful as well. For a few examples among many, see the treatment of romance in *The Girl in Her Trust* (1912), of the often complexity of apparent antagonism in *The Musketeers of Pig Alley* (1912), of despair and its effects in *Death's Marathon* (1913), of marital conflict and the workings of sorrow in *The Mothering Heart* (1913); see also contemporaneous work by the likes of Max Linder, Louis Feuillade, August Blom, Lois Weber, Cecil B. DeMille, or Maurice Tourneur.

16. See the synopsis in Usai, *Griffith Project 1*, 58. David Mayer points out that the play in question was actually *Drink*, an 1879 adaptation of Zola's novel by the English dramatist Charles Reade. Ibid., 58–60.

17. See Stanislavsky, *An Actor Prepares*, as well as Chekhov, entire.

18. *Biograph Bulletin*, No. 245, June 3, 1909, in Usai, *Griffith Project 2*, 124–25.

19. Usai, *Griffith Project 4*, 148.

20. Usai, *Griffith Project 1*, 163

21. Griffith was far from alone in generating this kind of material. Thomas Edison's film company produced hundreds and hundreds of films from its inception in the early 1890s to the end of World War I. As was typical of this film-industrial period, these productions were extremely wide ranging in setting and subject matter. Race was part of a hodgepodge of conversations that were not always carefully considered. To key on just a couple of particular manifestations—the plots of which the reader can well imagine—burlesques like *The Chicken Thieves* (1896), *Watermelon Eating Contest* (1896, Musser 233, Edison, 207), *Watermelon Contest* (1900, Musser 601–2, Edison 836), *The Chicken Thief* (1904), and *The Watermelon Patch* (1905) suggest the power and prevalence of insistent racial stereotypes in films during this period. Predictably, children of color were not immune from stereotypical assumptions and disrespectful treatment in these films. Edison's *A Morning Bath* (1896) features a young black woman bathing a protesting black baby. Charles Musser elaborates: "A remake of rival Biograph's popular *A Hard Wash*,

this film's 'joke' plays with racist clichés as well as theatrical conventions where blacks, whether impersonated by white actors or played by African Americans, performed using burnt cork as masks. No matter how vigorous the bath, the baby's skin remains dark and corky." From the online supplementary material for *Edison: The Invention of the Movies* available at http://www.kinolorber.com/edison/pdfs/FilmNotes_DVD1.pdf. See also Musser, 1990, 148–49, 380–81.)

22. As we have seen, child idealization was a powerful, long-standing, cross-cultural trend. It was urged and articulated in innumerable stories of this period, and for some time leading up to it. If this idealization could be sentimental or hyperbolic, then it was still true and real, originating as it did in the actual experiences that so many of its adherents—writing or reading, filming or viewing—had had with the children in their lives. It is remarkable that, as powerfully over-arching as the idealization of children may have been, race prejudice could be more powerful still. After all, child-loving had been a devotion of practically religious magnitude. For so many, children had the attributes of angels and were objects of near-worship; however, a few of these believers did not extend their reverence to black children, who became at best fallen angels, ever to remain so.

23. *Biograph Bulletin*, No. 1551, July 14, 1908. In Usai, *Griffith Project 1*, 59–60.

24. Ibid.

25. Ibid. It is important to recognize that these attitudes toward Gypsies and others do not necessarily go unchallenged or unsatirized. *The Peachbasket Hat*, a Mr. and Mrs. Jones comedy released in June 1909, raises the alarm over yet another Gypsy child-snatching. Eventually it comes out that the Gypsies are entirely innocent—and completely inoffensive. The bourgeois protagonists themselves had accidentally misplaced the child under a basket. Scott Simmon in Usai, *Griffith Project 2*, 146.

26. See Patrick Loughney, *Griffith Project 3*, 7–8, on numerous ethnic conflicts in the Griffith Biograph films produced during 1909.

27. Tramp films were also extremely common in this period. See Griffith's, *A Beast at Bay* (released May 1912, Biograph No. 409), or Lois Weber's justifiably celebrated *Suspense* (Rex Motion Picture Company—distributed by Universal—1913). While serving to deepen dramatic conflict, these stock characters also reflected and occasionally inflamed attitudes regarding the unfortunates that existed outside of the movie theater. Scott Simmon discusses the presence of unsympathetic tramps in Griffith's *The Adventures of Billy*. He finds an energy or animus in their antagonism that is more than merely melodramatic. Pictures like this, Simmon says, "might support the frequent observation that American films by 1911 were, in their push for a higher class clientele, becoming less sympathetic to the poor and to what we would now call the homeless." (*Griffith Project 5*, 134–5.) Endangered cinematic children only served to further these aims and to exacerbate this insensitivity.

28. For instance, the devastating homecoming of the Little Colonel (Henry Walthall) at the end of the Civil War, into the midst of material devastation and his mournful family's loving arms.

29. For example, gender problematics in the otherwise ideological advance of Jean-Luc Godard's films from the 1960s or the stock portrayal of Native Americans in the otherwise spectacular psychological subtlety of Budd Boetticher's Ranown Westerns.

30. Eileen Bowser cites precedents that would then have been very familiar to Griffith's audiences: *The Lost Child* (1904/Biograph), *Raffles the Dog* and *Stolen by Gypsies* (1905/Edison), *Rescued by Rover* (1905/Hepworth), *Rescued by Carlo* (1906/Lubin). Usai, *Griffith Project 1*, 17.

31. Also, theatrical conventions related to fairy tales. These may not have been intentionally or aggressively racist, so much as a muddled connection to their European sources. Usai, *Griffith Project 1*, 169.

32. *Biograph Bulletin*, No. 156, July 28, 1908, in Usai, *Griffith Project I*, 65.

33. For similarly sympathetic treatment see *The Mended Lute* (August 1909, Biograph No. 170), *The Indian Runner's Romance* (August 1909, Biograph No. 171), *The Redman's View*, (December 1909), and *A Mohawk's Way* (August 1910, Biograph No. 285).

34. The "noble savage" is discussed, though without the use of that particular phrase, in Rousseau's *Discourse on the Arts and the Sciences*.

35. Again, as explained in Aristotle, *Poetics*, op. cit., 10–17.

Chapter 5

1. As in *The Zulu's Heart* (October 1908, Biograph No. 176), in which a Zulu tribesman buries his just-deceased four-year-old daughter, and is immediately summoned to battle the Boers. In this battle, Zulu forces cut off a Boer family, kill the father, and take his little four-year-old. Remembering his own lost child, the Zulu's heart is softened, and he courageously returns the child to her mother. *The Zulu's Heart* and the advertising copy from the Biograph Bulletin are both in conflict

with themselves. The Zulus are collectively referred to as "merciless black brutes." Later, they are described as "prancing, jibbing, gibbering barbarians." It is at this point that the Boer child toddles toward the Zulu chief, and softens his heart. But while sympathetically describing the chief's change, the text continues to deride his companions, who are next described as "wily devils." Usai, *Griffith Project*, 1:110–11. In the socially affirmative films, the individual Other is not only redeemable, but often exemplary. See also the extremely well-meaning, exceedingly problematical *His Trust* (January 1911, Biograph No. 310) and its sequel *His Trust Fulfilled* (also released in January 1911, Biograph No. 311). It is often true, however, that the collective Other continues to strike fear and reflect inadequate understanding.

2. An example of the potentially profound depths of Victorian sentimentality is the English painter Sir Luke Fildes' iconic 1887 painting, *The Doctor*. A pensive physician watches faithfully over the sickbed of a little child. The painting contains many of the conventions that Moderns may most resist in the Victorian. The Tate Britain's 2012 display on the subject of sentimental Victorian art, which prominently featured Fildes' painting, identified many of its most now-questionable emblems and motifs: "art that appeals to popular taste … emotive themes [like] childhood and especially child death, forsaken love, animals, sunsets, heart-rending stories and pathetic themes" (Smith, Alison, et al. "Focus: Victorian Sentimentality," Tate Britain: Display). The display was devised by Nicola Brown, Victoria Mills, and Alison Smith, who acknowledge that much of this now seems hackneyed and that the techniques in use could often manipulate the viewer into an unwarranted or unfairly earned emotional response. However they do not simply condemn or dismiss Victorian sentimentality; rather, they concentrate on how sophistication and sincerity both often coexisted with its suspect parts. As for Fildes' painting—emphatic but not without restraint, accomplished and powerful—dismissive critical impulse might diminish somewhat when it finds that all of this craft and conviction was not simply or even directed to forcing viewer response, but rather to the depiction of the years' previous death of Fildes' own child, as well as the skilled and faithful physician who attended it (Birchall, Heather. "Sir Luke Fildes: *The Doctor* Summary," Tate Britain: Display). What can seem and be experienced as a pulling of the heart strings might just as well be the speaking of sorrow, and conviction.

3. Mendelssohn, *Songs Without Words*, Book 5, Op. 62, No. 6.

4. For example, see Kirsh, "Cartoon Violence," 547–57; Place-Verghnes, *Tex Avery*, 71–77; and Thompson, "Meep-Meep," in Nichols, *Movies and Methods*, 126–35.

5. Avery had, in fact, worked at Warner Bros.' studio years previously until a run-in with producer Leon Schlesinger over perceived and very actual excesses in *The Heckling Hare* (1941) had precipitated his removal and his relocation to MGM. On that controversy, see Greg Ford's second track commentary on the film. "The Heckling Hare," in *Looney Tunes Golden Collection*, vol. 2.

6. Browning's heroine is of a somewhat indeterminate age, though she must work for a living and she lives alone. Griffith's Pippa has a husband, far in the background. A common ambiguity, bordering on impropriety, justifies the character's inclusion in this discussion. See chapter 4, note 12.

7. Bowser, *GP*, 53; see also Gunning, *D. W. Griffith*, 177–83.

8. *The Girls and Daddy* (February 1909), as described in the *Biograph Bulletin*: "the smiling faces of children in the household, shed a light more radiant than the sun, a warmth that dispels the chill of misfortune." *Biograph Bulletin*, February 1, 1909, in Usai, *Griffith Project*, 2: 13.

9. The *Bulletin*, on *Two Little Waifs* (October 1910, Biograph No. 295): "There is nothing wordly [sic] that makes a stronger appeal to the human heart than the grief of the little child. Children are so seldom made to feel the weight of woe, that when they do suffer real sorrows we are sure to weep with them. One of the most important of God's lessons is taught by the child—sincerity, and the child's tears will wash from our soul the stain of indifference, selfishness and artifice." *Biograph Bulletin* [?], October 31, 1910, in Usai, *Griffith Project*, 4:201.

10. The *Biograph Bulletin* on *His Last Burglary* (February 1910, Biograph No. 235): "How a Baby's Presence regenerates him. The Scottish poet, Robert Pollock, called children 'Living jewels dropped unstained from heaven,' and this esteem is backed by Scriptural evidence, for the Saviour came to us as a child. He ever specialized the child. He taught that a little child should lead them. And so it is; the tiny hand of the baby has ever been the propelling force of the universe. Never was this more vividly portrayed than in this Biograph subject." *Biograph Bulletin*, February 21, 1910, in Usai, *Griffith Project*, 4:4. See also the *Biograph Bulletin* on *A Child's Impulse*, in Usai, *Griffith Project*, 4:102.

11. Merritt, in Usai, *Griffith Project*, 2:168. In Griffith's *Behind the Scenes* (September 1908, no Biograph number), an actress's child

is dying. The actress's manager forces her to leave the child and perform, or else lose the position for which she has worked so hard, which she has so desired, and on which she and her family so depend. The actress complies, and has to maintain a jolly front for the cheering crowds, though her heart breaking inside. After her triumph the actress returns home, and finds that her child has died. *The Country Doctor* (July 1909, Biograph No. 158) concerns a doctor who successfully treats the ailing child of a poor family while his own daughter, at home, dies of the exact same malady.

12. Isaiah 1:17.
13. Matthew 5:48.
14. Print: *Woodhouse's English-Greek Dictionary*, s.v. "perfect." Online: *Woodhouse's English-Greek Dictionary*, s.v. "perfect," http://artflsrv02.uchicago.edu/cgi-bin/efts/dicos/woodhouse_test.pl?keyword=^Perfect,%20adj.
15. In Holzapfel and Pheysey, *The Master's Hand*, passim.
16. Holzapfel and Pheysey, *The Master's Hand*, 86.
17. Holzapfel and Pheysey, *The Master's Hand*, 80.
18. Cf. Matthew 6:28–29.
19. Hiyao Miyazaki, *Porco Rosso* (Japan, 1992).
20. Mark 9:24.
21. Lefebvre, *The L. M. Montgomery Reader*, 57, 84.
22. The estimation in which the inconvenient Anne is held in the eyes of her minders is very movingly portrayed in Montgomery, *Anne of Green Gables*, chapters 34 and 37.
23. As discussed in chapter 3, herein. See note 3.
24. Sartre, *Existentialism is a Humanism*, 49.
25. Harold Bloom, *Shakespeare: The Invention of the Human*; Francis Bacon, *Novum Organum*; René Descartes, *Discourse on Method*; David Hume, *An Enquiry Concerning Human Understanding*; Georg Wilhelm Friedrich Hegel, *The Phenomenology of Spirit*; Albert Camus, *The Plague*; Jacques Lacan, *Ecrits: A Selection*, (New York: Norton, 1977), 3–9, 31–106, 281–312; Louis Althusser, "Ideology and Ideological State Apparatuses" in *Lenin and Philosophy, and Other Essays*, (New York: Monthly Review Press, 2001).
26. As previously mentioned (chapter 2, note 19) Bertolt Brecht, for one, objects strenuously to this formulation.
27. Aristotle, *Poetics*, trans. Malcolm Heath, 10–17.
28. St. Thomas Aquinas, *Summa Theologica*, trans. Fathers of the English Dominican Province, III, Q. 1, Art. 3.

29. John Milton, *Paradise Lost*, (New York: Norton, 2004), Book X, lines 245–649.
30. In a way, we are now entering into the jurisdiction of mythology, of the folk and fairy tale, of genres and archetypes and the deepest of narrative structures, and their actual implications. All of these things fall outside of the purview of this modest study.
31. See Milos Forman's film adaptation of Ken Kesey's *One Flew Over the Cuckoo's Nest* (1975).
32. Dreyer, *Ordet*, 1955.
33. *Ibid.* This is Inger, miraculously raised from the dead, responding to her equally revivified husband.
34. Job 42:10, 12.
35. Discussed in *Poetics*, trans. Malcolm Heath, 20–22. See also Heath's introduction, xxxi–xxxv.
36. Isabel Hyde, "The Tragic Flaw: Is it a Tragic Error?" 1963.
37. Aristotle, *Poetics*, opp. cit., 10–17.
38. Thwaite, *Waiting For the Party*, 142.
39. Mrs. Sowerby, Martha and Dickon's mother, is a nurturing exception to the pattern of unhelpful adults. She operates effectively as a healthy alternative to adult inadequacy and also as another species of sincerely intended, slightly condescending idealization, this time of the rural working classes.
40. Thwaite, *Waiting For the Party*, 142.
41. Matthew 10:39
42. Jansson, *Moominland Midwinter*.
43. For more on the whirlwind see this study's sixth chapter, on bad children.
44. *Biograph Bulletin*, June 13, 1910, in Usai, *Griffith Project*, 4:94.
45. Kipling, *Wee Willie Winkie and Other Child Stories*.
46. Macbeth 4.2.70.
47. *Ibid.*, lines 83–88.
48. Dardagan and Salama, *Stolen Futures*. See also the following drops in this enormous bucket: UN News Centre, "Afghan conflict"; Seymour Hersh, "The Massacre at Mi Lai" in Pilger, ed., *Tell Me No Lies*; and Anne Frank's famously optimistic benediction, contrasted with the Afterword's account of her subsequent death in *The Diary of a Young Girl*, 263–64, 277–80.
49. Dovzhenko, *Poet as Filmmaker*, 1.
50. *The Crowd*, directed by King Vidor. See also Kotlowitz, *There Are No Children Here*; Kozol, *Death at an Early Age*; London, *The People of the Abyss*; Riis, *How the Other Half Lives*; Wiesel, *Night*; Richard Cardinal: *Cry from the Diary of a Métis Child*, directed by Alanis Obomsawin; and *Hoop Dreams*, *Stevie*, and *The Interrupters*, directed by Steve James.
51. Barrie, *Peter Pan*, 72.

52. Kafka, "A Little Fable," in *Complete Fables and Stories*, 445.
53. Kafka, "Absent-minded Window Gazing," in *Complete Fables and Stories*, 387.
54. In fact, with the final 15 words, Kafka's little story pulls this child back from the brink. This is not always the case in his anxious, impending oeuvre. (e.g., "The Knock at the Manor Gate," in Kafka, *Complete Fables and Stories*, 418–19.)
55. Valgardson, "Red Dust," in *Red Dust*, 115–16.
56. Jansson, *Moominsummer Madness*, 69–77. Similarly, in *Moominland Midwinter*, Little My goes recklessly skating across the ice just as it starts breaking up. This time it is Moomintroll who has to rescue her, receiving never a word of thanks (116–25).
57. Wilder, *Little House on the Prairie*, 20–24
58. Deraniyagala, *Wave*.
59. Other glad, glad-ish, or proto-glad novels include Charles Dickens' *The Old Curiosity Shop* (1841), Harriet Beecher Stowe's *Uncle Tom's Cabin* (1852), George Eliot's *Silas Marner* (1861; see chapter 3), Louisa May Alcott's *Little Women* (1869) and sequels, Susan Coolidge's *What Katy Did* (1872) and sequels, Joanna Spryri's *Heidi* (1980), Margaret Sidney's *The Five Little Peppers and How they Grew* and sequels (1881), Kate Douglas Wiggin's *Rebecca of Sunnybrook Farm* (1903), Gene Stratton Porter's *A Girl of the Limberlost* and sequels (1909) and, of course, Eleanor Porter's *Pollyanna* (1913) and sequels. Tremendously popular for some time, the glad girls' stock is not as high as it once was. Humphrey Carpenter discusses the "aggressive femininity" of these young women, which allowed them to "charm hearts and get their own way.... This produced the 'Pollyanna' or 'glad girl' school of writing, featuring girls of unbearable cheerfulness." Carpenter, *Secret Gardens*, 98. As Carpenter suggests, the term "glad girl," and much of that unbearable cheerfulness, comes from Eleanor H. Porter's 1913 novel, *Pollyanna*. *Pollyanna* and its numerous sequels came to be known as "glad books," and the term "glad girls" was subsequently applied to this species of pluckily virtuous literary heroines. Pollyanna arrives on the scene in Porter's third chapter: "'Oh, I'm so glad, GLAD, GLAD to see you,' cried an eager voice in her ear. 'Of course I'm Pollyanna, and I'm so glad you came to meet me!'" The emphasis, very emphatically, is in the original.

Unsurprisingly, Pollyanna's credo is "Just be glad." The 1920 film version, starring Mary Pickford, begins with the following title card:

This is really not a story ... it's a rainbow—born of the sunshine of a little girl's smile glistening through her tears ... it's a fantasy of children's laughter, of hope, of gladness ... for Pollyanna's "Glad Game" holds forth this message—

Be thou the rainbow to the storms of life, the joyous beam that smiles the clouds away.

This intertitle is obviously cut from the same cloth as the heightened advertising copy from the *Biograph Bulletin*, which we have already considered at great length (see chapter 4). Eleanor Porter's protagonist says the word "glad" 181 times (at least according to an exhaustive, possibly slightly inaccurate tabulation, generated by a word search of Project Gutenberg's Pollyanna file); additional characters say "glad" many more times, and Porter herself subjects her readers to all manner of sentimental and manipulative buffeting in order to convert them to her Gospel of Gladness.

60. Franklin K. Mathiews, "Blowing Out the Boy's Brains," 1914; Chris Crowe, "Young Adult Literature," 2002.
61. Krakauer, *From Caligari to Hitler*; 223–226
62. Strindberg, *The Father*, in *Five Plays*, 24.
63. Matthew 10:16.
64. In *Tweetie-Pie* the not quite fully formed Sylvester is called "Thomas."
65. Samuel Beckett, *Waiting for Godot*, 1.
66. Matthew 22:39.

Chapter 6

1. Wilder, *On the Banks of Plum Creek*, 156.
2. Wilder, *By the Shores of Silver Lake*, 76.
3. Shaw, quoted in Jones, *Chuck Amuck*, 41. This piquant sentiment is quite thoroughly explored in the work of Hilaire Belloc, including *The Bad Child's Book of Beasts* (1896), *More Beasts for Worse Children* (1897), *A Moral Alphabet* (1899), and *Cautionary Tales for Children* (1907).
4. Philip, *Book of Children's Verse*, 231.
5. Plato, *Republic*: Subsection, in Hofstadter and Kuhns, *Philosophies of Art and Beauty*, 35.
6. Pascal, *Pascal's Pensées*, 85.
7. Ibsen, *Hedda Gabler*. Hedda's pistols are introduced in the second part of Ibsen's first act, going on to serve as shadow and threat—Act 2 part 1, Act 3 part 2—until they conduct the action to its final conclusion (Act 4 part 2).
8. See *Unknown Chaplin*, Kevin Brownlow and David Gill's 1983 television documentary, for an illuminating record of Chaplin's refined improvisatory method and the finely tooled comic constructions that resulted from it.

9. As with a similar situation that was referenced in this book's second chapter, a close look at Riesner's face at this moment seems to reveal a delighted smile.
10. Chaplin, *My Autobiography*, 295.
11. Robinson, *Chaplin*, 297–98.
12. See note three of this chapter.
13. Refer to section one of chapter three (q.v.).
14. Barrie, *Peter Pan*, 18, 20.
15. Collodi, *Pinocchio*, 13.
16. Schrader, *Transcendental Style in Film*, 159–66.
17. Collodi, *Pinocchio*, 13.
18. Collodi, *Pinocchio*, 15.
19. *Ibid.*
20. *Ibid.*
21. Twain, *Complete Short Stories*, 7, 81.
22. See also the extremely effective 1961 film adaptation, *The Innocents*, written by William Archibald and Truman Capote, photographed by Freddie Francis, and directed by Jack Clayton.
23. Golding, *Lord of the Flies*, 152.
24. Hughes, *A High Wind in Jamaica*, 38–39.
25. Hughes, *A High Wind in Jamaica*, 36. See also 185, 277.
26. Hughes, *A High Wind in Jamaica*, 39
27. Hughes, *A High Wind in Jamaica*, 45.
28. Hughes, *A High Wind in Jamaica*, 24–26.
29. Hughes, *A High Wind in Jamaica*, 35.
30. This type of romantic, winking piracy is present in James Barrie's Captain Hook, Johnny Depp's Captain Jack Sparrow, or Aardman Animation's *The Pirates! Band of Misfits* (2010).
31. The alternatives explored by Hughes are very effectively translated and communicated by film director Alexander Mackendrick, in his 1967 film adaptation of Hughes' novel.
32. Hughes, *A High Wind in Jamaica*, 158. In the same vein: "It is true that [babies] look human—but not so human, to be quite fair, as many monkeys" (159).
33. Hughes, *A High Wind in Jamaica*, 158–59.
34. Hughes, *A High Wind in Jamaica*, 177.
35. It is similar in effect to Arthur C. Clark's classic science fiction novel, *Childhood's End* (first published 1953). Clark's tale ends with an intergalactic intervention and an evolutionary leap that sees earth's children abandon their parents, and their families, and any awareness of or even reason for the existence of either.
36. See, for example, Camus, *The Plague*, which features powerful examples of both these impulses.
37. Eliot, *Middlemarch*, 682.
38. Conrad, *Heart of Darkness*, 2006.
39. Norris, *McTeague*, 210.
40. Tennyson, *In Memoriam A.H.H.*, 36.
41. Hughes, *A High Wind in Jamaica*, 190.
42. Hughes, *A High Wind in Jamaica*, 275–76.
43. Hughes, *A High Wind in Jamaica*, 236.
44. See extended discussions of these characters in chapter three, q.v.
45. *Macbeth* 3.7.58–63.
46. Eliot, *Four Quartets*, 59.
47. Hughes, *A High Wind in Jamaica*, 250.
48. Hughes, *A High Wind in Jamaica*, 279.
49. Shakespeare, *Julius Caesar*, 3.1.273.
50. Cain, *Double Indemnity*. In Billy Wilder's 1944 film, the fatal female's name was changed to Phyllis Dietrichson.
51. Thomas Harris and Jonathan Demme, *The Silence of the Lambs* (1988, 1991).
52. Charles Dickens, *A Christmas Carol*.
53. *King Lear*, 3.4.96–103.
54. Much of naturalism's original disposition is contained in the painter Gustave Courbet's famous provocation, uttered in response to the French Academy's staid, idealist conventions: "I have never seen an angel. Show me an angel and I'll paint one." As quoted by Vincent van Gogh in Kleiner, *Gardner's Art through the Ages*, 2:631.
55. Taine, *History of English Literature*, trans. H. Van Laun, 6.
56. Van Laun's translation renders these as "race, surroundings and epoch." Taine, *History of English Literature*, 10.
57. In this way great artists are never greater than or independent of the influence or the determinations of heritage and setting, broadly speaking. It is on this basis that Taine proceeds to isolate patterned typicalities through the long march of English literature. These ideas are also quite productively developed in Matthew Arnold's *On the Study of Celtic Literature* (1867).
58. Andrew Rothwell, in his introduction to Émile Zola, *Thérèse Raquin*, xiii–xiv.
59. Zola's project was prefigured by Honoré de Balzac and Gustave Flaubert, and further elaborated by writers like Guy de Maupassant, Thomas Hardy, Frank Norris, Jack London, and Theodore Dreiser. Naturalist filmmakers are manifold: Erich von Stroheim, Jean Renoir, De Sica, Rossellini and Visconti, Luis Buñuel, Jacques Becker, Henri-Georges Clouzot, Satyajit Ray, John Cassavetes, Ermanno Olmi, Nelson Pereira dos Santos, Robert Altman, Bill Douglas, Krzysztof Kieslowski, Martin Scorsese, Abbas Kiarostami, Aki Kaurismaki, the Dardennes brothers. All have contributed to and often complicated this conversation.
60. This celebrated sentiment was spoken by the haplessly decent character of Octave,

played by Renoir himself in his 1939 masterpiece, *Rules of the Game*.
61. Luke 23:34.
62. See Dickens, *Oliver Twist* (1837–38), *Little Dorrit* (1857) and *Bleak House* (1852–53).
63. Eclecticism was vigorously opposed by Hippolyte Taine. Encyclopaedia Britannica Online, s.v. "Hippolyte Taine."
64. Zola, *La Bête Humaine*, 88–89.
65. Zola, *L'Assommoir*, 7.
66. Zola, *L'Assommoir*, 9.
67. Zola, *L'Assommoir*, 21.
68. Zola, *L'Assommoir*, 49.
69. Zola, *L'Assommoir*, 278–79.
70. Zola, *L'Assommoir*, 112.
71. Zola, *L'Assommoir*, 160.
72. Zola, *L'Assommoir*, 161.
73. Zola, *L'Assommoir*, 161.
74. Zola, *L'Assommoir*, 246–47.
75. Zola, *L'Assommoir*, 21.
76. Zola, *L'Assommoir*, 126.
77. Zola, *L'Assommoir*, 266.
78. Zola, *L'Assommoir*, 268.
79. Zola, *L'Assommoir*, 268.
80. The process continues. For Nana's similarly crass response to death, see Zola *L'Assommoir*, 289. For her professional initiation, at first in the floral trade, and finally, permanently, as a libertine and eventual prostitute, see Zola *L'Assommoir*, 315, 346–48, 358. For the results of all of this grossly inadequate nurture, see Zola's *Nana* (1880).
81. Zola, *L'Assommoir*, 322.
82. Zola, *L'Assommoir*, 323–26.
83. Zola, *L'Assommoir*, 340.
84. Zola, *L'Assommoir*, 388.
85. Zola, *La Bête Humaine*, 66.

Chapter 7

1. Barrie, *Peter Pan*, 69.
2. Dante, *Inferno*, Canto XI, 99, lines 80–84.
3. John 8:1–11.
4. John 2:1–11. Chapter 5 referenced a couple of religious paintings by Carl Bloch, with a couple of inoffensively inattentive children that were portrayed therein. On the same subject, with regard to the wedding at Cana, and upping the ante, consider the positively Dionysian child looking directly out at the viewer in Jan Steen's 1676 rendering. Jan Steen, *Marriage at Cana*, 1676, oil on canvas, Norton Simon Museum, Pasadena. Similarly, see Judith Leyster, *A Boy and a Girl with a Cat and an Eel*, ca. 1635; Nicolas Maes, *Christ Blessing the Children*, 1652–53; and William Hogarth, *The Graham Children*, 1742; all National Gallery, London.
5. Jeffers, *Stuck*, n.p.
6. *Ibid*.
7. London, *The Call of the Wild, White Fang, and Other Stories*, 229.
8. London, *The Call of the Wild, White Fang, and Other Stories*, 282.
9. Jansson, "The Invisible Child," in *Tales from Moominvalley*, 118.
10. *Ibid*.
11. Referring to *Moominpappa at Sea* (1965), Glyn Jones speaks thusly: "My ... has been the voice of unadorned down-to-earth reality, bringing back all the members of the family from their frequent flights of fancy. It has throughout been her task to remove illusions, check pretensions, and blurt out the unadorned truth. She is completely ruthless in her actions, completely devoid of ... sentimentality and emotionalism." (Jones, *Tove Jansson*, 83.) In other words, My is only superficially, only seemingly naughty. Deeper down, she is independence, conscience, and freedom.
12. Laura Ingalls joins her family in a swimming excursion to the deep pool that lies nearby their house, *On the Banks of Plum Creek*. Her mother instructs her, and her sister, to stay near the edge, and not go where it is deep. She responds by splashing, and disturbing her more circumspect older sister. She loses her balance momentarily, and takes a ducking. She is frightened. She likes it. She keeps going, deeper and deeper, until suddenly something grabs her foot and she is pulled under the water. "She grabbed and could not get hold of anything. Water filled her ears and her eyes and her mouth." (24) When she resurfaces her father is holding her. "'Well, young lady,' Pa said, 'You went out too far, and how did you like it?'" Laura is too startled and too out of breath to respond. Her father remonstrates her for her disobedience and recklessness. "'You deserved a ducking, and I ducked you. Next time you'll do as you're told.'" "'Y-yes, Pa!' Laura spluttered. 'Oh, Pa, p-please do it again!'" "Pa said, 'Well, I'll—!' Then his great laughter rang among the willows." (26)
13. Luke 10:38–42.
14. Anthony Trollope, *The Warden*, 64–65.
15. Anthony Trollope, *The Warden*, 65
16. *Ibid*.
17. *Ibid*.
18. *Ibid*.
19. Anthony Trollope, *The Warden*, 66.
20. *Ibid*.
21. Examples of Trollope's richly rendered female characters include Mary Thorne and Martha Dunstable in *Doctor Thorne* (1858), Lily Dale in *The Small House at Allington* (1864), Alice Vavasor and Lady Glencora in *Can You Forgive Her?* (1864), Lady Glencora, interspersed throughout Trollope's subsequent Palliser novels (1869, 1873, 1874, 1876,

1879), Madame Max Goesler in *Phineas Finn* (1869), Mary Lowther, in *The Vicar of Bullhampton* (1870), and so on. The subject of Trollope's female characters is addressed, for instance, in Jane Nardin, *He Knew She Was Right*, 1989.

22. Similarly, see "Aboriginals" (1873), Trollope's strikingly problematical, of-its-time essay about Australia's indigenous peoples, in Elleke Boehmer, ed., *Empire Writing*, 20–32. Further to the present point, it is very important to recognize and counter unfortunate expressions, and at the same time resist reducing a mind, or a life, to its most unfortunate expression. This is especially true when considering the pressures then operating, and the perceptions that then prevailed. As Taine averred (q.v.), we are products.

23. Bettelheim, *Uses of Enchantment*, 9.
24. Bettelheim, *Uses of Enchantment*, 69.
25. Bettelheim, *Uses of Enchantment*, 135.
26. Bettelheim, *Uses of Enchantment*, 69. See also his analysis of the Grimms' "brother and sister" on pages 78–83.
27. Bettelheim, *Uses of Enchantment*, 172.
28. Lang, "Beauty and the Beast," in *Blue Fairy Book*, 100–119. For a similarly healthful, joyous view of growing up and moving on, especially as pertaining to adult initiation, see Miyazaki et al., *Ponyo* (Japan, 2010).
29. DeMille, ever confident, gleefully takes a number of outlandish liberties with the source's plotting and character relationships.
30. This is an adaptation of the exchange recounted in John 9:13–38, especially verses 24–25.
31. Acts 23:3.
32. Mark 10:13–16.
33. Usai, *Griffith Project*, 5:196.
34. Anonymous review, quoted by Merritt in Usai, *ibid*.
35. Andersen, *Complete Fairy Tales and Stories*, 631.
36. Andersen, *Complete Fairy Tales and Stories*, 632.
37. This concept also brings to mind Geoffrey Chaucer's expansively antical bestiary in *The Canterbury Tales* (ca. 1387–1400). His numerous characters describe, enact and embody all manner of perfidy and virtue and yet, combined, are still quite properly described as "God's plenty" (Chaucer, *The Canterbury Tales*, 88). John Dryden keyed on Chaucer's phrase of in his own noted celebration in the preface to his own *Fables, Ancient to Modern*. (Dryden, *Selected Poetry and Prose*, 531). As with Hans Christian Andersen's short-coming and yet always validated children, Inez Seabury's seeming extremity is mitigated and actually neutralized when considered as part of a collective, or totality. Similarly, see John Ford's deepening of "Shirley Temple" in the midst of an uncharacteristically abundant cast of characters/*mis-en-scene* in *Wee Willie Winkie* (op. cit.).

38. Shakespeare, *Romeo and Juliet*, 2.3.17–22.
39. *Ibid.*, 2.3.23–30.
40. Aristotle, *Nicomachean Ethics*, trans. David Ross, 40.
41. See chapter 1.
42. Grahame, *Wind in the Willows*, 20–21.
43. Grahame, *Wind in the Willows*, 25.
44. Grahame, *Wind in the Willows*, 16.
45. Grahame, *Wind in the Willows*, 108–9.
46. Dickens, *David Copperfield*, chapters 2–5, 8, 10, 14.
47. Grahame, *Wind in the Willows*, 108–9.
48. Grahame, *Wind in the Willows*, 89.
49. Mark 12:41–44; Luke 21:1–4.
50. Grahame, *Wind in the Willows*, 206.
51. Collodi, *Pinocchio*, 1.
52. Collodi, *Pinocchio*, 15.
53. See discussion, chapter 6.
54. Collodi, *Pinocchio*, 31–33, 38. Similarly: "That is why I have forgiven you. As you were really sorry, I knew that you had a good heart; and if a child has a good heart, even if he is mischievous and full of bad habits, there is hope that he will mend his ways. That is why I came here to look for you. I shall be your mamma." Collodi, *Pinocchio*, 149. And also: "Then [Pinocchio] went to bed, and fell asleep. As he slept, he dreamed he saw the fairy, lovely and smiling, who gave him a kiss, saying, 'Brave Pinocchio! In return for your good heart I forgive you all your past misdeeds. Children who love their parents, and help them when they are sick and poor, are worthy of praise and love, even if they are not models of obedience and good behavior. Be good in future, and you will be happy.'" Collodi, *Pinocchio*, 258.
55. Frank, *Anne Frank: The Diary of a Young Girl*, 6.
56. Frank, *Anne Frank: The Diary of a Young Girl*, 33.
57. Frank, *Anne Frank: The Diary of a Young Girl*, 77.
58. Frank, *Anne Frank: The Diary of a Young Girl*, 41.
59. Frank, *Anne Frank: The Diary of a Young Girl*, 61.
60. Frank, *Anne Frank: The Diary of a Young Girl*, 197.
61. Skretvedt, *Laurel and Hardy*, 190.
62. A very partial selection of Laurel and Hardy's home-destroying films includes *The Finishing Touch* (1928), *A Perfect Day* and *Big Business* (both 1929), *Hog Wild* (1930), *Our Wife* (1931), and the utterly cataclysmic *Helpmates* (1932).
63. Comparing Laurel and Hardy to Samuel Beckett has become something of a common-

place: *Guardian*, http://bit.ly/1oFoqvo; Canby, http://bit.ly/1jgBH7W 2006 vol:378 iss:8469 pg:82US; *Economist*, http://www.economist.com/node/5624852. A commonplace, perhaps, but a productive one; *Waiting for Godot*, for instance, recalls Laurel and Hardy's knockabout very distinctly (Beckett, *Waiting for Godot*, 26, 30), their tender regard, made more affecting by the bleak setting, very movingly (*ibid.*, 22, 45).

64. McCabe, *Mr. Laurel and Mr. Hardy*, 210.
65. McCabe, *Mr. Laurel and Mr. Hardy*, 210–11.
66. Skretvedt, *Laurel and Hardy*, 55.
67. Skretvedt, *Laurel and Hardy*, 63.
68. Skretvedt, *Laurel and Hardy*, 88.
69. Skretvedt, *Laurel and Hardy*, 97.
70. *Ibid.*, 150.
71. *Ibid.*
72. *Ibid.*
73. Skretvedt, *Laurel and Hardy*, 377.
74. Skretvedt, *Laurel and Hardy*, 66. Leonard Maltin and Dick Bann begin their book-length history/appreciation of Roach's *Our Gang* series with the very same essential, familial point. Everyone on the lot loved what they were doing, working "in remarkable harmony to create the most endearing, enduring short films ever made.... The love showed, and the care showed; Roach comedies have unmistakable charm and style. They're comedies not only of slapstick and spectacular gags, but often tender feeling and whimsy too." Maltin and Bann, *Life and Times of Our Gang*, 1.

Chapter 8

1. David Buckingham has sharply criticized the nature in which adults impose themselves upon children in these settings: "Like children's literature, children's television is not produced *by* children but *for* them. As such, it should be read as a reflection not so much of children's interests or fantasies or desires but of adults'. The texts which adults produce for children represent adult constructions, both of childhood and (by implication) of adulthood itself. They are one of the means by which 'we' attempt to regulate our relationships with 'them' and—perhaps also our relationships with those 'childlike' aspects of our own identities." Buckingham, "On the Impossibility of Children's Television," in Bazalgette and Buckingham, eds., *In Front of the Children*, 47. In that same volume, see also Buckingham, "Introduction: The Invisible Audience," 10, and Messenger Davies, "Babes 'n' the Hood," 22–23.
2. Nesbit, *Five Children and It*, 5.
3. 1 Corinthians 12:4–9.
4. Pascal, *Pensées*, 257–59.
5. Saint-Exupéry, *Little Prince*, 2.
6. Saint-Exupéry, *Little Prince*, 10.
7. Wordsworth, "Ode: Intimations of Immortality," in *William Wordsworth*, 281.
8. Saint-Exupéry, *Little Prince*, 29. Similarly, see the episode of the grasping, suffocating baobabs on page 49.
9. Saint-Exupéry, *Little Prince*, 63.
10. Hebrews 11:1.
11. Saint-Exupéry, *Little Prince*, 64.
12. Saint-Exupéry, *Little Prince*, 65.
13. To touch the very tip of a vast iceberg, see Matthew 6:28–29, "Consider the lilies of the field, how they grow; they toil not, neither do they spin: And yet I say unto you, That even Solomon in all his glory was not arrayed like one of these."
14. Cf. Matthew 4:8–11; Matthew 11:28–30.
15. Allan and Janet Ahlberg's *Bye-bye, Baby: A Sad Story with a Happy Ending* (1989) illustrates this counterview very effectively. It is a picture book in which the manifold complexity of family life is rendered from the perspective of a very little child. On the surface the child's needs, and his wants as well, take precedence above all other considerations. As with the bigotry into which Twain's Huckleberry Finn was born, Ahlberg's book knows that there is more, and better. However it also accepts that the child can't know any of this yet, nor need he. Since this is the case, the adults quite happily submit themselves to his service. The gentle implication is that adult readers, women and men alike, could do worse than following suit, at least while the child is in this particular developmental stage. It passes quickly, after all.
16. Saint-Exupéry, *Little Prince*, 83.
17. Carpenter, *Secret Gardens*, x.
18. Carpenter, *Secret Gardens*, 13.
19. See discussion in chapter 7.
20. Grahame, *Wind in the Willows*, 11–12.
21. Carpenter, *Secret Gardens*, 13–17.
22. See Lurie, *Don't Tell the Grown-Ups*, passim.
23. Alison Lurie holds that "it is the particular gift of some writers to remain in a sense children all their lives: to continue to see the world as boys and girls see it and to take their side instinctively." *Don't Tell the Grown-Ups*, 14. Her book holds that this is a very positive thing, partly because of the way that the literary manifestations of this childlike gift continue to contribute to the subversion of, say, Patriarchal Capitalism. However, at the same time that she celebrates the texts and their resonances, Lurie also spares some time to consider the serious problems that developmental arrest brought to the lives of the actual writers, for all the richness of their works.

24. Certain stridently blockbusting commercial films, with their combinations of the regressive-infantile and the indulgent-sophomoric, are obvious culprits. Many now–proliferating publications for tweens and teens, particularly of the serial-fantasy variety, also fit this profile.

25. Barrie, *Peter Pan*, 56. Similarly, "'You see, Wendy, when the first baby laughed for the first time, its laugh broke into a thousand pieces, and they all went skipping about, and that was the beginning of fairies.' Tedious talk this, but being a stay-at-home she liked it." *Peter Pan*, 42. In addition to speaking a great deal of utter nonsense, Peter, and *Peter Pan*, communicates a constant, more than just plot-derived sense of foreboding on the subject of growing up: "While [Wendy] sewed they played around her; such a group of happy faces and dancing limbs lit up by that romantic fire. It had become a very familiar scene, this, in the home under the ground, but we are looking on it for the last time." *Peter Pan*, 193. "'I don't want to go to school and learn solemn things,' [Peter] told her passionately. 'I don't want to be a man. O Wendy..., if I was to wake up and feel there was a beard!'" *Peter Pan*, 229. "In the old days at home the Neverland had always begun to look a little dark and threatening by bedtime." *Peter Pan*, 62. Barrie's uncanny, unsettling 1920 play *Mary Rose* ups this particular ante as it explores the dire consequences of excessive childhood nostalgia.

26. "The 'secondary world' in Peter Pan does not exist except in the children's imaginations.... There is no question about it being real. Unlike his predecessors who created Arcadias, Barrie is constantly stating that his dream-land *is* a dream. The play is a detailed map of the earthly paradise, the secret garden, more detailed than that made by another writer. But at the same time it is a statement that such a territory is only to be found in the imagination. Barrie invokes religious belief in his creation only to dismiss it as childish nonsense." Carpenter, *Secret Gardens*, 185–86, emphasis in the original. Peter Pan's arrested state and morbid self-absorption is most pointedly portrayed in the stunning last chapter of Barrie's novel, "When Wendy Grew Up." Barrie, *Peter Pan*, 226–42.

27. Tolkien, *Tree and Leaf*, 35.
28. Tolkien, *Tree and Leaf*, 44, 45.
29. Quoted in Butler, Francelia and Cott, *Victorian Color Picture Books*, xix.
30. Bettelheim, *Uses of Enchantment*, 79.
31. Bettelheim, *Uses of Enchantment*, 83.
32. Ibid.
33. Nesbit, *Five Children and It*, 54–81.
34. Nesbit, *Five Children and It*, 186.
35. Nesbit, *Five Children and It*, 200.
36. Nesbit, *Five Children and It*, 190.
37. Matthew 12:24.
38. Kipling, *Jungle Books*, 52–53.
39. Collodi, *Pinocchio*, 261–62.
40. See discussion in chapter 7.
41. Bettelheim, *Uses of Enchantment*, 84. Andrew Lang's retelling of the Sindbad story is especially successful in the way it balances these two inclinations; see *Tales from the Arabian Nights*, 101–53.
42. Bettelheim, *Uses of Enchantment*, 91.
43. Grahame, *Wind in the Willows*, 52.
44. Bettelheim, *Uses of Enchantment*, 127. Emphasis in the original.
45. Bettelheim, *Uses of Enchantment*, 156.
46. Bettelheim, *Uses of Enchantment*, 128.
47. Bettelheim, *Uses of Enchantment*, 275.
48. Grahame, *Wind in the Willows*, 254.
49. See Hebrews 12:1–13, or Proverbs, entire.
50. Bettelheim, *Uses of Enchantment*, 275.
51. The animal groom cycle is discussed by Bettelheim in *Uses of Enchantment*, 282–309. It is most famously and beautifully exemplified by Madame de Villeneuve's "Beauty and the Beast" (in Lang, 1965, 100–119).
52. Bettelheim, *Uses of Enchantment*, 279.
53. See this study's first part, and particularly its first chapter.
54. Bettelheim, *Uses of Enchantment*, 279.
55. "The Juniper Tree," in Grimm, *Complete Fairy Tales*, 171.
56. Grahame, *Golden Age*, 3–8.
57. Compare "The Roman Road" with Ratty's unsettling exchange with the wayfarer in chapter 9 of *The Wind in the Willows*. See also Farjeon, 1961, March 27, March 28, "Every Man loves the Tree that gives him Shelter" (109–10) and "An Old Man's Epitaph" (111). Both of these wise fragments evoke the beautiful expanse of familial and of human generations, effectively accomplishing the ideal anticipated at the end of the Book of Malachi, at the close of the Hebrew Bible/Old Testament: "The hearts of the children turn to the fathers and the hearts of the fathers turn to the children." Malachi 4:5–6.Similarly, see the celebrated, rapturous passing of the grandfather in Alexander Dovzhenko's pioneering Soviet film, *Earth* (1930).
58. Grahame, *Wind in the Willows*, 256.
59. Wilder, *By the Shores of Silver Lake*, 91–107.
60. Mary Ingalls is devoted to a smaller, more modest course of domestic industry. She doesn't understand why Laura is interested in such irrelevancies: "I've finished another quilt patch while you've been idling." Wilder, *By the Shores of Silver Lake*, 107.
61. Wilder, *By the Shores of Silver Lake*, 104.
62. Wilder, *By the Shores of Silver Lake*, 72.

63. *Ibid.*
64. Wilder, *By the Shores of Silver Lake*, 73.
65. *Ibid.*
66. Wilder, *Farmer Boy*, 310–11. See also the beautiful account of the Ingalls family's Christmas in *By the Shores of Silver Lake*, 175–201. Here we find the older Ingalls girls, Mary, Laura, and (to the extent of her capacities) Carrie, sewing, knitting, joyfully fashioning a number of very practical and pretty presents for each other; 175–77. In this account the girls' filial affections are symbolized by and equivalent to the industry they expend on each other's behalf. This deep feeling applies also to Wilder's very writings, which are just as lovingly detailed as those presents had been lovingly made, all those decades previous. "'Every Christmas is better than the Christmas before,' Laura thought. 'I guess it must be because I'm growing up.'" Wilder, *By the Shores of Silver Lake*, 201.
67. Cf. Cormac McCarthy's *The Road*.
68. Kipling, *Jungle Books*, 95.
69. Among Jaenzon's most celebrated films are *A Man There Was* (1917), *The Sons of Ingmar* (1919), and *The Phantom Carriage* (1919), all directed by Victor Sjostrom, as well as Mauritz Stiller's *Sir Arne's Treasure* (1919) and *Gösta Berlings Saga* (1923).
70. On home movies and domestic amateur filmmaking in general, see Zimmerman, *Social History of Amateur Film*, Citron, *Home Movies*, Doherty, *Pre-Code Hollywood*, Ishizuka/Zimmerman ed., *Mining the Home Movie*, Craven ed., *Movies on Home Ground*, and Morner, 2011, "Dealing with domestic films."
71. Confucius, *Analects*, 2:3 (54). See also the three abstentions discussed in 16:7 (162).
72. Matthew 10:39.

Bibliography

Achebe, Chinua. *Chike and the River.* Cambridge: Cambridge University Press, 1966.
Adams, Richard. *Watership Down.* New York: Macmillan, 1974.
Ahlberg, Allan. *The Baby in the Hat.* Illustrated by Andre Amstutz. Cambridge, MA: Candlewick Press, 2008.
_____. *Big Bad Pig.* Illustrated by Colin McNaughton. New York: Random House, 1985.
_____. *Bravest Ever Bear.* Illustrated by Paul Howard London: Walker Books Ltd., 1999.
_____. *Monkey Do!* Illustrated by Andre Amstutz. Cambridge, MA: Candlewick Press, 1998.
_____. *Mrs. Jolly's Joke Shop.* Illustrated by Colin McNaughton. London: Viking Kestrel, 1988.
_____. *Tell Us a Story.* Illustrated by Colin McNaughton. London: Walker, 1986.
Ahlberg, Janet, and Allan Ahlberg. *The Baby's Catalogue.* Boston: Little, Brown, 1982.
_____, and _____. *Burglar Bill.* New York: Greenwillow Books, 1977.
_____, and _____. *Cops and Robbers.* New York: Greenwillow Books, 1978.
_____, and _____. *Funnybones.* New York: Greenwillow Books, 1980.
_____, and _____. *Peepo!* Harmondsworth, UK: Puffin Books, 1981.
_____, and _____. *Starting School.* London: Viking Kestrel, 1988.
Alexander, Lloyd. *The Black Cauldron.* New York: H. Holt and Co., 1999.
_____. *The Book of Three.* New York: H. Holt and Co., 1999.
_____. *The Castle of Llyr.* New York: H. Holt and Co., 1999.
_____. *The High King.* New York: H. Holt and Co., 1999.
_____. *Taran Wanderer.* New York: H. Holt and Co., 1999.
Althusser, Louis. "Ideology and Ideological State Apparatuses." In *Lenin and Philosophy, and Other Essays,* 85–126. New York: Monthly Review Press, 2001.
Andersen, Hans Christian. *The Complete Fairy Tales and Stories.* Translated by Erik Christian Haugaard. Garden City, NY: Anchor Press, 1983.
Anthony, Barry. "Biograph Fiction." *Griffithiana* 1 (1999/2000): 66–70, 116–45.
Ardizzone, Edward. *Little Tim and the Brave Sea Captain.* 2nd ed. New York: H. Z. Walck, 1955.
_____. *Sarah and Simon and No Red Paint.* 1st American ed. New York: Delacorte Press, 1965.
_____. *Tim All Alone.* 1st American ed. New York: H. Z. Walck, 1957.
_____. *Tim and Ginger.* New York: H. Z. Walck, 1965.
_____. *Tim to the Lighthouse.* New York: H. Z. Walck, 1968.
_____ *Tim to the Rescue.* New York: Lothrop, Lee & Shepard Books, 2000.
Aristotle. *Eudemian Ethics.* Translated by Anthony Kenny. Oxford: Oxford University Press, 2011.
_____. *The Nicomachean Ethics.* Translated by William David Ross. New York: Oxford University Press, 2009.
_____. *Nicomachean Ethics: Book II.* Translated by W. D. Ross. In Albert Hofstadter and Richard Kuhns, 93–94. Chicago: University of Chicago Press, 1976.
_____. *Poetics.* Translated by Malcolm Heath. New York: Penguin, 1996.
Arnett, Jeffrey Jensen, ed. *Encyclopedia of Children, Adolescents, and the Media.*

Thousand Oaks, CA: SAGE Publications, 2007.
Arnheim, Rudolf. *Film as Art.* Berkeley: University of California Press, 1957.
——. *Film Essays and Criticism.* Madison: University of Wisconsin Press, 1997.
Arnold, Matthew. *Culture & Anarchy.* New York: Oxford University Press, 2006.
——. *On the Study of Celtic Literature.* New York: E. P. Dutton, 1910.
Arvidson, Linda. *When the Movies Were Young.* New York: B. Blom, 1968.
Ashcroft, Bill, and Gareth Griffiths. *Post-Colonial Studies: The Key Concepts.* London: Routledge, 2000.
Aufderheide, P. *Media Literacy: A Report of the National Leadership Conference on Media Literacy.* Aspen: Aspen Institute, 1992. http://www.medialit.org/reading-room/aspen-media-literacy-conference-report-part-ii.
Aymé, Marcel. *The Magic Pictures: More about the Wonderful Farm.* Illustrated by Maurice Sendak. New York: Harper, 1954.
——. *The Wonderful Farm.* Illustrated by Maurice Sendak. Translated by Norman Denny. New York: Harper, 1951.
Babbitt, Natalie. *The Devil's Other Storybook: Stories and Pictures.* New York: Farrar, Straus, Giroux, 1987.
——. *Tuck Everlasting.* New York: Farrar, Straus, Giroux, 1975.
——, Cynthia Krupat, and Robert L. Egolf. *The Devil's Storybook.* New York: Farrar, Straus, Giroux, 1974.
Bakhtin, M. M., and Caryl Emerson. *Problems of Dostoevsky's Poetics.* Minneapolis: University of Minnesota Press, 1984.
Bakhtin, M. M., and Michael Holquist. *The Dialogic Imagination: Four Essays.* Austin: University of Texas Press, 1981.
Baldwin, James. *Fifty Famous Stories Retold.* New York: American Book Co., 1896.
Banks, Lynne Reid. *The Indian in the Cupboard.* Garden City, NY: Doubleday, 1980.
Bannerman, Helen. *The Story of Little Black Sambo and the Story of Little Black Mingo.* London, 1899, 1901. Project Gutenberg, 2008. http://www.gutenberg.org/files/1330/1330-h/1330-h.htm.
Barnett, Mac. *Extra Yarn.* Illustrated by J. Klassen. New York: Balzer & Bray, 2012.
Barrie, J. M. *Auld Licht Idylls.* 1888. New York: Scribner, 1918.
——. *Mary Rose: A Play in Three Acts.* 1914. New York: Scribner's Sons, 1947.
——. *Peter Pan.* 1911. London: Puffin Books, 1994.

Barry, Lynda. *The Greatest of Marlys!* Seattle: Sasquatch Books, 2000.
Barthes, Roland. *Mythologies.* New York: Hill and Wang, 1972.
Bauer, Jutta. *Grandpa's Angel.* Cambridge, MA: Candlewick Press, 2005.
Baum, L. Frank. *The Wonderful Land of Oz.* New York: Quality Paperback, 1998.
Bazin, André. *Jean Renoir.* New York: Simon and Schuster, 1973.
——. *What Is Cinema?* Translated by Hugh Gray. 2 vols. Berkeley: University of California Press, 2005.
Beckett, Samuel. *Three Novels: Molloy, Malone Dies, The Unnamable.* New York: Grove Press, 1965.
——. *Waiting for Godot.* New York: Grove Press, 1954.
Bell, J. J. *Wee MacGreegor: A Scottish Story.* New York: Ogilvie, 1903.
Belloc, Hilaire. *Hilaire Belloc's Cautionary Verses.* Illustrated by Nicolas Bentley. Illustrated album ed. New York: A. A. Knopf, 1941.
Bentley, E. C. *Trent's Last Case.* London, 1913. Project Gutenberg, 2009. HTML e-book.
Berenstain, Stan, and Jan Berenstain. *The Bears' Picnic.* New York: Beginner Books, 1966.
——, and ——. *The Berenstain Bears and Too Much TV.* New York: Random House, 1984.
Bergman, Ingmar. *Sunday's Children: A Novel.* New York: Arcade Publishing, 1994.
Bernanos, Georges. *Mouchette.* New York: Holt, Rinehart and Winston, 1966.
Bettelheim, Bruno. *The Uses of Enchantment: The Meaning and Importance of Fairy Tales.* New York: Vintage, 1989.
Bhabha, Homi K. *The Location of Culture.* London: Routledge, 1994.
Birchall, Heather. "Sir Luke Fildes: *The Doctor* Summary." Tate Britain: Display. http://www.tate.org.uk/art/artworks/fildes-the-doctor-n01522/text-summary.
Bierhorst, John. *The Dancing Fox.* New York: HarperCollins, 1997.
——. *Latin American Folktales: Stories from Hispanic and Indian Traditions.* New York: Pantheon Books, 2003.
——. *The Mythology of Mexico and Central America.* New York: Oxford University Press, 2002.
Black, Gregory. *Hollywood Censored: Morality Codes, Catholics, and the Movies.* Cambridge: Cambridge University Press, 1994.
Blake, Quentin. *Clown.* New York: H. Holt, 1996.

_____. *Mrs. Armitage and the Big Wave.* San Diego: Harcourt Brace, 1997.
_____. *Mrs. Armitage on Wheels.* New York: Knopf, 1988.
_____. *Zagazoo.* New York: Orchard Books, 1998.
Blake, William. *Songs of Innocence and Songs of Experience.* New York: Dover Publications, 1984.
Blatty, William Peter. *The Exorcist.* New York: Harper & Row, 1971.
Bloom, Harold. *Shakespeare: The Invention of the Human.* New York: Riverhead, 1998.
Bloor, Edward. *London Calling.* New York: Alfred A. Knopf, 2006.
_____. *Tangerine.* San Diego: Harcourt Brace, 1997.
Bluestone, George. *Novels into Film.* Baltimore, MD: Johns Hopkins University Press, 2003.
Boehmer, Elleke, ed. *Empire Writing: An Anthology of Colonial Literature, 1870–1918,* 20–32. Oxford: Oxford University Press, 1998.
Bottigheimer, Ruth B. *Grimms' Bad Girls & Bold Boys: The Moral & Social Vision of the Tales.* New Haven: Yale University Press, 1987.
Bottomore, Stephen. "'Every Phase of Present-Day Life': Biograph's Non-Fiction Production." *Griffithiana* 2 (1999/2000): 146–211.
Bowser, Eileen. *Biograph Bulletins, 1908–1912.* New York: Octagon, 1973.
Brannigan, John. *New Historicism and Cultural Materialism.* London: Macmillan, 1998.
Braudy, Leo, and Marshall Cohen. *Film Theory and Criticism: Introductory Readings.* 6th ed. New York: Oxford University Press, 2004.
Brecht, Bertolt. *Brecht on Theatre: The Development of an Aesthetic.* Translated by John Willett. New York: Hill and Wang, 1964.
Brett, Jan. *Daisy Comes Home.* New York: Putnam Juvenile, 2002.
_____. *On Noah's Ark.* New York: Putnam Juvenile, 2003.
Briggs, Raymond. *The Bear.* New York: Random House, 1994.
_____. *Ug: Boy Genius of the Stone Age and His Search for Soft Trousers.* New York: Alfred A. Knopf, 2002.
Brontë, Charlotte. *Jane Eyre.* New York: Modern Library, 1997.
Brontë, Emily. *Wuthering Heights.* New York: Oxford University Press, 1995.
Brown, George Mackay. *Beside the Ocean of Time.* London: J. Murray, 1994.
_____. *For the Islands I Sing: An Autobiography.* London: J. Murray, 1997.
Browne, Anthony. *Gorilla.* New York: Knopf, 1983.
_____. *How Do You Feel?* Somerville, MA: Candlewick Press, 2011.
_____. *Into the Forest.* Cambridge, MA: Candlewick Press, 2004.
_____. *My Dad.* New York: Farrar Straus Giroux, 2001.
_____. *My Mom.* New York: Farrar Straus Giroux, 2005.
_____. *Piggybook.* New York: Knopf, 1986.
_____. *Silly Billy.* Cambridge, MA: Candlewick Press, 2006.
_____. *The Tunnel.* New York: Knopf, 1989.
_____. *Willy and Hugh.* New York: A. A. Knopf, 1991.
_____. *Willy the Wimp.* New York: Knopf, 1984.
Browning, Robert. "Pippa Passes." In *Pippa Passes and Other Poems,* 19–112. Boston: Educational Publishing Co., 1901.
Brownlow, Kevin. *David Lean: A Biography.* New York: Wyatt Book for St. Martin's Press, 1996.
Brunhoff, Jean de. *Babar and Father Christmas.* Translated by Merle Haas. New York: Random House, 1940.
_____. *Babar the King.* Translated by Merle Haas. New York: Random House, 1963.
_____. *The Story of Babar, the Little Elephant.* Translated by Merle Haas. New York: Random House, 1960.
Buckingham, David. *After the Death of Childhood: Growing Up in the Age of Electronic Media.* Malden: Polity Press, 2000.
Bunyan, John. *Grace Abounding to the Chief of Sinners.* 1666. Project Gutenberg, 2013. http://www.gutenberg.org/files/654/654-h/654-h.htm.
_____. *The Pilgrim's Progress.* Harmondsworth, UK: Penguin Books, 1987.
_____. "The Shepherd Boy Sings in the Valley of Humiliation." In *The Oxford Book of English Verse, 1250–1918,* edited by A. T. Quiller-Couch, 414. Oxford: Clarendon, 1939.
Burch, Noël. *Life to Those Shadows.* Edited and translated by Ben Brewster. Berkeley: University of California Press, 1990.
Burgess, Thornton W. *The Adventures of Grandfather Frog.* 1915. Original illustrations by Harrison Cady, adapted by Thea Kliros. New York: Dover Publications, 1992.
_____. *The Adventures of Jerry Muskrat.* 1914. Original illustrations by Harrison Cady, adapted by Thea Kliros. New York: Dover Publications, 1993.

———. *The Adventures of Jimmy Skunk*. 1918. Original illustrations by Harrison Cady, adapted by Thea Kliros. New York: Dover Publications, 1994.

———. *The Adventures of Johnny Chuck*. 1913. Original illustrations by Harrison Cady, adapted by Thea Kliros. New York: Dover Publications, 1994.

———. *The Adventures of Poor Mrs. Quack*. 1917. Original illustrations by Harrison Cady, adapted by Thea Kliros. New York: Dover Publications, 1993.

———. *The Adventures of Prickly Porky*. 1916. Original illustrations by Harrison Cady, adapted by Thea Kliros. New York: Dover Publications, 1996.

———. *The Adventures of Reddy Fox*. 1913. Original illustrations by Harrison Cady, adapted by Thea Kliros. New York: Dover Publications, 1991.

Burningham, John. *Borka: The Adventures of a Goose with No Feathers*. New York: Random House, 1963.

———. *The Cupboard*. New York: Crowell, 1976.

———. *The Friend*. New York: Crowell, 1976.

———. *Mr. Gumpy's Motor Car*. New York: T. Y. Crowell, 1976.

———. *Mr. Gumpy's Outing*. New York: Holt, Rinehart and Winston, 1970.

———. *The Shopping Basket*. New York: Crowell, 1980.

———. *Where's Julius?* New York: Crown Publishers, 1986.

Burns, Robert. "The Cotter's Saturday Night." In *The Works of Robert Burns*, 26–31. Ware, UK: Wordsworth Poetry Library.

Butler, Francelia, and Jonathan Cott, eds. *Victorian Color Picture Books*. Vol. 7, *Masterworks of Children's Literature*. New York: Stonehill Pub. Co., 1983.

Butler, Judith P. *Gender Trouble: Feminism and the Subversion of Identity*. London: Routledge, 1990.

Buzzeo, Toni. *One Cool Friend*. Illustrated by David Small. New York: Dial Books for Young Readers, 2012.

Cai, Xiaomei. "TV-Turnoff Week." In *Encyclopedia of Children, Adolescents, and the Media*, edited by Jeffrey Jensen Arnett, 835. Thousand Oaks, CA: SAGE Publications, 2007.

Cain, James M. *Double Indemnity*. New York: Vintage Crime/Black Lizard, 1992.

Caldecott, Randolph. *Come Lasses and Lads*. Danbury, CT: Grolier Educational Corp., 1988.

———. *The Three Jovial Huntsmen*. New Orchard ed. Danbury, CT: Grolier Educational Corporation 1989.

Calvino, Italo. *Marcovaldo*. Edited by Zita Vaccaro. Translated by William Weaver. London: Secker and Warburg, 1983.

Campbell, Joseph. "Folkloristic Commentary." In *The Complete Grimm's Fairy Tales*, 833–39, 846–56. New York: Pantheon, 1944.

Camus, Albert. *The Plague*. Translated by Stuart Gilbert. New York: Quality Paperback Book Club, 1995.

Card, Orson Scott. *Ender's Game*. Revised ed. New York: Tor, 1991.

———. *Speaker for the Dead*. New York: Tor, 1986.

———. *Xenocide*. New York: Tor, 1991.

Carle, Eric. *The Artist Who Painted a Blue Horse*. New York: Philomel Books, 2011.

———. *Hello, Red Fox*. New York: Simon & Schuster Books for Young Readers, 1998.

———. *Mister Seahorse*. New York: Philomel Books, 2004.

———. *Rooster's Off to See the World*. Natick, MA: Picture Book Studio, 1987.

———. *"Slowly, Slowly, Slowly," Said the Sloth*. New York: Philomel Books, 2002.

———. *The Tiny Seed*. Natick, MA: Picture Book Studio, 1987.

———, and Julian Waters. *A House for Hermit Crab*. Saxonville, MA: Picture Book Studio, Ltd., 1987.

Carlson, Marvin. *Theories of the Theatre: A Historical and Critical Survey, from the Greeks to the Present*. Ithaca, NY: Cornell University Press, 1993.

Carpenter, Humphrey. *Secret Gardens: The Golden Age of Children's Literature*. Boston: Houghton Mifflin, 1985.

Carr, Emily. *Klee Wyck*. Vancouver, BC: Douglas & McIntyre, 2003.

Carroll, Lewis. *The Annotated Alice: Alice's Adventures in Wonderland & Through the Looking Glass*. Introduction and notes by Martin Gardner. New York: C. N. Potter, 1960.

Carter, Anne Laurel. *Under a Prairie Sky*. Illustrated by Alan Daniel and Lea Daniel. Victoria, BC: Orca Book Publishers, 2002.

Causley, Charles. *Jack the Treacle Eater*. Illustrated by Charles Keeping. London: Macmillan Children's Books, 1987.

———, and Vera Gray. *The Gift of a Lamb: A Shepherd's Tale of the First Christmas Told as a Verse-Play*. Illustrated by Shirley Felts. London: Robson Books, 1978.

Cervantes, Miguel de. *Don Quijote*. Translated by Burton Raffel. New York: W. W. Norton, 1999.

Chaplin, Charles. *My Autobiography.* New York: Simon and Schuster, 1964.

Chaucer, Geoffrey. *The Canterbury Tales.* Translated by Nevill Coghill. London: Penguin, 1977.

Chesterton, G. K. "A Christmas Carol." In *Stories, Essays, & Poems,* 294. London: J. M. Dent, 1935.

Citron, Michelle. *Home Movies and Other Necessary Fictions.* Minneapolis: University of Minnesota Press, 1999.

Clark, Arthur C. *Childhood's End.* New York: Ballantine Books, 1953.

Cleary, Beverly. *Beezus and Ramona.* New York: Morrow, 1955.

———. *Ramona and Her Father.* Illustrated by Alan Tiegreen. New York: Morrow, 1977.

———. *Ramona and Her Mother.* Illustrated by Alan Tiegreen. New York: Morrow, 1979.

———. *Ramona Forever.* Illustrated by Alan Tiegreen. New York: Morrow, 1984.

———. *Ramona Quimby, Age 8.* Illustrated by Alan Tiegreen. New York: Morrow, 1981.

———. *Ramona the Brave.* Illustrated by Alan Tiegreen. New York: Morrow, 1975.

Collington, Peter. *The Angel and the Soldier Boy.* New York: A. A. Knopf, 1987.

———. *Little Pickle.* New York: E. P. Dutton, 1986.

———. *The Midnight Circus.* New York: Alfred A. Knopf, 1992.

Collodi, Carlo. *Pinocchio.* 1883. London: Puffin Books, 2011.

Confucius. *The Analects of Confucius.* Translated by Chichung Huang. New York: Oxford University Press, 1997.

Conrad, Joseph. *Heart of Darkness.* New York: W. W. Norton, 2006.

———. *Lord Jim.* Harmondsworth, UK: Penguin, 1990.

———. *Youth.* 1898. Project Gutenberg, 2009. HTML e-book.

Coolidge, Susan. *What Katy Did.* London: Puffin Classics, 2009.

Cooney, Barbara. *Island Boy: Story and Pictures.* New York: Viking Kestrel, 1988.

Cormier, Robert. *Beyond the Chocolate War.* New York: Knopf, 1985.

———. *The Chocolate War.* New York: Pantheon Books, 1974.

———. *I Am the Cheese.* New York: Knopf, 1977.

Cosme, Nadine. *Big Wolf & Little Wolf.* Translated by Claudia Zoe Bedrick. Illustrated by Olivier Tallec. New York: Enchanted Lion Books, 2009.

Couenhoven, Jess. "St. Augustine's Doctrine of Original Sin." *Augustinian Studies* 36, no. 2 (2005): 359–96.

Craven, Ian. *Movies on Home Ground: Explorations in Amateur Cinema.* Newcastle upon Tyne, UK: Cambridge Scholars, 2009.

Crowe, Chris. "Young Adult Literature." *English Journal* 91, no. 6 (2002): 116–18.

Dahl, Roald. *The BFG.* Illustrated by Quentin Blake. New York: Farrar, Straus, Giroux, 1982.

———. *Matilda.* Illustrated by Quentin Blake. New York: Viking Kestrel, 1988.

———. *The Witches.* Illustrated by Quentin Blake. New York: Farrar, Straus, Giroux, 1983.

Dalgliesh, Alice. *The Bears on Hemlock Mountain.* Illustrated by Helen Sewell. New York: Scribner, 1952.

Damjan, Mischa. *The Clown Said No.* Illustrated by Christa Fischer. New York: North-South Books, 2002.

Dante. *Inferno.* Translated by Allen Mandelbaum. New York: Bantam, 1982.

Dardagan, Hamit, and Hana Salama. "Stolen Futures: The Hidden Toll of Child Casualties in Syria." Oxford Research Group. November 24, 2013. http://www.oxfordresearchgroup.org.uk/publications/briefing_papers_and_reports/stolen_futures.

Hersh, Seymour. "The Massacre at Mi Lai." In *Tell Me No Lies,* edited by John Pilger, 87–119. New York: Basic Books, 2005.

Darton, F. J. Harvey. *Children's Books in England: Five Centuries of Social Life.* 3rd ed., revised by Brian Alderson. New York: Cambridge University Press, 1982.

Darwin, Charles. *The Expression of the Emotions in Man and Animals.* 1872. London; New York: Penguin, 2009.

Dawood, N. J, trans. *The Koran.* London: Penguin, 1997.

Day, Aidan. *Romanticism.* New York: Routledge, 1996.

Day-Lewis, Cecil. *The Otterbury Incident.* Illustrated by Edward Ardizzone. London: Putnam, 1948.

Deacon, Alexis. *A Place to Call Home.* Illustrated by Viviane Schwarz. Somerville, MA: Candlewick Press, 2011.

———. *While You Are Sleeping.* New York: Farrar, Straus and Giroux, 2006.

DeMause, Lloyd. *The History of Childhood.* New York: P. Bedrick Books, 1988.

DePaola, Tomie. *The Baby Sister.* New York: Putnam's Sons, 1996.

———. *Big Anthony and the Magic Ring: Story and Pictures.* New York: Harcourt Brace Jovanovich, 1979.

———. *Big Anthony: His Story.* New York: Putnam Juvenile, 1998.

———. *Nana Upstairs & Nana Downstairs*. New York: Putnam, 1973.
———. *Strega Nona*. New York: Simon & Schuster, 1998.
Deraniyagala, Sonali. *Wave*. New York: Alfred A. Knopf, 2013.
Descartes, René. *Discourse on the Method*. Translated by Ian MacLean. New York: Oxford University Press, 2006.
Desai, Anita. *The Village by the Sea*. London: Puffin, 1982.
Dickens, Charles. *The Adventures of Oliver Twist*. 1837–39. New York: Heritage Press, 1939.
———. *Bleak House*. 1852–53. New York: Oxford University Press, 1996.
———. *A Christmas Carol*. 1843. Project Gutenberg, 2004. HTML e-book.
———. *David Copperfield*. 1849–50. New York: Oxford University Press, 1999.
———. *Great Expectations*. 1860–1861. New York: Norton, 1999.
———. *Little Dorrit*. 1855–57. New York: Penguin Books, 1998.
———. *Nicholas Nickleby*. 1838–1839. New York: Penguin Books, 1999.
———. *The Old Curiosity Shop*. 1840–41. New York: Oxford University Press, 1997.
———. *The Pickwick Papers*. 1836–37. New York: Oxford University Press, 1988.
———. *A Tale of Two Cities*. 1859. New York: Oxford University Press, 2008.
Dobson, Clive. *Fred's TV*. Willowdale, ON: Firefly Books, 1989.
Doherty, Thomas. "No Longer Home Movies." *The Chronicle Review* 52 no. 2 (2005): B11.
Doherty, Thomas Patrick. *Pre-code Hollywood: Sex, Immorality, and Insurrection in American Cinema, 1930–1934*. New York: Columbia University Press, 1999.
Dovzhenko, Alexander. *The Poet as Filmmaker*. Cambridge, MA: MIT Press, 1973.
Doyle, Brian. *Easy Avenue*. Toronto, ON: Douglas & McIntyre, 1995.
Doyle, Roddy. *The Giggler Treatment*. Illustrated by Brian Ajhar. New York: Arthur A. Levine Books, 2000.
———. *Her Mother's Face*. Illustrated by Freya Blackwood. New York: Arthur A. Levine Books, 2008.
———. *Rover Saves Christmas*. Illustrated by Brian Ajhar. New York: Arthur A. Levine Books, 2001.
Dr. Seuss. *Bartholomew and the Oobleck*. New York: Random House, 1977.
———. *The Cat in the Hat*. New York: Random House, 2007.
———. *The Cat in the Hat Comes Back!* New York: Beginner Books, 1958.
———. *Dr. Seuss's Sleep Book*. New York: Random House, 1962.
———. *The 500 Hats of Bartholomew Cubbins*. New York: Random House, 1989.
———. *Green Eggs and Ham*. New York: Beginner Books, 1960.
———. *Hop on Pop*. New York: Beginner Books, 1991.
———. *Horton Hears a Who!* New York: Random House, 1982.
———. *I Had Trouble in Getting to Solla Sollew*. New York: Random House, 1993.
———. *Marvin K. Mooney, Will You Please Go Now!* New York: Random House, 1972.
———. *One Fish Two Fish Red Fish Blue Fish*. New York: Beginner Books, 1988.
———. *The Sneetches and Other Stories*. New York: Random House, 1989.
———. *Yertle the Turtle and Other Stories*. New York: Random House, 1986.
Drummond, V. H. *Mrs. Easter and the Storks*. London: Faber & Faber, 1957.
Dryden, John. *Selected Poetry and Prose of John Dryden*. Edited by Earl Miner. New York: The Modern Library, 1985
Du Bois, William Pène. *The Alligator Case*. New York: Harper & Row, 1965.
———. *The Twenty-One Balloons*. New York: Viking Press, 1947.
Duncan, Lisa. *The Image Trap*. Salt Lake City: Bookcraft, 1991.
Dundes, Alan. "Bruno Bettelheim's Uses of Enchantment and Abuses of Scholarship." *Journal of American Folklore* 194 (1991): 74–83.
Economist. "Samuel Beckett: Try Again. Fail Again. Fail Better." March 16, 2006. http://www.economist.com/node/5624852.
Edgerton, Gary, ed. *Film and the Arts in Symbiosis: A Resource Guide*. Westport, CT: Greenwood, 1988.
Eisenstein, Sergei. "Dickens, Griffith, and the Film Today." In *Film Form: Essays in Film Theory*, 195–255. Translated by Jay Leyda. New York: Harcourt, 1969.
Eleftheriotis, D. "Early Cinema as Child: Historical Metaphor and European Cinephilia in Lumiere & Company." *Screen* 46, no. 3 (2005): 315–28.
Eliot, George. *Middlemarch*. 1871–72. New York: Oxford University Press, 1990.
———. *Silas Marner*. 1861. London: Penguin Popular Classics, 1994.
Eliot, T. S. *Four Quartets*. 1943. London: Faber & Faber, 1960.
———. "Hamlet and His Problems." In *The Sacred Wood*. 1921. Bartleby, 2000. HTML e-book.
Elkind, David. *The Hurried Child: Growing*

Up Too Fast Too Soon. Reading, MA: Addison-Wesley Publishing, 1981.
Elsaesser, Thomas. *Early Cinema: Space, Frame, Narrative*. London: BFI Publishing, 1990.
Erasmus, Desiderius. *The Praise of Folly and Other Writings*. Edited by Robert M. Adams. New York: W. W. Norton, 1987.
Ets, Marie Hall. *Mr. Penny*. New York: Viking, 1967.
_____, and Robert L. Egolf. *Mister Penny's Race Horse*. New York: Viking Press, 1956.
Falconer, Rachel. *The Crossover Novel: Contemporary Children's Fiction and Its Adult Readership*. New York: Routledge, 2009.
Farjeon, Eleanor. *Eleanor Farjeon's Poems for Children*. New York: J. B. Lipincott, 1951.
_____. *The New Book of Days*. Illustrated by Philip Gough and M. W. Hawes. 1st American ed. New York: H. Z. Walck, 1961.
_____. *Elsie Piddock Skips in Her Sleep*. Illustrated by Charlotte Voake. Cambridge, MA: Candlewick Press, 2000.
Faulkner, William. *Intruder in the Dust*. New York: Random House, 1948.
_____. *Light in August: The Corrected Text*. Vintage international ed. New York: Vintage Books, 1990.
_____. *The Reivers: A Reminiscence*. New York: Random House, 1962.
_____. *The Unvanquished*. New York: Random House, 1965.
Feiffer, Jules. *A Barrel of Laughs, A Vale of Tears*. New York: HarperCollins Publishers, 1998.
Fitzhugh, Louise. *Harriet, the Spy*. New York: Harper & Row, 1964.
Flaherty, Frances Hubbard. *The Odyssey of a Film-maker: Robert Flaherty's Story*. Centennial edition. Putney, VT: Threshold Books, 1984.
Forman, Henry James. *Our Movie Made Children*. New York: The Macmillan Co., 1933.
Frank, Anne. *The Diary of a Young Girl*. New York: Bantam, 1995.
Freud, Sigmund. *The Interpretation of Dreams*. 1900. Translated by James Strachey. London: G. Allen & Unwin, 1954.
Gaiman, Neil. *The Graveyard Book*. Illustrated by Dave McKean. New York: HarperCollins Publishers, 2008.
Garfield, Leon. *The Apprentices*. 1st American ed. New York: Viking Press, 1978.
_____. *Black Jack*. Illustrated by Antony Maitland. New York: Pantheon Books, 1969.
_____. *The Sound of Coaches*. New York: Viking Press, 1974.
Garner, Alan. *The Stone Book Quartet*. London: Collins, 1983.

Garnett, Eve. *The Family from One End Street and Some of Their Adventures*. New York: Vanguard Press, 1960.
Gauntlett, David. *Moving Experiences: Understanding Television's Influence and Effects*. 2nd ed. Bloomington: Indiana University Press, 2005.
Gill, Stephen. *William Wordsworth*. Oxford: Oxford University Press, 2010.
Godden, Rumer. *The Doll's House*. Illustrated by Tasha Tudor. New York: Viking Press, 1962.
_____. *Four Dolls*. Illustrated by Pauline Baynes. New York: Greenwillow Books, 1983.
_____. *The Mousewife*. Illustrated by William Pène du Bois. New York: Viking Press, 1951.
_____. *The River*. Boston: Little, Brown, 1946.
Golding, William. *The Lord of the Flies*. London: Faber and Faber, 1962.
Gorbachev, Valeri. *Shhh!* New York: Philomel Books, 2011.
Gorey, Edward. *The Beastly Baby*. New York: Fantod Press, 1962.
_____. *The Pious Infant*. New York: Fantod Press, 1966.
Graham, Bob. *April and Esme, Tooth Fairies*. Somerville, MA: Candlewick Press, 2010.
_____. *Crusher Is Coming!* New York: Viking Kestrel, 1988.
_____. *Greetings from Sandy Beach*. Brooklyn, NY: Kane/Miller Bk. Publishers, 1992.
_____. *Has Anyone Here Seen William?* London: Walker Books, 1989.
_____. *"Let's Get a Pup!" Said Kate*. Cambridge, MA: Candlewick Press, 2001.
_____. *Oscar's Half Birthday*. Cambridge, MA: Candlewick Press, 2005.
_____. *The Red Woolen Blanket*. Boston: Little, Brown, 1988.
_____. *Rose Meets Mr. Wintergarten*. Cambridge, MA: Candlewick Press, 1992.
_____. *"The Trouble with Dogs," Said Dad*. Cambridge, MA: Candlewick Press, 2007.
Grahame, Kenneth. *Dream Days*. London; New York: John Lane, 1909.
_____. *The Golden Age*. London: John Lane, 1905.
_____. *The Reluctant Dragon*. 1898. Illustrated by Michael Hague, Marc Cheshire, Trent Duffy, Karen Gillis, and Robert L. Egolf. New York: Holt, Rinehart and Winston, 1983.
_____. *The Wind in the Willows*. 1908. New York: Scribners, 1987.
Greenaway, Kate. *Under the Window*. London: Frederick Warne & Co., 1900.
Grey Owl. *The Adventures of Sajo and the*

Beaver People. Toronto, ON: Macmillan of Canada, 1958.

Grimm, Jacob, and Wilhelm Grimm. *The Complete Fairy Tales of the Brothers Grimm.* Translated by Jack Zipes. New York: Bantam, 1992.

Gunn, Neil M. *Highland River.* Edinburgh, UK: Canongate, 1991.

Gunning, Tom. *D. W. Griffith and the Origins of American Narrative Film: The Early Years at Biograph.* Urbana: University of Illinois Press, 1991.

Guy, Alice. *The Memoirs of Alice Guy Blaché.* Edited by Anthony Slide. Translated by Roberta Blaché and Simone Blaché. Metuchen, NJ: Scarecrow Press, 1986.

Haggard, H. Rider. *She.* Edited by Daniel Karlin. Oxford: Oxford University Press, 1991.

Hall, Donald. *Ox-Cart Man.* Illustrated by Barbara Cooney. New York: Viking Press, 1979.

Harris, Thomas. *The Silence of the Lambs.* New York: St. Martin's Press, 1988.

Haugaard, Erik Christian. *Portrait of a Poet: Hans Christian Andersen and His Fairytales.* Washington, D.C.: Library of Congress, 1973.

Haughton, Chris. *Oh No, George!* Somerville, MA: Candlewick Press, 2012.

———. *Shh! We Have a Plan.* Somerville, MA: Candlewick Press, 2014.

Hawthorne, Nathaniel. *The Scarlet Letter.* 1850. New York: Penguin Books, 2003.

Heaney, Seamus. "The Plantation." In *Door into the Dark.* London: Faber, 1972.

Hegel, G. W. F., *The Phenomenology of Spirit.* 1807. Translated by A. V. Miller. Oxford: Clarendon Press, 1977.

Heide, Florence Parry, and Judith Heide Gilliland. *The Day of Ahmed's Secret.* Illustrated by Ted Lewin. New York: Lothrop, Lee & Shepard Books, 1990.

——— and ———. *The House of Wisdom.* Illustrated by Mary GrandPré. New York: DK Ink, 1999.

Heinlein, Robert A. *Podkayne of Mars, Her Life and Times.* New York: Putnam, 1963.

Henkes, Kevin. *Chester's Way.* New York: Greenwillow Books, 1988.

———. *Jessica.* New York: Greenwillow Books, 1989.

———. *Julius, the Baby of the World.* New York: Greenwillow Books, 1990.

———. *Lily's Purple Plastic Purse.* New York: Editorial Everest, S. A., 1996.

———. *Sheila Rae, the Brave.* New York: Greenwillow Books, 1987.

———. *A Weekend with Wendell.* New York: Greenwillow Books, 1986.

Herbert, George. *The Temple.* London: Cassell & Co., 1887.

Hesse, Karen. *Spuds.* Illustrated by Wendy Watson. New York: Scholastic Press, 2008.

Hest, Amy. *When Jessie Came across the Sea.* Illustrated by Patrick James Lynch. Cambridge, MA: Candlewick Press, 1997.

Hoban, Russell. *The Sorely Trying Day.* Illustrated by Lillian Hoban. New York: Harper & Row, Publishers, 1964.

Hobbes, Thomas. *Leviathan.* New York; Oxford: Oxford University Press, 1996.

Hobbs, R. *Digital and Media Literacy: A Plan of Action.* Washington, D.C.: The Aspen Institute, 2010. http://www.knightcomm.org/wp-content/uploads/2010/12/Digital_and_Media_Literacy_A_Plan_of_Action.pdf.

———. "The Seven Great Debates of the Media Literacy Movement." *Journal of Communication* 48, no. 1 (1998). http://mediaeducationlab.files.wordpress.com/2011/09/hobbs-joc-seven-great-debates-1998.pdf.

Hofstadter, Albert, and Richard Kuhns, eds. *Philosophies of Art and Beauty: Selected Readings in Aesthetics from Plato to Heidegger.* Chicago: University of Chicago Press, 1976.

Holling, Holling C. *Paddle-to-the-Sea.* Boston: Houghton, Mifflin, 1941.

Houghton Mifflin Company. "A Teacher's Guide for *The Wretched Stone* by Chris Van Allsburg." Accessed January 1, 2014. http://www.houghtonmifflinbooks.com/features/thepolarexpress/tg/stone.shtml.

———. "A Teacher's Guide for *Zathura* by Chris Van Allsburg." Accessed January 1, 2014. http://www.houghtonmifflinbooks.com/features/thepolarexpress/tg/zathura.shtml

Houston, James. *James Houston's Treasury of Inuit Legends.* Orlando: Harcourt, 2006.

Howe, James. *The Watcher.* New York: Atheneum Books for Young Readers, 1997.

Huck, Charlotte S. *The Black Bull of Norroway: A Scottish Tale.* Illustrated by Anita Lobel. New York: Greenwillow Books, 2001.

Hughes, Monica. *Invitation to the Game.* New York: Simon & Schuster Books for Young Readers, 1990.

———. *The Keeper of the Isis Light.* New York: Atheneum, 1981.

Hughes, Richard. *A High Wind in Jamaica.* 1929. New York: NYRB Classics, 1999.

Hughes, Shirley. *Alfie and the Big Boys.* London: Bodley Head, 2007.

———. *Alfie Gets in First.* New York: Lothrop, Lee & Shepard Books, 1982.

———. *Alfie Gives a Hand.* New York: Lothrop, Lee & Shepard Books, 1983.

____. *Alfie's Feet*. New York: Lothrop, Lee & Shepard Books, 1982.
____. *The Big Alfie and Annie Rose Storybook*. New York: Lothrop, Lee & Shepard Books, 1989.
____. *Chips and Jessie*. New York: Lothrop, Lee & Shepard, 1986.
____. *The Christmas Eve Ghost*. Somerville, MA: Candlewick Press, 2010.
____. *Dogger*. New York: Lothrop, Lee & Shepard Books, 1988.
____. *An Evening at Alfie's*. New York: Lothrop, Lee & Shepard Books, 1984.
____. *The Lion and the Unicorn*. New York: DK Publishing, 1999.
____. *Moving Molly*. Englewood Cliffs, NJ: Prentice-Hall, 1979.
____. *Olly and Me*. Cambridge, MA: Candlewick Press, 2004.
Hughes, Ted. *The Iron Man*. London: Faber, 2005.
Hume, David. *An Enquiry Concerning Human Understanding and Other Writings*. Cambridge; New York: Cambridge University Press, 2007.
Hunt, Peter, ed. *International Companion Encyclopedia of Children's Literature*. 2nd ed. London: Routledge, 2004.
Hunter, Mollie. *The King's Swift Rider: A Novel on Robert the Bruce*. New York: HarperCollins Publishers, 1998.
____. *The Pied Piper Syndrome, and Other Essays*. New York: HarperCollins Publishers, 1992.
____. *A Sound of Chariots*. New York: Harper & Row, 1972.
____. *A Stranger Came Ashore: A Story of Suspense*. New York: Harper & Row, 1975.
____. *The Stronghold*. New York: Harper & Row, 1974.
Hutchins, Pat. *Rosie's Walk*. New York: Macmillan, 1968.
____. *Titch*. New York: Macmillan, 1971.
____. *The Very Worst Monster*. New York: Greenwillow Books, 1985.
____. *Where's the Baby?* New York: Greenwillow Books, 1988.
Hyde, Isabel. "The Tragic Flaw: Is it a Tragic Error?" *The Modern Language Review* 58, no. 3 (1963): 321–25.
Ibsen, Henrik. *A Doll's House*. 1879. In *Four Major Plays, Volume I*, 39–114. Translated by Rolf Fjelde. New York: Signet Classic, 1992.
____. *Hedda Gabler*. 1890. In *Four Major Plays, Volume I*, 217–304. Translated by Rolf Fjelde. New York: Signet Classic, 1992.
Ishizuka, Karen L., and Patricia R. Zimmermann, eds. *Mining the Home Movie Excavations in Histories and Memories*. Berkeley: University of California Press, 2007.
Jacobs, James S., and Michael O. Tunnell. *Children's Literature, Briefly*. Englewood Cliffs, NJ: Merrill, 1996.
Jacobs, Lewis. *The Rise of the American Film: A Critical History*. New York: Teacher's College Press, 1968.
Jacques, Brian. *Redwall*. New York: Philomel Books, 1986.
James, Henry. *The Turn of the Screw*. 1898. Waiheke Island, New Zealand: Floating Press, 2009.
Jameson, Frederick. *Postmodernism, or the Cultural Logic of Late Capitalism*. London: Verso, 1991.
Jansson, Tove. *Comet in Moominland*. London: Penguin Books, 1990.
____. *Finn Family Moomintroll*. London: Penguin Books, 1973.
____. *Moominland Midwinter*. London: Penguin Books, 1973.
____. *Moominpappa at Sea*. London: Puffin Books, 2011.
____. *Moominpappa's Memoirs*. London: Penguin Books, 2005.
____. *Moomins and the Great Flood*. London: Sort of Books, 2012.
____. *Moominsummer Madness*. London: Puffin Books, 1973.
____. *Moominvalley in November*. London: Puffin Books, 1991.
____. *The Summer Book*. London: Sort of Books, 2003.
____. *Tales from Moominvalley*. London: Puffin Books, 1973.
____, and Sophie Hannah. *Moomin, Mymble and Little My*. Montreal, QC: Enfant, 2009.
Jeffers, Oliver. *The Heart and the Bottle*. New York: Philomel Books, 2010.
____. *Lost and Found*. New York: Philomel Books, 2005.
____. *Stuck*. New York: Philomel Books, 2011.
____. *Up and Down*. New York: Philomel Books, 2010.
Jenkins, Henry. *Convergence Culture: Where Old and New Media Collide: Updated and with a New Afterword*. New York: New York University Press, 2008.
Johnson, Steven. *Everything Bad Is Good for You: How Today's Popular Culture is Actually Making Us Smarter*. New York: Riverhead Books, 2006.
Johnston, Tony. *The Quilt Story*. Illustrated by Tomie dePaola. New York: Putnam, 1985.
Jones, Chuck. *Chuck Amuck: The Life and*

Times of an Animated Cartoonist. New York: Farrar Straus Giroux, 1989.
Jones, W. Glyn. *Tove Jansson*. Boston: Twayne Publishers, 1984.
Jowett, Garth, I. C. Jarvie, and Kathryn Seeley. *Children and the Movies: Media Influence and the Payne Fund Controversy*. Cambridge: Cambridge University Press, 1996.
Joyce, James. *A Portrait of the Artist as a Young Man*. 1916. New York: Viking Press, 1964.
Joyce, William. *A Day with Wilbur Robinson*. New York: Harper & Row, 2006.
_____. *George Shrinks*. New York: Harper & Row, 1985.
Juster, Norton. *Alberic the Wise*. Illustrated by Leonard Baskin. Saxonville, MA: Picture Book Studio, 1992.
_____. *The Odious Ogre*. Illustrated by Jules Feiffer. New York: Michael di Capua Books, 2010.
_____. *The Phantom Tollbooth*. Illustrated by Jules Feiffer. New York: Epstein & Carroll, 1961.
Kafka, Franz. *Complete Fables and Stories*. New York: Quality Paperback, 1983.
Kästner, Erich. *Emil and the Detectives*. Translated by Eileen Hall. London: Red Fox, 2001.
_____. *Emil and the Three Twins*. London: Vintage Classic, 2012.
Katz, John. *Virtuous Reality: How America Surrendered Discussion of Moral Values to Opportunists, Nitwits, and Blockheads like William Bennett*. New York: Random House, 1997.
Kazantzakis, Nikos. *The Last Temptation of Christ*. New York: Simon and Schuster, 1960.
Keeping, Charles. *Adam and Paradise Island*. Oxford: Oxford University Press, 1989.
Keller, Helen. *The Story of My Life*. Garden City, NY: Doubleday, 1954.
Kellner, D., and J. Share. "Critical Media Literacy, Democracy and the Reconstruction of Education." In *Media Literacy: A Reader*, Macedo and Steinberg eds. New York: Peter Lang, 2007
Kimmel Eric A. *The Adventures of Hershel of Ostropol*. Illustrated by Trina Schart Hyman. New York: Holiday House, 1995.
_____, Leonard Everett Fisher, and Miguel de Saavedra. *Don Quixote and the Windmills*. New York: Farrar, Straus and Giroux, 2004.
Kimmel, Haven. *A Girl Named Zippy*. New York: Broadway Books, 2002.
Kingsley, Charles. "Child Ballad." In *Andromeda, and Other Poems*. 1858. Project Gutenberg, 2004. http://www.gutenberg.org/ebooks/11064.
_____. *The Heroes*. Reprint of the 1889 London edition, Project Gutenberg, 1996. http://www.gutenberg.org/ebooks/677.
_____. *The Water Babies, and Glaucus*. London: J. M. Dent, 1908.
Kipling, Rudyard. *The Jungle Books*. 1894, 1895. London: Penguin Classics, 1987.
_____. *Kim*. 1901. London: Penguin, 1987.
_____. *Puck of Pook's Hill*. 1906. Mineola, NY: Dover Publications, 2006.
_____. *Wee Willie Winkie, and Other Stories*. 1888. London: Standard Book, 1930.
Kirk, Katie. *Eli, No!* New York: Abrams Books for Young Readers, 2011.
Kirsh, Steve J. "Cartoon Violence and Aggression in Youth." *Aggression and Violent Behavior* 11 (2006): 547–57.
Klassen, J. *I Want My Hat Back*. Somerville, MA: Candlewick, 2011.
Klein, Melanie. *The Selected Melanie Klein*. Edited by Juliet Mitchell. New York: Free Press, 1986.
Knerr, H. H. *The Katzenjammer Kids*. New York: Dell, 1939.
Konigsburg, E. L. *From the Mixed-Up Files of Mrs. Basil E. Frankweiler*. New York: Atheneum, 1967.
Kooser, Ted. *House Held Up by Trees*. Illustrated by J. Klassen. Somerville, MA: Candlewick, 2012.
Kosinski, Jerzy. *The Painted Bird*. 2nd ed. New York: Grove Press, 1995.
Kotlowitz, Alex. *There Are No Children Here: The Story of Two Boys Growing Up in the Other America*. New York: Doubleday, 1991.
Kozol, Jonathan. *Death at an Early Age*. Boston: Houghton Mifflin, 1967.
_____. *Ordinary Resurrections: Children in the Years of Hope*. New York: Crown, 2000.
_____. *Savage Inequalities*. Uncorrected proof. New York: Crown, 1991.
_____. *The Shame of the Nation: The Restoration of Apartheid Schooling in America*. New York: Crown Publishers, 2005.
Krahn, Fernando. *April Fools*. New York: E. P. Dutton, 1974.
_____. *Here Comes Alex Pumpernickel!* Boston: Little, Brown, 1981.
_____. *Sleep Tight, Alex Pumpernickel*. Boston: Little, Brown, 1982.
Kuhn, Reinhard Clifford. *Corruption in Paradise: The Child in Western Literature*. Hanover, NH: University Press of New England, 1982.

Kurelek, William. *A Prairie Boy's Summer.* Boston: Houghton Mifflin, 1975.
———. *A Prairie Boy's Winter.* Boston: Houghton Mifflin, 1973.
———, and Margaret S. Engelhart. *They Sought a New World: The Story of European Immigration to North America.* Montreal, QC: Tundra Books, 1985.
Lacan, Jacques. *Ecrits: A Selection.* Translated by Alan Sheridan. New York: Norton, 1977.
Lagerlöf, Selma. *From a Swedish Homestead.* Freeport, NY: Books for Libraries Press, 1970.
———. *The Wonderful Adventures of Nils.* Translated by Velma Swanston Howard. Illustrated by Hans Baumhauer. New York: Pantheon Books, 1947.
Lang, Andrew. *The Blue Fairy Book.* New York: Dover, 1965.
———. *Tales from the Arabian Nights.* Ware, UK: Wordsworth Classics, 1993.
Larsson, Carl. *A Family: Paintings from a Bygone Age.* Edinburgh, UK: Floris Books, 2007.
———. *A Farm: Paintings from a Bygone Age.* Edinburgh, UK: Floris Books, 2008.
Lebeau, Vicky. *Childhood and Cinema.* London: Reaktion, 2008.
Lee, Harper. *To Kill a Mockingbird.* Philadelphia: Lippincott, 1960.
L'Engle, Madeleine. *The Glorious Impossible.* New York: Simon and Schuster Books for Young Readers, 1990.
Lester, Alison. *Clive Eats Alligators.* Boston: Houghton Mifflin, 1986.
Lewis, C. S. *An Experiment in Criticism.* Cambridge: Cambridge University Press, 1961.
———. *The Horse and His Boy.* New York: HarperTrophy, 2000.
———. *The Lion, the Witch, and the Wardrobe.* New York: HarperTrophy, 2000.
———. *The Voyage of the Dawn Treader.* New York: HarperTrophy, 2000.
Lindenbaum, Pija. *Bridget and the Gray Wolves.* Stockholm: R & S Books, 2001.
———. *Else-Marie and Her Seven Little Daddies.* Adapted by Gabrielle Charbonnet. New York: H. Holt, 1991.
Lindgren, Astrid. *Lotta's Bike.* Illustrated by Ilon Wikland. Stockholm: R & S Books, 1989.
———. *Pippi Goes On Board.* New York: Viking, 1957.
———. *Pippi in the South Seas.* New York: Viking, 1959.
———. *Pippi Longstocking.* New York: Viking, 1950.
Lindsay, Norman. *The Magic Pudding.* North Rydem, Australia: Angus and Robertson, 1985.
Lindsay, Vachel. *The Art of the Moving Picture.* New York: Macmillan, 1915.
Lionni, Leo. *A Color of His Own.* New York: Pantheon Books, 1975.
———. *It's Mine!* New York: Knopf, 1986.
———. *Swimmy.* New York: Pantheon Books, 1963.
Littlewood, Karin. *Immi's Gift.* Atlanta: Peachtree, 2010.
Lobel, Anita. *Nini Here and There.* New York: Greenwillow Books, 2007.
Lobel, Arnold. *Frog and Toad All Year.* New York: Harper & Row, 1976.
———. *Frog and Toad Are Friends.* New York: Harper & Row, 1970.
———. *Frog and Toad Together.* New York: Harper & Row, 1972.
Locke, John. *An Essay Concerning Human Understanding.* 1690. Oxford: Clarendon, 1975.
———. *Some Thoughts Concerning Education.* 1693. Oxford: Clarendon, 1989.
———. *Two Treatises of Government; and, A Letter Concerning Toleration.* 1689–1690. London: Yale University Press, 2003.
Lofting, Hugh. *Doctor Dolittle.* New York: Scholastic, 2004.
———. *Doctor Dolittle's Caravan.* Philadelphia: J. B. Lippincott, 1954.
———. *Doctor Dolittle's Circus.* Philadelphia: Lippincott, 1952.
———. *Doctor Dolittle in the Moon.* Philadelphia: Lippincott, 1956.
———. *Doctor Dolittle's Post Office.* Philadelphia: Lippincott, 1951.
———. *Doctor Dolittle's Zoo.* New York: Fred A. Stokes, 1925.
———. *The Voyages of Doctor Dolittle.* New York: Dell Yearling, 1988.
London, Jack. *The Call of the Wild, White Fang, and Other Stories.* New York: Penguin Books, 1986.
———. *Klondike Tales.* New York: Modern Library, 2001.
———. *The People of the Abyss.* Brooklyn: L. Hill Books, 1995.
———. *The Sea Wolf.* New York: Dover, 1999.
Longfellow, Henry Wadsworth. *Song of Hiawatha.* 1855. New York: Dover, 2006.
Lottridge, Celia Barker. *Ticket to Curlew.* Illustrated by Wendy Wolsak-Frith. Vancouver, BC: Douglas & McIntyre, 1994.
Lundin, Anne H. *Constructing the Canon of Children's Literature beyond Library Walls and Ivory Towers.* New York: Routledge, 2004.

Lurie, Alison. *Don't Tell the Grown-Ups: Subversive Children's Literature*. Boston: Little, Brown, 1990.

Lury, K. "The Child in Film and Television: Introduction." *Screen* 46, no. 3 (2005): 307–14.

MacDonald, George. *The Golden Key*. Illustrated by Maurice Sendak. New York: Farrar, Straus and Giroux, 1967.

———. *The Light Princess*. Illustrated by William Pène du Bois. Glenview, IL: Scott Foresman, 1962.

Macedo, Donaldo, and Shirley R. Steinberg, eds. *Media Literacy: A Reader*. New York: Peter Lang, 2007.

Machiavelli, Nicolo. *The Prince*. In *The Portable Machiavelli*. Edited and translated by Peter Bondanella and Mark Musa. New York: Penguin, 1979.

Mackey, Margaret. "Media Adaptations." In *The Routledge Companion to Children's Literature*, edited by David Rudd, 112–24. London: Routledge, 2010.

MacLachlan, Patricia. *Sarah, Plain and Tall*. New York: Harper & Row, 1985.

MacLeod, Alistair. *No Great Mischief*. New York: W. W. Norton, 2000.

Madsen, Susan Arrington. *Growing Up in Zion: True Stories of Young Pioneers Building the Kingdom*. Salt Lake City: Deseret Book, 1996.

Mahy, Margaret. *Bubble Trouble*. Illustrated by Polly Dunbar. New York: Clarion Books, 2009.

———. *The Catalogue of the Universe*. New York: Atheneum, 1986.

———. *The Changeover: A Supernatural Romance*. New York: Atheneum, 1984.

———. *The Great White Man-Eating Shark: A Cautionary Tale*. Illustrated by Jonathan Allen. New York: Dial Books for Young Readers, 1990.

———. *A Summery Saturday Morning*. Illustrated by Selina Young. New York: Viking, 1998.

Maltby, Richard. "Censorship and Self-Regulation." In *The Oxford History of World Cinema*, edited by Geoffrey Nowell-Smith, 235–48. New York: Oxford University Press, 1996.

Maltin, Leonard, and Richard Bann. *The Little Rascals: The Life and Times of Our Gang*. New York: Crown, 1992.

Mander, Jerry. *Four Arguments for the Elimination of Television*. New York: Morrow, 1978.

Mann, Thomas. *Joseph and His Brothers*. Translated by H. T. Porter. New York: A. A. Knopf, 1948.

March, William. *The Bad Seed: A Novel*. Hopewell, NJ: Ecco, 1997.

Markandaya, Kamala. *Nectar in a Sieve*. New York: J. Day, 1955.

Marsden, John. *Tomorrow, When the War Began*. Boston: Houghton Mifflin, 1995.

Marshall, David. "Frankenstein, or Rousseau's Monster: Sympathy in Speculative Eyes." In *The Surprising Effects of Sympathy: Marivaux, Diderot, Rousseau, and Mary Shelley*, 178–226. Chicago: University of Chicago Press, 1988.

Marshall, Donald R. *The Rummage Sale: Collections and Recollections*. Santa Barbara, CA: Peregrine Smith, 1975.

Martel, Yann. *Life of Pi*. New York: Harcourt, 2001.

Mathews, Nancy Mowll. *Mary Cassatt: A Life*. New York: Villard Books, 1994.

Martins, Isabel Minhos. *When I Was Born*. Illustrated by Madalena Matoso. London: Tate, 2010.

Mathiews, Franklin K. "Blowing Out the Boy's Brains." *The Outlook*, November 18, 1914, 652–53.

Mayer, Mercer. *East of the Sun and West of the Moon*. New York: Four Winds, 1980.

McCabe, John. *Mr. Laurel and Mr. Hardy: An Affectionate Biography*. New York: Robson Books, 1976.

McCarthy, Cormac. *The Road*. New York: Alfred A. Knopf, 2006.

McCaughrean, Geraldine, and Sophy Williams. *The Nativity Story*. London: Lion's Children, 2007.

McCloskey, Robert. *Blueberries for Sal*. New York: Viking, 1948.

———. *Homer Price*. New York: Viking Press, 1943.

———. *Make Way for Ducklings*. New York: Viking Press, 1941.

McCully, Emily Arnold, Nanette Stevenson, and David Gatti. *Mirette on the High Wire*. New York: G. P. Putnam's Sons, 1992.

McFarlane, Brian. *Novel to Film: An Introduction to the Theory of Adaptation*. Oxford: Oxford University Press, 1996.

McGavran, James Holt. *Romanticism and Children's Literature in Nineteenth-Century England*. Athens: University of Georgia Press, 1991.

McGillis, Roderick. *The Nimble Reader: Literary Theory and Children's Literature*. New York: Twayne, 1996.

McPhail, David. *Fix-It*. New York: E. P. Dutton, 1984.

———. *Weezer Changes the World*. New York: Beach Lane Books, 2009.

McPherson, Scott. *Marvin's Room*. New York: Plume, 1993.

McWhir, Anne. "Teaching the Monster to Read." In *The Educational Legacy of Romanticism*, edited by John Willinsky, 73–92. Waterloo, ON: Wilfrid Laurier University Press, 1990.

Meddaugh, Susan. *Beast*. Boston: Houghton Mifflin, 1981.

———. *Martha Speaks*. Boston: Houghton Mifflin, 1992.

Medved, Michael. *Hollywood vs. America: Popular Culture and the War on Traditional Values*. New York: HarperCollins, 1992.

Meek, Margaret. *The Cool Web: The Pattern of Children's Reading*. London: Bodley, Head, 1977.

Metz, Christian. *Film Language: A Semiotics of the Cinema*. New York: Oxford University Press, 1974.

Meyrowitz, Joshua. *No Sense of Place: The Impact of Electronic Media on Social Behavior*. New York: Oxford University Press, 1985.

Milne, A. A. *The House at Pooh Corner*. Illustrated by Ernest H. Shepard. London: Methuen, 1928.

———. *Winnie the Pooh*. Illustrated by Ernest H. Shepard. London: Puffin, 1992.

Milton, John. "Sonnet (On His Blindness)." In *The New Oxford Book of Christian Verse*, edited by Donald Davie, 95–96. Oxford: Oxford University Press, 1990.

Mitchell, W. O. *Jake and the Kid*. Toronto, Ont.: Macmillan of Canada, 1974.

———. *The Kite*. Toronto, Ont.: Macmillan of Canada, 1974.

———. *Who Has Seen the Wind*. Illustrated by William Kurelek. Toronto, ON: Macmillan of Canada, 1976.

More, Thomas. *Utopia*. 1516. Translated and edited by Robert M. Adams. New York: W. W. Norton, 1992.

Morner, Cecilia. "Dealing with Domestic Films: Methodological Strategies and Pitfalls in Studies of Home Movies from the Predigital Era." *Moving Image* 11, no. 2 (2011): 22–45.

Muir, John. *The Story of My Boyhood and Youth*. Edinburgh, UK: Birlinn, 2006.

Münsterberg, Hugo. *Hugo Münsterberg on Film: The Photoplay: A Psychological Study, and Other Writings*. Edited by Allan Langdale. New York: Routledge, 2002.

Musser, Charles. *Before the Nickelodeon: Edwin S. Porter and the Edison Manufacturing Company*. Berkeley: University of California Press, 1991.

———. *The Emergence of Cinema: The American Screen to 1907*. New York: Scribner, 1990.

Muybridge, Eadweard. *The Human Figure in Motion*. New York: Dover Publications, 1955.

Myers, Mitzi. "Impeccable Governesses, Rational Dames and Moral Mothers: Mary Wollstonecraft and the Female Tradition in Georgian Children's Books." *Children's Literature* 14 (1986): 31–58.

Myers, Walter Dean. *Bad Boy: A Memoir*. New York: HarperCollins, 2001.

Napier, Susan J. *Anime from Akira to Howl's Moving Castle: Experiencing Contemporary Japanese Animation*. Rev. ed. Basingstoke: Palgrave Macmillan, 2005.

Nardin, Jane. *He Knew She Was Right: The Independent Woman in the Novels of Anthony Trollope*. Carbondale: Southern Illinois University Press, 1989.

Naylor, Phyllis Reynolds. *The Agony of Alice*. New York: Atheneum, 1985.

Needle, Jan. *Wild Wood*. Illustrated by William Rushton. London: Deutsch, 1981.

Nesbit, E. *Five Children and It*. London: Puffin Books, 2008.

———. *The Railway Children*. London: Puffin Books, 2011.

Nichols, Bill, ed. *Movies and Methods*. Oakland: University of California Press, 1976.

Nilsson, Ulf. *Adieu, Herr Muffin*. Illustrated by Anna-Clara Tidholm. Frankfurt, Germany: Moritz, 2003.

Nodelman, Perry. *The Hidden Adult: Defining Children's Literature*. Baltimore: John Hopkins University Press, 2008.

———. *Touchstones Reflections on the Best in Children's Literature*. West Lafayette: Children's Literature Association, 1985.

Nordqvist, Sven. *Pancakes for Findus*. Stroud: Hawthorn, 2007.

Norris, Frank. *McTeague*. New York: W. W. Norton & Co., 1977.

Noyes, Alfred. *The Highwayman*. Illustrated by Charles Mikolaycak. New York: Lothrop, Lee & Shepard Books, 1983.

Oberstein, Karin. *Children's Literature: Criticism and the Fictional Child*. Oxford: Clarendon, 1994.

———. *Children's Literature: New Approaches*. New York: Palgrave, 2004.

Oppel, Kenneth. *Silverwing*. New York: Simon and Schuster Books for Young Readers, 1997.

Ormerod, Jan. *Lizzie Nonsense*. New York: Clarion Books, 2005.

———. *Maudie and Bear*. Illustrated by Freya Blackwood. New York: G. P. Putnam's Sons, 2012.

_____. *Moonlight.* New York: Lothrop, Lee & Shepard Books, 1982.
_____. *Sunshine.* New York: Lothrop, Lee & Shepard Books, 1981.
_____. *Water Witcher.* Surry Hills, Australia: Little Hare, 2006.
Page, Michael F. *The Great Bullocky Race.* Illustrated by Robert Ingpen. New York: Dodd, Mead, 1988.
Papert, Seymour. *The Connected Family: Bridging the Digital Generation Gap.* Atlanta: Longstreet, 1996.
Parten, Mildred. "Social Participation among Preschool Children." *Journal of Abnormal and Social Psychology, 28* (1932): 136–47.
Pascal, Blaise. *Pascal's Pensées.* New York: E. P. Dutton, 1958.
Paulsen, Gary. *Hatchet.* New York: Bradbury, 1987.
Pearson, Kit. *Awake and Dreaming.* Toronto, ON: Viking, 1996.
Penrose, Antony *The Boy Who Bit Picasso.* New York: Abrams Books for Young Readers, 2011.
Perkins, Lynne Rae. *Pictures from our Vacation.* New York: Greenwillow Books, 2007.
Pheysey, Dawn C., and Richard Neitzel Holzapfel. *The Master's Hand: The Art of Carl Heinrich Bloch.* Salt Lake City: Deseret Book, 2010.
Philip, Neil, ed. *The New Oxford Book of Children's Verse.* New York: Oxford University Press, 1998.
Pinkwater, Daniel Manus. *At the Hotel Larry.* Illustrated by Jill Pinkwater. New York: Marshall Cavendish, 1997.
_____. *Beautiful Yetta: The Yiddish Chicken.* Illustrated by Jill Pinkwater. New York: Feiwel and Friends, 2010.
_____. *Ice-Cream Larry.* Illustrated by Jill Pinkwater. New York: Marshall Cavendish, 1999.
_____. *The Neddiad.* Prince Frederick: Recorded Books, 2007.
_____. *Sleepover Larry.* Illustrated by Jill Pinkwater. New York: Marshall Cavendish, 2007.
_____. *Young Larry.* Illustrated by Jill Pinkwater. New York: Marshall Cavendish, 1997.
Place-Verghnes, Floriane. *Tex Avery: A Unique Legacy.* Eastleigh: John Libbey, 2006.
Plato. *The Republic.* Translated by Benjamin Jowett. Mineola, NY: Dover Publications, 2000.
_____. *The Republic,* Book II. In *Philosophies of Art and Beauty,* edited by Albert Hofstadter and Richard Kuhns, 8–14. Chicago: University of Chicago Press, 1976.
_____. *The Republic,* Book III. In *Philosophies of Art and Beauty,* edited by Albert Hofstadter and Richard Kuhns, 14–29. Chicago: University of Chicago Press, 1976.
_____. *The Republic:* Book X. In *Philosophies of Art and Beauty,* edited by Albert Hofstadter and Richard Kuhns, 30–45. Chicago: University of Chicago Press, 1976.
_____. *Statesman* (283b–285b). In *Philosophies of Art and Beauty,* edited by Albert Hofstadter and Richard Kuhns, 5–8. Chicago: University of Chicago Press, 1976.
Polacco, Patricia. *Aunt Chip and the Great Triple Creek Dam Affair.* New York: Philomel Books, 1996.
_____. *Babushka Baba Yaga.* New York: Philomel Books, 1993.
_____. *Betty Doll.* New York: Philomel Books, 2001.
_____. *Chicken Sunday.* New York: Philomel Books, 1992.
_____. *The Keeping Quilt.* New York: Simon & Schuster Books for Young Readers, 1988.
_____. *Mrs. Mack.* New York: Philomel Books, 1998.
_____. *Thunder Cake.* Illustrated by Nanette Stevenson. New York: Philomel Books, 1990.
_____. *When Lightning Comes in a Jar.* New York: Philomel Books, 2002.
Porter, Eleanor H. *Pollyanna.* 1913. Project Gutenberg, 2008. HTML e-book.
Portis, Charles. *True Grit.* New York: Simon and Schuster, 1968.
Postman, Neil. *Amusing Ourselves to Death: Public Discourse in the Age of Show Business.* New York: Viking, 1985.
_____. *The Disappearance of Childhood.* New York: Delacorte Press, 1982.
_____. *Technopoly: The Surrender of Culture to Technology.* New York: Knopf, 1992.
Potter, Beatrix. *The Story of a Fierce Bad Rabbit.* 1906. London: F. Warne, 1987.
_____. *The Story of Miss Moppet.* 1906. London: F. Warne, 1987.
_____. *The Tale of Benjamin Bunny.* 1904. Harmondsworth, UK: F. Warne, 1987.
_____. *The Tale of Mr. Tod.* 1912. London: F. Warne, 1987.
_____. *The Tale of Mrs. Tittlemouse.* 1910. Harmondsworth, UK: F. Warne, 1987.
_____. *The Tale of Peter Rabbit.* 1902. Harmondsworth, UK: F. Warne, 1987.
_____. *The Tale of Samuel Whiskers, or, The Roly-Poly Pudding.* 1908. London: F. Warne, 1987.
_____. *The Tale of Squirrel Nutkin.* 1903. London: F. Warne, 1987.

____. *The Tale of the Flopsy Bunnies*. 1909. London: F. Warne, 1987.

____. *The Tale of Tom Kitten*. 1907. New York: F. Warne, 1935.

____. *The Tale of Two Bad Mice*. 1904. Harmondsworth, UK: F. Warne, 1987.

Pratchett, Terry. *Reaper Man*. London: Victor Gollancz, 1991.

____. *The Wee Free Men*. New York: HarperCollins, 2003.

____. *Wyrd Sisters: A Novel of Discworld*. New York: HarperTorch, 1988.

Provensen, Alice, and Martin Provensen. *An Owl and Three Pussycats*. New York: Atheneum, 1981.

Pullman, Philip. *The Amber Spyglass*. New York: Alfred A. Knopf, 2001.

____. *Fairy Tales from the Brothers Grimm: A New English Version*. New York: Viking, 2012.

____. *The Golden Compass*. New York: Alfred A. Knopf, 1995.

____. *The Good Man Jesus and the Scoundrel Christ*. New York: Canongate, 2010.

____. *The Subtle Knife*. New York: Alfred A. Knopf, 2001.

Queneau, Raymond. *Zazie in the Metro*. Translated by Barbara Wright. New York: Penguin Books, 2001.

Quiller-Couch, A. T., ed. *The Oxford Book of English Verse, 1250–1918*. Oxford: Clarendon, 1939.

Rayner, Catherine. *Iris and Isaac*. London: Little Tiger, 2010.

Rayner, Mary. *Wicked William*. London: Macmillan Children's Books, 1996.

Reid, Barbara. *The Party*. New York: Scholastic, 1997.

____. *Perfect Snow*. Chicago: Albert Whitman, 2011.

Rey, H. A. *Curious George*. Boston: Houghton Mifflin, 1973.

____. *Curious George Rides a Bike*. Boston: Houghton Mifflin, 1973.

____. *Curious George Takes a Job*. Boston: Houghton Mifflin, 1947.

Ridgman, Jeremy. *From River Bank to South Bank: "The Wind in the Willows" and the Staging of National Identity*. Oxford: Peter Lang, 2006.

Riis, Jacob. *How the Other Half Lives*. New York: Hill and Wang, 1966.

Risom, Ole. *I Am a Bunny*. Illustrated by Richard Scarry. New York: Golden Press, 1963.

Robinson, David. *Chaplin: His Life and Art*. New York: McGraw-Hill, 1985.

Robinson, Marilynne. *Housekeeping*. New York: Farrar, Straus and Giroux, 1980.

Rose, Gerald. *The Bag of Wind*. London: Bodley Head, 1983.

Rose, Jacqueline. *The Case of Peter Pan, or, The Impossibility of Children's Fiction*. London: Macmillan, 1984.

Rosen, Michael. *Michael Rosen's Sad Book*. Illustrated by Quentin Blake. Cambridge, MA: Candlewick, 2005.

Rosen, Michael, and Bob Graham. *This Is Our House*. Cambridge, MA: Candlewick, 1996.

Rosen, Michael, and Helen Oxenbury. *We're Going on a Bear Hunt*. New York: Margaret K. McElderry Books, 1989.

Ross, Tony. *I Don't Want to Go to Bed*. La Jolla, CA: Kane/Miller, 2004.

____. *I Want My Dinner*. San Diego, CA: Harcourt Brace, 1996.

____. *I Want to Be*. Brooklyn, NY: Kane/Miller, 1993.

Rousseau, Jean-Jacques. *A Discourse on Inequality on the Origin and Basis of Inequality among Men*. 1755. Waiheke Island, New Zealand: Floating Press, 2009.

____. *Émile, or On Education*. 1762. New York: Basic Books, 1979.

____. *Julie, or, the New Heloise*. 1761. Hanover: Dartmouth College, 1997.

____. *The Social Contract, and Discourses by Jean-Jacques Rousseau*. New York: E. P. Dutton, 1950.

Rudd, David. *The Routledge Companion to Children's Literature*. London: Routledge, 2010.

Rushkoff, Douglas. *Playing the Future: How Kids' Culture Can Teach Us to Thrive in an Age of Chaos*. New York: HarperCollins, 1996.

Rustin, Margaret, and Michael Rustin. *Narratives of Love and Loss: Studies in Modern Children's Fiction*. Rev. ed. London: Karnac, 2001.

Sachar, Louis. *Holes*. New York: Farrar, Straus and Giroux, 1998.

Sacks, Janet. *Victorian Childhood*. Oxford: Shire, 2010.

Salinger, J. D. *The Catcher in the Rye*. Boston: Little, Brown, 1951.

____. *Franny and Zooey*. Boston: Little, Brown, 1961.

____. *Raise High the Roof Beam, Carpenters; and, Seymour, an Introduction*. Boston: Little, Brown, 1963.

Sanders, Barry. *A Is for Ox: The Collapse of Literacy and the Rise of Violence in an Electronic Age*. New York: Vintage Books, 1994.

Saramago, José. *Cain*. Translated by Margaret Jull Costa. Boston: Houghton Mifflin Harcourt, 2011.

Sartre, Jean-Paul. *Existentialism Is a Human-*

ism. New Haven: Yale University Press, 2007.

———. *No Exit and Three Other Plays*. New York: Vintage International, 1989.

Saussure, Ferdinand de. *Course in General Linguistics*. Rev. ed. London: Fontana, 1974.

Scanlon, Elizabeth Garton. *All the World*. Illustrated by Marla Frazee. New York: Beach Lane Books, 2009.

Schickel, Richard. *D. W. Griffith: An American Life*. New York: Simon and Schuster, 1984.

Schrader, Paul. *The Transcendental Style in Film: Ozu, Bresson, Dreyer*. Berkeley: University of California Press, 1972.

Schulz, Charles M. *The Peanuts Treasury*. New York: Holt, Rinehart and Winston, 1968.

Sendak, Maurice. *In the Night Kitchen*. New York: Harper & Row, 1970.

———. *Outside Over There*. New York: Harper & Row, 1981.

———. *Where the Wild Things Are*. New York: Harper & Row, 1963.

Seton, Ernest Thompson. *Wild Animals I Have Known*. Toronto, ON: McClelland & Stewart, 2009.

Shakespeare, William. *William Shakespeare: The Complete Works*. Edited by Alfred Harbage. Baltimore: Penguin Books, 1969.

———. *Hamlet*. In *The Complete Works*, edited by Alfred Harbage, 930–76. Baltimore: Penguin Books, 1969.

———. *Henry V*. In *The Complete Works*, edited by Alfred Harbage, 741–79. Baltimore: Penguin Books, 1969.

———. *Julius Caesar*. In *The Complete Works*, edited by Alfred Harbage, 895–929. Baltimore: Penguin Books, 1969.

———. *King Lear*. In *The Complete Works*, edited by Alfred Harbage, 1060–1106. Baltimore: Penguin Books, 1969.

———. *Macbeth*. In *The Complete Works*, edited by Alfred Harbage, 1107–35. Baltimore: Penguin Books, 1969.

———. *Romeo and Juliet*. In *The Complete Works*, edited by Alfred Harbage, 855–93. Baltimore: Penguin Books, 1969.

Sheldon, Charles. *In His Steps*. Uhrichsville, OH: Barbour, 2002.

Shelley, Mary. *Frankenstein*. 1818. New York: Penguin, 2003.

Shulevitz, Uri. *How I Learned Geography*. New York: Farrar, Straus and Giroux, 2008.

Silvey, Anita, ed. *Children's Books and Their Creators*. Boston: Houghton Mifflin, 1995.

Simmon, Scott. *The Films of D. W. Griffith*. New York: Cambridge University Press, 1993.

Singer, Isaac Bashevis. *A Day of Pleasure: Stories of a Boy Growing Up in Warsaw*. New York: Farrar, Straus and Giroux, 1969.

Sís, Peter. *The Conference of the Birds*. New York: Penguin, 2011.

———. *Madlenka*. New York: Frances Foster Books, 2000.

———. *Madlenka's Dog*. New York: Farrar, Straus and Giroux, 2002.

———. *An Ocean World*. New York: Greenwillow Books, 1992.

———. *Tibet: Through the Red Box*. New York: Farrar, Straus and Giroux, 1998.

Skretvedt, Randy. *Laurel and Hardy: The Magic behind the Movies*. Beverly Hills, CA: Moonstone Press, 1987.

Small, David. *Imogene's Antlers*. Decorah, IA: Dragonfly Books, 1988.

———. *Ruby Mae Has Something to Say*. New York: Crown, 1992.

Smith, Alexander. *Akimbo and the Elephants*. Illustrated by LeUyen Pham. New York: Bloomsbury Children's Books, 2005.

Smith, Alison, and Nicola Brown and Victoria Mills. "Focus: Victorian Sentimentality." Tate Britain: Display. http://www.tate.org.uk/whats-on/tate-britain/display/focus-victorian-sentimentality.

Smith, Betty. *A Tree Grows in Brooklyn*. New York: Harper, 1947.

Smith, Dick. *George Speaks*. Illustrated by Judy Brown. Brookfield, CT: Roaring Brook, 2002.

Smith, Iain Crichton. "Seordag's Interview with the BBC." In *Murdo: The Life and Works*, edited by Stewart Conn, 124–25. Glasgow, UK: Birlinn, 2001.

Smith, Les. "Theatre: Waiting for Godot; Liverpool." *Guardian*, March 15, 1993. http://bit.ly/1oFoqvo.

Smith, Lindsay. *The Politics of Focus: Women, Children and Nineteenth-Century Photography*. Manchester, UK: Manchester University Press, 1998.

Sophocles. *The Three Theban Plays: Antigone; Oedipus the King; Oedipus at Colonus*. Translated by Robert Fagles. Harmondsworth, UK: Penguin Books, 1984.

Speare, Elizabeth George. *The Bronze Bow*. Boston: Houghton Mifflin, 1961.

Spencer, Margaret Meek. *How Texts Teach What Readers Learn*. Stroud, UK: Thimble, 1988.

Spier, Peter. *Oh, Were They Ever Happy!* Garden City, NY: Doubleday, 1978.

———. *Peter Spier's Christmas!* Garden City, NY: Doubleday, 1983.

Spinelli, Jerry. *Maniac Magee*. Boston: Little, Brown, 1990.

———. *Stargirl*. New York: Knopf, 2000.

Bibliography

Spyri, Johanna. *Heidi*. Translated by Helen B. Dole. New York: Grosset & Dunlap, 1945.

Stanislavski, Constantin. *An Actor Prepares*. 1936. Translated by Elizabeth Reynolds Hapgood. New York: Routledge, 1989.

Steichen, Edward. *The Family of Man: The Photographic Exhibition*. Rev. ed. New York: Simon and Schuster, 1955.

Steig, William. *Abel's Island*. New York: Farrar, Straus and Giroux, 1976.

———. *The Amazing Bone*. New York: Farrar, Straus and Giroux, 1976.

———. *Brave Irene*. New York: Farrar, Straus and Giroux, 1986.

———. *Doctor De Soto*. New York: Farrar, Straus and Giroux, 1982.

———. *Gorky Rises*. New York: Farrar, Straus and Giroux, 1980.

———. *Roland, the Minstrel Pig*. New York: Windmill Books, 1968.

———. *Sylvester and the Magic Pebble*. New York: Windmill Books, 1969.

———. *The Toy Brother*. New York: HarperCollins, 1996.

———. *Zeke Pippin*. New York: HarperCollins, 1994.

Steinbeck, John. *East of Eden*. New York: Penguin, 2002.

———. *Of Mice and Men*. New York: Penguin, 1993.

Steinberg, Shirley, and Joe Kincheloe. *Kinderculture: The Corporate Construction of Childhood*. Rev. ed. Boulder, CO: Westview, 2004.

Stephens, John. *Language and Ideology in Children's Fiction*. London: Longman, 1992.

———. *Not By Words Alone: Language, Intertextuality, Society*. London: Longman, 1992.

Stevenson, Robert Louis. *A Child's Garden of Verses*. 1913. New York: HarperCollins, 2011.

———. *Kidnapped*. 1886. London: Penguin, 1994.

———. *Treasure Island*. 1883. New York: Penguin, 2010.

Stewart, Joel. *Dexter Bexley and the Big Blue Beastie*. New York: Holiday House, 2007.

———. *Me and My Mammoth*. London: Macmillan, 2005.

Stewart, Sarah. *The Friend*. Illustrated by David Small. New York: Farrar, Straus and Giroux, 2004.

———. *The Gardener*. Illustrated by David Small. New York: Farrar, Straus and Giroux, 1997.

———. *The Journey*. Illustrated by David Small. New York: Farrar, Straus and Giroux, 2001.

———. *The Library*. Illustrated by David Small. New York: Farrar, Straus and Giroux, 1995.

Stockton, Frank Richard. *The Bee-Man of Orn*. Illustrated by Maurice Sendak. New York: Holt, Rinehart and Winston, 1964.

———. *The Griffin and the Minor Canon*. Illustrated by Maurice Sendak. New York: Holt, Rinehart and Winston, 1963.

———. *The Lady or the Tiger? And Other Stories*. New York: Charles Scribner's Sons, 1914.

Stowe, Harriet Beecher. *Uncle Tom's Cabin*. New York: Oxford University Press, 2002.

Stretton, Hesba. *Jessica's First Prayer*. New York: Garland, 1976.

———. *Jessica's Mother*. Philadelphia: Henry Altemus, 1898.

Strindberg, August. *The Father*. In *Strindberg: Five Plays*, 19–62. Translated by Harry G. Carlson. Berkeley: University of California Press, 1983.

Studlar, Gaylyn. "Oh, 'Doll Divine': Mary Pickford, Masquerade and the Pedophilic Gaze." *Camera Obscura* 16, no. 3 (2001): 197–227.

Sutcliff, Rosemary. *The Eagle of the Ninth*. New York: Farrar, Straus and Giroux, 1993.

———. *Outcast*. Illustrated by Richard Kennedy. New York: Farrar, Straus and Giroux, 1995.

———. *Tristan and Iseult*. New York: Dutton, 1971.

———. *Warrior Scarlet*. New York: H. Z. Walck, 1958.

Swift, Jonathan. *Gulliver's Travels*. 1726. London: Penguin, 2001.

Taine, Hippolyte. *History of English Literature*. Translated by H. Van Laun. Reprint of the 1886 New York edition. Hathi Trust Digital Library, n.d. http://hdl.handle.net/2027/loc.ark:/13960/t5s75zf3g.

Tapscott, Don. *Grown Up Digital: How the Net Generation is Changing Your World*. New York: McGraw-Hill, 2009.

Tagore, Rabindranath. *The Post Office*. New York: Macmillan, 1914.

Tarkington, Booth. *The Magnificent Ambersons*. Charleston, SC: Bibliolife, 2008.

———. *Penrod*. Garden City, NY: Doubleday, 1926.

———. *Penrod and Sam*. Bloomington: Indiana University Press, 2003.

Tatar, Maria. *The Hard Facts of the Grimms' Fairy Tales*. Princeton, NJ: Princeton University Press, 2003.

———. *Off With Their Heads! Fairy Tales and the Culture of Childhood*. Princeton, NJ: Princeton University Press, 1992.

Tate. "Focus: Victorian Sentimentality." Tate Britain: Display. Accessed July 10, 2012.

http://www.tate.org.uk/whats-on/tate-britain/display/focus-victorian-sentimentality.
———. "Sir Luke Fildes: The Doctor Summary." Tate Britain: Display. Accessed August 14, 2012. http://www.tate.org.uk/art/artworks/fildes-the-doctor-n01522/text-summary.
Taylor, Roger, and Edward Wakeling. *Lewis Carroll, Photographer: The Princeton University Library Albums*. Princeton, NJ: Princeton University Press, 2002.
Tennyson, Alfred. *Enoch Arden*. 1864. In *Tennyson's Poetry*, edited by Robert W. Hill, Jr., 250–70. New York: W. W. Norton & Co., 1971.
———. *In Memoriam A.H.H.* 1849. New York: W. W. Norton & Co., 1973.
Thomas à Kempis. *The Imitation of Christ*. Translated by B. J. H. Biggs. Oxford: Oxford University Press, 1997.
Thomas Aquinas, Saint. *Summa Theologica*. 5 vols. Translated by Fathers of the English Dominican Province. New York: Benziger Brothers, 1948.
Thomas, Dylan. *A Child's Christmas in Wales*. Illustrated by Trina Schart Hyman. New York: Holiday House, 1985.
Thompson, Richard. "Meep-Meep." In *Movies and Methods*, edited by Bill Nichols, 126–35. Oakland: University of California Press, 1976.
Thurber, James. *The Wonderful O*. Illustrated by Marc Simont. New York: Simon and Schuster, 1957.
Thwaite, Ann. *Waiting for the Party: The Life of Frances Hodgson Burnett*. Boston: D. R. Godine, 1991.
Tibbetts, John, and James Welsh. *The Encyclopedia of Novels into Film*. New York: Facts on File, 2005.
Tillich, Paul. *The Dynamics of Faith*. New York: HarperOne, 2001.
Tolkien, J. R. R. *The Hobbit*. London: HarperCollins, 2012.
———. "Leaf, by Niggle." In *Tree and Leaf*, 75–95. Boston: Houghton Mifflin Co., 1989.
———. *The Return of the King*. New York: Ballantine Books, 2003.
———. *Tree and Leaf*. Boston: Houghton Mifflin, 1965.
Townsend, John Rowe. *Written for Children: An Outline of English-Language Children's Literature*. 2nd ed. New York: Lippincott, 1983.
Travers, P. L. *Mary Poppins*. Illustrated by Mary Shepard. New York: Harcourt, Brace & World, 1962.
Trites, Roberta Seelinger. *Waking Sleeping Beauty: Feminist Voices in Children's Novels*. Iowa City: University of Iowa Press, 1997.

Trollope, Anthony. "Aboriginals." In *Empire Writing*, 20–32, edited by Elleke Boehmer. Oxford: Oxford University Press, 1998.
———. *The Warden*. London: Penguin Classics, 1986.
Tucker, Nicholas. "Depressive Stories for Children." *Children's Literature in Education* 37, no. 3 (2006): 199–210.
———. *Suitable for Children? Controversies in Children's Literature*. London: Chatto and Windus for Sussex University Press, 1976.
Tunnell, Michael O. *Mailing May*. Illustrated by Ted Rand. New York: Greenwillow Books, 1997.
Turkle, Brinton. *Thy Friend, Obadiah*. New York: Viking, 1969.
Turner, Ethel. *Seven Little Australians*. Ringwood, Australia: Puffin, 1994.
Twain, Mark. *The Complete Short Stories of Mark Twain*. New York: Bantam Classics, 1984.
———. *A Connecticut Yankee in King Arthur's Court*. Reprint of the 1889 New York edition, Project Gutenberg, 2004. http://www.gutenberg.org/files/7249/7249-h/7249-h.htm.
Ungerer, Tomi. *Christmas Eve at the Mellops.'* New York: Harper & Brothers, 1960.
———. *The Mellops Go Diving for Treasure*. New York: Harper, 1957.
———. *The Mellops Go Spelunking*. New York: Harper & Row, 1963.
———. *The Mellops Strike Oil*. New York: Harper, 1958.
———. *No Kiss for Mother*. New York: Harper & Row, 1973.
———. *Otto: The Autobiography of a Teddy Bear*. London: Phaidon, 2010.
Usai, Paolo Cherchi, ed. *The Griffith Project*. 12 vols. London: British Film Institute, 1999–2008.
Vaage, Carol. *Bibi and the Bull*. Illustrated by Georgia Graham. Red Deer, AB: Red Deer College Press, 1998.
Valgardson, W. D. "Red Dust." In *Red Dust*. Ottawa, ON: Oberon Press, 1978.
Van Allsburg, Chris. *Jumanji*. Boston: Houghton Mifflin, 1981.
———. *The Polar Express*. Boston: Houghton Mifflin, 1985.
———. *The Sweetest Fig*. Boston: Houghton Mifflin, 1993.
———. *The Wreck of the Zephyr*. Boston: Houghton Mifflin, 1983.
———. *The Wretched Stone*. Boston: Houghton Mifflin, 1991.
———. *Zathura: A Space Adventure*. Boston: Houghton Mifflin, 2002.

Varon, Sara. *Robot Dreams*. New York: First Second, 2007.

Velthuijs, Max. *Crocodile's Masterpiece*. New York: Farrar, Straus and Giroux, 1992.

———. *Frog and the Birdsong*. New York: Farrar, Straus and Giroux, 1991.

———. *Frog and the Stranger*. New York: Tambourine Books, 1994.

———. *Frog and the Wide World*. London: Andersen, 1998.

———. *Frog in Love*. New York: Farrar, Straus and Giroux, 1989.

———. *Frog in Winter*. New York: Tambourine Books, 1993.

———. *Frog Is Frightened*. New York: Tambourine Books, 1995.

———. *Frog Is Frog*. London: Andersen, 1996.

———. *Little Man Finds a Home*. New York: North-South Books, 1985.

———. *Little Man to the Rescue*. New York: North-South Books, 1986.

Viorst, Judith. *I'll Fix Anthony*. Illustrated by Arnold Lobel. New York: Harper & Row, 1969.

Voltaire. *Candide*. Reprint of the 1918 New York edition, Project Gutenberg, 2006. http://www.gutenberg.org/files/19942/19942-h/19942-h.htm.

———. *A Pocket Philosophical Dictionary*. 1764. Translated by John Fletcher. New York: Oxford University Press, 2011.

———. *Treatise on Tolerance*. 1763. Translated by Brian Masters. Cambridge: Cambridge University Press, 2000.

Waddell, Martin. *Can't You Sleep, Little Bear?* Illustrated by Barbara Firth. 2nd ed. Cambridge, MA: Candlewick, 1992.

———. *Let's Go Home, Little Bear*. Illustrated by Barbara Firth. Cambridge, MA: Candlewick, 1993.

Waldron, Kevin. *Mr. Peek and the Misunderstanding at the Zoo*. Somerville, MA: Candlewick, 2010.

Wallace, Lew. *Ben-Hur: A Tale of the Christ*. New York: Modern Library, 2002.

Wayland, April Halprin. *Girl Coming In for a Landing*. Illustrated by Elaine Clayton. New York: Alfred A. Knopf, 2002.

Webster, Jean. *Daddy Long-Legs*. New York: Grosset & Dunlap, c1940.

Weing, Drew. *Set to Sea*. Seattle: Fantagraphics, 2010.

Wells, H. G. *Love and Mr. Lewisham*. 1899. London: Everyman, 1994.

Wells, Paul. *Animation: Genre and Authorship*. London: Wallflower, 2002.

Westcott, Nadine Bernard. *I Know an Old Lady Who Swallowed a Fly*. Boston: Little, Brown, 1980.

White, E. B. *Charlotte's Web*. Illustrated by Garth Williams. New York: Harper, 1952.

———. *Stuart Little*. Illustrated by Garth Williams. New York: Harper & Row, 1973.

———. *The Trumpet of the Swan*. Illustrated by Edward Frascino. New York: Harper & Row, 1970.

White, T. H. *The Once and Future King*. New York: Putnam, 1958.

Wiebe, Rudy Henry. *Of This Earth: A Mennonite Boyhood in the Boreal Forest*. Intercourse, PA: Good Books, 2007.

Wiesel, Elie. *Night*. Translated by Marion Wiesel. New York: Hill and Wang, 2006.

Wilde, Oscar. *The Picture of Dorian Gray*. 1891. New York: Modern Library, 1992.

Wilder, Laura Ingalls. *By the Shores of Silver Lake*. New York: Harper, 1953.

———. *Farmer Boy*. New York: Harper, 1953.

———. *Little House on the Prairie*. New York: Harper, 1953.

———. *Little Town on the Prairie*. New York: Harper, 1953.

———. *The Long Winter*. New York: Harper, 1953.

———. *On the Banks of Plum Creek*. New York: Harper, 1953.

———. *These Happy Golden Years*. New York: Harper, 1953.

Wilkie-Stibbs, Christine. "Intertextuality and the Child Reader." In *International Companion Encyclopedia of Children's Literature*, edited by Peter Hunt, 179–90. New York: Routledge, 2004.

Willis, Jeanne. *Big Bad Bun*. Illustrated by Tony Ross. London: Andersen, 2009.

Wilson, E. "Children, Emotion and Viewing in Contemporary European Film." *Screen* 46, no. 3 (2005): 329–40.

Winn, Marie. *Children without Childhood*. Harmondsworth, UK: Penguin, 1984.

———. *The Plug-In Drug*. Rev. ed. New York: Viking, 1985.

Winterfeld, Henry. *Detectives in Togas*. New York: Harcourt, Brace, 1956.

Wood, Sarah. *Museum of Childhood: A Book of Childish Things*. London: V&A Publishing, 2012.

Wordsworth, William. *Michael*. In *William Wordsworth*, edited by Stephen Gill, 134–46. Oxford: Oxford University Press, 2010.

———. *Ode: Intimations of Immortality from Recollections of Early Childhood*. In *William Wordsworth*, edited by Stephen Gill, 281–86. Oxford: Oxford University Press, 2010.

Wyndham, John. *The Midwich Cuckoos*. London: Michael Joseph, 1957.

Yeats, W. B. *The Celtic Twilight*. In *Mythologies*, 3–141. New York: Touchstone, 1998.

———. *W. B. Yeats: The Poems.* Edited by Daniel Albright. London: J. M. Dent & Sons, 1990.

———, ed. *Irish Fairy and Folk Tales.* New York: Modern Library, 2003.

Yolen, Jane. *Elsie's Bird.* Illustrated by David Small. New York: Philomel Books, 2010.

Young, Ed. *I, Doko: The Tale of a Basket.* New York: Philomel Books, 2004.

Zemach, Margot. *Self Portrait: Margot Zemach.* Reading, MA: Addison-Wesley, 1978.

Zimmermann, Patricia R. *Reel Families: A Social History of Amateur Film.* Bloomington: Indiana University Press, 1995.

Zimnik, Reiner. *The Bear and the People.* New York: Harper & Row, 1971.

Zipes, Jack. *The Enchanted Screen: The Unknown History of Fairy Tale Films.* New York: Routledge, 2011.

———. "Once There Were Two Brothers Named Grimm." In *The Complete Fairy Tales of the Brothers Grimm,* xvii–xxxi. New York: Bantam, 1992.

———. *The Outspoken Princess and the Gentle Knight.* New York: Bantam Books, 1994.

Filmography

Accatone. Directed by Pier Paolo Pasolini. 1961. Brandon Films.
The Adventures of Baron Munchausen. Directed by Terry Gilliam. 1988. Columbia Pictures.
The Adventures of Billy. Directed by D. W. Griffith. 1911. Biograph Co.
Ain't She Tweet. Directed by Friz Freleng. 1952. Warner Bros.
All a Bir-r-r-rd. Directed by Friz Freleng. 1950. Warner Bros.
"And a Little Child Shall Lead Them." Directed by D. W. Griffith. 1909. Biograph Co.
Angels with Dirty Faces. Directed by Michael Curtiz. 1938. Warner Bros.
Anne Frank Remembered. Directed by Jon Blair. 1995. Sony Pictures Classics.
Annie. Directed by John Huston. 1982. Columbia Pictures.
Anvil! The Story of Anvil. Directed by Sacha Gervasi. 2008. Abramorama.
Aparajito. Directed by Satyajit Ray. 1956. Merchant Ivory Production.
As in a Looking Glass. Directed by D. W. Griffith. 1911. Biograph Co.
Babe: Pig in the City. Directed by George Miller. 1998. Universal Pictures.
The Baby and the Stork. Directed by D. W. Griffith. 1912. Biograph Co.
Baby Bottleneck. Directed by Robert Clampett. 1951. Warner Bros.
Ballet Adagio. Directed by Norman McLaren. 1972. National Film Board of Canada.
Bambi. Directed by James Algar, Samuel Armstrong, David Hand, Graham Heid, Bill Roberts, Paul Satterfield, and Norman Wright. 1942. RKO Radio Pictures.
The Banker's Daughters. Directed by D. W. Griffith. 1910. Biograph Co.
The Battle at Elderbush Gulch. Directed by D. W. Griffith. 1913. Biograph Co.

A Bear for Punishment. Directed by Chuck Jones. 1951. Warner Bros.
A Beast at Bay. Directed by D. W. Griffith. 1912. Biograph Co.
Beauty and the Beast. Directed by Paul Thomas. 1988. VCA Pictures.
The Bellboy. Directed by Jerry Lewis. 1960. Paramount Pictures.
Big Drive. Directed by Anita Lebeau. 2011. National Film Board of Canada.
Bigger Than Life. Directed by Nicholas Ray. 1956. Twentieth Century Fox.
Billy's Stratagem. Directed by D. W. Griffith. 1912. Biograph Co.
A Bird in a Guilty Cage. Directed by Friz Freleng. 1952. Warner Bros.
Black Beauty. Directed by Caroline Thompson. 1994. Warner Bros.
The Black Stallion. Directed by Carroll Ballard. 1979. United Artists.
The Broken Cross. Directed by D. W. Griffith. 1911. Biograph Co.
The Broken Doll. Directed by D. W. Griffith. 1910. Biograph Co.
Broken Leghorn. Directed by Robert McKimson. 1959. Warner Bros.
Bugs Bunny and the Three Bears. Directed by Chuck Jones. 1944. Warner Bros.
The Cabbage-Patch Fairy. Directed by Alice Guy. 1896. Gaumont.
Canary Row. Directed by Friz Freleng. 1950. Warner Bros.
Canned Feud. Directed by Friz Freleng. 1951. Warner Bros.
A Chairy Tale. Directed by Claude Jutra and Norman McLaren. 1957. National Film Board of Canada.
The Children's Friend. Directed by D. W. Griffith. 1909. Biograph Co.
A Child's Faith. Directed by D. W. Griffith. 1910. Biograph Co.

A Child's Impulse. Directed by D. W. Griffith. 1910. Biograph Co.
A Child's Remorse. Directed by D. W. Griffith. 1912. Biograph Co.
A Child's Stratagem. Directed by D. W. Griffith. 1910. Biograph Co.
Circle of the Sun. Directed by Colin Low. 1961. National Film Board of Canada.
City Lights. Directed by Charles Chaplin. 1931. United Artists.
The Country Doctor. Directed by D. W. Griffith. 1909. Biograph Co.
Crac!. Directed by Frederic Back. 1981. East-West Entertainment.
The Crooked Road. Directed by D. W. Griffith. 1911. Biograph Co.
The Cruel Mother. Directed by Alice Guy. 1908. Gaumont.
Custody of the Child. Directed by Louis Feuillade. 1909. Gaumont.
The Danish Poet. Directed by Torill Kove. 2006. Magnolia Pictures, National Film Board of Canada.
The Day I Became a Woman. Directed by Marzieh Makhmalbaf. 2000. Olive Films.
Death's Marathon. Directed by D. W. Griffith. 1913. Biograph Co.
Dr. Zhivago. Directed by David Lean. 1965. MGM.
A Dog's Life. Directed by Charles Chaplin. 1918. First National Exhibitors' Circuit.
The Doll. Directed by Ernst Lubitsch. 1919. Universum Film.
Drink's Lure. Directed by D. W. Griffith. 1913. Biograph Co.
A Drunkard's Reformation. Directed by D. W. Griffith. 1909. Biograph Co.
Easy Street. Directed by Charles Chaplin. 1917. Mutual.
Electrick Children. Directed by Rebecca Thomas. 2012. Phase 4 Films.
Elephant Boy. Robert Flaherty and Zoltan Korda. 1937. United Artists.
Elmer Elephant. Directed by Wilfred Jackson. 1936. United Artists.
"The Emperor's New Clothes." Directed by Peter Medak. In *Faerie Tale Theatre*, Showtime, 1982.
Endless Summer. Directed by Bruce Brown. 1966. Monterey Media.
The Enemy's Baby. Directed by D. W. Griffith. 1913. Biograph Co.
Enoch Arden (pts. 1 and 2). Directed by D. W. Griffith. 1911. Biograph Co.
Every Child. Directed by Eugene Fedorenko. 1979. National Film Board of Canada.
Examination Day at School. Directed by D. W. Griffith. 1910. Biograph Co.
The Ex-Convict. Directed by Edwin S. Porter. 1904. Edison Manufacturing Company.
A Fair Exchange. Directed by D. W. Griffith. 1909. Biograph Co.
The Fallen Idol. Directed by Carol Reed. 1948. Selznick Releasing Organization.
The Family Jewels. Directed by Jerry Lewis. 1965. Paramount Pictures.
Fantasia. Directed by Norman Ferguson. 1940. Walt Disney Productions.
Fantasia 2000. Directed by James Algar and Gaetan Brizzi. 1999. Buena Vista Pictures.
Fantastic Mr. Fox. Directed by Wes Anderson. 2009. Twentieth Century Fox Film Corporation.
Fat and Lean Wrestling Match. Directed by Georges Méliès. 1903. Star-Film.
Fate. Directed by D. W. Griffith. 1913. Biograph Co.
Feed the Kitty. Directed by Chuck Jones. 1952. Warner Bros.
The Female of the Species. Directed by D. W. Griffith. Biograph Co.
The Feud and the Turkey. Directed by D. W. Griffith. 1908. Biograph Co.
A Feud in the Kentucky Hills. Directed by D. W. Griffith. 1912. Biograph.
Fighting Blood. Directed by D. W. Griffith. 1911. Biograph Co.
The Final Settlement. Directed by D. W. Griffith. 1910. Biograph Co.
Finding Nemo. Directed by Andrew Stanton. 2003. Buena Vista Pictures.
The 5000 Fingers of Dr. T. Directed by Roy Rowland. 1953. Columbia Pictures Corporation.
The Foghorn Leghorn. Directed by Robert McKimson. 1948. Warner Bros.
Frankenweenie. Directed by Tim Burton. 2012. Walt Disney Studios.
The Freshman. Directed by Fred C. Newmeyer. 1925. Pathé Exchange.
Friends. Directed by D. W. Griffith. 1912. Biograph Co.
From Up on Poppy Hill. Directed by Goro Miyazaki. 2011. Studio Ghibli.
Frozen. Directed by Chris Buck and Jennifer Lee. 2013. Walt Disney Studios Motion Pictures.
Gangs of New York. Directed by Scorsese. 2002. Miramax Films.
Gasman. Directed by Lynne Ramsay. 1996. The Criterion Collection.
Gentlemen Broncos. Directed by Jared Hess. 2009. Fox Searchlight Pictures.
Gerald McBoing-Boing. Directed by Robert Cannon. 1950. Columbia Pictures.
Get a Horse. Directed by Lauren MacMullan. 2013. Walt Disney Studios Motion Pictures.

Gift Wrapped. Directed by Friz Freleng. 1952. Warner Bros.
The Girl and Her Trust. Directed by D. W. Griffith. 1912. Biograph Co.
The Girls and Daddy. Directed by D. W. Griffith. 1909. Biograph Co.
The God Within. Directed by D. W. Griffith. 1912. Biograph Co.
Gold and Glitter. Directed by D. W. Griffith. 1912. Biograph Co.
The Golden Louis. Directed by D. W. Griffith. 1909. Biograph Co.
Gorilla My Dreams. Directed by Robert McKimson. 1948. Warner Bros.
Grave of the Fireflies. Directed by Isao Takahata. 1988. Studio Ghibli.
Harry Potter and the Half-Blood Prince. Directed by David Yates. 2009. Warner Bros.
Harry Potter and the Order of the Phoenix. Directed by David Yates. 2007. Warner Bros.
Harry Potter and the Prisoner of Azkaban. Directed by Alfonso Cuarón. 2004. Warner Bros.
Harvest of Shame. Directed by Fred W. Friendly. 1960. Columbia Broadcasting System.
Her Mother's Oath. Directed by D. W. Griffith. 1913. Biograph Co.
Heredity. Directed by D. W. Griffith. 1912. Biograph Co.
High Diving Hare. Directed by Friz Freleng. 1949. Warner Bros.
His Last Burglary. Directed by D. W. Griffith. 1910. Biograph Co.
His Trust. Directed by D. W. Griffith. 1911. Biograph Co.
His Trust Fulfilled. Directed by D. W. Griffith. 1911. Biograph Co.
House: After Five Years of Living. Charles Eames and Ray Eames. 1955. Image Entertainment.
How to Train Your Dragon. Directed by Dean DeBlois and Chris Sanders. 2010. Paramount Pictures.
Howl's Moving Castle. Directed by Hayao Miyazaki. 2004. Buena Vista International.
Hud. Directed by Martin Ritt. 1963. Paramount Pictures.
The Hutterites. Directed by Colin Low. 1964. National Film Board of Canada.
I Did It. Directed by D. W. Griffith. 1909. Biograph Co.
I Know Where I'm Going. Directed by Michael Powell and Emeric Pressburger. 1945. Universal Pictures.
I Love to Singa. Directed by Tex Avery. 1936. Warner Bros. DVD.
I Remember Mama. Directed by George Stevens. 1948. RKO Radio Pictures.
I Was Born, but ... Directed by Yasujiro Ozu. 1932. Janus Films.
I Wish. Directed by Hirokazu Koreeda. 2011. The Criterion Collection.
The Iconoclast. Directed by D. W. Griffith. 1910. Biograph Co.
If We Only Knew. Directed by D. W. Griffith. 1913. Biograph Co.
The Illusionist. Directed by Sylvain Chornet. 2010. Sony Pictures Classics.
The Immigrant. Directed by Charles Chaplin. 1917. Mutual.
In a Hempen Bag. Directed by D. W. Griffith. 1909. Biograph Co.
In the Border States. Directed by D. W. Griffith. 1910. Biograph Co.
In the Street. Directed by James Agee, Helen Levitt, and Janice Loeb. 1948. Museum of Modern Art Film Library.
The Incredibles. Directed by Brad Bird. 2004. Buena Vista Pictures.
The Infernal Cake-Walk. Directed by Georges Méliès. 1903. Star-Film.
The Inn Where No Man Rests. Directed by Georges Méliès. 1903. Star-Film.
The Inner Circle. Directed by D. W. Griffith. 1912. Biograph Co.
The Interrupters. Directed by Steve James. 2011. The Cinema Guild.
Jupiter's Thunderbolts. Directed by Georges Méliès. 1903. Star-Film.
Justin Bieber: Never Say Never. Directed by Jon M. Chu. 2011. Paramount Pictures.
The Karate Kid. Directed by John G. Avildsen. 1984. Columbia Pictures.
Kick-Ass. Directed by Mathew Vaughn. 2010. Lionsgate.
The Kid. Directed by Jon Turteltaub. 2000. Buena Vista Pictures.
The Kid Brother. Directed by Ted Wilde. 1927. Paramount Pictures.
Kung Fu Panda. Directed by Mark Osborne and John Stevenson. 2008. Paramount.
Late Spring. Directed by Yasujiro Ozu. 1949. The Criterion Collection.
The Landlady. Directed by Alice Guy. 1900. Gaumont.
Le Havre. Directed by Aki Kaurismaki. 2011. Janus Films.
The LEGO Movie. Directed by Phil Lord and Christopher Miller. 2014. Warner Bros.
Let the Right One In. Directed by Tomas Alfredson. 2008. Magnet Releasing.
The Little Fugitive. Directed by Ray Ashley, Morris Engel, Ruth Orkin. 1953. Joseph Burstyn.

The Little Teacher. Directed by D. W. Griffith. 1909. Biograph Co.
The Little Tease. Directed by D. W. Griffith. 1913. Biograph Co.
Little Women. Directed by Gillian Armstrong. 1994. Columbia Pictures.
The Lonedale Operator. Directed by D. W. Griffith. 1911. Biograph Co.
The Lonely Villa. Directed by D. W. Griffith. 1909. Biograph Co.
Lorenzo's Oil. Directed by George Miller. 1992. Universal Pictures.
Louise. Directed by Anita Lebeau. 2003. National Board of Canada.
Make Way for Tomorrow. Directed by Leo McCarey. 1937. Paramount Pictures.
The Medicine Bottle. Directed by D. W. Griffith. 1909: Biograph Co.
The Melomaniac. Directed by Georges Méliès. 1903. Star-Film.
The Message. Directed by D. W. Griffith. 1909. Biograph Co.
Midwife to the Upper Class. Directed by Alice Guy. 1902. Gaumont.
A Misappropriated Turkey. Directed by D. W. Griffith. 1913. Biograph Co.
Mr. Magorium's Wonder Emporium. Directed by Zach Helm. 2007. Fox-Walden.
Mixed Babies. Directed by Wallace McCutcheon. 1908. American Mutoscope & Biograph.
The Modern Prodigal. Directed by D. W. Griffith. 1910. Biograph Co.
Modern Times. Directed by Charles Chaplin. 1936. United Artists.
Mon Oncle. Directed by Jacques Tati. 1958. Continental Distributing.
Monsters Inc. Directed by Pete Docter. 2001. Buena Vista Pictures.
Moonbird. Directed by John Hubley, 1959. EastWest Entertainment.
Moonfleet. Directed by Fritz Lang. 1955. MGM.
More Kittens. Directed by David Hand and Wilfred Jackson. 1936. United Artists.
A Morning Bath. Directed by James H. White. 1896. Edison Manufacturing Company.
Mother Pluto. Directed by David Hand. 1936. United Artists.
The Mothering Heart. Directed by D. W. Griffith. 1913. Biograph Co.
The Mountaineer's Honor. Directed by D. W. Griffith. 1909. Biograph Co.
Munro. Gene Deitch. 1961. Paramount Pictures.
The Muppets Take Manhattan. Directed by Frank Oz. 1984. TriStar Pictures.
My Baby. Directed by D. W. Griffith. 1912. Biograph Co.
My Grandmother Ironed the King's Shirts. Directed by Torill Kove. 2001. National Film Board of Canada.
Nanook of the North. Directed by Robert J. Flaherty. 1922. The Criterion Collection.
The Nativity. Directed by Louis Feuillade. 1910. Gaumont.
Nausicaa of the Valley of the Wind. Directed by Hayao Miyazaki. 1984. Studio Ghibli.
Never Cry Wolf. Directed by Carroll Ballard. 1983. Buena Vista Distribution.
The Night of the Hunter. Directed by Charles Laughton. 1955. United Artists.
Oil and Water. Directed by D. W. Griffith. 1913. Biograph Co.
The Old Confectioner's Mistake. Directed by D. W. Griffith. 1911. Biograph Co.
One Magic Christmas. Directed by Phillip Borsos. 1985. Buena Vista Pictures.
One Potato Two Potato. Directed by Leslie Daiken. 1957. British Film Institute.
The One She Loved. Directed by D. W. Griffith. 1912. Biograph Co.
One Touch of Nature. Directed by D. W. Griffith. 1909. Biograph Co.
Ordet. Directed by Carl Theodor Dreyer. 1995. Kingsley International Pictures.
Ordinary People. Directed by Robert Redford. 1980. Paramount Pictures.
Orphans of the Storm. Directed by D. W. Griffith. 1921. United Artists.
Oz the Great and Powerful. Directed by Sam Raimi. 2013. Walt Disney Studios Motion Picture.
A Pain in the Pullman. Directed by Jack White. 1936. Columbia Pictures.
Patinoire. Directed by Gilles Carle. 1962. National Film Board of Canada.
The Peachbasket Hat. Directed by D. W. Griffith. 1909. Biograph Co.
Peter Pan. Directed by Herbert Brenon. 1924. Paramount Pictures.
Le Petit Nicolas. Directed by Laurent Tirard. 2009. M6 Metropole Television.
The Pilgrim. Directed by Charles Chaplin. 1923. Associated First National Pictures.
Pinocchio. Directed by Normon Ferguson, T. Hee, Wilfred Jackson, Jack Kinney, Hamilton Luske, Bill Roberts, and Ben Sharpsteen. 1940. RKO Radio Pictures.
Pippa Passes. Directed by D. W. Griffith. 1909. Biograph Co.
Ponyo. Directed by Hayao Miyazaki. 2008. Studio Ghibli.
Poor Little Rich Girl. Directed by Maurice Tourneur. 1917. Artcraft Pictures Corporation.

Pop Goes the Easel. Directed by Del Lord. 1935. Columbia Pictures.

Porco Rosso. Directed by Hayao Miyazaki. 1992. Studio Ghibli.

Il Posto. Directed by Ermanno Olmi. 1960. Cowboy Pictures.

A Pueblo Legend. Directed by D. W. Griffith. 1912. Biograph Co.

Putty Tat Trouble. Directed by Friz Freleng. 1951. Warner Bros.

Quai des Orfèvres. Directed by Henri-Georges Clouzot. 1947. Rialto Pictures.

Ratatouille. Directed by Brad Bird. 2007. Buena Vista Pictures.

The Red Man and the Child. Directed by D. W. Griffith. 1908. Biograph Co.

The Red Man's View. Directed by D. W. Griffith. Biograph Co.

Ride the High Country. Directed by Sam Peckinpah. 1962. Metro-Goldwyn-Mayer.

The Rocky Road. Directed by D. W. Griffith. 1910. Biograph Co.

The Root of Evil. Directed by D. W. Griffith. 1912. Biograph Co.

The Ruling Passion. Directed by D. W. Griffith. 1911. Biograph Co.

Rushmore. Directed by Wes Anderson. 1998. The Criterion Collection.

A Salutary Lesson. Directed by D. W. Griffith. 1910. Biograph Co.

Schneider's Anti-Noise Crusade. Directed by D. W. Griffith. 1909. Biograph Co.

Scott Pilgrim vs. the World. Directed by Edgar Wright. 2010. Universal Pictures.

The Secret Garden. Directed by Fred Wilcow. 1949. Metro-Goldwyn-Mayer.

The Secret of Kells. Directed by Tomm Moore and Nora Twomey. 2009. Gkids.

The Secret of Roan Inish. Directed by John Sayles. 1994. The Samuel Goldwyn Company.

The Secret World of Arriety. Directed by Hiromasa Yonebayashi. 2010. Studio Ghibli.

The Seventh Day. Directed by D. W. Griffith. 1909. Biograph Co.

The Sheriff's Baby. Directed by D. W. Griffith. 1913. Biograph Co.

Signs. Directed by M. Night Shyamalan. 2002. Buena Vista Pictures.

Silver Linings Playbook. Directed by David O. Russell. 2012. The Weinstein Company.

Sita Sings the Blues. Directed by Nina Paley. 2008. Gkids.

Small Deaths. Directed by Lynne Ramsay. 1996. The Criterion Collection.

The Smile of a Child. Directed by D. W. Griffith. 1911. Biograph Co.

Snow Business. Directed by Friz Freleng. 1953. Warner Bros.

The Sorrowful Example. Directed by D. W. Griffith. 1911. Biograph Co.

Sparrows. Directed by William Beaudine. 1926. United Artists.

Speed Racer. Directed by the Wachowski brothers. 2008. Warner Bros.

Spirited Away. Directed by Hayao Miyazaki. 2001. Studio Ghibli.

Standing Alone. Directed by Colin Low. 1982. National Film Board of Canada.

Stella Dallas. Directed by Henry King. 1937. UA.

Stevie. Directed by Steve James. 2002. Kartemquin Films.

The Stories We Tell. Directed by Sarah Polley. 2012. Roadsite Attractions.

Strange Cargo. Directed by Frank Borzage. 1940. Loew's.

Strange Invaders. Directed by Cordell Barker. 2002. National Film Board of Canada.

A String of Pearls. Directed by D. W. Griffith. 1912. Biograph Co.

The Sunbeam. Directed by D. W. Griffith. 1912. Biograph Co.

Sunshine Sue. Directed by D. W. Griffith. 1910. Biograph Co.

The Telephone Girl and the Lady. Directed by D. W. Griffith. 1913. Biograph Co.

The Ten Commandments. Directed by Cecil B. DeMille. Paramount Pictures, 1923.

The Terrible Kids. Directed by Wallace McCutcheon and Edwin Porter. 1906. Edison Manufacturing Company.

There Was a Father. Directed by Yasuiro Ozu. 1942. Shochiku Eiga.

Those Boys. Directed by D. W. Griffith. 1909. Biograph Co.

Thou Shalt Not. Directed by D. W. Griffith. 1910. Biograph Co.

Three Bad Men. Directed by John Ford. 2005. Fox Film Corporation.

Three Friends. Directed by D. W. Griffith. 1913. Biograph Co.

Three Orphan Kittens. Directed by David Hand. 1935. United Artists.

Through the Breakers. Directed by D. W. Griffith. 1909. Biograph Co.

Tokyo Godfathers. Directed by Satoshi Kon. 2003. Columbia TriStar.

A Town Called Panic. Directed by Vincent Patar and Stephane Aubier. 2009. Zeitgeist Films.

Toy Story 2. Directed by John Lasseter and Ash Brannon. 1999. Walt Disney Studios Motion Pictures.

Toy Story 3. Directed by John Lasseter and

Andrew Stanton. 2010. Walt Disney Studios Motion Pictures.
The Traveler. Directed by Abbas Kiarostami. 1974. Kanoon.
The Tree of Life. Directed by Terrence Malick. 2011. Fox Searchlight Pictures.
Treeless Mountain. Directed by So Yong Kim. 2008. Oscilloscope Pictures.
True Grit. Directed by Ethan Coen. 2010. Paramount Pictures.
True Grit. Directed by Henry Hathaway. 1969. Paramount Pictures.
Tweetie Pie. Directed by Friz Freleng. 1947. Warner Bros.
Tweety's S.O.S. Directed by Friz Freleng. 1951. Warner Bros.
Two Daughters of Eve. Directed by D. W. Griffith. 1912. Biograph Co.
The Two Sides. Directed by D. W. Griffith. 1911. Biograph Co.
Tzaritza. Directed by Theodore Ushev. 2007. National Film Board of Canada.
Ugetsu Monogatari. Directed by Kenji Mizoguchi. 1953. Daiei International Film.
The Ugly Duckling. Directed by Wilfred Jackson. 1931. Walt Disney Productions.
An Unseen Enemy. Directed by D. W. Griffith. 1912. Biograph Co.
The Unwelcome Guest. Directed by D. W. Griffith. 1913. Biograph Co.
Up. Directed by Pete Docter. 2009. Walt Disney Studios Motion Pictures.
The Vagabond. Directed by Charles Chaplin. 1916. Mutual Film.
The Valet's Wife. Directed by D. W. Griffith. 1908. Biograph Co.
Village of Idiots. Directed by Eugene Fedrenko and Rose Newlove. 1999. National Film Board of Canada.
I Vitelloni. Directed by Federico Fellini. 1953. Janus Films.
The Voice of the Child. Directed by D. W. Griffith. 1911. Biograph Co.
Wanted, a Child. Directed by D. W. Griffith. 1909. Biograph Co.
War Horse. Directed by Steven Spielberg. 2011. Touchstone Pictures.
Watermelon Eating Contest. Produced by Siegmund Lubin. 1903. S. Lubin.
The Watermelon Patch. Directed by Wallace McCutcheon and Edwin Porter. 1905. Edison Manufacturing Company.
The Way to Shadow Garden. Directed by Stan Brakhage. 1954. Canyon Cinema.
The Way, Way Back. Directed by Nat Faxon and Jim Rash. 2013. Fox Searchlight Pictures.
A Welcome Intruder. Directed by D. W. Griffith. 1913. Biograph Co.
What Drink Did. Directed by D. W. Griffith. 1909. Biograph Co.
Where the Wild Things Are. Directed by Spike Jonze. 2009. Warner Bros.
The White Balloon. Directed by Jafar Panahi. 1995. October Films.
White Mane. Directed by Albert Lamorisse. 1953. United Artists.
The White Rose of the Wilds. Directed by D. W. Griffith. 1911. Biograph Co.
Wild Strawberries. Directed by Ingmar Bergman. 1957. Janus Films.
Wreck-It-Ralph. Directed by Richard Moore. 2012. Walt Disney Studios.
The Yearling. Directed by Clarence Brown. 1946. Metro-Goldwyn-Mayer.
Young America. Directed by Frank Borzage. 1932. Twentieth Century Fox Film Corporation.
The Zulu's Heart. Directed by D. W. Griffith. 1908. Biograph Co.

Index

A Is for Ox 27
Abel 86–87
Abraham 86, 95, 105
Academy Award (Oscar) 12
Achebe, Chinua 37
Adaptation 37–40, 53–57
Adeimantus 31–32
The Adventures of Dollie 109–110, 113, 129
The Adventures of Huckleberry Finn 151
Aesop 13, 134, 137
Afghan Alphabet 220
Ahlberg, Allan 64, 238*ch*8*n*15
Ahlberg, Janet 238*ch*8*n*15
Alfie Gets In 129–130
Alfie Gives a Hand 130
Alfie series 129–130, 190; *see also* Hughes, Shirley
Alice in the Cities 218
All a Bir-r-r-rd 137–138
All My Babies 219
Althusser, Louis 14
Amelia and the Angel 157, 220
American Medical Association 27
American Mutuoscope and Biograph Company (Biograph) 47, 71, 102–114; *see also* D. W. Griffith
Amusing Ourselves to Death 28–30, 33
Analects 78
And a Little Child Shall Lead Them 103
Andersen, Hans Christian 58–59, 65, 73–74, 93–96, 99, 100, 107, 184–185, 203
Angels with Dirty Faces 219
Anna from 6 to 18 220
Anne of Green Gables 123–124
Anne Shirley 107, 123–124, 135–136
Aparajito 220
Apollo and Dionysus 192
Apology (Socrates) 78
The Apple 220
Apu trilogy 48
Aquinas, Thomas 126
Aristotle 4, 19, 42, 44, 49, 66, 125, 187, 202, 224*n*27; on adaptation 53–57; the mean 4, 42–53, 177–187; *Poetics* 50–52, 125–126, 127; *see also Poetics*
Arnheim, Rudolf 223*ch*1*n*2
The Art of the Moving Picture 54
Artaud, Antonin 14
As in a Looking Glass 106
L'Assomoir (Zola) 107, 163–169
Au Revoir, les Enfants 220
Augustine 126
Auld Licht Idylls 75
Aunt Chip and the Great Triple Creek Dam Affair 36–37
Avery, Gillian 65
Avery, Tex 116–117

Babe: Pig in the City 220
Babes in Arms 137
Babes on Broadway 137
The Baby and the Stork 110
Baby Takes a Bow 136
Bachelor Mother 219
Badger (*The Wind in the Willows*) 187–191, 207
Ballet Adagio 220
Balzac, Honoré de 14
Banks, Lynne Reid 186
Bann, Richard 7
Baran 220
Barbauld, Anna Laetitia 107
Barnet, Boris 47
Barrie, James 62, 75, 107, 133, 172, 200, 207, 239*n*25, 239*n*26; *see also* Peter Pan
Battleship Potemkin 47, 69
Baudrillard, Jean 14, 48
Baum, L. Frank 107
Bazin, André 1–2, 3, 33, 162; on realism 1–2, 6; on the reciprocal influence of the arts 75–76
Beckett, Samuel 61, 139
Beethoven, Ludwig van 8, 147
Behind the Scenes 233*n*11

267

Bellissima 219
Belloc, Hillaire 148
Ben-Hur (book) 107
Benigni, Roberto 57
Bentley, E. C. 13
Bernard, Dorothy 112
La Bête Humaine 137, 163, 165, 169
Betsy Trotwood (*David Copperfield*) 189
Bettelheim, Bruno 44, 180, 208–209; on character splitting 180–187; on graduation 211–214
The Bible 5, 29, 80–89, 91, 115, 118, 139
Bicycle Thieves 219
Bierhorst, John 64
The Big City 48
Big Drive 220
Billy's Stratagem 110
Biograph Bulletin 102–114, 131
Birth of a Nation 69, 110, 111
Birth of a Notion 139
The Black Stallion 219
Blake, William 105
Blatty, William Peter 186
Bleak House 163
Bloch, Carl 119–121, 139
Blockheads 196–197
Blotto 195
The Bluebird (film) 219
Bluestone, George 54
Bluto 116
Bobbsey Twins 136
Boccaccio 13
Book of Genesis 85–88
Book of Judges 105
Book of Ruth 105
Born into Brothels 220
Borzage, Frank 48
Bosko 116
Boudu Saved from Drowning 48
Bowser, Eileen 117
Boys Town 219
Bradbury, Ray 35
Brando, Marlon 146
Brats 194–195
Brave New World 35
Brecht, Bertolt 13, 226*n*19
Bresson, Robert 48
Bright Eyes 136
Bringing Up Baby 219
Brittain, Donald 34
The Broken Doll 113
Brooke, Dorothea 155–156
"Brother and Sister" (Grimms) 209
The Brothers Karamazov 8
Browning, Robert 75, 117, 170
Brubeck, Dave 8
Buckingham, David 31, 33
Bugs Bunny 4
Buñuel, Luis 137
Bunyan, John 4, 20–22, 41, 90, 107; *see also The Pilgrim's Progress*

Burger, Peter 14
Burnett, Frances Hodgson 127, 130, 142
Burningham, John 173
Burns, Robert 62
Burnt by the Sun 220
The Butcher Boy 220
By the Law 47
By the Shores of Silver Lake 216–217, 240*n*66
Bye-Bye Birdie 220
BYU Bookstore 54

Cain 86–87
Cammina, Cammina (Keep Walking) 122–123
Candide 14
Carpenter, Humphrey 206, 207
Cassavetes, John 48
Causley, Charles 143–144
The Celtic Twilight 62, 63–64
Central Station 219
Cervantes, Miguel de 13, 34
Chaplin, Charles 47, 65–66, 144–149, 192, 218; *see also The Pilgrim*
Chaplin, Sydney 144
Charles James Grantly (*The Warden*) 178
Charulata 48
The Chase 146
Chatman, Seymour 57
Chaucer, Geoffrey 13
Chekhov, Anton 107
Chesterton, G. K. 91
"Child Ballad" (Kingsley) 77
A Child Is Waiting 219
The Childhood of Maxim Gorky 219
Children from Overseas 219
Children Learning by Experience 219
The Children of Fogo Island 219
Children Without Childhood 27
"Children's Prattle" 184–185
A Child's Impulse 103
A Child's Stratagem 104
A Christmas Carol (Chesterton) 91
A Christmas Carol (Dickens) 159–161
Christopher Robin 91
"Cinderella" 56
Cineguild 73
City of Gold 48
Clair, René 48
Clouzot, Henri-Georges 219
Collodi, Carlo 149–150, 191–193, 210
The Color of Paradise 220
Confucius 78, 124, 222, 227*ch*3*n*1
A Connecticut Yankee in King Arthur's Court 92
Conrad, Joseph 156
"The Cotter's Saturday Night" 62
The Country Doctor 233*n*11
Coupeau (*L'Assommoir*) 166–167
Crac! 219
"A Cradle Song" (Yeats) 77

Crichton-Smith, Iain 62
The Crime of M. Lange 48
Crooklyn 219
The Crowd 133
Curly Top 136

Daguerre, Louis 29
Dahl, Roald 60–61, 93
The Danish Poet 220
Dante 172
David 82
The Dawn of Tomorrow 136
The Day I Became a Woman 220
Dead End 219
De Brunhoff, Jean 148
Delphi 59
deMause, Lloyd 45
DeMille, Cecil 181–183
Deraniyagala, Sonali 135
Deren, Maya 48
De Sica, Vittorio 48
Desmond, Paul 8
Devi 48
Diana Barry (Anne of Green Gables) 123
A Diary for Timothy 219
The Diary of Anne Frank (book) 193–194
Dickens, Charles 71–72, 169
"Dickens, Griffith, and the Film Today" (Eisenstein) 71–73
The Disappearance of Childhood 28, 45
"Discourse on the Arts and the Sciences" (Rousseau) 62
Disney, Walt 149, 191, 192
Disney Corporation 57
Distant Voices, Still Lives 220
Do Detectives Think? 196
The Doctor (painting) 232n2
Dr. Zhivago (1965 film) 74
Dodge, Mary Mapes 107
A Doll's House (play) 230n12
Don Quixote 91, 124–125, 215
Donald Duck 116
Dostoyevsky, Fyodor 8, 157
Double Whoopee 197
Dovzhenko, Alexander 47, 133
Dream Days 214, 228n48
Dreyer, Carl Theodor 34, 48, 89
A Drunkard's Reformation 106
Durbin, Deanna 136

E.T. 205
Ealing Studios 137
Ebenezer Scrooge 159–161
Edgeworth, Maria 107
Eisenstein, Sergei 47, 71–3
Eliot, George 96–99, 100, 103, 149, 155–156, 159, 168, 173, 184, 218; *see also Silas Marner*
Eliot, T. S. 158
Elisa ("The Wild Swans") 94–95
Elisha 84, 89

Elkind, David 27
Emil and the Detectives (book) 137
Emil and the Detectives (film) 137
Emil and the Three Twins 137
Émile (Rousseau) 78, 79, 105
The Emperor's New Clothes (1985 television film) 65
"The Emperor's New Clothes" (story) 65
The End of St. Petersburg 47
L'Enfant 220
Engels, Friedrich 14
Erasmus, Desiderius 13
Être et Avoir 219
Eulalie and the Hopping Head 173
Every Child 124, 220
"The Evolution of the Language of Cinema" 1–2
Ewing, Juliana 107
The Exorcist 186
The Exterminating Angel 137
The Extraordinary Adventures of Mr. West in the Land of the Bolsheviks 46

Faces of Children 74, 219
Fahrenheit 451 (book) 35
A Fair Exchange 103
Fairy and Folk Tales of Ireland (Yeats) 62
Falkner, J. Meade 153
Family Guide to Media Violence 27
Fanchon, the Cricket 136
Faraway, So Close 126
Farmer Boy 217
The Father (Strindberg) 138
A Father's Lesson 106
Feed the Kitty 218
Felix the Cat 116
The Female of the Species 105
Feuillade, Louis 47
Feyder, Jacques 74
Fielding, Henry 13
Fighting Blood 110
Fildes, Sir Luke 232n2
"The Fisherman and His Wife" 186
The Five Children and It 209–210
The 5,000 Fingers of Dr. T. 220
Flaherty, Robert 1, 47
Flawed 220
Flynn, Errol 154
Forbidden Games 219
Ford, John 131
Forman, Henry James 23–27
Foster Child 220
The Foundling 136
The 400 Blows 219
Four Quartets 158
A Four-Year-Old Hero 128–129
Fox Sunshine Kiddies 7
Frank, Anne 193–194
Frankenstein (book) 80
Frankenstein (film) 148, 219
Franklin, Sidney 7

Freleng, Friz 139
Freud, Sigmund 64
Friar Lawrence (*Romeo and Juliet*) 185
Frog and the Wide World 173
From Up on Poppy Hill 220

Garfield, Leon 44–45, 73
Garland, Judy 138
Gasman 220
Gauntlett, David 27
Genesis, Book of 85–88
Gerda (*The Snow Queen*) 95–96, 157, 203
Germany, Year Zero 219
Gervaise Macquart 164–169
Gilbert Blythe 123–124
Il Giornate del Cinema Muto 221
The Girl and Her Trust 111–112
The Girl Who Hated Books 220
Gish, Dorothy and Lillian 111
Glad Girls 135, 234*ch*5*n*59
Globe Theatre 56
The God Within 104
Godard, Jean-Luc 48
The Golden Age 214–215, 228*n*48
The Golden Coach 48
Golding, William 152
Good Morning 219
Gospel of John 172
Grahame, Kenneth 187–191, 214–215, 228*n*48
Gramsci, Antonio 14
Granny 135, 140
The Grapes of Wrath 219
Grave of the Fireflies 220
The Great Adventure 219
Great Expectations (book) 56, 219
Great Expectations (1946 film) 56
Greed 74–75
Green, Guy 73
The Green Wall 220
Griffith, D. W. 47, 71–72, 115, 117, 118, 128–129, 136, 139–140, 142, 160, 162, 206, 230*n*13, 230*n*14, 230*n*15, 230–231*n*21; child films at the Biograph Film Company 102–114; the portrayal of girls and women 229*ch*4*n*12; *The Sunbeam* 183–185; *see also* American Mutuoscope and Biograph Company
Grimm, Jacob, and Wilhem 7, 64, 107, 211
Growing Up Digital 45–46
Guaraldi, Vince 8
Guest, Edgar 107
Guitry, Sacha 34
Gulliver's Travels 13, 15
Gunning, Tom 108–109
The Guns of Navarone (book) 62
Guy, Alice 128–129, 131

Hair Raising Hare 139
Hamartia 127
Hamlet 162

Hannibal Lecter 159
"Hansel and Gretel" (Grimm) 181
Happy Feet 220
Hardy, Oliver 48, 194–199; *see also* Laurel, Stan
Hardy Boys 136
Harvest of Shame 124, 219
Haugaard, Erik 59
Hays, Will 24, 25
Healing the Blind Man (Carl Bloch) 120
Heart o' the Hills 136
Heartland 219
Hedda Gabler 145
Hegel, Georg Wilhelm Friedrich 9, 78, 125, 177
Heidi (book) 229*ch*3*n*77
Heidi (1937 film) 136
Henry V (1989 film) 56
Henry V (play) 56
Henry Grantly (*The Warden*) 178–179
Herbert, George 15
The Heroes 90–91
Hezekiah 82
A High Wind in Jamaica 151–159, 167, 173
Highsmith, Patricia 157
The History of Childhood 45
Hitchcock, Alfred 69, 148
Hitler, Adolf 137
Hobbes, Thomas 13
The Hockey Sweater (film) 219
Hoffmann, Heinrich 148
Holling, Holling C. 66–67, 69
Hollywood vs. America 27
Home Alone 205
Homer 53
Homework 220
The Hoodlum 136
Hoop Dreams 220
The House at Pooh Corner 215
Housing Problems 219
How Green Was My Valley 219
How to Train Your Dragon 219
Howl's Moving Castle 220
Huck, Charlotte 37
Hud 219
Hue and Cry 137
Hughes, Richard 151–159, 162, 168; *see also A High Wind in Jamaica*
Hughes, Shirley 129–130, 131, 190; *see also* Alfie series
Hugo, Victor 164
Hume, David 125
Las Hurdes 219
The Hurried Child 27
The Hutterites 219
Huxley, Aldous 35

I Was Born, but... 219
I Wish 219
Ibsen, Henrik 14, 230*n*12
The Iconoclast 104

Index

Imitation of Christ 15
In the Border States 131
In the Labyrinth 219
In the Street 219
"Inchelina" 94, 157
"Infant Song" (Causley) 143–144
Ingeborg Holm 219
Ingram, Rex 47
The Inner Circle 110
The Interpretation of Dreams 64
The Interrupters 220
Intruder in the Dust 219
"The Invisible Child" (Tove Jansson) 175–177
The Iron Giant 219
Isaac 105
Isaiah 83, 119
Israel (Jacob) 85–88

Jackson, Stanley 34
Jacques Lantier (*La Bête Humaine*) 165, 169
Jaenzon, Julius 221–222
Jaenzon home movies 221–222
James 92, 119
James, Henry 151
Jameson, Frederic 14
Jansson, Tove 130–131, 134, 175
Jason and the Argonauts 220
Jeffers, Oliver 173
Jefferson, Joseph 26
Jennings, Humphrey 48
Jeremiah 14
Jesus Christ 22, 80, 81, 83, 86, 88, 90, 92, 94, 96, 103, 119–120, 135, 147, 168, 172, 205
John, Gospel of 172
Johnston, Joe 59–60
Joseph 85–88, 117
Joseph and His Brothers 87
Josiah 82
Judah 88
Judges, Book of 105
Jumanji (book) 59–60
Jumanji (1995 film) 59–60
The Jungle Book (1942 film) 219
Juvenal 13

Kafka, Franz 133–134
Kai (*The Snow Queen*) 95–96, 203
Kästner, Erich 137
Katz, Jon 46
Kauffman, Stanley 53–54
Kazantzakis, Nikos 87
Keaton, Buster 47
Keil, Charlie 103
Kes 219
The Kid (1921 film) 148, 218
The Kid with a Bike 219
Kiki's Delivery Service 220
Kikujiro 219
Killer of Sheep 219

Kincheloe, Joe 27
Kinderculture 27
King Lear 161
King of Kings (1927 film) 181–183
Kingsley, Charles 77, 90–91
Kipling, Rudyard 131–132, 210, 220
Kitano, Hideshi 219
Ko-Ko 116
The Koran 91
Kozintsev, Grigori 34
Kracauer, Siegfried 137
Kubrick, Stanley 194
Kuleshov, Lev 46
Kung Fu Panda 219
Kyle Apotegan 68

Labyrinth 48
Lady Macbeth 158
Lady MacDuff 132
Laemmle, Carl 148
Lalie (*L'Assommoir*) 168–169
Lamentations of Jeremiah 14
Lamprecht, Gerhard 137
Landscape in the Mist 220
Lang, Fritz 34, 148
Lantier (*L'Assommoir*) 166–167
Lassie (2005 film) 220
The Last Temptation of Christ (book) 87
Last Train Home 220
Laurel, Stan 48, 194–199; *see also* Hardy, Oliver
Le Havre 219
Lean, David 56, 73, 74
Lear, Edward 206
Lebeau, Vicky 101
Legg, Stewart 48
Les Misérables (Hugo) 164
Leviathan 13
Lewis, Jerry 48
Life, and Nothing More ... 219
Lindsay, Norman 58
Lindsay, Vachel 54
Literary Naturalism 159–169, 235–236n59
Little Dorrit 163
The Little Fugitive 220
"Little Gidding" (Eliot) 158
The Little Girl Who Sold the Sun 220
Little House on the Prairie (book) 134–135
Little Lord Fauntleroy (film) 136
Little Miss Broadway 136
Little Miss Marker 136
Little Nell 160, 169
The Little Prince (book) 142, 202, 205, 206, 207
The Little Princess (1917 film) 136
The Little Princess (1939 film) 136
"Little Red Riding Hood" (Grimm) 181
The Littlest Rebel 136
Locke, John 79, 202
London, Jack 137, 174–175
Looney Tunes 116

The Lord of the Flies (book) 152
Lorenzo's Oil 219
Louisiana Story 219
Lovecraft, H. P. 152
Luke (writer of the New Testament gospel) 81
Lumière, Louis, and Auguste 47, 101, 170–171
Luther, Martin 14
Lye, Len 48

M 148
M. Hulot's Holiday 140–142
Macbeth 132, 162
Machiavelli, Niccolo 13, 179
MacPherson, Jeannie 181–183
The Magic Pudding 58
Maltby, Richard 26
Maltin, Leonard 7
The Man Who Planted Trees (film) 4
The Man with the Movie Camera 47
Mandy 219
Mankiewicz, Herman 34
Mankiewicz, Joseph 34
Mann, Thomas 87
Marcus Aurelius 215
Marilla Cuthbert 123
Mark (*King of Kings*) 182–183
Marker, Chris 34, 223ch2n2
Marx, Karl 9, 14, 78, 177
Mary Magdalene (*King of Kings*) 182
Mary Poppins (book) 200
Mason, Bill 67–71
The Matrix 48
Matthew (writer of the New Testament gospel) 81
McCabe, John 195–196
McCutcheon, Wallace, Sr. 109
McLaren, Norman 48
McTeague 74–75, 105, 156
The mean (Aristotle) 4, 42–53, 177–187
Medea 158
Medved, Michael 27
Medvedev, Alexander 47
Meet Me in St. Louis 219
Méliès, Georges 47
Melodrama 71
Mendelssohn, Felix 116
Merritt, Russell 117–118, 184
Merry Melodies 116
Metropolis 69
Metz, Christian 34
Meyrowitz, Joshua 45
MGM 198
Mickey Mouse 116
Mikkel Borgen 127
Milne, A. A. 149
Milton, John 126
The Mirror 219
Les Misérables (Hugo) 164
Miss Honey 93

Mr. Gumpy's Outing 173
Mr. Murdstone (*David Copperfield*) 189
Mr. Toad (*The Wind in the Willows*) 91, 107, 187–191, 207, 211, 212–213, 215–216
Mixed Babies 109
Miyazaki, Hiyao 97, 121–122, 139
Mizoguchi, Kenji 48
M'liss 136
The Modern Prodigal 104
Mole (*The Wind in the Willows*) 107, 187–191, 207, 212
Molière 14
Moloch 69
Mon Oncle 219
Mon Oncle Antoine 220
Montgomery, Lucy Maud 123–124, 135–136, 139
Moominland Midwinter 130–131
Moominsummer Madness 134
Moomintroll (Tove Jansson) 130–131, 176
Moonfleet (book) 153
More, Hanna 107
More, Thomas 13
Moses 99, 122
Mother (film) 47
The Motion Picture Research Council (MPRC) 23
Mouchette 219
Movie Made America 23–27; *see also* Payne Fund Studies
Moving Experiences 27
Moving Picture World 184
Mowgli (*The Jungle Book*) 210, 221
Mulligan, Gerry 8
Munk, Kaj 89
The Muppets Take Manhattan 137
Murnau, F. W. 1, 34
The Music Room 48
My Ain Folk 220
My Childhood 220
My Grandmother Ironed the King's Shirts 220
My Home Is Copacabana 219–220
My Name Is Ivan 219

Nana (*L'Assommoir*) 165–168
Nancy Drew 136
Nanook of the North 219
National Film Board of Canada 48, 67, 124
National Theatre, London 56
The Navigator 219
Neame, Ronald 73
Nesbit, E. 201, 202, 209
The New Heoloise 105
The Nicomachean Ethics 42–43
Ninny ("The Invisible Child") 175–177
No Exit 61, 137
No Sense of Place 45
Nobody Knows 220
Nordquvist, Sven 173
Norris, Frank 74–75, 156

Index 273

North, Sir Thomas 65
Not One Less 219
Novels into Film 54
Now and Forever 136

O. Henry 107
Objective correlative 63–4
October 47
Oedipus 60
"The Old Street Lamp" 58–59
Old Testament 82
Oliver Twist (book) 71–72, 74, 78, 107, 163
Oliver Twist (character) 219–220
Oliver Twist (1948 film) 73
Los Olividados 219
Olmi, Ermanno 48, 122–123, 139
"On Fairy-Stories" (Tolkien) 208
On the Banks of Plum Creek 236ch7n12
On the Waterfront 146
One-Eyed Jacks 146
One Flew Over the Cuckoo's Nest (film) 126–127
One Hundred Men and a Girl 219
One Potato, Two Potato 219
One Sixth of the World 47
One Touch of Nature 110
Ordet (1955 film) 89, 127
Ordet (play) 89
Original Sin 78–79, 126
Oscar's Half Birthday 228n60
Oswald the Rabbit 116
Othello 162
Our Gang 7
Our Little Girl 136
The Owl's Legacy 223ch2n2
Oxford Research Group 132–133
Ozu, Yasujiro 48, 219

Paddle to the Sea (1941 book) 66–71
Paddle to the Sea (1966 film) 67–71
Palme d'Or 12
Paper Moon 219
Paradise Lost 126
Pascal, Blaise 144, 202
Pasolini, Pier Paolo 48
Pasternak, Boris 74
Pathé Frères film production company 47
Pather Panchali 219
Patinoire 219
Paul 84–85, 89, 135, 202
The Payne Fund Studies 22–27; *see also* Movie Made America
Peanuts 8
Peirce, Charles Sanders 34
Perfect Snow 174
Peter Pan (book) 62–63, 75, 149, 171–172, 200, 207–208, 239n25, 239n26
"The Philosopher's Stone" 93–94
The Philosophical Dictionary 14
Phyllis Nirdlinger 159
Pickford, Mary 136, 230n12

The Picture of Dorian Gray (book) 107
The Pilgrim (1924 film) 65–66, 144–149, 192
The Pilgrim's Progress 20–22
Pinocchio (book) 57, 149–150, 191–193, 210–211, 214, 237n54
Pinocchio (1940 film) 57, 149, 191
Pinocchio (2002 film) 57
Piper at the Gates of Dawn 97, 149
Pippa Passes (film) 117
Pippa Passes (poem) 117, 170
Piscator, Erwin 13
Pixote 220
Plato 23, 24, 25, 28, 29, 30, 31, 32, 41, 50–53, 124–125, 144, 186–187; on narrative 15–20; the Parable of the Cave 11–13, 14, 15, 16, 17, 21, 37, 48; *The Republic* 16–18, 24, 31–33, 42, 50
Please Vote for Me 219
The Plug-In Drug 27
Plutarch 65
Plutarch's Lives 65
Poetics 19, 50–52, 125–126, 127; *see also* Aristotle
Polacco, Patricia 36–37, 44
The Polar Express (book) 142, 205, 214
Pollyanna (film) 136
Ponyo 220
The Poor Little Rich Girl 136
Porco Rosso 121–122
Postman, Neil 27–30, 31, 33, 34, 41, 54, 70, 223ch1n8
Il Posto 220
Powell, Michael 48
The Praise of Folly 13
The Prince 13
Professor Branestawm (character created by Norman Hunter) 4
Proverbs 84
Pudovkin, V. I. 47
Putty Tat Trouble 139

Quai des Orfevres 219
The Quiet One 219

Rabelais, François 13
Rachel Lynde 124
Rags 136
Randall Patrick McMurphy 126–127
Ratcatcher 220
Ratty (*The Wind in the Willows*) 187–191, 207, 211, 212
Ray, Satyajit 34, 48
Rebecca of Sunnybrook Farm 136
The Red Balloon 219
The Redman and the Child 112
Reid, Barbara 174
Renoir, Jean 1, 34, 48, 162
The Republic (Plato) 16–18, 24, 31–33, 42, 50
The Return 220
Reuben (Genesis) 87–88

Riesner, Dean 144–149
Rip Van Winkle 26
The River (Renoir film) 48, 219
Roach, Hal 7, 196–199
Robinson, David 148, 195
Rocha, Glauber 48
Rohmer, Eric 34
"The Roman Road" 215
Rome, Open City 219
Romeo and Juliet (play) 185–186
Room, Abram 47
Rooney, Mickey 137
Rosetta 220
Rossellini, Roberto 34; war trilogy 48
Rousseau, Jean-Jacques 62, 79, 105, 202
Rules of the Game 48
Rushmore 220
Russell, Ken 157
Ruth, Book of 105

Sabatini, Rafael 154
Sabotage 148
Saint-Exupéry, Antoine de 202–205, 206
Salaam Bombay! 220
A Salutary Lesson 108
Sammy Going South 219
Samuel 82
Samuel Grantly (*The Warden*) 179
Sanders, Barry 27
Saramago, José 86
Sartre, Jean-Paul 61, 137
Saussure, Ferdinand de 34
Schickel, Richard 71
Schmidlin, Rick 74
School of Rock 219
Schrader, Paul 150
Schulz, Charles 8
Seabury, Inez 183–184
Searching for Bobby Fisher 219
Seawright, Roy 198
The Second 100 Years 196
The Secret Garden 127, 142
The Secret of Roan Inish 219
The Secret World of Arietty 220
Sendak, Maurice 7, 208
Sermon on the Mount (Carl Bloch) 120
Sewell, Anna 107
Shakespeare, William 34, 56, 59, 124, 132
Shaw, George Bernard 14, 143
Shawn, Dick 65
Shelley, Mary 80
"The Shepherd Boy Sings in the Valley of Humiliation" 90, 204
Sherwood, Mary Martha 107
The Shining (film) 194
Shklovsky, Viktor 13
Shockheaded Peter 148
Shoeshine 219
Shub, Esfir 47
Silas Marner 96–99, 103, 149, 218; *see also* Eliot, George

Simmon, Scott 104
Sindbad the Porter 211
Sindbad the Seaman 211
Skretvedt, Randy 196–197
Small, David 173
Smart, Christopher 75
The Smile of a Child 104
The Snow Queen 95–96, 157
"The Social Contract" 79
Socrates 11, 31, 32, 41, 42, 78, 178, 186–187, 227*ch*3n1
Solomon 82
The Son 220
The Sons of Ingmar 219
Sophocles 53, 60
The Sound of Coaches 44–45
The Southerner 48, 219
Sparrows 219
Speed Racer 220
Spielberg, Steven 205
The Spirit of the Beehive 220
Spirited Away 220
"Spring Song" 116
Springville High School 37–40, 54
Spyri, Johanna 107
Stanislavski, Konstantin 107
Steinbeck, John 86
Steinberg, Shirley 27
Stevenson, Robert Louis 153
Stevie 220
"A Story from the Dunes" 59
The Story of Babar 148
"The Story of the Bad Little Boy" 151
"The Story of the Good Little Boy" 151
Stowaway 136
Stratemeyer Literary Syndicate 136
Stretton, Hesba 107
Strike 47
Strike Up the Band 137
Strindberg, August 14, 138
Stuck 173
Sturges, Preston 34
The Sunbeam 183–185
Susannah of the Mounties 136
Swift, Jonathan 13, 155

Tabula rasa (blank slate) 79
Taine, Hippolyte 161
A Tale of Two Cities (book) 107
Talmud 91
Tancock, Leonard 164
Tapscott, Don 45
Tati, Jacques 140–142; *see also M. Hulot's Holiday*
Taxi Driver 220
Taylor, Ann, and Jane 107
Technopoly 223*ch*1n8
Tell Us a Story 64
Temple, Shirley 131, 136
Tess of the Storm Country (1914 film) 136
Tess of the Storm Country (1920 film) 136

Testament 220
Thackeray, William Makepeace 13
Theorem 48
Thérèse Raquin 161–162
Things Fall Apart 38
Thomas à Kempis 15
Thoughts of Murdo 62
The 3 Godfathers 219
Three Smart Girls 136
Thwaite, Ann 127
Tiny Tim (Dickens) 160
To Kill a Mockingbird 219
Tokyo Godfathers 219
Tolkien, J. R. R. 208
Tom and Jerry 116
Tom Jones (film) 219
Tom Ripley 157
Tom Sawyer (book) 151
Tom Swift 136
Toni 48
Tootles (*Peter Pan*) 133
A Town Called Panic 4
Transylvania 6-5000 139
The Traveler 219
The Traveling Companion 73–74
Travers, P. L. 200
Treasure Island 153
Treatise on Tolerance 14
A Tree Grows in Brooklyn 219
The Tree of Life 220
Trent's Last Case 13
Trimmer, Sarah 107
Trollope, Anthony 177–180, 236–237ch7n21, 237n22
Trubloff 173
A Turn of the Screw (book) 151
TV Turn-Off Week 36
Twain, Mark 92, 107, 123, 151
Tweetie Pie 135, 139
Tweety and Sylvester 135, 137–140
20th Century Fox 198
"The Two Brothers" (Grimm) 211
The Two Sides 113–114
2001: A Space Odyssey 220
Two Treatises on Government 79
Tzaritza 219

Umberto D. 48
Uncle Bob's Hospital Visit 220
Uncle Tom's Cabin (book) 107, 205
UNICEF 124
An Unseen Enemy 111
Up films (Apted) 220
The Uses of Enchantment 44, 180–187; *see also* Bettelheim, Bruno
Utopia 13

The Valet's Wife 109
Van Allsburg, Chris 35–36, 37, 44, 59–60, 66, 205

Van Dyke, Henry 107
Velthuijs, Max 173
Vertov, Dziga 47
Victoria and Albert Museum 7
Vidas Secas 219
Virtuous Reality 46
The Voice of the Child 104
Voltaire 14
Von Stroheim, Erich 1, 47, 74–75

Wachowski, Andy, and Larry/Lana 48
The War Game 219
The Warden (book) 177–180
Warner Brothers cartoons 48, 137–140; *see also* Tweety and Sylvester
Warrendale 219
Watts, Isaac 107
Wee Willie Winkie (film) 131–132
"Wee Willie Winkie" (short story) 131–132
Welles, Orson 1
Wells, Mai 144
Wenders, Wim 126, 218
What Drink Did 108
What the Whole Family Said 59
When Findus Was Little and Disappeared 173
Where Eagles Dare 62
Where Is My Friend's House? 220
The White Balloon 220
White Fang 174–175
White Mane 219
The White Ribbon 220
The Wild Child 219
The Wild Knight and Other Poems 91
Wild Strawberries 221
"The Wild Swans" 94–95, 228n56
Wilder, Almanzo 217
Wilder, Billy 34
Wilder, Laura Ingalls 134, 216–217, 236ch7n12
The Wind in the Willows 187–191, 206–207, 212, 228n48
A Window in Thrums 75
Wings of Desire 126
Winn, Marie 27
Winnie the Pooh 149
The Witches (book) 60–61
The Witches (1990 film) 60–61
The Wizard of Oz 219
Wordsworth, William 105, 203–204
The Wretched Stone 35–36

The Yearling (1948 film) 219
Yeats, William Butler 62, 63, 64, 77
Young America 219

Zathura (book) 60
Zathura (2005 film)
Zola, Émile 14, 107, 137, 161–169
Zukor, Adolph 34
The Zulu's Heart 231–232ch5n1

www.ingramcontent.com/pod-product-compliance
Ingram Content Group UK Ltd.
Pitfield, Milton Keynes, MK11 3LW, UK
UKHW041928140426
5217IPUK00014B/374